Contents

Preface and Acknowledgements

This volume is very much a companion volume to *Language in Geographic Context* (Williams, 1988) and reflects the steady growth over the past decade in the development of geographers' interest in language. In this context, the first international seminar on Geolinguistics was held in the Department of Geography and Recreation Studies, Staffordshire Polytechnic, in May 1987. The seminar was the initiative of the permanent members of the Department's Centre for Geolinguistic Research, Dr John Ambrose, Professor Colin H. Williams and Dr Stephen Wyn Williams.

The central theme of the seminar was the manner in which geolinguistic analysis could further our undertanding of the plight of linguistic minorities in Western Europe and Canada. Inevitably, given the under-developed state of comparative geolinguistics, there was an undue emphasis on case-study material, and less formal attention was paid to theory. However, we believe that the resulting chapters, together with other publications which were encouraged by the seminar, will contribute to the production of a wider base for geolinguistic studies. The ten papers presented at the seminar have been revised for publication, and I wish to thank the authors for their co-operation in the preparation of this volume. I would also like to thank Mr. M. Hellyer of the Canadian High Commission, London, for a grant towards the hosting of the seminar, and Professor George Kay for making the facilities of the Department available to seminar participants.

Much of the re-drafting of cartographic material has been accomplished by Paul Taylor, former cartographer at Staffordshire Polytechnic, with expert assistance and advice offered by Dr J. Ambrose throughout. My thanks to them both for their willingness to speculate on how best to represent the images portrayed in this volume. I am also grateful to Mrs Jane Williams, former cartographer at Staffordshire Polytechnic for her work, together with the work of the departmental cartographers in the home colleges of the various contributors. We are grateful to the Highlands and Islands Development Board (1982) for their permission to quote from their report 'Language, Community and Development' in Chapter Seven.

Preparation and thinking on the issues raised by the seminar have been aided by a British Academy Award in 1987 for research on Breton cultural reproduction, and a Swedish Institute Visiting Fellowship at the University of Lund in the autumn of 1988 which allowed me to discuss these issues with Professor Sven Tägil and his colleagues in the Department of International History. I am grateful to both organisations for their support.

Finally I wish to thank Derrick Sharp, and Mike and Marjukka Grover of Multilingual Matters for their encouragement and assistance.

Colin H. Williams

Reference

WILLIAMS, C. H. (ed.) 1988, *Language in Geographic Context*. Clevedon: Multilingual Matters.

1 Linguistic Minorities: West European and Canadian Perspectives

COLIN H. WILLIAMS

Introduction

It is now commonplace for most accounts of language decline and ethnic politics to rehearse the failings of social scientists in not recognising the salience of cultural factors in determining the character of the modern state. The dominance of the modernisation paradigm from the late 1950s to the early 1970s, which marginalised ethnicity and culture, has now given way to a convergence which focuses on the state as a prime influence on the formation of ethnic identity. The vast extension of the powers of the state, and of its penetration into all aspects of communal life, has resulted in a vigorous debate on the 'true' nature of statehood, on the relative autonomy of the state, and on the exercise of state power as a means of exalting some groups at the expense of others. Central to this debate has been the waxing and waning of the fortunes of constituent cultural groups in the modern state. Whilst intellectuals within advanced industrial states were arguing about the withering away of ethnicity, and of the primacy of individualism over collectivism, everyday reality in the rest of the world brought home to us the continued significance of ethnic consciousness in shaping life's opportunities. Thus situations as diverse as South Africa's 'segregated' Group Areas and 'independent' Homelands, Beirut's divided neighbourhoods, and the disputed Nagorno-Karabakh region of the USSR, all have in common the fundamental assertion of the rights of groups to exist and flourish despite a depressingly restrictive context. A central element of many such disputes is the relationship between language reproduction and territorial affiliation, between communication, power and space. Language is often both the symbol and the substance of group resistance to assimilation or annihilation and thus becomes inherently politicised as a group marker, suggestive of a far wider socio-cultural reality. Characteristically, one of the first reforms of the newly independent state or ethnic-region is to declare its language (or a dominant autochthonous tongue) as the official state medium, even if functionally the former 'colonial', or 'majoritarian' language still holds sway. This was the experience of post-colonial Africa and Asia and is the current reality in the increasingly autonomous parts of Central and Eastern Europe (Kozlov, 1988).

But Western intellectuals were too quick to relegate non-state languages to the domains of history, for despite the obvious appeals of supra-state economic and political integration, as represented in the development of the European Community, for example, declining linguistic minorities have refused to lie down and pass out of existence. It is debatable as to whether or not the development of a supra-state and global appreciation of our common problems has actually quickened or arrested the decline of minority cultures in the West. There is ample and conflicting evidence for both viewpoints. What is not in conflict, however, is that the situation of groups such as the Basques, the Welsh or the Catalans has improved out of all recognition since the granting of fundamental concessions by their respective dominant state majorities. Legal recognition of minority cultural rights has led to an extension and development of bilingualism and biculturalism in these nations, and has been accompanied by increased political pressure, from many quarters, for the granting of greater measures of autonomy. Cultural identity has been tied closer than ever before to questions of political authority, and the state has emerged as the central actor in this struggle for survival. Many within the European Community recognise that there is a positive worth in mobilising the resource of ethnicity to create a stronger Europe, a Europe of the Nations rather than a Europe of the Nation-State. Current trends offer a more promising future to the better organised and politically astute non-state nations, for in a reconstituted Europe, territories such as Catalonia and Euskadi would surely become integral elements in a federal structure (Williams, 1989d).

But what of those communities whose language, culture and economic base have already atrophied under the twin weights of an often oppressive, unresponsive state and world economy which dictated to them their role in the global division of labour? What future do they have? Are their languages and cultures already doomed? Need they necessarily become 'open museums' where a once virulent cultural heritage is repackaged to make it palatable to consumers, in a Disney-like theme homeland? Are the sons and daughters of slate quarry workers in North Wales destined to become industrial heritage guides, with an occasional smattering of Welsh thrown in to prove to the tourist that they are indeed in a 'foreign' land? Is crofting in the Scottish Highlands to be preserved so that eager youngsters from Strathclyde, let alone all the Celtic descendants abroad, can undertake interesting history projects and relive the past through the ingenuity of marketing consultants who sanitise history so as not to cause offence or discomfort?

Though exaggerated, these are by no means spurious questions, for they strike at the heart of what role declining languages and their associated cultures are to play within a modern, or indeed post-modern, society. Questions about power, control, legitimacy, adequate employment, demography, development and planning are as central to the future of lesser-used language communities as are the more conventional elements of education, literature and communal values and behaviour. The main object of this volume is to examine selected declining language minorities within Western Europe and Canada from this geolinguistic perspective. It is my conviction that the issues addressed are not qualitatively different from many of the issues of identity and relative cultural autonomy which characterise other parts of the world with a far shorter history of state integration and nation-building. Thus, for example, the decline of Gaelic in Scotland should not be viewed as a unique phenomenon, but as a very early example of systematic cultural extinction by a powerful set of interests operating in a marginal and fragmented territory. Its effects are not dissimilar to that which obtain in many creole, pidgin or indigenous communities, as examined in Dorian's (1989) superb collection of essays. However, there is a certain irony in that such displaced Europeans were part of the colonial process which in turn caused the cultural annihilation of Cayugas, Haida, and Kutenai in the New World without too much regard for the very right to existence which they had failed to secure in their own homelands.

We have concentrated our attention in this volume on a sub-set of lesser-used languages, some of which appear to be doomed to disappear by the early part of the twenty-first century, unless revivalist efforts now underway make remarkable progress. In truth, there is little sign that such efforts will prove successful in the long term, though other lesser-used languages have been effectively reinvigorated as a result of both political autonomy and economic autarchy, the twin pre-conditions in my view of successful language regeneration based upon resistance. These chapters are thus designed both as a contribution to the developing field of geolinguistics and to the understanding of declining cultural communities in an increasingly pressing world system.

Identity, Warfare and Nation-State Formation

Though I recognise that the current position of Europe's lesser-used languages has much to do with economic factors and demographic trends in history, it is quite evident that their role in the European order has been determined essentially by national political considerations and by warfare. Questions of a language's relevance, legitimacy and survival are socially constructed, not naturally ordained. Languages in contact are often languages in competition, and the ecology of language has much to do with questions of power, of control over resources, people and land, and of the granting or abrogating of social rights throughout history. Central to this process of legitimising some cultures and alienating others, has been the rise of the 'territorial nation-state'. The complex process of state development has resulted in the inexorable integration of diverse culture groups into 'national populations', who, in turn, become the constituent citizens of the modern state system. In time state and nation, two enigmatic concepts in both the real world and the social sciences, were to become coextensive entities in the formation of national congruence (Williams, 1989a). Inevitably perhaps, most histories of state-formation and nation-building, have involved the institutional denial of minority group rights, initially in regard to religious freedoms from the Reformation to the Enlightenment in Western Europe, and culminating in the periodic purges of 'dissident cultures and individuals' in Eastern Europe. Exile was often the fate of religious minorities in Protestant territories, execution too often the fate of dissenters in Catholic Europe.

In post-Enlightenment Europe when the religious question was eased by the safety valve of emigration to the New World and beyond, new minority problems took over. Chief of these was the case of minority language groups who did not share the culture of the dominant majority which animated state development. In an age of nationalism and state expansion, the destruction of minority cultures was deemed to be a necessary concomitant of modernity and progress. As the uneven effects of capitalism penetrated into the marginal, ethnically differentiated peripheries of Europe, outmoded cultures were considered to be anathema to the realisation of a fully integrated national market, let alone the platform for an ever expanding overseas empire. Thus the diffusion of state-wide ideals, carried through a common language, became the urgent programme of nineteenth-century Europe. The key agencies of this national socialisation programme were compulsory education and mass conscription, which together did more to seal the populous into a citizenry than any other earlier state-inspired necessity. The militarisation of society in the latter half of the century was made possible by the accumulated surpluses of industrial organisations and by their military technologies. Its social impact was felt most keenly in the widespread practice of conscription, which in my view is a chronically under-researched aspect of language spread in modern society.

Some previous scholars have noted the significance of conscription for shaping national consciousness (Smith, 1981; Seton-Watson, 1977). In earlier works (Williams, 1984; 1989a) I have referenced the role of the French Revolution in exporting both the ideals of national uniformity and the means by which such uniformity was to be achieved, namely the military structure in civilian clothes, i.e. the territorial, bureaucratic state with its appeal to obedience, regulation and standardisation. Mass education, conscription and taxation were all prime requisites of a mobile, technocratic society. But the experience of being caught up in this ferment of social change also had its effects on diluting regional cultures and strengthening identification with a common culture in the modern state. State activities had created a new set of opportunities for incorporated peoples, influencing their socio-economic levels of material well-being and political representation at the centre. Superordinate nations came to dominate unrepresented nationalities and used the power of the state to buttress their own cultural apparatus as the orthodox, legitimised value system. The new opportunities were often glimpsed as a result of serving in the armed forces, or as a result of civilians engaged in preparation for war-making. Recently John Keegan (1989: 20) has related these features to the three principle ideals of the French Revolution: liberty, equality and fraternity.

He argues that 'military service became popular in the nineteenth century first because it was an experience of *equality*' (Keegan, 1989: 20). Conscription was relatively egalitarian in both class and ethnic terms so that 'emancipation' in military terms was an agency for national socialisation.

> The universality of conscription swept up every nationality in the Hapsburg lands. Poles and Alsace-Lorrainers in Germany, Basques, Bretons and Savoyards in France. All, by being soldiers were also to be Austrians, Germans or Frenchman. (Keegan, 1989).

The commonality of conscription was also an instrument for *fraternity*.

> Conscription took young adults from their locality and plunged them into the experience of growing up — confronting them with the challenge of separation from home, making new friends, dealing with enemies, adjusting to authority, wearing strange clothes, eating unfamiliar food, shifting for themselves. It was a genuine *rite de passage*, intellectual, emotional, and, not least of all, physical. Nineteenth-century armies, told that they were 'schools of the nation', took on many of the characteristics of contemporary schools, not only testing and heightening literacy and numeracy but also teaching, swimming, athletics, and cross-country sports as well as shooting and the martial arts. (Keegan, 1989: 20–1).

However, the appeal of liberty was by no means universally shared, for many of the excesses unleashed by Napoleon's revolutionary armies destroyed older traditions and freedoms and replaced them with rational, humanistic reforms which served the modern state apparatus. Keegan's observations at the mass political level have significant force. He argues that

> the ultimate importance of universal conscription in changing attitudes to military service was that it ultimately connected with *liberty*, in its political if not its personal sense. The old armies had been instruments of oppression of the peoples by the kings; the new armies were to be instruments of the people's liberation from the kings, even if that liberation was to be narrowly institutional in the states which retained monarchy. (Keegan, 1989: 21).

From henceforth the call to arms was made in the name of the *nation*, its people, language, values and resources were the principal attributes of the emerging nation-state system.

What of cultural minorities in this process of nation-state-building? Their freedom was often severely limited, for its bounds were set by the logic of assimilation and compliance with the new state order. Attempts by minorities to resist assimilation were deemed to be expressions of primordial sentiments and a spurning of the individual's opportunity to advance within the liberalising framework of the new, open society, where rationalism displaced parochialism. Why should one want to remain Breton, backward and superstitious when the possibility existed to become a fully-fledged member of a modern, progressive and fully-civilised French society? The nationalist intelligentsia of nineteenth-century Europe were not only reporting upon the withering away of tribalism and primordialism in the nether regions of their new states, they were formulating new principles for cultural imperialism which would hasten the demise of alternative socio-cultural formations which threatened to arrest the progress of their national plans. Such logic was not new. It was a reflection of a form of cultural imperialism, commonplace at least since the French Revolution which promoted French throughout the hexagon of France in order to seal the patriotism of the liberated through forced linguistic unification. This early form of state language planning occurred for, by now, quite familiar reasons, in order to undermine the influence of clericalism, of tradition, and to stifle anti-revolutionary (anti-state) challenges from the ethnic peripheries. This was the fear which led Bertrand Barrere in his *Sur les idiomes étrangers et l'enseignment de la langue française* (27th January 1794) to assert that 'Federalism and supersition speak Breton; emigration and hatred of the Republic speak German; the counter-revolution speaks Italian; and fanaticism speaks Basque' (quoted in Gordon, 1978: 30).

In European history the attempt to anchor whole societies to specific places, to 'nationalise space' so to speak, has been a recurrent theme of socio-political development. It has also been a major contributory cause of inter-state warfare and of inter-group conflict which has had a profound significance on the formation of states and on the creation of national peoples. The intimate connection between a particular territory and its people has been a fascinating theme of social history, capable of being interpreted in a slightly different fashion by each generation. The politicisation of territory reached its most intense expression in the Age of Nationalism and induced a complex process we may term 'the national construction of social space'. Williams & Smith (1983) argue that this has been one of the most influential processes in creating identities, and in producing a consciousness which could be mobilised to serve the aspirations of leaders of the new nation-states. Williams & Smith (1983: 504) argue that if 'the nation' represents a mode of moulding and interpreting social space, 'nationalism' as an ideology and political movement may be viewed as the dominant mode of politicising space by treating it as a distinctive and historic territory. This volume concentrates on the attempts of linguistic minorities to maintain control of their historic territories and so thereby guarantee some degree of success in reproducing their cultures, ideologies and interests in the face of enormous assimilatory pressures from majority cultures. The focus is on declining linguistic minorities who, by and large, have been excluded from the process of constructing their own national spaces, largely because of their political subordination to more powerful neighbours.

Central to this subordination was the myriad processes we now call state formation. We may, following Binder (1971), Young (1976), and

Williams (1980), summarise this process as the successive resolution of a series of crises, as depicted in Figure 1.1.

The outcome of the crises posed by issues of identity, legitimacy, participation, distribution and penetration structure the relationship between the state and its constituent minorities. Three consequences flow from the state's attempt to politicise its territory (Williams & Smith, 1983). The first is the increase in society's control over and ability to manipulate the environment. In the past this has included such strategic and grandiose schemes as 'nationalising society and space' where both the majority and minority communities are engaged in projects to activate their respective environments as a resource base for the collective goals of the community. Physically this is manifest in the construction of the built environment, in the development of a state-wide infrastructure for the rapid movement of goods and ideas and in furthering the distribution and activation goals of society. Socially this has involved the construction of a new citizenry through mass education, political orientation and degrees of participation. It can also occasion population exchanges with neighbours as a means by which homogeneous national communities are

State Development

The successive resolution of a series of crises

1 **Identity**: the extension of an active sense of membership in the national state community to the entire populace; in essence this is the issue of making state and nation coterminous.

2 **Legitimacy**: securing a generalised acceptance of the rightness of the exercise and structure of authority by the state so that its routine regulations and acts obtain compliance.

3 **Participation**: the enlargement of the numbers of persons actively involved in the political arena, through such devices as voting for parties and extending involvement ideally to the entire polity.

4 **Distribution**: ensuring that the valued resources in society such as material well-being and status are available on equal terms to all persons and that the re-distributive policies inhibit the heavy concentrations of wealth in a few hands or a specific region.

5 **Penetration**: extending the effective operation of the state to the farthest periphery of the system.

Source: Binder (1971), Young (1976), Williams (1980)

FIGURE 1.1 *The state development process*

created, witness the Greco–Turkish exchanges after 1922, the problem of the German border areas in 1919–21 (Tägil, *et al.*, 1984) and again in the period 1922–39 (Kaiser, 1968; Keegan, 1989; Gilbert, 1989). We are currently witnessing the same process of 'ethnic purification', albeit at various degrees of intensity, in many parts of the USSR, particularly in Azerbaijan, Armenia and Georgia, and also in Romania and Bulgaria. At a more local level control over the social environment can concern itself with questions of in-migration to linguistically endangered areas, such as Brittany, Scotland and Ireland discussed below, or with threats to communal cultural cohesion when external factors such as resource extraction, tourism, regional development programmes and strategic defence and energy installations are imposed upon the local community for national (state-wide) considerations (Williams, 1987; 1989e).

A second consequence has been the 'hardening of space', that is the filling out of power vacuums and the utilisation of all areas for social benefit and communal power. This relates to the state's concern with identity and penetration of all its territory. National leaders have been unremitting in this task, especially in Western Europe, and the lasting evidence is the virulent state system we share today, though, of course, this system represents the interests of the victors in this struggle for statehood. The vanquished, the so-called 'stateless nations' or 'unrepresented nationalities' unable to achieve political sovereignty within the status quo, pin their hopes on various regional level and federal-type multinational associations being created in the future: a Europe of the Nations, rather than a Europe of the Nation-State (Williams, 1989a; Veiter, 1989). Successful élites have constructed the territorial bureaucratic state (Smith, 1985) which is both autonomous and self-sustaining. They have sought

> to present to the world the face of a united and mobilised community securely based throughout a compact territory, which brooks no external interference or internal subversion, and which is able to unleash a collective energy for development that can utterly transform the environment and deter aggressors. (Williams & Smith, 1983: 513)

Thirdly, there has been a growing 'abstraction of the land' that has been given new meaning as the total environment, both physical and social, becomes re-interpreted to suit the exigencies of the age. This is evidenced in a number of ways, for example in the zest for linguistic revivals and the protection of threatened homelands which have spiritual as well as material significance. It is reflected in the manner in which popular writers and artists have re-interpreted society's relationship with nature and in the whole movement to understand both the origins and diversity of all species. It is represented in the scientific search for archaeological remains, in the reconstruction of past environments and in the attempts to relate linguistic origins to specific places (Renfrew, 1987). Most obviously it is exhibited in the post-war experiential search for primitive authenticity in the 'return to nature movement' and in the environmentalist and deep ecology thrust of sections of contemporary society.

Clearly society–environment relations have achieved a new critical and self-conscious awareness, unanticipated barely a generation ago. Minority groups, conscious of their relative powerlessness, have tended to argue on moral grounds that their rights to have a separate language or religious status in the modern state are an expression of universal human rights. They echo the nineteenth-century liberal call for tolerance and equality for disadvantaged groups, and assert that the modern multicultural state not only has an obligation to guarantee them freedom *from* oppression, but also freedom *to* expression and participation. This new conception of freedom and social rights places a responsibility on the state to construct the conditions of possibility whereby a minority culture may be permitted to operate in formal, public domains. Hence the whole thrust of minority language agitation in Western Europe of late has been for bilingual education provision, for simultaneous translation services in legal and public administration services, for official recognition of language rights both on the statute book and in the market-place. That such proposals are nearly always accompanied by both conflict and counter-claims that cultural pluralism is inefficient or subversive of state integrity should come as no surprise.

We recognise that legislating for the freedom to use a minority language in several domains has been a major political breakthrough in many of the states of western Europe. This was the battle of the 1960s and 1970s. The challenge facing such minorities in the 1990s is to transform the legal recognition institutionalised in the past two decades into actual routine social behaviour. This involves reform at two levels. First, many minority language speakers have to be encouraged to make use of the new opportunities which are now available. Paradoxically this is not as self-evident as one might expect. After decades or centuries of being socialised into accepting that their culture is second-rate, of limited utility in a burgeoning world economy, many within the minority communities are reluctant to take advantage of the opening up of new domains, whether they be in formal education or in dealings with local and civil authorities in the autochthonous tongue. Reversing this status differential and inducing more self-confident use of the lesser-used language is clearly far more difficult in some contexts, such as Breton and Arberesch, than in others, such as Catalan. Secondly, in order to allow these new domains to function there has to be corresponding reform of the public sector to enable bi- or multilingual practices to be instituted, for there is little justice in legislating for the use of the minority language in the courts of law, for example, if there are not also facilities for simultaneous translations. Similarily the employment and training of personnel must be a key factor in the success of bilingual reforms, for initially it often happens that the demand for language usage in a wide range of domains threatens to outstrip the supply of competent bilinguals in specialist fields. Thus we are lead to conclude that the recognition of minority language rights places a new obligation on the modern state to provide the context within which such rights may be exercised. This context should be seen from an holistic perspective for it involves all aspects of the local state's apparatus if language equality is to be a norm. Conventionally, attention has been focused on formal education as the chief agency of language reproduction, but increasingly we are recognising the potency of regional planning, of economic development and of social policy in structuring the conditions which influence language vitality.

The literature on linguistic minorities is rich in relation to social and socio-psychological aspects of identity formation, the cognitive, social and linguistic development of bilinguals and multilinguals. However, it is less informative about the environment or context within which such elements flourish or flounder. This volume seeks to add to our understanding of that context by examining the interrelationship between society and territory, between behaviour and place at all scales, macro, meso and micro.

Contemporary Trends

As a result of these macro-political and demographic changes there are currently over 40 million citizens in the European Community whose mother tongue is a language other than the main official language of the member state in which they live. The European Bureau for Lesser Used Languages, established by the European Parliament, and located in Dublin since 1984, has categorised the various language communities as follows:

(1) Small independent nation-states whose languages are not widely used

by European standards and which are not official, working languages of the European Community (e.g. the Irish and Letzeburgers).
(2) Small nations without their own state (e.g. the Welsh, the Bretons, and the West-Frisians) who reside in one or other member-state.
(3) Peoples such as those in (2) who reside in more than one member-state (e.g. the Catalans, the Occitans who can be found in France, Spain and Italy).
(4) Trans-frontier minorities, i.e. communities within one country who speak a majority language of another, be that country a member-state of the EC or not, e.g. the German-speakers of North-Schleswig, the Slovenes of Trieste, the francophones of the Vallée d'Aoste. (Ó Riagáin, 1989: 511).

The constituent language groups are represented on Figures 1.2 and 1.3. They vary tremendously in their size, constitutional recognition, socio-economic levels of material well-being, internal cohesion and susceptibility to contraction and decline. However, despite their many individual problems, which I would not wish to underplay, collectively they face a brighter future than any other time in the post-war period and that for a number of reasons. First, several initiatives taken in the past decade have brought the common plight of Europe's minority cultures to the attention of key decision-making bodies who have established in turn representative agencies to promote the use of lesser-used languages. Thus the European Community's Bureau for Lesser Used Languages has in a very short space of time mobilised a large number of previously disparate and often overlapping organisations to co-operate with it in its general aim of safeguarding and promoting minority cultures. It has pursued three broad strategies as described by its Secretary General Dónall Ó Riagáin:

(1) To press for the bringing into being of legal and political structures which would protect lesser-used language communities;
(2) To engage in and promote work programmes which would be of practical assistance to those it is endeavouring to serve; and
(3) To facilitate an exchange of information and experiences between the various lesser-used language communities and thus help bring about a greater sense of collective awareness. (ÓRiagáin, 1989: 514)

Through its international links and national representative committees the Bureau has been very active in the following areas. It has prepared reports for the European Parliament on the necessity for legislation permitting constituent language groups to make more use of their language in formal affairs, and on the cultural aspects of minority life. Further initiatives have involved a comparative analysis of pre-school

Europe's Lesser Used Languages

(1) Ireland
Irish

(5) UK
Gaelic
Scots
Cornish
Irish
Welsh

(7) France
Breton
Catalan
Basque
Corsican
Dutch
German/Alsatian
Occitan

(4) Greece
Arvinite
Turkish
Macedonian
Vlak

(0) Portugal

(4) Spain
Catalan
Gallego
Basque
Occitan

(11) Italy
French (Franco-Provencal)
Occitan
German
Ladin
Slovene
Friulan
Sard
Catalan
Greek
Croatian
Albanian

(1) Denmark
German

(1) Belgium
German

(1) Luxemburg
Letzebuergesch

(4) Germany
North Frisian
East Frisian
Danish
Polish

(1) Netherlands
West Frisian

Figure in brackets indicates number of minority languages

Source: EBLUL

FIGURE 1.2 *Europe's lesser used languages*

education in the EC's lesser-used languages, a project on primary school education, the preparation of an EC map of the lesser used languages and several investigations into the relationship between the media, particularly broadcasting and lesser-used languages. These activities are means of sponsoring research findings which feed in to practical policies, and also permit the co-operation and closer understanding of shared problems, thus raising the general standard of discussion and prescription for the resolution of these problems.

Parallel initiatives have been taken by the Council of Europe,

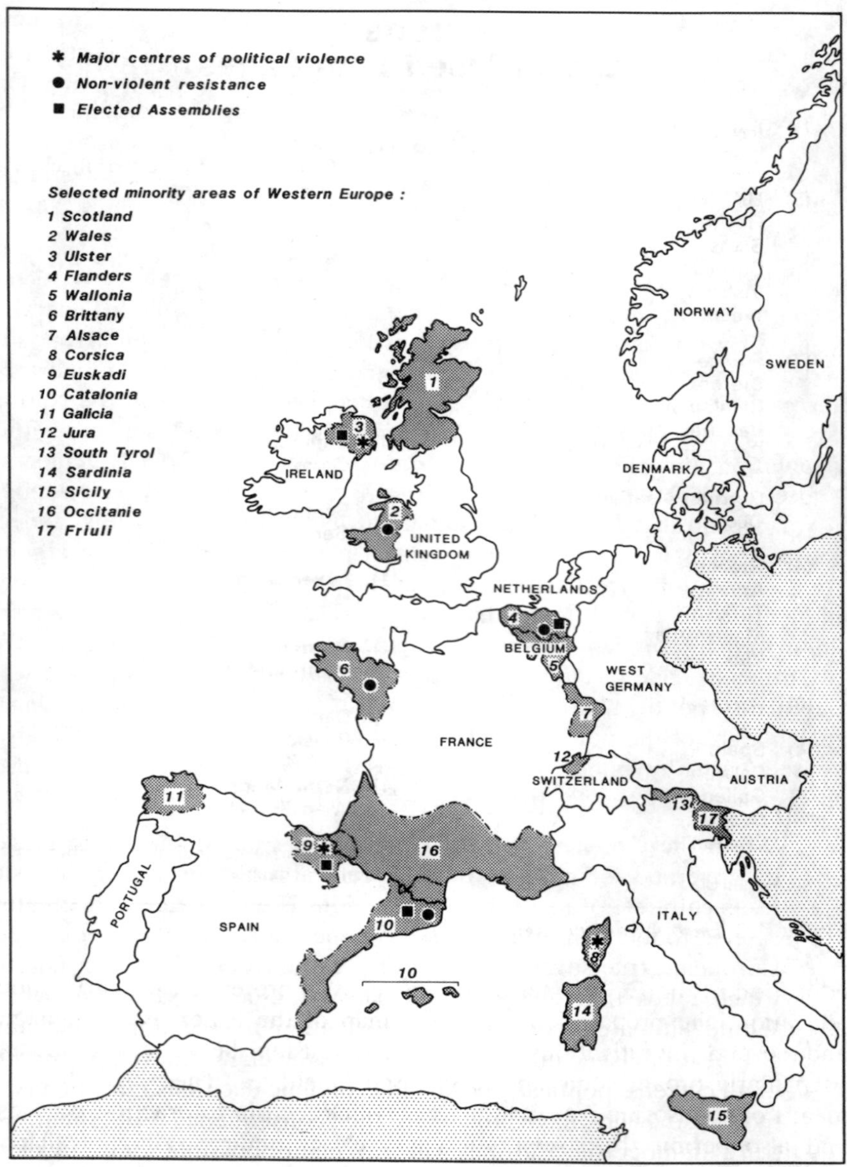

FIGURE 1.3 *Selected minority areas in Western Europe*

through its Conference on Local and Regional Authorities of Europe, which has drafted a Charter on European Regional and Minority Languages, and the UN Commission on Human Rights, which is preparing a universal declaration of the rights of members of national, ethnic, religious and linguistic minorities (Ó Riagáin, 1989: 515). In addition there has been a proliferation of interest groups, quasi-political organisations and lobby associations to promote the activities of, for example, the Federal Union of European Nationalities or the Bureau of Unrepresented Nations in Brussels.

The effectiveness of such organisations is enhanced by a second trend in European political life, namely the recognition that a Federal or United Europe, however conceived, is likely to be more democratic and more responsive to the needs of its citizens. Traditionally the call for a reconstituted Europe of the People, rather than a Europe of the Nation-State, has come from Nationalist parties and Liberals interested in regional devolution and electoral reform. More recently both Social Democrats and Green Party members across Europe have also added their support for a decentralised Europe, based upon its constituent regions. Indeed the ecologists have taken up the central plank of nationalists in arguing for a devolution of power to lower levels in the political hierarchy. Their motivation may be different from nationalists, but the effect may bring about remarkably similar results if enacted in a reformed Europe. Too often the struggle of language minorities has been overly associated with nationalist political mobilisation. Increasingly though we are seeing a realignment of the political ranks which will have far-reaching normative consequences for minority groups. Consider the following declaration of the European Green Parties in 1984.

> We in the Green movement believe that Europe should no longer be governed, or misgoverned, by central authorities. The diversity of its cultures, of its peoples and regions is one of Europe's greatest assets, to be conserved and developed for the benefit of every European; true sovereignty can only come from a federal structure, which takes that diversity into account. Such a structure, which should ultimately consist of regions rather than nation-state, must also be established in a way that respects the dignity and responsibility of all citizens: political, social and economic decisions must be taken by those who have to bear the consequences of them. A truly democratic Europe will be made possible only through decentralisation of institutions, constant dialogue between citizens and those making decisions at various levels, open discussion of problems, free access to all official documents and files, referenda

> at the will of the people, and the granting of the vote to immigrants, which is a matter of importance in elections to the European Parliament. (European Green Parties (1984), quoted in Parkin, 1989: 327–8)

A new alignment of Ecologists, Liberals, Nationalists and Social Democrats on the central issue of European parliamentary representation and the structure of a 'Europe without Frontiers' (Dankert & Kooyman, 1989) represents a challenge to the status quo whose force is only now being recognised.

The third promising trend is something of a two-edged sword. It is conventional to belabour the point that technology has so empowered majoritarian languages such as English and French, that they become irresistible forces in the modern world. Beginning with print capitalism, which Anderson (1983) has demonstrated conferred 'economic advantage, social position and political privilege' on new languages of power, we have witnessed the 'possibility of a new form of imagined community, which in its basic morphology set the stage for the modern nation' (Anderson, 1983: 49). Rapid communication methods have enabled the cultural values of imperial states in both the nineteenth and twentieth centuries to set the agenda of world politics and global aspirations. Television and mass rapid air transport have created a 'shrinking world', a 'global village', but they have also threatened the very survival of minority cultural groups by exposing them to external influences and realisable alternative life-styles.

However, it is not the technology itself which threatens, but its social control and political determination. Thus within Catalonia, Euskadi and Wales we have seen the rapid development of radio and television services operating within the national language and serving as a focus of ideas, news, entertainment and discussion which has far-reaching normative consequences for the lesser-used language. Similarlily in the field of bilingual education the introduction of computer-aided learning in the weaker languages, the preparation of a diverse set of teaching materials across the curriculum and the interaction between educators and administrators which relatively inexpensive software now affords, is a major breakthrough in making the best material available to staff and pupils in bilingual education. I recognise that often the stumbling block to the full implementation of such programmes is the cost of releasing full-time teachers/researchers to develop such initiatives, but even so the computerisation of knowledge within the lesser-used language is a healthy embracing of modern technology. In time when speech-wise computers will enable the identification of thousands of words and the adoption of models of speech blocks in any language it is possible that lesser-used languages will be employed more generally within the public administration and commercial life of hitherto disadvantaged communities.

The fourth and most vital trend is the renewal of commitment, and sense of urgency which animates many within the communities we are discussing to act for the collective good of their fellow-nationals. To date most of the successful programmes of language reform, whether they be in education, the media or in the workplace, have been extensions of ventures which were pioneered by committed volunteers, who gave of their time, energies and resources to the cause they most valued. A second stage has been the institutionalisation of the bilingual or mother tongue practices which the pioneers advocated. The fact such practices are in the hands of professionals drawn from within the lesser-used language communities, has induced critics to suggest that there are both class implications and tendencies toward positive discrimination arising from this new situation (Williams, 1989c). There is some merit to such observations, but there is greater merit in reporting that it is now normal for a young Welsh person or a Catalan to anticipate using his/her bilingual capacity as a bone fide qualification in everyday work. Sadly the same cannot be said for the majority of the cases reported upon in this volume, they are simultaneously more threatened and less able to construct the conditions which would permit the extension of bilingualism as a situational norm in the workplace.

These four trends, among others, offer some hope for the better organised and resourceful lesser-used language communities, but the pressure for assimilation and conformity are still as great as ever. What lessons may we draw from an analysis of such communities within the modern western state? This is the burden of the remainder of this introductory chapter.

Themes and Issues of this Volume

The chapters which follow will each address several of the five themes outlined below in question form.

(1) How adequate are the key concepts and theoretical approaches in describing the plight of lesser-used languages within advanced industrial societies? Are our typlogies, basic constructs such as

culture region and speech community, and conventional models able to capture the reality of change which we are describing? Is our language of 'explanation' a sufficient explanation of our language situation?

(2) What is the origin of most of our data on lesser-used languages? Is such data reliable and comprehensive? How accurate are our methods of measuring aggregate language change over space and through time? Are cross-cultural comparisons of the effects of universal processes on small language communities possible, given the paucity of data and its lack of standardisation?

(3) Are our interpretations of the various causal factors which induce language switching and language decline ideologically tainted by our desire to see such language groups thrive? Are we in danger of over-exaggerating the baneful effects of language competition, and guilty of taking for granted the liberating force of being able to communicate with a much larger audience in an international language? Do we tend to analyse within a primarilty consensus or conflict approach to language change?

(4) What are the policy and planning implications of our analyses? Should scholars and researchers merely let the data speak for itself? Or should they advocate a particular set of planning proposals which would ameliorate particularly harmful situations? Is language planning itself sufficiently widely conceived to be of maximum use? Or should linguists take a far greater account of the socio-economic and political context within which the reforms they advocate can flourish?

(5) How are our ideas and descriptions best represented in geolinguistic analysis? Do we have innovative or methodologically appealing techniques which others may adopt to their advantage? Is our representation of a complex reality within a two-dimensional spatial frame, such as a map or a diagram, a genuine contribution to understanding, or a partial exercise in irrelevancy? How have we been able to manipulate new forms of data interrogation and computer-aided cartography to extend the bounds of our analyses? Is there sufficient communication of the results of academic investigation to a wider, more influential and concerned audience, who can in turn effect change?

These questions have animated much of the work in geolinguistics for over two decades, but it is only rather recently that collaborative work has begun to focus on appropriate answers such as those found in the case studies treated herein.

Spatial Preliminaries: Italy and Ireland

In the first case study, Paul White asks a fundamental question. Why do some minority language situations become politically sensitive and even state-threatening, whilst others have had very little effect on the political equilibrium of their respective states? When one considers that most linguistic minorities are also relatively under-developed in economic and political terms, it is clear that questions of language, culture and identity are no mere appendages to 'normal socio-economic processes', but can themselves constitute the very essence of a minority's relationship with both the majority and the state, in whose name the majority wield power. What it means to be Estonian, Basque, Québécois or Catalan today is essentially captured by their construction of a 'political culture', for it is through struggle, readjustment and national assertion that such identities are being recast. This is not necessarily true for other minorities such as the Breton, Gaelic Scots, or Gallicians, for much of their ethnicity, as John Edwards (1984b) has demonstrated, is symbolic and not essentially a platform for a wider political assertion of group rights in a plural society.

In seeking to answer this political mobilisation issue, Paul White applies a typology of minority language situations to Italian history, focusing on eleven minority languages and their relationship with the state. He frames his geolinguistic interpretation around three key elements of his typology, viz.: whether the minority is an absolute or a local one; the degree of connection between the minority and other speakers of the same language; and the extent of the spatial cohesion between speakers of the minority language. In effect this is a geographical perspective supplementing earlier analyses as provided by de Vries (1984) and Stephens (1976) among others. The most fundamental aspect of the Italian situation is the extent to which many of the minorities described herein will survive well into the twenty-first century. Unless there is a radical re-structuring of the European Community which will accord greater recognition and power to many of the ethno-regional communities described by White there are little grounds for overall optimism for Italy's linguistic minorities.

A common feature of most shrinking linguistic minorities is a concern, amounting to a daily crisis, over the loss of their territorial heartland, homeland, core area, national hearth. Territorial concerns are at the heart of the debate and operate at a number of scales from the national right down to the local and the immediate. Accurate description precedes policy prescription for the amelioration of the myriad problems faced by linguistic minorities, and Reg Hindley is expressly concerned with the problems which innaccurate definition of the official Irish-speaking regions of Ireland, the Gaeltacht, posed for the Irish governments' successive attempts to resuscitate the national tongue. In chapter three Hindley argues that in the initial definition of the Gaeltacht in 1926 the size of the 'true Irish' core was greatly exaggerated because of defective survey work and official benevolence. As a consequence of this liberal delimitation, in the first flush of a nationalist-inspired return to the primal West, the heart of Irish identity was rooted in the land and peasant society of the pre-anglicised past. This was, of course, a parallel from Irish history in the contemporary power struggle of the new state. The western Gaeltacht was to be the putative bastion of Irish uniqueness, the inspiration of Fianna Foil's attack on an English-influenced, Dublin-rooted *étatist* oligarchy (Williams, 1989b). The exaggeration of the Gaeltacht compromised subsequent language policies and brought discredit on the whole Gaeltacht concept, adding confusion and inaccuracy to the very poor material resource base of this outpost of European culture.

In an attempt to correct its earlier mistakes and to match the reality of continued language decline, the Gaeltacht boundaries were greatly reduced by the government's second official delimitation of 1956. However, Hindley draws from both his own original fieldwork at the time and subsequent analysis to argue that even the 1956 delimitation 'rounded up' the Irish-speaking areas to about 50% more than was strictly warranted at the time. The boundaries of the Gaeltacht took little account of the actual interaction between communities, they failed to reflect the functional dependence of the Gaeltacht on the Galltacht (the English-speaking areas) and they did not constitute a meaningful social or geographical entity, which would form an integral element in language-related regional development policies. That the inner core of the predominantly Irish-speaking areas remained reasonably intact until the 1970s may be attributed, in part, to initial delimitation faults. The chapter argues that 'Gaeltacht industries' and other state-inspired schemes which were designed to help, were misdirected by faulty definition to already anglicised central places which were nominally in the Gaeltacht.

Rural-urban friction, place-insensitive policies and grandiose rescue schemes seem to be the norm when governments seek to revive or protect shrinking language communities, without adopting either an holistic perspective or involving the linguistic minority itself in whose name such reforms are being promulgated (Williams, 1988b). Clearly, such attempts fail to recognise that at root language decline is a reflection of a far wider majority–minority power relationship, and one which often goes much deeper than prescriptions based upon the expedient palliatives of a short-term government plan will allow. Of course, I am not arguing that all aspects of language shift and language decline are aggregate in nature and political in origin. I am as conscious as other social scientists of the dangers of adopting a reductionist stance on language competition. However, it is evident that when faced with language stabilisation as a state ideal, too often governments wittingly fail to place the language issue within a realistic socio-economic context at local, national and international levels. One can do as great a disservice to a language minority by exaggerating its capacity to act and to fulfil state expectations, as one can by denying the legitimacy of its claims and neglecting the requisite provision of resources so as to allow language reproduction. The lesson from this chapter is that poor diagnoses will follow from an exaggerated report of the health of the language and the extent of its geographical dominance.

Unsurprisingly, given their geopolitical position as neighbours of the imperial cultures of the modern world system, all of the Celtic peoples share similar characteristics as struggling minorities. Despite having the comfort of their own state, with its declaration of Irish as the first official language, supporters of Irish readily admit that the forces of modernisation and of anglicisation threaten to overwhelm them, turning a living identity and culture into an historical curiosity and base for little more than a symbolic ethnicity in the modern period. Despite over 60 years of state and private language reforms which has seen the numerical potential of the Irish-speaking community grow from 540,802 in 1926 to 1,018,413 in the latest 1981 census, there is a very real sense in which numbers alone provide a misleading impression of the state of the Irish language today. We know to our cost that there is an abyss between the self-report ability recorded on a language question and the reality of language use and functional bilingualism in modern Ireland. However, no matter how relatively disappointing the data may be, at the very least there are ample data upon which estimations of growth and decline may be based, and indeed some successes in the field of education and of commerce may now be recorded accurately. Government surveys on the use, quality, attainment levels and evaluation of Irish in a wide number of social domains, together with a plethora of academic and interest group research reports, now enable us to measure the role of Irish with a far greater degree of accuracy and confidence than ever before. Unfortunately the same cannot be said for most other European linguistic minorities including Breton, the subject of Chapter 4.

Brittany

Territorial considerations lie at the core of Humphrey Lloyd Humphreys' reconstruction of the historical landscape of the Breton language area. In the total absence of census-derived data for the language he is forced to tease out the patterns of language change from various social, geographical and historical sources which, in truth, act as surrogate measures for Breton culture. His first task is to identify the outward extension of the Breton culture area and to trace the vicissitudes of the French–Breton language divide. Paralleling the experience of all the other Celtic language groups, Breton has moved inexorably westward, a retreat reported by Sébillot (1886), Panier (1942), Ambrose (1979) and Timm (1980). Humphreys is careful to note that the construction of linguistic divides, an essential feature of geolinguistics, involves a high degree of generalisation. But it can also lead to confusion, as Ambrose and I suggested in an earlier study of Breton and other linguistic divides (Williams & Ambrose, 1988).

> In some circumstances, as a means of measurement of the language area, such divides can lead to confusion because there is no general convention about what stage of transition across the language boundary they are seeking to outline. Amongst the possible stages the following could be cited: (a) the area where Breton is the only, or (b) the preferred, everyday language of the majority; (c) the line at which French asserts itself as the usual language for the majority of the people; (d) the edge of the area where only a minority of people can speak Breton, or (e) where they do so in a reduced selection of circumstances; and (f) the point at which French becomes the only everyday language. (Williams & Ambrose, 1988: 110)

A second related problem of linguistic divides is that such linear features fail to recognise the range of processes which take place across the language border, further reducing the dynamism inherent in the situation and suggesting the existence of two monolithic entities either side of the line, whereas in fact most linguistic divides in Celtic societies are cartographic representations which have little significance on the ground in terms of a changing topography, or of a break in style of such material cultural artefacts as vernacular architecture or farming patterns. This is not to deny the existence of very radical changes which accompany linguistic divides in many other parts of the world, such as India, West Africa or Soviet Central Asia. However, in well integrated western societies we need to be careful of over-exaggerating the significance of revealed linguistic divides on actual social behaviour and language switching in bi- or multicultural communities.

Having established the linguistic divide, Humphreys traces the dynamic variations in the vitality of Breton within its core area. Lack of a consistent data base over time is a major handicap here and he is perforce obliged to rely upon less consistent surrogate measures, chief of which is the use of Breton in the Catechism as compared with the Sermon. In 1927, for example, the language of religious instruction in both Church and Convent School tended to be French in and around urban areas, with girls being more likely than boys to be taught in French. The 'social demotion of Breton' which accompanied modernisation and urbanisation is but part of a general tendency throughout France and other centralising polities in Europe after the industrial revolution. However, we should not automatically assume that Breton was the language of the rural peasantry only. We acknowledge that though the French Revolution inspired the policy of linguistic and cultural standardisation, its full-scale realisation occurred only during the first decades of the Third Republic (1870–1914). Weber (1976) argued that until then France consisted of separate, often isolated communities, each with its own variety of French, let alone the lesser-used languages, such as Breton, Corsican or Flemish. A sense of national identity and of state cohesion was thus not achieved until the end of the nineteenth century. Mordrel (1981) goes further and argues that the exultation of France as a classic nation-state is a misreading of history, the propagation of what he calls *le mythe de l'hexagone* which seeks to deny

> l'histoire de toutes les contrées de l'Hexagone: de la Flandre à la Guyenne, de la Corse à la Normandie, de la Franche-Comté au Pays Basque, de la Bourgogne au Languedoc, de l'Alsace à la Bretagne, de la Savoie au Pays Toulousain. (Mordrel, 1981)

However, Charles Tilly (1979) demonstrates in his critique of Weber's version of the modernisation thesis, that France and other continental European countries did not consist of 'congeries of isolated, immobile agrarian societies' at the beginning of the nineteenth century. Even before the mid-nineteenth century and the penetration of industrial capitalism and the revolutions in mass communications, villages contained a diverse population and not just the peasantry. Rural should not be equated with peasantry. Coastal Brittany, for example, had a long maritime association with other parts of Europe and the North Atlantic fisheries trade guaranteed regular contact with francophones in North America, particularly in Québec and Acadia. Furthermore, as far back as the Revolutionary period, conscription due to Napoleon's imperial designs (Williams, 1989a) had begun to wrench peasants and artisans from their villages, while national politics reached deep into rural France. The nationalisation of the citizenry through formal education, conscription, print capitalism, social and physical communications and the social construction of state space was an essential, if debatable, element in the transition from localism, to provincialism and beyond to state nationalism (Kofman & Williams, 1989: 10).

As a result of both state integration and of social modernisation, Breton was increasingly confined to private domains, to the rural, scattered hamlets. Even the Church, for so long the one domain within which Breton had a formal, public role, began by the turn of the century to abandon Breton wholesale in favour of French. Without an institutional framework, languages in decline typically lose their relevance and potency for expressing the most fundamental of human desires, hopes and fears. Unless such a loss can be turned into a mobilising force whereby the language becomes a symbol of resistance, as Sartre characterised the Basque struggle against Spanish fascism, then language death will quickly follow.

How alive is the Breton language today? What are the signs of its ethnolinguistic vitality? How may we measure such features in the absence of reliable and systematic information? These are the questions which lie behind Humphreys' third contribution, perhaps the most unique and controversial part of his chapter, namely a numerical estimate of the size of the Breton-speaking population. Past estimates have ranged from the 1,300,000 suggested by Sébillot in 1886, to the 685,250 reported by Bozec in 1974. Denez (1983) sounded a characteristically cautious note on present estimates: 'I wonder who, today, would give a fair guess? Between the 20,000 given by the Préfecture and the 700,000 given by the Breton activists there is bound to be a lot of wishful thinking.' Humphreys' method produces a figure of 686,000 speakers and Figure 4.3 maps this estimate. This will come as a surprise to many Breton experts, let alone the many detractors of the language in France, who will challenge this figure as being rather high. Regardless of the actual figure, it is patently obvious that two features serve to reduce the impact which a critical mass of about 600,000 Breton speakers should make on the culture and social life of Brittany. The first is that the vast majority of such people are very reticent to use their Breton in public, even with others they know to be fluent or comfortable with Breton. The second is the steep fall in the proficiency and self-confidence of Breton communication from the older to the younger generation — hardly conducive to the survival of an autonomous Breton culture into the twenty-first century!

Kuter (1989: 75–6) has recently examined the ambiguity of Breton attitudes to the transmission of their language in terms of a competition between opposing languages (see also Wardaugh (1987) for a fine overview of this phenomenon at the global level). He suggests that there are three basic oppositions between Breton and French:

(1) The political symbolism of French as the 'national' language opposed to Breton as the 'regional' language.
(2) The socio-economic symbolism of French as the language of civilisation, progress and the future, opposed to Breton as a language of the past, fit only for backward peasants.
(3) The cultural symbolism of French as an international, urban language, opposed to Breton as a marker of a uniquely local, rural identity. (Kuter, 1989: 76)

His analysis of the conflict between the ideologies which are suggested by these opposites, points to the strong political and economic symbolism of French as a 'useful', 'practical' and 'international' language. The 'one and indivisible' French state has promoted its language as the bearer of civilisation and education, the harbinger of modernity in underdeveloped societies at home and abroad. The contrasts are familiar, and are repeated in other cases discussed in this volume, e.g. Gaelic versus English, Friulian or Slovene versus Italian, Faroese versus Danish. However, when two international cultures penetrate a third territory, such as English and French have settled in Canada, then it is quite possible for the language of modernity in one context (i.e. French in Europe under Napoleon) to be labelled the language of the *ancien régime* and of parochial conservatism (i.e. French in Canada until the 'quiet revolution' of the Lesage administration of the early 1960s). It is the context and socio-economic structure of the respective society which determines the relative power and attraction of languages in competition, not necessarily the languages themselves. That said, of course, it is far easier for a language minority speaking an international language to gain sustenance, material cultural products and personnel from outside its geographical situation, than it is for an original, autochthonous group as the chapters which follow ably demonstrate.

Scotland

The contraction of the cultural heartland, historically persistent out-migration and the inexorable decline of the minority language is a pattern repeated for Scotland also. In the next three chapters different aspects of this pattern are examined by a sociolinguist, an historical geographer and a professional planner. Kenneth MacKinnon charts the pattern of language-retreat over the past century as revealed by the census questions on Gaelic from 1881–1981. In the first census of 1881 officials who were asked to estimate the numbers 'in the habit of making colloquial use of the Gaelic language' suggested a total of 231,594 speakers (for details see Withers, 1984). By 1981 only 79,307 were recorded as Gaelic speaking (see Figure 5:1), by far the weakest of the four popular Celtic languages. Geographically, also, the location of the Gaelic speaking population has shifted. The core of the Gaelic-speaking region has shrunk north-westwards to Tiree, Skye and the Western Isles, while the urban areas of the Lowlands now account for 41%, or 32,342 (1981 figure) of all Gaelic speakers resident in Scotland. (How many reside in the rest of the UK and abroad would make a fascinating, not to say ingenious, research project.)

The traditional cultural divide in Scottish history has been the Highland–Lowland divide, and though no one would suggest that the Lowlands offers a more promising hope for the reproduction of Gaelic in the future, it is remarkable how little research has been done into the Gaelic-speaking communities of the Lowlands. MacKinnon suggests with a mixture of wishful thinking and cynicism that were the colonies of Gaelic speakers in the Lowlands true communities, they would constitute a Gaelic Archipelago in a Lowlands Sea of greater consequence than that of the Hebrides themselves. Relative isolation afforded by the physical distance from the centres of power, commerce and influence had in the past kept many Gaelic-speaking communities distinct from the mainstream Anglo-Scottish culture and material patterns. However, as a result of a wide variety of factors which characterise a modern society, many individuals are now more autonomous and more directly receptive to outside influences. Processes such as in-migration of non-Gaelic speakers, language shift, the decline in organised religion, the revolution in telecommunications and access to the mass media, the development of tourism and of capital-intensive resource exploitation all reduce the probability of Gaels inhabiting settled, Gaelic-speaking communities as a local majority. The old domains no longer apply in language reproduction, and new domains have yet to be fully established. Following the Welsh example, MacKinnon suggests that if viable Gaelic-speaking communities are to be encouraged then the twin agencies of language reproduction, i.e. education and a sensitive environmental policy which takes account of the needs of the language and Gaelic culture, have to be established as a matter of urgency. Only then will *coimhearsnachdan ura Gaidhealach* — new Gaelic communities — based upon a partnership of local popular commitment and government direction of resources and finance be fully realised. His thesis rests on a policy of positive discrimination in favour of Gaelic speakers and their communities. He warns that 'unless attention is given to the means of securing the maintenance of economic health and social well-being of the Gaelic communities, there may well be no truly Gaelic communities left by the end of the century'. The detailed planning proposals spelling out his regenerative call are taken up by Clive James in chapter seven. Earlier I alluded to the neglect of the Lowland Gaelic-speaking communities in previous research. Charles Withers attempts to redress the balance somewhat in his investigation of the lessons to be learned from the 1891 census source. He focuses on the four Lowland cities of Aberdeen, Dundee, Perth and Stirling to reconstruct elementary aspects of the urban Gaelic-speaking population of Scotland. First he discusses the significance of the numbers of Gaelic speakers according to the published census volumes and the unpublished enumerators' books. Secondly, he considers where the Gaelic speaking residents of urban Lowland Scotland were born. Thirdly, he examines differences by age and sex in the levels of Gaelic speaking in the four urban areas.

His detailed enquiry casts severe doubts on the conventional interpretation of the Highland–Lowland divide, and guards against overgeneralising about language use from the census source. His analysis offers four conclusions which are in varying degrees applicable to other Celtic societies. First, a familiar argument in socio- and geolinguistics: the census is not necessarily an accurate guide to the numbers speaking Gaelic, let alone to their social use of the language. It 'is of little or no use in investigating how Gaelic was used, to whom, when and why, or in exploring processes of language transmission'. Second, an analysis of the enumerators' books reveals that the Gaelic-speaking population of the 'urban Gaidhealtachd' was drawn from particular areas within the Highlands; not themselves necessarily highly Gaelic speaking, and from parishes not in the Highlands proper. Third, as with the Breton and Irish cases discussed above, important variations were found in the relative strength by age, sex and location of Gaelic speakers. Fourth, Charles Withers argues for further research on the survival of the minority outside the traditional heartland area, a call echoed in Ireland, Wales, Brittany and Québec by others in this volume.

What future, then, for the Gaelic-speaking communities? Clive James is well-placed to offer an answer, for he is a planner with Gwynedd County Council, and has been active in grappling with the question of how to include language considerations in local authority planning policy.

James concentrates his attention on providing a sustainable resource base for community development in the Gaelic-speaking areas. He traces the initiatives of agencies such as the Highlands and Islands Development Board in establishing local co-operatives and in institutionalising the use of Gaelic in a business environment, albeit at a very limited level. Commending the development of tourism and other activities James is adamant that it is the community and its needs which should determine the rate and extent of additional employment opportunities. To this end he advocates a policy of holistic development, which is very akin in aim, if not in execution, to policies of sustainable development produced for the Third World, where rural poverty and resource exploitation also threaten to destroy communal cohesion and cultural vitality (Redclift, 1987). Central to this process is the preparation of a sympathetic, yet realistic, Structure Plan, particularly for the Western Isles. Much of the remainder of the chapter is an astute explication of the necessary preconditions which have to be met now so as to ensure the future economic and cultural viability of the Gaelic communities.

This detailed set of proposals is an important contribution to the general debate on the survival of shrinking lesser-used languages. We have enough evidence to date about the linguistic changes which occur in threatened minority contexts, and more than enough public beating of the chest from 'bleeding heart liberals.' What is needed above all else is a realistic assessment of what can be done now, in concrete, material terms to strengthen the socio-economic structure of already emaciated minority communities. The old maxim from the Gaeltacht 'no jobs, no people; no people, no Gaeltacht' points to the fact that regional planners, government agencies and corporate enterprises are vital actors in any revitalisation programme for threatened language groups. Too often, however, such actors are perceived as the principal authors of the very processes which accelerate the emasculation of the minority culture.

Political control is the key, at the local level at least, as to whether such holistic planning will be implemented. One may question James's faith in the planning process, for it is debatable as to whether structure planning is a sufficiently sensitive instrument to deal with such complex issues as language preservation and community development. But in the absence of binding legislation to control the deleterious influences in linguistically sensitive areas, recognising the legitimacy of, and planning for the Gaelic language as a communal resource would be a major step forward.

Canada

In contrast to West European societies Canada has had a far more tolerant attitude to the cultural traditions and aspirations of its constituent peoples, many of whom were fleeing from the very conditions of poverty, discrimination and exclusion which were described at the beginning of this chapter. Three periods of inter-ethnic interaction are conventionally portrayed in post-Confederation Canadian history. Following the accommodation reached by the Fathers of Confederation in 1867, Canada was subjected to successive policies of Anglo-Conformity which sought to give a geographical basis to national unity, based upon the English language and culture, commercial exploitation of land and resources and the development of a British-style parliamentary democracy. Successive generations of French-Canadian leaders felt betrayed by the lack of respect for their rights embodied in Confederation and adopted various degrees of nationalism in order to bring about a restitution of the co-equal position of francophones in Canadian statehood. The Federal government's most comprehensive response to these demands was to institute a coast-to-coast policy of Bilingualism and Biculturalism, following the recommendations of the Royal Commission on Bilingualism and Biculturalism in 1969. Unable to assuage both Québécois separatism and the rise of the 'new ethnics', the government broadened its policy to invoke a commitment to Multiculturalism within a bilingual framework as the new and lasting basis for Canadian citizenship and identity.

In the early 1960s the fear was expressed that the French language would be lost in the heartlands of Québec, let alone in the outlying districts of *la francophonie* in North America. Two decades on the vitality of French in Québec has been increased through government regulation and social change, but even so the French language in Canada is still in a precarious position, considering its formal role as a co-equal language of society (see Figure 1.4). Successive Federal Governments have sought to refine the original Official Languages Act passed in 1969, supplementing it by the 1973 Parliamentary Resolution, and specifying in more detail the rights and obligations of the state in respect of the linguistic provisions of the 1982 Charter of Rights and Freedoms, which enshrined English and French as Canada's two official languages (D'Iberville Fortier, 1988: 4). Sections 16 to 22 of the Charter confirmed the previously central concepts of the 1969 Act as having constitutional status but added a new rider: from henceforth in addition to the existing test of significant demand for bilingual service it also recognised that 'the nature of the office' held by a federal employee could also require knowledge of both

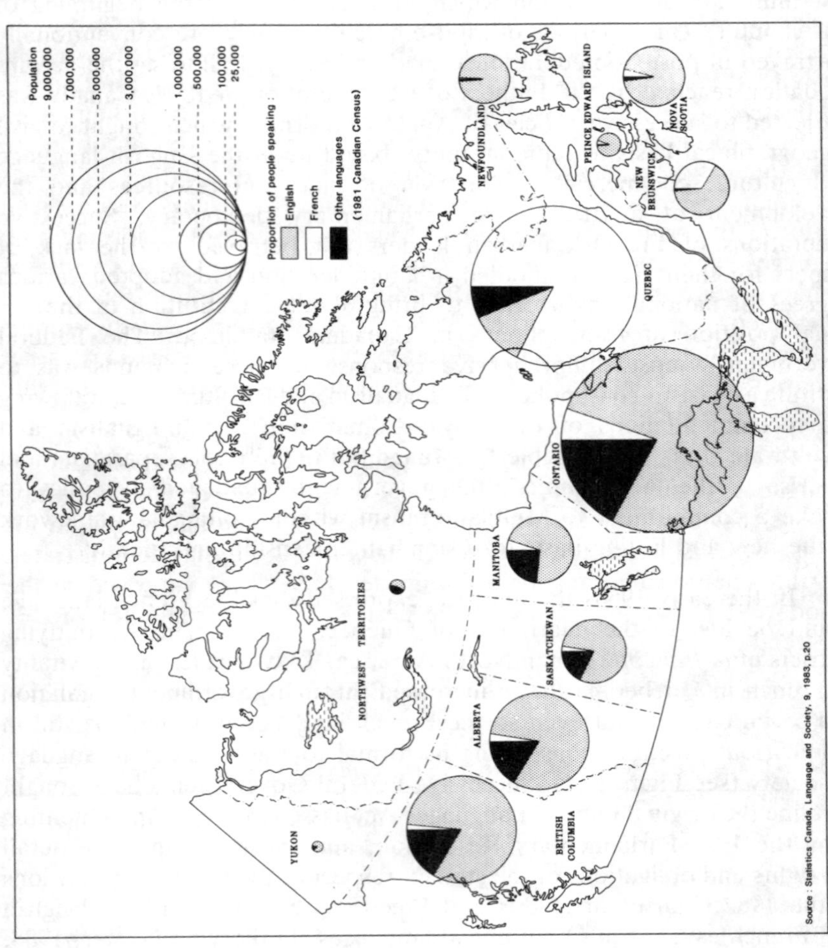

FIGURE 1.4 *The proportion speaking English, French and 'Other' Languages in Canada, 1981*

languages. The 1988 Annual Report of the Commissioner of Official Languages (1988: 27) illustrated the type of office thus envisaged: 'where a federal office is of such immediate importance to the citizen (for example, a customs office at the border), the service it offers will have to be made available, in some manner in both languages, regardless of demand'. This new obligation required a new and more comprehensive Language Act, and in June 1987 the government tabled a new Bill, C-72, just a few weeks after the Meech Lake accord was signed by the majority of the provinces. Improvements and amendments followed much political debate and on 15th September 1988 the new Official Languages Act was proclaimed. It has three fundamental requirements according to the Commissioner of Official Languages. First, it 'clarifies both the obligations of federal institutions and the rights of citizens'. Secondly, 'it reinforces the principle of equality of English and French, according both languages equal status before the courts and giving most of its provisions primacy over other legislation'. Thirdly, 'it also calls for the federal government to co-operate closely with provincial governments in support of official language minorities and to advance the knowledge and use of both our official languages throughout Canadian society' (D'Iberville Fortier, 1988: 4).

Québec continues to fear for the cultural survival of francophones throughout North America, but may take comfort from recent data which suggests that the numbers who speak French at home has increased for the rest of Canada outside Québec. Henripin (1988: 6) has demonstrated that the situation of francophones outside Québec has improved in the period 1981–6 as compared with the period 1971–81. Table 1:1 reveals this trend.

It is evident also that the annual rate of increase for Anglo-

TABLE 1.1 *Mother tongue and home language: annual rates of increase*

	1971–1981	1981–1986
French, outside Québec		
mother tongue	+1.2%	+0.1%
home language	−0.1%	+0.2%
English, Québec		
mother tongue	−1.2%	−0.8%
home language	−0.9%	−0.3%

Source: Henripin (1988: 6)

Québecers suggests that they are losing less ground if one considers the language spoken at home rather than the mother tongue, whereas the opposite is true of francophones outside Québec in 1971–81 (Henripin, 1988: 6). In addition he argues that the rate of decrease of Anglo-Québecers has fallen by one-third if one considers mother tongue and by two-thirds for home language. He attributes this to the fact that the net emigration of Québecers whose mother tongue was English declined from 16,000 a year in 1971–81 to 8,000 a year in 1981–6. However, the most encouraging feature for both Québec and the Federal commitment to a balanced bilingual society is that the number of those who habitually speak French at home outside Québec has increased, whereas it had declined in the period 1971–81.

Further evidence of the changes in demography, migration and language legislation affecting patterns of home language use and mother tongue retention are evidenced in Table 1.2. The main conclusion from this census evidence released in April 1988 is that both cultural regions are becoming more homogeneous. In Québec in 1986, 82.8% of the population was French-speaking (mother tongue or home language), that is 2% more than it was 15 years earlier. Henripin (1988: 7) also observes that this trend is more marked in Montreal and its environs than in Québec as a whole (Table 1.2): whereas in the rest of Canada, English has made almost equivalent gains. In 1986, 88.6% of the population of 'English Canada' spoke mainly English at home, and 80% had English as their mother tongue.

Is this homogenisation process constructive for the attainment of Canadian language and political goals? Would Québec feel more secure within the Canadian federation if she were undoubtedly unilingual French in character and social practice? Or would such unilingualism serve to differentiate her further from the rest of Canada? The passage of the controversial Law 178 which enforces the use of French only within Québec in the spheres of public notices and commercial publicity on the outside of establishments, certainly seeks to reduce the trans-Canadian element of Québec public spaces (Leclerc, 1989). Québec is more obviously French now than at any other time in the twentieth century in formal, institutional terms. The debate now focuses on whether or not the undoubted gains made in Québec are at the expense of goodwill and constructive co-operation with the rest of Canada on a whole range of socio-political, commercial and resource-environmental issues. The failure of the Meech Lake accord and the backlash against Québec in parts of English-Canada was sufficient testimony to the fact that many still believe that the role of Québec within Canadian federation is still ambigious, to

TABLE 1.2 *Percentage of certain linguistic groups, Canada, Québec, rest of Canada, Montreal, Toronto, 1971, 1981 and 1986*

Regions and languages	*Mother tongue*			*Home language*		
	1971	*1981*	*1986*	*1971*	*1981*	*1986*
Canada						
English	60.1	61.3	62.1	67.0	68.2	68.9
French	26.9	25.7	25.1	25.7	24.6	24.0
Others	13.0	13.0	12.8	7.3	7.2	7.1
Québec						
English	13.1	11.0	10.4	14.7	12.7	12.3
French	80.7	82.4	82.8	80.8	82.5	82.8
Others	6.2	6.6	6.8	4.5	4.8	4.9
Rest of Canada						
English	78.3	79.4	80.0	87.2	88.2	88.6
French	6.0	5.3	5.0	4.3	3.8	3.6
Others	15.7	15.4	14.9	8.5	8.1	7.8
Montreal						
English	21.7	18.2	17.0	24.9	21.7	20.8
French	66.3	68.8	69.7	66.3	68.9	69.7
Others	12.0	13.0	13.4	8.8	9.3	9.5
Toronto						
English	73.8	72.0	72.1	81.8	81.6	82.2
French	1.7	1.5	1.6	0.8	0.7	0.8
Others	24.5	26.5	26.3	17.4	17.7	16.9

Source: 1981 and 1986 censuses (1986 figures 'adjusted'). Reproduced with permission from Henripin, 1988: 7.

say the least. Professor Don Cartwright adds a specifically geographical element to this debate, focusing on the significance of a cultural zone of transition between the 'two solitudes' of Québec and English Canada. Stemming from his earlier work on bilingual districts and linguistic accommodation (Cartwright, 1980; 1987; Cartwright & Williams, 1982) he develops a dynamic model of cultural interaction in transition zones which stresses the interactive, consensual dimension to language issues in Canada. His thesis is that bicultural accommodation within cultural transitional zones may serve to lessen the social and cognitive distance which engenders ethnic conflict in Canada. His research is policy-oriented, as befits his former role as Research Director of the Bilingual Districts Advisory Board. His detailed analysis in eastern Ontario and eastern

Québec charts the manner in which migration, education and self-perception can all be influenced by central and provincial government policies. Thus he advocates a more constructive recognition of the need to promote bicultural interaction in many domains so as to reduce the possibility of linguistic territorialisation becoming the norm in Canada. By comparison with other linguistically divided societies, legislators in Canada can still point with pride to their record of support for bilingualism and biculturalism. If Canada is to avoid the fate of Belgium (Murphy, 1988) or Yugoslavia, where linguistic boundaries are entrenched, it has to recognise the critical importance of the cultural transition zone as a key to national unity.

We have noted above that the census-based language statistics suggest that Québec continues to become more French and the rest of Canada to become more English confirming a functional, if not a formal, linguistic territorialisation. The most recent census of 1986 confirmed well-established trends reported earlier by Lachapelle & Henripin (1982). These general features of Canada's language situation are well understood; they include the following salient points: (1) the English-speaking population of Québec has declined; (2) the francophone minorities outside Québec are increasingly vulnerable, only in New Brunswick is there sustained resistance to linguistic assimilation; (3) English–French bilingualism throughout Canada is increasing apace. In 1971, Henripin (1988: 9) reports, 13.4% of Canadians were bilingual; in 1981, 15.3%; in 1986, 16.2%; (4) bilingualism is a geographically uneven phenomenon. In Québec, 34.5% of the population is bilingual: in the rest of Canada the figure is 9.9%; (5) the minority groups are clearly losing ground. Henripin (1988: 9) suggests that

> in the course of time, persons who have another mother tongue adopt English at home, and this language of adoption becomes the mother tongue of their children. French just manages to hold its ground, and only in Qúebec, where its losses to English are almost exactly compensated for by the gains it makes at the expense of third languages. (Henripin, 1988: 9)

In Chapter 9 Professor John de Vries develops our understanding of these trends since 1971 by adopting methodologically sophisticated demographic techniques of analysis. Using changes in language data, 1971–81, de Vries shows that subtle variations in the data are often masked by overall marginal stability of language affiliation in Canada. By employing the statistical decomposition methodology he demonstrates that the further one moves either east or west from Québec, the stronger the association between province and English mother tongue (the exception is Ontario). A similar pattern is revealed, though of opposite signs, by the values of French mother tongue. Only Alberta is an exception to this pattern for it has received positive migration flows of francophones since 1971. Further analysis of differential growth rates suggests that the English mother tongue population increased its share of the total population through net migration, language shift and differential natural increase with a slight increase of those who were monolingual in 1971 becoming bilingual in 1981. In contrast, the French mother tongue segment grew by 6.6%, but French monolinguals increased by only 2.2% (well below what might be expected on the basis of natural increase). De Vries argues from this data that there was a considerable movement from French monolingualism to bilingualism, but that this took place largely outside Québec. Bilinguals increased by 27%, well above the growth rate for the other groups. He comments that

> it is likely that much of this growth may be attributed to second-language acquisition during the intercensal period (rather than higher new migration balances, or lower death rates among bilinguals). Much of this increase may have come from official language minorities. (de Vries, this volume)

His analysis suggests that the period 1971–81 showed slight relative loss for the French mother tongue population, for those speaking French only, and for those speaking neither English nor French. Much of this intercensal change could be 'explained' by changes in marginal distributions of a statistical nature, that is, they explained the 'how' question of language ecology. The more debatable 'why' question is less amenable to interpretation by recourse to census data alone. Recognising this, de Vries concludes with a number of questions that highlight the limitations of sophisticated aggregate census analysis. For example, in noting the confirmation of Canada as a more bilingual society by the 1980s, he asks was this

> increase in bilingualism due to higher rates of natural increase, or to the effects of international migration or to the acquisition of the second official language by persons who in 1971 were able to speak one (only) or neither of the official languages?

One way of resolving such questions is by undertaking research at a more localised and detailed scale of analysis, according to de Vries. In the penultimate chapter, Professor John Edwards provides us with a model case study of such micro-level investigations. The focus of his chapter is the survival of Gaelic in Nova Scotia. His illustration has two merits in the context of this volume. It demonstrates some specific applications of his more generalised interpretation of language-group relations *per se*, for Gaelic is an historically significant 'other language' in the cultural mosaic of Canada. It thus offers a useful counter to the more familiar examples of French-speakers outside Québec, and of the more recent Eastern European and Asian minority languages, used whenever minority–majority relations are discussed. Secondly, because Gaelic is a transplanted language, and Nova Scotia has been described as still the most populous Celtic speech community in the New World (MacKinnon, 1985), the chapter offers some useful comparisons with the Scottish perspectives on language survival discussed earlier in Chapters 5, 6 and 7.

For scholars interested in language contraction and death, Edwards's comments about the possibility of language survival in threatened environments will be particularly significant. I have reproduced his ten observations below because they are pertinent to all the situations discussed in this volume of essays on endangered linguistic minorities. They also have the great merit of recognising that change is inherent in any social relationship, and we should not necessarily interpret the 'abandonment of original or static positions as decay or loss' (Edwards, 1985: 86).

Ten observations on declining linguistic minorities

(1) Languages in decline typically have a predominance of middle-aged or elderly speakers; there is a lack of transmission to the younger generation.
(2) Weakening languages are often confined to rural areas, and associations are often made between the language and poverty, isolation and lack of sophistication of its speakers.
(3) Bilingualism in the declining language and its powerful linguistic neighbour is often only a temporary phenomenon, to be ultimately replaced with dominant-language monolingualism.
(4) Language decline can be understood properly only as a *symptom* of minority–majority contact; it is thus extremely unlikely that efforts directed towards language preservation alone will be successful.
(5) *Active* desires to stem the decline of threatened languages are usually operative only for a minority within a minority group. Indeed, revivalists are sometimes *non*-group members who have become apologists for language maintenance.
(6) There are important and obvious differences, for the ultimate fate of a language, between native speakers and those who study and learn the language on a more self-conscious basis.

(7) Cultural activities and symbolic manifestations of ethnicity often continue long after group language declines. They support a continuing sense of groupness yet do not hinder successful movement in the mainstream.
(8) The media are two-edged swords for declining languages. It is, on the one hand, desirable that minority languages be represented in them; on the other hand, however, the media act to channel dominant-language influence to the minority group.
(9) Language change, rather than stasis, is the historical pattern and ordinary people are largely motivated by practical necessity in linguistic matters.
(10) It is important to realise that there can exist a distinction between communicative and symbolic aspects of a language. For majority speakers of majority languages, both aspects generally co-exist, but they can become separated; minority-group speakers who no longer use the original language for ordinary, communicative purposes often retain an attachment which involves the language as group symbol. (Edwards, this volume)

Evidence for the verification of most of these points in respect of the Gaelic-speaking community of Nova Scotia in general and Cape Breton in particular is available from the many studies and popular investigations which Edwards reviews. The main conclusion is that the Gaelic language has lost its communicative role for the vast majority of those with Scottish ancestry and has been absorbed into a larger cultural configuration we may call the symbolic ethnicity of Scottishness. This transformation from an active communicative function to a passive symbolic function is a very characteristic process in those situations of language contraction and death (for a comparative treatment see the studies in Dorian, 1989). However, Edwards sought to investigate the sociolinguistic characteristics of those who either used Gaelic, or who were studying Gaelic, by means of a direct measurement of a sample of 159 residents of Nova Scotia. His study revealed interesting results on the sample's demographic information and Gaelic background, its Gaelic competence and use, evaluations of Gaelic, its current status, the transmission and survival potential of Gaelic, and the reasons which led to the learning of the language.

The chief element that I wish to emphasise is that many of his respondents did not see themselves as providing active support for a Gaelic revival. They were interested, sympathetic but ultimately not *responsible* for the survival of the language. In an earlier work (Edwards, 1985: 51), it was found that the 'reasons behind non-transmission are not related to some personal repudiation of the language but rather to pragmatic assessments of the likely utility of competing varieties'. The practical difficulties surrounding language reproduction, in the absence of a well-organised and routine set of domains, is a major consideration in language switching behaviour. Too often language romantics rebuke their compatriots for not joining the 'heroic language struggle', for not supporting the writings of poets, authors and propagandists in the threatened tongue. They also appeal to their countrymen to return to the homeland and bolster the ethnolinguistic vitality of the culture core area. Emyr Llewelyn of *Adfer*, an organisation to invigorate Welsh-speaking areas, phrased it thus:

> Colonisation. That is the key to it all. You must return from exile in the non-Welsh-speaking areas, there is no vigour, no energy, no vision, no power there — nothing will emerge from there. . . . In the west, awaiting your leadership, is our unassuming peasantry — thoroughly lost, and voices from all sides deafening and confusing them. Materialistic English voices shout at them from all sides. Everything surrounding an ordinary Welshman tells him that English not Welsh should prevail, tells him to forget his language and his people and adopt foreign ones. My battle is not to create more bourgeois to inhabit suburbia, but in order to raise a generation of young people who are heroic and cultured, true to the people and civilised. (Llewelyn, 1986: 249)

This link between the mystical purity of the western lands, the spiritual simplicity of the peasantry waiting to be led by enlightened activists who forgo the pleasures of Sodom and Gomorrah (actually Cardiff and Swansea, the Welsh Cities of the Plain wherein Mammon succours the 'exiled' Welsh speakers) and the historic role of the language activist in leading his people to a new era of autochthonous freedom, is a common theme among language nationalists (Williams, 1988a).

Edwards notes the same phenomenon in Nova Scotia, though not to the same degree, where Gaelic is infused with righteousness, truth, honour and spirituality. Why is it that declining languages conjure up these images of spirituality and of primitive religious feelings? Is it their antiquity? Surely not, for many of their direct competitors are equally old. Is it that, because they are in danger of passing out of existence, we attach an element of uniqueness and rarity value to them, so that when they disappear a certain amount of our common humanity also disappears? If so, then the 'ecology of language' needs to be recast as a more fundamental species-wide imperative. Indeed, there are signs that the current concern with deep ecology and with environmental issues now embraces declining languages and cultures as evidence that humankind has failed in its stewardship role. If in addition to the 'Save the Whales' campaign we also popularise the 'Save the Welsh' campaign we will immediately gain the support of at least three strands of a dissenting culture: the ecologists, the religious fundamentalists, and the language activists — a powerful combination in contemporary Britain. In truth, we need not be so coy or tongue-in-cheek for it is likely that a combination of nationalists, ecologists, religionists and socialists will emerge in the future as the basis of a communal defence of threatened environments (both natural and social) in contrast to state-centralist and market-driven forces of the left and right. Their emphasis on decentralised community action and responsibility is already having an influence on certain sectors of society, e.g. environmental pollution, food production and safety, the anti-nuclear movement and the peace protests in the West. Most clearly of all is the call in Eastern Europe to make glasnost and perestroika a reality. The key actors in Poland, Hungary, the former East Germany and the various regions of the USSR, most notably Estonia, Lithuania, Latvia and the Ukraine, are the former outlawed members of the nationalist intelligentsia and the Catholic or Orthodox Church, together with new activists mobilised on the basis of environmental issues, such as industrial pollution in southern Poland, nuclear catastrophe in the Ukraine and forest degradation and water pollution in Hungary. In an attempt to construct a communal democratic programme for their reforms such activists often champion the cultural symbols of language and religion, and point to their demise or banning as evidence of the intransigence of a hostile or uncaring central state apparatus. We need not necessarily agree with the demands of Ukranian nationalists to re-establish the 'Uniate' Catholic Church which Stalin banned, nor need we endorse the autonomist push in western Ukraine or Estonia to sympathise with the question how free are individuals if they are not free to use their own language in their own land? The interrelationship between national identity, language defence and environmental concern, all within the greater push for democratic representation, makes Eastern and Central Europe a fascinating, if at times perilous contrast to the cases discussed herein. But we should not lose sight of the fact that the fundamental issue which unites such disparate cases is the call for greater control over the basics of life, food, shelter, employment and security all mediated through one's own culture, precisely because it is one's own.

The final chapter analyses the role and function of maps and diagrams in geolinguistics. We are unlikely to advance our understanding of the relationship between linguistic minorities and their environments if our means of representing such relationships are poor. Therefore John Ambrose and I discuss the strengths and the weaknesses of current common practice in geolinguistic illustrations and interpretations. We survey the commonly-used language-mapping techniques concentrating on point, line and area symbols. We also discuss the relevance of the scale factor in linguistic research and illustrate its applicability in measuring the changes in the bilingual communities of the Welsh borderland. A concluding case study examines the difficulties at the other end of the scale continuum in preparing a European Community map of the lesser-used languages and the associated difficulties, both in terms of data and political considerations, which such an undertaking entails.

We have sought to answer several of the questions raised earlier in this introduction as regards new forms of data interrogation and computer-aided cartography, but must conclude that ultimately our methodologically sophisticated techniques will stand or fall on the basis of the quality of the data itself. Whilst we are heartened that more research than ever before is being undertaken by scholars and interest groups concerned with the fate of linguistic minorities, we must perforce end on a note of caution. There is a disturbing trend in modern industrial society for governments to sanction the collection of essential census data only, and to consider data on language and religion as being private rather than public concerns. It would be ironic indeed if at the very time when we need accurate, systematic and state-wide data on the linguistic composition of advanced industrial societies, the ruling élites should suspend their public obligation to survey the multilingual character of society, all in the name of efficiency and state integration.

References

AMBROSE, J. E. 1979, A geographical study of language borders in Wales and Brittany. University of Glasgow doctoral thesis.

ANDERSON, B. 1983. *Imagined Communities*. London: Verso Editions.

BINDER, L. 1971, *Crises and Sequences in Political Development*. Princeton: Princeton University Press.

BOZEC, J.-C. 1974, Survey of Breton speaking: Results communicated to the *Telégramme de Brest* by R. Laovénan, 21 February 1974.

CARTWRIGHT, D. G. 1980, *Official Language Populations in Canada*. Montreal: The Institute for Research on Public Policy.

— 1987, Accommodation among the anglophone minority in Quebec to official language policy. *Journal of Multilingual and Multicultural Development* 8(1), 85–103.

CARTWRIGHT, D. G. and WILLIAMS, C. H. 1982, Bilingual districts as an instrument of Canadian language policy. *Transactions I.B.G.* 7, 474–93.

COMMISSIONER OF OFFICIAL LANGUAGES (Canada) 1988, *Annual Report*. Ottawa: Ministry of Supply and Services Canada.

DANKERT, P. and KOOYMAN, A. (eds.) 1989, *Europe Without Frontiers*. London: Mansell.

DENEZ, P. 1983, The present state of the Celtic languages: Breton. *Proceedings of the 6th International Congress Celtic Studies* (pp. 73–81). Dublin: Institute of Advanced Studies.

DORIAN, N. C. (ed.) 1989, *Investigating Obsolescence: Studies in Language Contraction and Death*. Cambridge: Cambridge University Press.

EDWARDS, J. 1984a, Irish and English in Ireland. In P. TRUDGILL (ed.) *Language in the British Isles* (pp. 480–99). Cambridge: Cambridge University Press.

— (ed.) 1984b, *Linguistic Minorities, Policies and Pluralism*. London: Academic Press.

— 1985, *Language, Society and Identity*. Oxford: Blackwell.

FORTIER, D'IBERVILLE 1988, The new Act and one of its aspects. *Language and Society* 24, 4.

GORDON, D. C. 1978, *The French Language and National Identity*. The Hague: Mouton.

HENRIPIN, J. 1988, The 1986 Census: some enduring trends abate. *Language and Society* 24, 6–9.

KAISER, K. 1968, *German Foreign Policy*. Oxford: Oxford University Press.

KEEGAN, J. 1989, *The Second World War*. London: Hutchinson.

KOFMAN, E. and WILLIAMS, C. H. 1989, Culture, community and conflict. In C. H. WILLIAMS and E. KOFMAN (eds) *Community Conflict, Partition and Nationalism* (pp. 1–24). London: Routledge.

KOZLOV, V. 1988, *The Peoples of the Soviet Union*. London: Hutchinson.

KUTER, L. 1989, Breton vs. French. Language and the opposition of political, economic, social and cultural values. In N. C. DORIAN (ed.) *Investigating Obsolescence: Studies in Language Contraction and Death* (pp. 75–89). Cambridge: Cambridge University Press.

LACHAPELLE, R. and HENRIPIN, J. 1982, *The Demolinguistic Situation in Canada: Past Trends and Future Prospects*. Montreal: The Institute for Research on Public Policy.

LECLERC, J. 1989, *La guerre des langues dans l'affichage*. Montreal: VLB Editeur.

LLEWELYN, E. 1986, What is Adfer? In I. HUME and W. T. R. PRYCE (eds) *The Welsh and Their Country* (pp. 244–52). Llandysul: Gomer.

MACKINNON 1985, Gaelic in Cape Breton: Language maintenance and cultural loyalty in the case of a Canadian 'non-official' language. Canadian Studies in Wales Conference. Gregynog Hall, University of Wales.

MORDREL, O. 1981, *Le mythe de l'hexagone*. Paris: Jean Picollec.

MURPHY, A. B. 1988, *The Regional Dynamics of Language Differentiation in Belgium*. Chicago: The University of Chicago, Geography Research Paper No. 227.

Ó RIAGÁIN, D. 1989, The European Bureau for Lesser Used Languages: Its role in creating a Europe, united in diversity. In T. VEITER (ed.) *Fédéralisme, Régionalisme, et Droit des Groupes Ethniques en Europe* (pp. 511–17). Vienna: Braumüller.

PANIER, R. 1942, Les limites actuelles de la langue bretonne; leur evolution depuis 1886. *Le Français moderne* 10, 97–115.

PARKIN, S. 1989, *Green Parties: An International Guide*. London: Heretic.

REDCLIFT, M. 1987, *Sustainable Development*. London: Methuen.

RENFREW, C. 1987, *Archaeology and Language*. London: Jonathan Cape.

SÉBILLOT, P. 1886, La langue bretonne: limites et statistique. *Revue d'ethnographie* 15, 1–29.

SETON-WATSON, H. 1977, *Nations and States*. London: Methuen.

SMITH, A. D. 1981, *The Ethnic Revival*. Cambridge: Cambridge University Press.

— 1985, *The Ethnic Origin of Nations*. Oxford: Blackwell.

STEPHENS, M. 1976, *Linguistic Minorities in Western Europe*. Llandysul: Gomer.

TÄGIL, S. *et al*. 1984, *Regions in Upheaval*, Lund Studies in International History. Stockholm: Esselte Studium.

TILLY, C. 1979, Did the cake of custom break? In J. MERRIMAN (ed.) *Consciousness and Class Experience in Nineteenth Century Europe* (pp. 19–42). New York: Holmes and Meier.

TIMM, L. A. 1980, Bilingualism, diglossia and language shift in Britanny. *International Journal of the Sociology of Language* 25, 29–41.

VEITER, T. (ed.) 1989, *Fédéralisme, Régionalisme, et Droit des Groupes Ethniques en Europe*. Vienna: Braumüller.

DE VRIES, 1984, Factors affecting the survival of linguistic minorities: A preliminary comparative analysis of data for Western Europe. *Journal of Multilingual and Multicultural Development* 5, 207–16.

WARDAUGH, R. 1987, *Languages in Competition*. Oxford: Blackwell.

WEBER, E. 1976, *Peasants into Frenchmen: The Modernisation of Rural France*. Stanford: Stanford University Press.

WILLIAMS, C. H. 1980, Ethnic separatism in Western Europe. *Tijdschrift voor Economische en Sociale Geografie* 71 (3), 142–59.

— 1984, Ideology and the interpretation of minority cultures. *Political Geography Quarterly* 3 (2), 105–25.

— 1987, The land in linguistic consciousness. *Sociolinguistica* I, 13–29.

— 1988a, Minority nationalist historiography. In R. J. JOHNSTON, D. KNIGHT and E. KOFMAN (eds) *Nationalism, Self-Determination and Political Geography* (pp. 203–22). London: Croom Helm.

— 1988b, Language planning and regional development: Lessons from the Irish Gaeltacht. In C. H. WILLIAMS (ed.) *Language in Geographic Context* (pp. 267–301). Clevedon: Multilingual Matters.

— 1989a, The question of national congruence. In R. J. JOHNSTON and P. TAYLOR (eds) *A World in Crisis?* (pp. 229–65). Oxford: Blackwell.

— 1989b, Political expressions of underdevelopment in the West European periphery. In. S. WRIGHT and H. BULLER (eds) *Rural Development: Problems and Practices* (pp. 227–47). Amersham: Avebury.

— 1989c, New domains of the Welsh language: Education, planning and the law. In G. DAY and G. REES (eds) *Contemporary Wales, 3*. (pp. 41–76). Cardiff: University of Wales Press.

— 1989d, Europe's linguistic minorities: The struggle for survival. Professorial Inaugural Lecture. Stoke on Trent: Staffordshire Polytechnic.

— 1989e, We are all ecologists now! The communal defence of threatened environments. Paper presented at the International Sociological Association, Social Ecology Research Committee Conference, Udine, June 1989.

WILLIAMS, C. H. and AMBROSE, J. 1988, On measuring language border areas. In C. H. WILLIAMS (ed.) *Language in Geographic Context* (pp. 93–135). Clevedon: Multilingual Matters.

WILLIAMS, C. H. and SMITH, A. D. 1983, The national construction of social space. *Progress in Human Geography* 7 (4), 502–18.

WITHERS, C. W. J. 1984, *Gaelic in Scotland 1698–1981: The Geographical History of a Language*. Edinburgh: John Donald.

Young, C. 1976, *The Politics of Cultural Pluralism*. Madison: University of Wisconsin Press.

2 Geographical Aspects of Minority Language Situations in Italy

PAUL WHITE

Introduction

The question to be addressed in this chapter is that of why certain minority language groups have raised issues that have disturbed the political equilibrium of the states concerned whilst others have had very little or no such effect. This is a topic that has been frequently addressed by political scientists and geographers in recent years (Foster, 1980; Rokkan & Urwin, 1982; Williams, 1985), yet most of the attention has been concentrated on minority situations that have become live political issues: the more 'dormant' minorities have been relatively overlooked. In seeking the forces underlying the regionalist and nationalist revival in parts of Western Europe recourse has commonly been made to explanations rooted in cultural, political and economic phenomena (see, for example, Petrella, 1980). Geographers have been influential in showing the significance of macro-scale spatial variables (Williams, 1980; 1985). However, as Trudgill (1975: 229) has observed, 'the relationship between language and geographical space is not an especially straightforward one': that relationship may operate at a variety of scales (Ambrose & Williams, 1981).

One of the most interesting discussions of the factors affecting the salience of a minority language issue is that by de Vries (1984) in which he examines the significance of a set of variables across a number of European language minorities. De Vries's variables fall into certain distinct groups, uncovered by factor analysis. These included demographic–ecological aspects of the minority language situation; language use and linguistic resources variables; and economic peripherality. However, the analysis included no specific geographical variable of spatial location and connections, other than consideration of whether or not the minority was unique (existing in no other country) or not.

The approach adopted here to the explanation of the salience of minority language issues is to produce a typology of minority situations along with certain propositions about the possible course of political and language change in the classes identified: this typology is based on geographical factors, and as such acts as a geographical critique of de Vries's analysis. The typology is then used as a basis for the discussion of the case of Italy, a unitary European state with a large number of minority language situations and with considerable variance in their political potency.

The phrase 'minority language' is apparently simple and unambiguous, yet general surveys of minority languages in Western Europe often disagree over the term. Price (1969), in an extensive bibliography of work on minority languages, confined himself to situations where the speakers of the language were in a minority in the country they lived in, and where there were no other countries where their language was spoken by the majority or had official status. Thus Price dealt with groups such as the Basques, Bretons and Catalans, but excluded from his analysis such minorities as the German speakers found in France (Alsace), Belgium (the three eastern cantons) or Italy (South Tirol and other areas).

On the other hand, Stephens (1976), in his comprehensive survey of the position of minority language groups in Western Europe, covered both types of situation, but noted that the origins and political implications of the two situations are generally rather different (Stephens, 1976: xiii–xv). The definition of minority language situation adopted in the present discussion follows Stephens in including all communities where the language used is not that of the majority of the state's citizens. However, recently developed language communities resulting from refugee or immigrant movement are not explicitly dealt with, although their existence and possible future development raise crucial questions about explanations of minority language strength, durability and social significance.

Geographical Factors in a Typology of Minority Language Situations

The factors to be considered here as a basis for a typology of minority language situations are all features of spatial significance related to the regional location of the minority language groups under consideration. Regional location is likely to have two effects: firstly in conditioning the degree of encapsulation or independence of the minority group within the surrounding hegemony of the overall nation state, and secondly by permitting, in certain cases, the development of autonomist, irredentist or separatist movements within the minorities.

The first criterion of the typology is that identified earlier: distinguishing cases (such as Welsh) where the minority language is not in a majority position in any state, from cases where the minority language is a majority or official tongue elsewhere. These two situations can have obviously different political implications. In the first case, of the absolute minority or 'nation without a state', the development of political consciousness on the basis of cultural cohesion may lead to claims for autonomy or separatism. Such claims are generally unlikely to receive support from other states since none will automatically gain from such a development. On the other hand, in the second case — that of the 'local minority' that is a majority elsewhere — political consciousness may lead to irredentist claims for the adjustment of boundaries and for the incorporation of the minority language area into the country where that language has official status. Such claims are obviously candidates for political support from the state that would gain by such boundary adjustments.

In the case of absolute minorities, such as Irish, Breton or Basque, there is a further potential division that can be made between those cases where the language is unique to one state (such as Irish or Breton) and those where the language-using group is a minority in more than one state (as with the case of Basque). This latter situation might raise interesting political potential for the rise of nationalist movements with specifically separatist objectives, since autonomy will not provide political unification for such split minorities. Historically, Western Europe witnessed the creation of new nation-states out of such minority situations after the First World War (for example in the case of Poland), but in more recent years minority situations of this type (such as the Basques in Spain and France) have not been notable for the unity of protest on both sides of a border (Williams, 1989).

A second important element in a geographical typology of minority language situations can thus be termed the 'external' geographical relationship. For the absolute minority unique to one state there is no external relationship. For other absolute minorities such a relationship exists but it can be either what we might term 'contiguous' or 'non-contiguous' — 'contiguity' meaning whether or not the minority language group is located against a border that permits access to similar speakers in another state. Politically, where contiguity exists the possibility of cohesion in the pursuit of demands may create a stronger scenario of protest, although at the same time reactions to such protest from the states concerned may be stronger since the outcome of 'giving in' is likely to be secession rather than just the granting of autonomy. Where external contiguity does not exist all forms of contact between groups are likely to be much weaker.

This question of external contiguity is, of course, also going to assume great significance for local minority situations where the language is used by a majority in another state. Where contiguity exists the possibilities of strong irredentist movements, supported by the state to which the minority would feel allegiance, are obviously greatly enhanced. Where external contiguity to other, majority, speakers of the same language does not exist the possibilities of real and effective external support for any demands put forward by the minority language group will be correspondingly less.

There is a third element that must be incorporated in any geographical typology of minority language situations, and this concerns the internal spatial structure of the minority community. This variable is of importance in any of the five minority situations so far given by the typology. A difference can be identified between 'close-knit' internal structures and 'diffuse' structures. There is certainly a danger here in thinking too strongly in spatial terms and in sanctifying a spatial explanation whilst ignoring other influences. Obviously purely social factors influence the answer to the classic question of sociolinguistics — that of 'who speaks what language to whom and when' (Fishman, 1965) — but the distribution of those able to speak a particular language is not without significance. If a minority is close-knit in local spatial structure this may mean, although not invariably, that the minority language can be used in a large variety of different speech situations or domains. Inevitably in almost all minority language situations certain linguistic transactions will not be possible in the minority language, for example discourse with national authorities originating from outside the local minority area, but where a minority group forms a cohesive spatial community — and, it should be added, is present in large enough numbers — there is the basis for continued cultural autonomy. Such autonomy will be weakened if other aspects of self-sufficiency, for example economic, political or demographic, are eroded, perhaps through the operation of general 'modernising' forces. In such an event erosion is likely to affect various social or economic groups differentially and result in the breaking-down of that cohesion and close-knit quality which gave stability to the minority group. The continued use of the minority language is only then possible in certain limited situations or domains tied to particular places or people, with fragmentation of the earlier close-knit spatial pattern. At such a stage we can define the situation as one of a diffuse internal spatial structure.

Although the focus of this chapter is on regional or rural minorities ('traditional' minorities) it is worth adding that the existence of spatial cohesion in new urban minorities is probably of lesser importance. Social cohesion here is less likely to be directly related to spatial structure such that a situation of diffused linguistic duality may exist whereby members of a linguistic minority can maintain their own speech community through urban activity spaces focusing on group-specific nodes, possibly reinforced by specialised communications networks such as radio stations (Sutcliffe, 1986).

The typology of minority language situations created here stresses geographical factors and emphasises three dimensions: the type of minority (absolute or local); the external structure of contact; and the internal spatial structure of the community. Before embarking on a detailed case-study of the use of the typology it is worth putting forward some general propositions about the potential problems created by these different types of situation and the possible significance of each type in raising political issues.

Absolute, unique and close-knit minorities (Type 1) are relatively common. Such a situation applies in the cases of Breton in France, Galician in Spain, and West Frisian in The Netherlands, as well as to Welsh. This is not the place to discuss the factors leading to the development of political consciousness, but where such consciousness exists its political expression may be either autonomist or secessionist.

Absolute, unique but diffuse minorities (Type 2) are in a very vulnerable position and are likely to be highly unstable. Without a close-knit internal spatial structure, cultural disintegration and assimilation to the majority tongue is a distinct probability. Certain languages now extinct, such as Cornish or Manx, went through a period of this sort of

TABLE 2.1 *A typology of minority language situations*

Type No.	Minority type	External structure	Internal structure
1	Absolute, unique to one state	—	Close-knit
2	Absolute, unique to one state	—	Diffuse
3	Absolute, minority tongue elsewhere	Contiguous	Close-knit
4	Absolute, minority tongue elsewhere	Contiguous	Diffuse
5	Absolute, minority tongue elsewhere	Non-contiguous	Close-knit
6	Absolute, minority tongue elsewhere	Non-contiguous	Diffuse
7	Local	Contiguous	Close-knit
8	Local	Contiguous	Diffuse
9	Local	Non-contiguous	Close-knit
10	Local	Non-contiguous	Diffuse

spatial disintegration in their final stages.

Absolute minorities which are part of an international minority community fall into a number of classes. Potentially the strongest is probably that of the minority that is internally close-knit and is also contiguous to a similar minority in an adjacent state (Type 3). In so far as much regionalist or nationalist upsurge results from the repressive activities of centralist states it is, however, quite possible that separatist sentiment with the objective of creating a new state will be quite different both in nature and strength on the two sides of the border. For example, both Catalan and Basque nationalism in Spain have been politically very much stronger than the equivalents in France where cultural rather than political regionalism has been the maximum extent of feeling among these groups (Busquet & Vidal, 1980; Jacob, 1975). Type 3 minorities are therefore of considerable, if variable, potential political significance.

Type 4 minorities, contiguous to others of the same minority group in another state but internally diffuse, are probably fairly rare, at least in Western Europe. They might result from national boundary-drawing which nearly, but not entirely, coincides with a linguistic frontier and which leaves certain individual communities stranded from the bigger group who, nevertheless, form a minority within the state they inhabit.

Being diffuse, their political power is likely to be weak, and their long-term continuity far from assured.

Absolute minorities which, whilst being close-knit, are not contiguous to other states within which they also form minorities (Type 5) are again likely to be rare, the most likely origin of such situations lying in migration, with the result that groups will often be fairly small. For example, in the Americas immigrants of common origins amongst minority peoples of Western Europe have congregated in specific areas. Such groups have become progressively assimilated to the language of the state concerned and their spatial and social cohesion has commonly broken up such that they have passed to a diffused structure (Type 6), possibly presaging ultimate extinction.

Local minorities for whom another state is composed of other, majority, speakers of their language may pose many more pressing political problems than absolute minorities. They are at once both in a more advantageous and a more vulnerable position than minorities of Types 1–6. The advantages lie in the fact that if threatened in any way by the government of their resident country the minority can seek support, even military support, from the nearby 'majority' state. However, vulnerability may occur if the government of a state sees its linguistic minorities of this type as a potential fifth column; then, particularly if the neighbouring majority state is thought to be weak, a campaign of minority persecution or discrimination may follow with the aim of rapid assimilation of the minority to the majority tongue of the country. Such is the case with the recent campaign in Bulgaria for the Bulgarianisation of that country's two million Turks.

The most significant situations are those of Type 7 in the typology where the minority group is close-knit and contiguous to the external majority state. Such situations are obviously prone to irredentist feeling, especially if the minority situation was originally created by a sudden change in frontiers divorcing a particular population from its linguistic and ethnic homeland. A common result may be political unrest aimed at revising the border.

Local minorities with a diffuse internal structure or with external non-contiguity (Types 8, 9 and 10) are likely to be less commonly found since the mechanisms for their creation cannot be general or straightforward. Type 8 situations might result, as with those of Type 4, from boundary drawing that does not quite reflect an ethnic border. Type 9 situations, with a close-knit community that is not in contiguous spatial contact with the majority homeland elsewhere, could come about through partial colonisation as, for example, in the case of the Swedish-speaking minorities in Finland who are concentrated in certain parts of the country in sets of communities that are close-knit at the local scale yet also diffused when viewed from the perspective of the country as a whole (Vuoristo, 1968). Similar communities of French speakers exist in the western provinces of Canada (Cartwright & Williams, 1982). At this latter scale such minorities could be viewed as being of Type 10, but this feature also characterises smaller local minorities that are rapidly being assimilated and broken up by centralist forces emanating from the hegemonic interests of the enveloping state.

The last part of this chapter will apply this ten-fold typology to the minority language communities of Italy. Before doing so, however, it is necessary briefly to consider the problem of the status and use made of languages in particular situations, taking a sociolinguistic viewpoint. Such status is an obvious further key factor in the maintenance of a minority language and is dealt with as such in the discussion of minority group salience by de Vries (1984).

In response to general requirements of a knowledge of the 'state' or official language, it would now be true to say that virtually the entire population of the various linguistic minorities of Western Europe is at least bilingual and in some cases plurilingual. The reduction in the numbers of monoglot minority language speakers has been the result of recent breaking down of older patterns of community isolation and the general operation of economic, social and political modernisation processes. The maintenance of minority language communities is now, therefore, a question of the maintenance of the separation of the use of particular languages in certain domains or between certain individuals (Fishman, 1968: 35). It has been shown how rigid this separation can be in individual speech communities (Denison, 1972), but if certain domains witness a change to another language then the 'minority' tongue is on the retreat. It can be accepted that changes in language use are often accompanied by general changes in social attitudes, since lexical change in one sphere of life may enhance the possibilities of total cultural penetration in that sphere (Fox, 1968: 456). It is therefore important to know something of the uses made of minority languages, since the simple index of ability to speak, or first known language (or mother tongue) is potentially highly misleading about the real strength of a language community (Cartwright, 1977: 17; Cartwright & Williams, 1982: 477).

The existence of these sociolinguistic issues does not alter the scope or utility of the typology of minority language situations put forward here, but a recognition of the situational language choices and constraints in what must be described as bilingual or multilingual communities provides a further basis for understanding the processes influencing the strength and vitality of minority groups.

Minority Language Situations in Italy

Italy provides a useful case in which to apply the typology of minority language situations suggested above since a large number of minority languages are found in a variety of different situations within the country. In addition to this complexity, the Italian case is interesting for other reasons. The first is that standard Italian is itself little more than an official language, an accepted form closest to Tuscan in grammatical structure, pronunciation and vocabulary (Devoto, 1978; Cardona, 1976). Throughout Italy a large number of regional variants is used, that we may refer to here as *koinés*: indeed it was only as recently as 1982 that a survey first showed the proportion of Italians speaking the standard form of the language to have surpassed 50%. The diversity of the *koinés* is such as to lead to some confusion in the identification of minority languages in Italy: Stephens (1976) identifies Piedmontese and Emilian as languages although most commentators see these as *koinés* or dialects, whilst Grassi (1976) regards Sard as an Italian *koiné* although others see it as a separate language. The present chapter follows the approach of Salvi (1975) in regarding Sard as the only one of this disputed group to have status as separate (see also Anon., 1982).

Further reasons for the interest of the Italian case lie in the recent political history of the country. The Fascist period of the inter-war years saw considerable persecution of linguistic minorities and attempts at the forced assimilation of groups identified as 'non-Italian' (Alcock, 1978; Gross, 1978), although recognition (for example in education policy) was officially given to certain Italian dialects and Italian-related languages (Hall, 1980). Then the post-war period of democratic government in Italy, with the rights of all citizens theoretically guaranteed regardless of language (Salvi, 1975: 9), has seen experiments with regional autonomy (King, 1987), certain of the cases involving minority language situations.

A survey of minority language use in Italy was instigated by parliament in 1971. Whilst detailed questions on domain language use were not included, the survey, carried out by questionnaires sent to all of Italy's municipal councils, elicited the information that 5.02% of the total population of the state formed part of a linguistic minority, on the basis of the fact that their

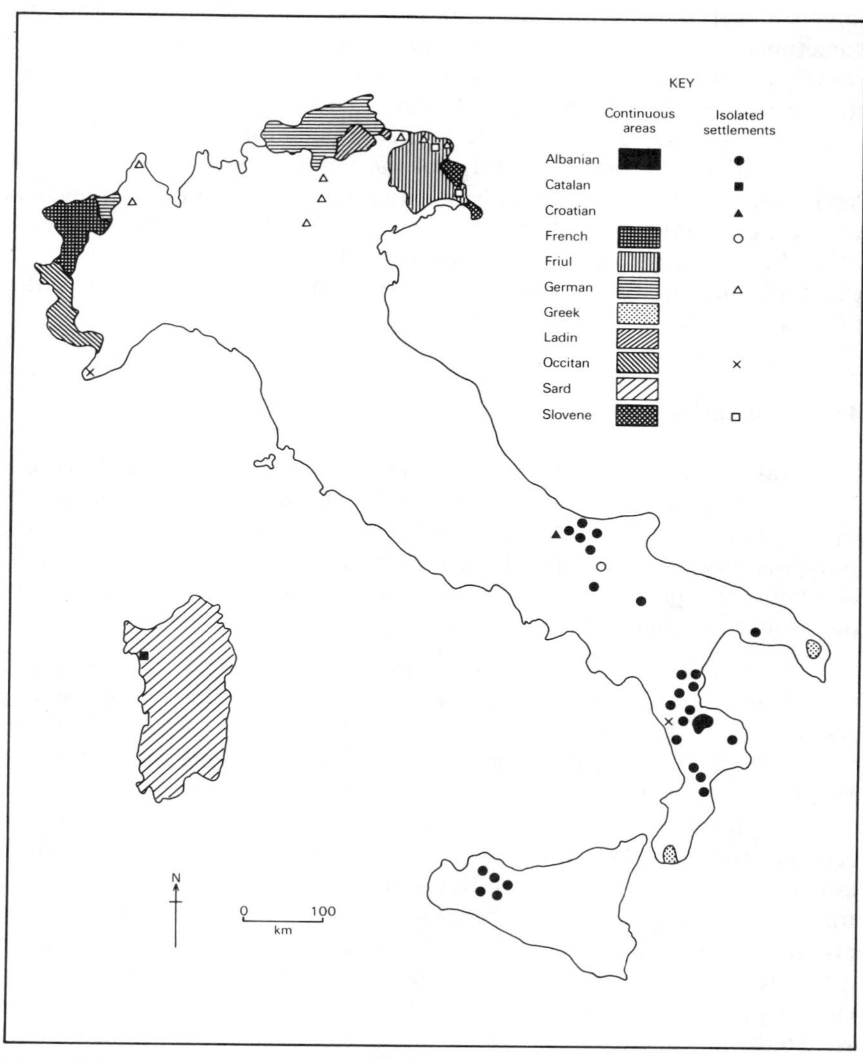

FIGURE 2.1 *Minority language areas in Italy*

most-used language was neither standard or official Italian, nor the regional *koiné* or dialect of Italian. It should also be noted that this figure is subject to disagreement among some authorities (e.g. Bonasera, 1985). Eleven different minority languages were in existence: from linguistic research it is known that within some of these there are considerable linguistic variations from place to place so that linguistic forms are sometimes extremely local (Grassi, 1976). The result in some cases is a complex plurilingualism involving the ability to speak a minority mother tongue of a local form, a regional dialect either of this or of Italian (in other words either a *koiné* of the mother tongue or a *koiné* of Italian), official Italian and a standard form of the minority tongue as used in its heartland. Of the ten types of minority language situation identified in the earlier typology, all but three occur within Italy: there is no case of a diffuse, absolute unique minority (Type 2), nor are there any cases of diffuse absolute minorities that also occur in other states (Types 4 and 6).

Type 1 minorities

Italy has three minority languages that are exclusive to her territory: Sard, Ladin and Friul. It must be noted that the latter two of these are closely related to the Romansch of eastern Switzerland, but they are now generally regarded as separate languages (Redfern, 1971; Grüll, 1965) although they probably share a common history as *koinés* of an earlier pan-Raeto-Romance (Dami, 1960).

The Ladins live in two separate areas in valleys to the east and west of Bolzano in the South Tirol. Here the use of Ladin has been progressively restricted to the more isolated communities (Grüll, 1965: 97) but within those the concentration of Ladin users has not been reduced. Plurilingualism is the norm, involving Ladin for local use, both the South Tirolean form of High German and the Veneto dialect of Italian for regional use and standard Italian or standard High German as official languages (Grassi, 1976: 49). In Bolzano province the regional and official forms used are German (see below), whilst in the other provinces they are Italian. The numbers of Ladin speakers have not been sufficient to generate any real political movement, although there has been a brief campaign amongst Ladin speakers in provinces other than Bolzano for an irredentist boundary change to take them into that province where the autonomy statute gives certain limited rights to the language, for example its use for one hour per week in elementary schools (Salvi, 1975: 138).

The position of the Friuls has been confused by the fact that during the Fascist period attempts were made to Italianise the area, one of the results of which was that Udine, the regional centre, became Italian-speaking. The church provided the main cultural bulwark against this

TABLE 2.2 *Minority language situations in Italy*

Language	*Italian regions involved*	*No. of speakers, 1974, in thousands (Source: Salvi, 1975)*	*Minority situation type no.*
Sard	Sardinia	1,200	1
Ladin	Trentino-Alto-Adige, Veneto	30	1
Friul	Friuli-Venezia-Giulia, Veneto	700	1
Occitan	Piedmont, Liguria	198	3
Catalan	Sardinia	15	5
Occitan	Calabria	1	5
French	Valle d'Aosta, Piedmont	88	7
German	Trentino-Alto-Adige	275	7
Slovene	Friuli-Venezia-Giulia	100	7
German	Piedmont, Valle d'Aosta, Friuli-Venezia-Giulia	14	8
French	Apulia	2	9
Croatian	Molise	4	9
Greek	Calabria, Apulia	20	9
German	Veneto, Trentino-Alto-Adige	1	10
Albanian	Sicily, Apulia, Molise, Campania, Calabria, Abruzzi Basilicata	100	10
Total		2,748	

campaign of cultural assimilation. After the war increasing political and cultural awareness (Grüll, 1965) led to the granting of a limited statute of autonomy in 1964, but the region has until recently been an economic backwater marked by out-migration and with little real cohesion or identity. Friul is not fully accepted as a separate language by the Italian authorities who regard it as a *koiné* of Italian: the autonomy statute for the region makes no provision for the language.

Sard is apparently the strongest minority language in Italy, but this appearance is misleading. It is represented by a vast variety of local forms, maintained through the historically high degree of self-sufficiency of the individual agricultural communities of the island, whilst there are a number of *koinés* of the language on the island, with particular problems over the adoption of a written standard (Rindler-Schjerve, 1982; Corvetto, 1980). Sardinia has consistently suffered political control from outside, with the symptoms of internal colonisation strong, and this led during the 1930s and 1940s to a strong separatist movement but without the language playing any particular unifying role — instead calls for separatism were based on a general feeling of cultural distinctiveness and economic and political oppression. Limited autonomy was granted in 1948 but without any guaranteed status for Sard which was officially still regarded as a *koiné* of Italian. However, linguistic revival has progressed strongly in more recent years, but is still hampered by the lack of a Sard standard.

All three Type 1 minority language situations in Italy have therefore been associated, albeit relatively weakly, with some local form of regional consciousness movement. In all three cases spatial cohesion is of importance in maintaining the viability of the speech communities concerned, but their relative isolation has hindered real cultural unity through the lack of a locally centralising impulse.

Type 3 minorities

Italy has one extensive minority of this type in the Occitan speakers of the southern Alps. This minority group is both internally cohesive (within several valleys but especially those of the Pellice and Germanasca), and in possible direct contact with speakers of the same tongue in neighbouring France. However, Occitan has not provoked any nationalist movement, neither in France where the strongest sentiment about the language tends to be academic and intellectual, nor in Italy. Indeed in Italy Occitan speakers are closely identified with the further cultural singularity of Protestantism which also singles them out from many in the larger Occitan community of southern France. The Occitans of Italy are Valdensians — members of a proto-Protestant sect dating from 1173 (Massucco-Costa, 1969). During the sixteenth century there were periodic suggestions for the formation of an independent Alpine state of Occitan speakers on the model of the Swiss cantons but, largely because of the relative isolation and the consequent social introversion of the valleys concerned, these ideals died out without result. The Occitan area is depopulating rapidly, and language use is quickly changing to the Piedmontese regional *koiné*. Although there were certain signs of a revival of interest in Occitan in the 1970s it is threatened on a number of fronts, not least by secularisation and the diminution of the power of the

Valdensian church to act as a cultural focus. Here, then, is a case where the existence of an absolute linguistic minority on both sides of a national frontier has not engendered any call for unity, largely because the potential unifying force of language is countered by fissiparous tendencies brought about by other cultural and social features and, not least, by the nature of the terrain which promotes isolation.

Type 5 minorities

There are two communities of this type in Italy. The first consists of a single village in Calabria in the deep south where Occitan is still used. Several Valdensian communities fled persecution in the southern Alps in the thirteenth century and settled in Calabria, and were able to retain their distinctive culture through the self-sufficiency of the settlements they set up, even though all contact with their homeland ceased after the instigation of the Inquisition in Naples in 1560. Progressively, language use has changed to the Calabrian dialect and today only one of the villages still has any Occitan speakers, numbering less than 500 (Grassi, 1976: 48; Salvi, 1975: 174).

The other minority situation of this type is that of the Catalan speakers of Alghero in Sardinia — a cultural reminder of the long period of Hispanic control over the island. Half of the town's population still habitually speaks Catalan, but this proportion is dwindling as the local Sard *koiné* and standard Italian take over (Salvi, 1975: Grassi, 1976).

As suggested earlier in connection with the construction of the typology, Type 5 situations created through migration appear unstable in the modern world: without real contact to a homeland and lacking the strength to obtain official recognition the erosion of minority language use in such communities now seems inevitable.

Type 7 minorities

It was suggested earlier that it is minorities of the seventh type that might be the most significant in generating political protest and in guaranteeing their own futures, assuming that they are not subjected to policies aimed at their elimination. The Type 7 minorities of Italy indicate the validity of these observations. Three of these minority language situations occur in Italy, involving close-knit communities contiguous to another state in which their language has official recognition or majority status. The French speakers of Valle d'Aosta and Piedmont have been within the unified Italian state since its inception in 1860, but the German speakers of South Tirol and the Slovenes of the north-east live in territory acquired by Italy at the end of the First World War. The Fascist period brought repression of these minorities, especially in the case of the Slovenes (Barbalić, 1936; Gross, 1978), and attempts at forced Italianisation. The best-known of these concerned South Tirol where basic geographical principles of town-hinterland dependence formed the basis for the policy of Italianisation of the main towns (Achenbach, 1974; 1975; Alcock, 1978). Fascist policies were aimed at the elimination of the minority language via the fragmentation of the originally spatially and functionally close-knit minority community.

It is worth looking at the post-war period in a little more detail for each of these groups, to tease out the potential political salience of minorities of this type. Each minority has been able to gain certain recognition, but this has been much more limited for the Slovenes than for the other two groups. Part of the reason for this lies in the lack of real cultural cohesiveness amongst the Slovenes, hampered by the wide variety of individual local dialects and the lack of an accepted regional standard of the language. Yugoslavia itself is an artificially created state to which the Slovenes of north-east Italy have no loyalty or attachment. The presence of a Slovene minority along a disputed boundary may therefore have been of political concern in the past but it is not of great cultural significance at the present day and there is no real irredentist feeling. The province of Trieste is officially bilingual, and the region of Friuli-Venezia-Giulia has an autonomy statute which accords some possibility of teaching in Slovene in schools, but the linguistic problem of disunity amongst the Slovenes and of continuing extreme localism is changing little.

In contrast the Valle d'Aosta in the western Alps is an example of a minority language situation that has achieved successful recognition and status. Undoubtedly this has been helped both by geographic and by linguistic factors. The Fascist ban on the use of French in the area in 1925 proved the catalyst for the creation of a clandestine movement for union with France: the fact of contiguity with France made this possible, and the valley had been a French *département* under Napoleon, although in practice the only routes into that country lie over high Alpine passes. To counter this irredentist movement the Fascists ceased their persecution but initiated the sort of Italianisation policies already being used in South Tirol — the creation of Italian industries employing Italian immigrants. During the Second World War Valle d'Aosta saw active partisan resistance with the leadership having strong ambitions to take the area into France. As a result of the perceived strength of these claims the newly democratised state of post-war Italy yielded autonomy to Valle d'Aosta in September 1945, effectively defusing the irredentist campaign. French and Italian were to be officially on a par. The use of French has been aided by the existence of a cohesive linguistic structure: local variants of the regional French *koiné* (in fact a form of Franco-Provençal) are relatively insignificant. Nevertheless, it is worth noting that continued economic development in the area has brought substantial immigration of Italians such that standard Italian often takes precedence in official use, even for mother tongue French speakers (Salvi, 1975: 112–13).

Much has been written about the case of the South Tirol (Alcock, 1978). In 1946 it was agreed by the Allies that Italy should give a measure of autonomy to the area but, in doing so, the Italians, in the autonomy statute of 1948, added the province of Trento (very largely Italian speaking) to that of Bolzano (two-thirds German, one-third Italian), thus ensuring that the autonomous region of Trentino–Alto-Adige had an Italian majority. In 1958 the German speaking South Tiroleans put forward a proposal for an alternative autonomy statute based on the province of Bolzano alone rather than the whole administrative region, and the case was raised by Austria at the United Nations in 1960, the resolution there obliging Italy to negotiate with Austria over the issue. There then followed a terrorist campaign lasting until 1967. Initially the aim was to bring Italy to negotiations, but once such negotiations started the campaign was taken over by pan-Germanic and neo-Nazi elements seeking to prevent any solution other than the reabsorption of South Tirol into Austria. However, the new autonomy statute of 1972 largely defused the issue, giving power to Bolzano province in which there is a German-speaking majority, but with a guaranteed role in decision-making for the Italian minority and the possibility of appeal to a Constitutional Court over disputes of interest. All three language levels of High German (local dialect, regional *koiné* and official version) exist, the last of these being standard literary High German, but all schools also instruct their pupils in standard Italian (Alcock, 1978).

It is instructive to look at the role of contiguous states in these three Type 7 minority language situations. Yugoslavia's role in the Slovene question was, in the past, the political one of seeking an adjustment of frontiers, but with that concern relating to territory rather than people. The people involved anyway had little reason to seek Yugoslav citizenship. In the case of Valle d'Aosta France played no role at all in encouraging or succouring irredentist feeling, but the strength of such feeling alone was sufficient to produce a solution in the form of autonomy. In the South Tirolean case Austria played a role at the behest of the South Tiroleans when progress in the dispute between Bolzano and Rome was blocked. Austria's frontiers had been guaranteed by the Allied powers so that there could be no question of irredentist claims succeeding; this also meant that the South Tiroleans had to work for an accommodation with Rome. But the external influence wielded by the contiguous state of Austria was sufficient to ensure that the rights of the minority were brought to international attention.

Type 7 minority situations are therefore in many ways the most sensitive of all, since the circumstances potentially exist for considerable political unrest with, at different times, both the centralist state and the minority groups feeling under threat. For real political objectives amongst the minority group to emerge, however, linguistic as well as spatial cohesion is needed, along with some feeling of sentiment towards the contiguous state across the frontier.

Type 8 minorities

Along the northern Alpine border of Italy there are a number of individual German-speaking communities which have historically had contact across Alpine passes into what is now Switzerland or Austria but which have no contact between each other within Italy. These German groups include both those of Alemannic speech in the west and those of High German in the east. The contact of these settlements with others across the watershed was of obvious significance in the past but has now virtually halted since none of the passes concerned has seen the construction of a motorable road: as a result these communities are now effectively almost Type 10 situations. The minorities are extremely fragile, threatened by depopulation or, in the case of those in tourist villages such as Macugnaga, by immigration of Italian speakers. German has no recognition or official status (Barbina, 1976: 537) and exists now solely as a home language for a rapidly diminishing number of people (Grassi, 1976: 50).

Type 9 minorities

Similar conclusions apply to the three Type 9 minority situations. Again there is no official recognition and the languages concerned are limited to use in a very few domains. Here, however, there is some cohesion in the communities concerned involving groups of settlements forming, in the past, autonomous and isolated economies and societies in which traditional cultures were maintained.

All three of these linguistic minorities have come about as a result of migration in the distant past. There are two adjacent villages in Apulia in the heel of Italy that have speakers of Franco-Provençal Alpine dialects: these communities are thought to have come about through migration in the fourteenth century (Salvi, 1975: 108). Croatian in three villages in the Molise region stems from settlement there by Slavs during the later Middle Ages (Ucchino, 1957). More uncertain is the origin of Greek settlements found in two blocks, one in the Salentine peninsula of Apulia and the other in southern Calabria (Rother, 1968: 2). Although all these different but very persistent linguistic communities have a certain amount of internal cohesion none has any contact with its original homeland, all are small in population, and in each case the minority language is today limited to home use with the *koiné* being the local variant of Italian (Grassi, 1976).

Type 10 minorities

One of Italy's two Type 10 minority language situations is on the point of extinction. This consists of a number of German-speaking 'islands' lying well to the south of the close-knit German area of the South Tirol, the result of settlement beyond the normal frontier of southwards Germanic migration several centuries ago. Certain of these German islands have been isolated from each other for very long periods, 700 years in the case of the village of Sauris (Denison, 1972: 65).

On the other hand, the other Type 10 minority situation in Italy, that of Albanians in the south, whilst declining, still retains some significance, largely because of the numbers of those still using Albanian in some aspect of everyday life. In 1974 Albanian speakers were present in 46 communes of southern Italy, split into 29 different non-contiguous geographic groups. The first Albanian settlement occurred in 1448 and further waves of migrants arrived in Italy until 1534, stimulated partly by demands for mercenary soldiers and also by the Turkish conquest of Albania (Parmegiani, 1962: 397–8; Rother, 1968: 3–5). At one time Albanian settlements were spread throughout the Kingdom of Naples and Sicily and in certain areas whole districts were once Albanian. Over the last 150 years the previously great isolation and self-sufficiency of the Albanian communities has been broken up. The language has not been accorded any educational or official status and, as with the Type 9 minority situations, Albanian use is now virtually entirely confined to home and a very limited number of other domains.

Discussion and Conclusions

This discussion of the minority language situations of Italy, utilising the geographically-based typology described in the first part of the chapter, has pointed out a number of contrasts between the levels of vitality and of political salience of minorities of different types. A number of tentative conclusions can be put forward which need further testing against situations elsewhere.

In the case of the smaller and more diffuse minority situations it is obvious that isolation in the past has preserved the culture, and that contact with external modernising influences at the present day presents a grave threat. When all language transactions are immediately local, linguistic variation from village to village is of little significance. However, once the need develops for contact at a regional scale the very isolation of the past becomes a drawback since such isolation may have prevented the emergence of a standard regional *koiné* or dialect of the minority language that can be accepted as a norm. Spatially diffuse minority language situations are therefore in an extremely vulnerable position in the modern world since the minority tongue can only be used in an extremely restricted number of domains. The fragility of Type 8 and 10 situations in modern Italy, and the non-existence of Types 2, 4 and 6, emphasises this conclusion. Only in the special case, discussed earlier in the chapter, of urban sub-communities displaying social and functional cohesion despite spatial fragmentation is language maintenance possible.

On the other hand the existence of a close-knit spatial structure to the minority situation does not necessarily guarantee successful language maintenance. Contiguity does not necessarily mean contact, and even within an extensive area widely different language forms may exist and hold back cultural cohesion — such as with Sard and Slovene. And localism can act against the creation of a feeling of regional sentiment or unity, leaving minority culture in a vulnerable position, as in the case of Occitan in the southern Alps. However, once cohesion is produced (possibly by economic or political rather than by cultural forces), then language use can become a rallying point and the rights of the language become part of a political platform. This has been partly characteristic of Type 1 minorities but much more so of those of Type 7.

The existence of a close-knit spatial and social structure is thus not enough to guarantee the future of a minority language situation. The circumstances for translating that close-knit quality into cultural cohesion, and hence, possibly, political cohesion, are needed. A further need is a sufficient population base — a threshold beyond which viability can be maintained. No figure can be given for the size of that threshold since it must vary with the economic basis of daily life and with the extent of penetration of regional or national influences. The close-knit minorities of Types 5 and 9 in Italy, both detached from more substantial communities elsewhere, appear now to be below that threshold such that essential contacts outside, or even increasingly within, local society must be carried out in other languages or dialects. Old minority communities of migrant origin therefore now appear doomed.

It is thus minority situations of Type 7 that are potentially the strongest and most viable in modern democratic states (although vulnerable to persecution under alternative types of government). All three Type 7 minorities enjoy some degree of official recognition with guarantees of freedom of language use for a range of official purposes (the most liberal being for the German speakers of the South Tirol). The only other minority language speakers with any form of recognition are the Ladins, as a result of their residence in the autonomous Bolzano province. None of the other linguistic minorities has any official recognition; even in the autonomous provinces of Sardinia and Friuli-Venezia-Giulia there is no linguistic recognition of Sard or Friul (Anon., 1982). From the argument of this paper, there are obvious geolinguistic reasons why less than 90,000 Franco-Provençal speakers in the Valle d'Aosta are protected whilst 1.2 million Sards are not.

The typology developed here relates simply to three criteria, two of them concerned with what we might call the external and internal spatial relationships of the minorities involved. It has been argued that the use of the typology needs to be paralleled by a consideration of the sociolinguistic circumstances of language use, and also by noting the total numbers of potentially interacting speakers. Such an approach could be achieved by the addition of spatial variables to existing typologies and discussions of minority language situations. Whilst the latter part of this chapter has shown how geolinguistic discussion can be usefully applied to the case of Italy, a next stage might be to evaluate the utility of the system against other examples, in the attempt to seek general geographical principles that contribute to the viability and strength of minority language situations elsewhere.

References

ACHENBACH, H. 1974, Urbane Wirtschaftsdynamik und ethnischer Dualismus, Dargestellt am Beispiel der Stadt Bozen. *Erdkunde* 28, 267–81.

— 1975, Bozen: Bevölkerungsdynamik und Raumgliederung einer zweisprachigen Stadt. *Die Erde* 106, 152–73.

ALCOCK, R. E. 1978, Three case-studies in minority protection: South Tyrol, Cyprus, Quebec. In A. C. HEPBURN (ed.) *Minorities in History* (pp. 189–225). London: Edward Arnold.

AMBROSE, J. E. and WILLIAMS, C. H. 1981, On the spatial definition of 'minority': Scale as an influence on the geolinguistic analysis of Welsh. In E. HAUGEN *et al.* (eds) *Minority Languages Today*. Edinburgh: Edinburgh University Press.

ANON. 1982, The alien language-speaking minorities of Italy: Brief notes on social and cultural questions. *Italy: Documents and Notes* 31, 37–47.

BARBALIĆ, F. 1936, The Jugoslavs in Italy. *Slavonic and East European Review* 15, 177–90.

BARBINA, G. 1976, Notizario — il congresso del'Associazione Internazionale per la Difesa delle Lingue e delle Culture Minacciate. *Bollettino, Società Geografica Italiana* 5, 537–8.

BONASERA, F. 1985, La Sicilia albanese. *Bollettino, Società Geografica Italiana* 2, 309–20.

BUSQUET, P. and VIDAL, C. 1980, *Le Pays Basque et sa Liberté*. Paris: Le Sycomore.

CARDONA, G. R. 1976, *Standard Italian* (Trends in Linguistics: State-of-the-Art Reports, 1). The Hague: Mouton.

CARTWRIGHT, D. G. 1977, The designation of bilingual districts in Canada through linguistic and spatial analysis. *Tijdschrift voor Economische en Sociale Geografie* 68, 16–29.

CARTWRIGHT, D. G. and WILLIAMS, C. H. 1982, Bilingual districts as an instrument in Canadian language policy. *Transactions, Institute of British Geographers* 7, 474–93.

CORVETTO, I. L. 1980, Variétés et minorités linguistiques en Sardaigne. *Peuples Méditerranéens, Mediterranean Peoples* 13, 3–24.

DAMI, A. 1960, Les Rhétoromances. *Le Globe* 100, 25–71.

DENISON, N. 1972, Some observations on language variety and plurilingualism. In J. B. PRIDE and J. HOLMES (eds) *Sociolinguistics* (pp. 65–77). Harmondsworth: Penguin.

DEVOTO, G. 1978, *The Languages of Italy*. Chicago: University of Chicago Press.

FISHMAN, J. A. 1965, Who speaks what language to whom and when. *La Linguistique* 2, 67–88.

— 1968, Sociolinguistic perspective on the study of bilingualism. *Linguistics* 39, 21–49.

FOSTER, C. R. (ed.) 1980, *Nations Without a State: Ethnic Minorities in Western Europe*. New York: Praeger.

FOX, R. 1968, Multilingualism in two communities. *Man* 3, 456–64.

GRASSI, C. 1976, Deculturization and social degradation of the linguistic minorities in Italy. *Linguistics* 191, 45–54.

GROSS, F. 1978, *Ethnics in a Borderland*. Westport, Conn.: Greenwood Press.

GRÜLL, J. 1965, Entwicklung und Bestand der Rätoromanen in den Alpen. *Mitteilungen, österreichischen Geographischen Gesellschaft* 107, 86–103 and 117.

HALL, R. A. 1980, Language, dialect and 'regional Italian'. *International Journal of the Sociology of Language* 25, 95–106.

JACOB, J. E. 1975, The Basques of France: A case of peripheral ethnonationalism. *Political Anthropology* 1, 67–87.

KING, R. L. 1987, Regional government: The Italian experience. *Environment and Planning C: Government and Policy* 5, 327–46.

MASSUCCO-COSTA, A. 1969, Torre Pellice and its people. In N. ANDERSON (ed.) *Studies in Multilingualism* (pp. 65–97). Leiden: E. J. Brill.

PARMEGIANI, R. 1962, L'Albania Salentina. *Bollettino, Società Geografica Italiana* 3, 397–408.

PETRELLA, R. 1980, Nationalist and regionalist movements in Western Europe. In C. R. FOSTER (ed.) *Nations Without a State: Ethnic Minorities in Western Europe* (pp. 8–28). New York: Praeger.

PRICE, G. 1969, *The Present Position of Minority Languages in Western Europe: A Selective Bibliography*, Cardiff: University of Wales Press.

REDFERN, J. 1971, *A Lexical Study of Raeto-Romance and Contiguous Italian Dialect Areas*. The Hague: Mouton.

RINDLER-SCHJERVE, R. 1982, Zweisprachigkeit in Sardinien: Ihre kultur- und schulpolitischen Auswirkungen. In J. CAUDMONT (ed.) *Sprachen in Kontakt: Langues en Contact* (pp. 283–99). Tübingen: Gunter Narr.

ROKKAN, S. and URWIN, D. (eds) 1982, *The Politics of Territorial Identity*. London: Sage.

ROTHER, K. 1968, Die Albaner in Süditalien. *Mitteilungen, österreichischen Geographischen Gesellschaft* 110, 1–20.

SALVI, S. 1975, *Le Lingue Tagliate*. Milan: Rizzoli.

STEPHENS, M. 1976, *Linguistic Minorities in Western Europe*. Llandysul: Gomer Press.

SUTCLIFFE, D. 1986, *The Language of the Black Experience: Cultural Expression Through Word and Sound in the Caribbean and Black Britain*. Oxford: Blackwell.

TRUDGILL, P. 1975, Linguistic geography and geographical linguistics. In C. BOARD *et al.* (eds) *Progress in Geography 7* (pp. 227–52). London: Edward Arnold.

UCCHINO, S. 1957, Le colonie slave nel Molise. *L'Universo* 37, 489–506.

DE VRIES, J. 1984, Factors affecting the survival of linguistic minorities: A preliminary comparative analysis of data for Western Europe. *Journal of Multilingual and Multicultural Development* 5, 207–16.

VUORISTO, K-V. 1968, On the language structure of the Finnish countryside with a Swedish-speaking majority. *Acta Geographica* 20, 365–88.

WILLIAMS C. H. 1980, Ethnic separatism in Western Europe. *Tijdschrift voor Economische en Sociale Geografie* 71, 142–58.

— 1985, Conceived in bondage — called unto liberty: Reflections on nationalism. *Progress in Human Geography* 9, 331–55.

— 1989, The question of national congruence. In R. J. JOHNSTON and P. J. TAYLOR (eds) *A World in Crisis?* (pp. 229–65). Oxford: Blackwell.

3 Defining the Gaeltacht: Dilemmas in Irish Language Planning

REG HINDLEY

Introduction

The Gaeltacht is the official name for all the Irish-speaking districts, whether referred to collectively or individually. It was first officially defined in 1926. Its extent was greatly reduced in 1956, creating what is popularly known as the *Nua-Ghaeltacht* (New Gaeltacht). The various Gaeltachtaí (plural) are separated from each other by *Galltacht* districts, i.e. English speaking areas.

The Gaeltacht Commission of 1925–6 recognised that the areas in which native Irish speakers were still to be found were considerably more extensive than those in which Irish was in regular everyday use. It therefore distinguished two tiers: the *Fíor-Ghaeltacht* where Irish was the normal language of everyday life, and the *Breac-Ghaeltacht* where Irish survived as a native language but in varying degrees of subordination to English. *Fíor* means true and *breac* means speckled. This distinction was officially abolished in 1956 but the terms remain in popular use.

Despite the census statistics it is universally accepted that there has been a continuous decline of *native* Irish speakers since 1926, masked by substantial accretions of school learners. This paper seeks to clarify the true extent of the habitually Irish speaking districts in 1926 and 1956 and their position now. It concentrates on the dilemmas and difficulties involved in any attempt to delimit a minority language so as *both* (a) to protect its heartland and (b) to include as many as possible of surviving native speakers regardless of their neglect of their mother tongue.

To understand how the errors of definition were made it is appropriate to examine them in sequence.

The Gaeltacht of 1926

Before criticising the work of the Gaeltacht Commission of 1925–6 it will be wise to state what it was asked to do. This was to distinguish and locate Irish-speaking and partly Irish-speaking districts so that the former could be immediately administered and educated entirely through Irish and the latter prepared for the eventual achievement of that goal. To do this it had first to decide how to determine which districts were Irish speaking in different degrees. It examined the language figures of the 1911 census (then most recent), found them a useful guide to where to seek surviving speakers, and then conducted its own census in the counties and parts of counties indicated. After careful study and local enquiry it decided that District Electoral Divisions (DEDs — equivalent to UK civil parishes) with 80% or more of Irish speakers warranted inclusion in the first category as Fíor-Ghaeltacht; and that those with less than 80% but a minimum 25% were the second-class Breac-Ghaeltacht (Coimisiún na Gaeltachta: Report, 1926).

The 80% base took into account the prevalence of bilingualism and was seen as providing 'a limited area over which concentrated effort would bring about the necessary changes in a short space of time . . . without inflicting appreciable inconvenience on any section of the people . . .'. The 25% minimum for the Breac-Ghaeltacht was accepted as tenuous but as about the lowest level possible for the survival of any native vigour in the language. The Commission's enumeration ignored a few genuine small pockets in the east and centre but this was nothing compared with the errors brought about by entrusting this special census to the Guards (the new police force).

The Guards were badly qualified to judge degrees of knowledge of Irish. Only 3.4% were native speakers and to make matters worse they were not allowed to serve in their own county or one adjacent. To judge 'ordinary conversational knowledge of Irish', as they were required, demanded sensitivity to the nuances of transitional bilingualism and the superficialities of 'school-Irish'. This they lacked, and the Secretary of the Department of Justice bore witness to their limited intellectual qualities (Coimisiún na Gaeltachta: Minutes, 21st May 1925).

Human fallibility was evident in their enumeration and comparison with the results of the normal censuses of 1911 and 1926 makes it easy to see where they made serious errors. My own conclusion is that they almost always exaggerated the strength of Irish where it was quite strong, lifting the 70% districts into the 80s or higher; and conversely they more often missed the lower range around 25%. In most cases they seem simply to have asked householders if they spoke Irish and accepted the answers. They had no time for long and careful cross-examination. In addition, post-independence national sentiment made anyone with a smattering keen to claim fluency, and the British background of the Guards was no position from which to challenge this. Also everyone knew that the Gaeltacht was being delimited with a view to state aid.

The inflation of the Guards' Irish figures thus resulted from a combination of ignorance, sentiment, self-interest and minimisation of effort. It was easiest for the Guards in strongly Irish districts to say everyone spoke Irish, omitting only the most blatant exceptions. This gave some DEDs 100% returns, never recorded in any other census. Conversely it was easiest to say none spoke Irish in districts where the Guards never heard a word of it. Some Guards corrected their preliminary returns on local advice, but this seems to have been infrequent and the Commission printed some grossly distorted figures.

In fairness to the Commission it must be noted that the decision to take a general census in April 1926 was made after the Gaeltacht census had been conducted; and they cannot be blamed for ignoring the 1926 language figures, not finally published until 1934. The Commission reported in August 1926. Its own Minutes of Evidence and the local knowledge of its members should nevertheless have saved it from the gross error of regarding the main fault in its figures as 'a small error due to under-enumeration . . . (which) . . . would not materially affect the figures' (Coimisiún na Gaeltachta: Report, 1926). This was untrue except at the very lowest end of the scale and even there it was admitted that many school learners of Irish had been counted as native speakers.

Figure 3.1 shows the areas defined as Fíor-Ghaeltacht and Breac-Ghaeltacht in the Commission's report, which was accepted as the basis for action by the state, but distinguishes within the Fíor-Ghaeltacht those areas whose inclusion was doubtful on one or more of the following grounds:

(a) Irish speakers fell below 80% in either 1925 (Commission's figures) or 1926 (national census);
(b) Irish speakers fell below 70% in 1911 (national census).
(c) Irish speakers fell below 70% in any one age-group in 1925.

In case (a) there is no reason to believe that the people themselves will

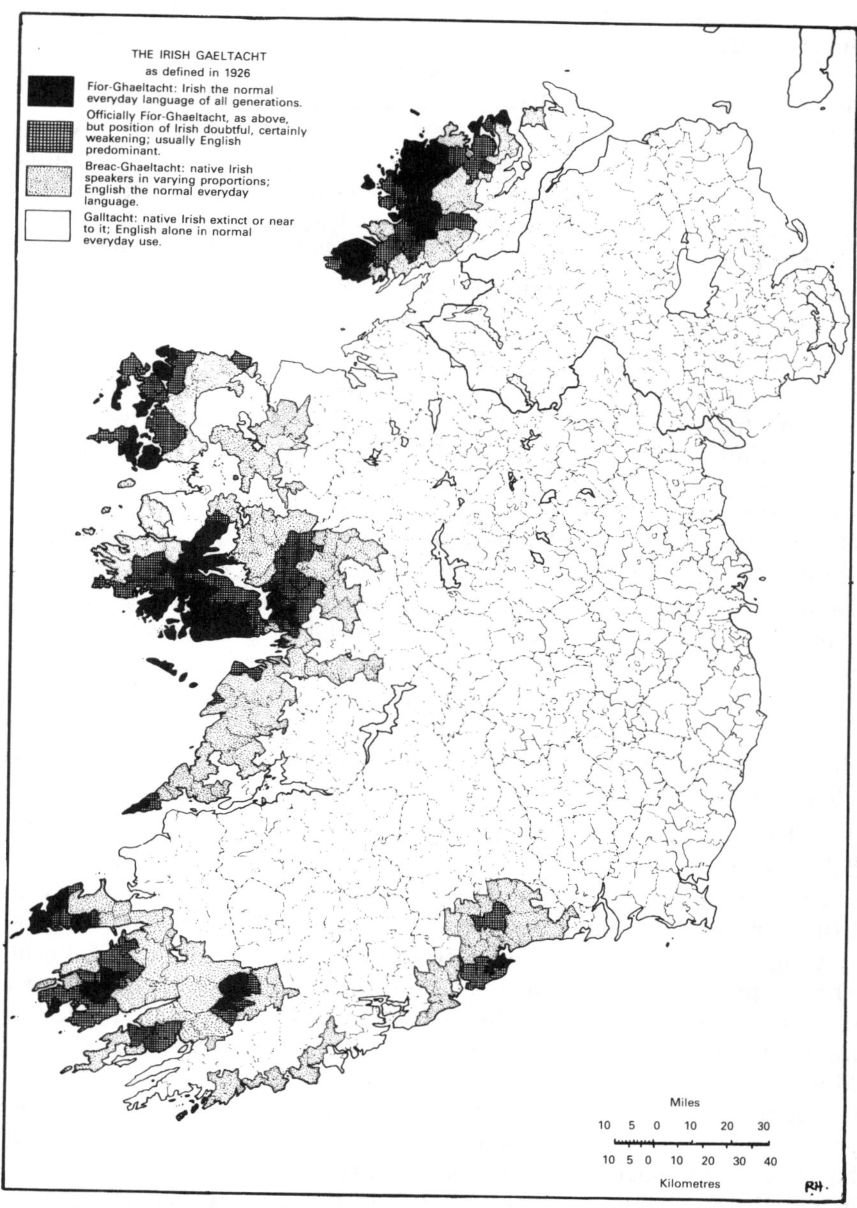

FIGURE 3.1 *Defining the Gaeltacht: The Irish Gaeltacht as defined in 1926*

have understated their Irish in 1926 and there is no evidence that the Guards understated it either. In case (b) there is no evidence that any increase beyond a small margin caused by the withdrawal of the 'garrison' element took place in the Irish-speaking proportions between 1911 and 1925. In case (c) the logic is that 30% of non-Irish speakers in any age-group means, in a closely knit and classless community, that a substantial part of the rest of the community cannot be using Irish in its daily dealings with this group. The point is most obvious when the non-Irish speakers are the younger children, and it has *normally* throughout this century been the pre-school children who have shown up in the censuses as weakest in Irish. Infants who do not speak Irish cannot have parents who are using Irish as the first language of the home.

Figure 3.2 is a more sophisticated attempt to indicate the anomalies resulting from the Gaeltacht Commission's ignoring of its own figures when defining the Fíor- and Breac-Ghaeltachtaí, and the different ways in which its delimitation and/or figures failed to correspond with the results of the 1926 census. Only the solid black areas were incontrovertibly Irish speaking on the Commission's own criteria. Note how badly fragmented they were already. It is clear from the map that the Commission erred entirely on the side of generosity, ignoring its own criteria to unify the different county Fíor-Ghaeltachtaí and otherwise allowing itself to be misled by the Guards. Often the discrepancy is only a few percentage points, but it must again be emphasised that in 1925 and 1926 both Guards and people were being generous in their assessments at this high end of the scale and any correction to both sets of figures would be downwards.

The Commission contended that it had not departed from its 80% criterion 'except in a small number of cases affected by the presence of a town' and argued that although towns and villages were weak spots for Irish their presence must not be allowed to hinder the application of language support measures necessary for the preservation of the Gaeltacht. This argument, recurrent in the history of the Gaeltacht, has at each point of decision resulted in the inclusion of anglicised central places in the very districts which needed protecting from them. Examples abound. Most of the case for the inclusion of these villages and towns was left unstated, but can be understood in terms of central place theory and growth-point policies. The Commission was explicit in relation to the one big town, Galway City (14,227 people in 1926), which they justly included in the Breac-Ghaeltacht. The city was to be given special attention in language policies because it provided the only large urban population within the Gaeltacht, was an important administrative, educational and commercial centre, and had therefore 'unique opportunities' for becoming 'an intellectual rallying ground for the language' (Coimisiún na Gaeltachta: Report, 1926).

The towns and villages were and mostly still are the little metropolises of their Gaeltacht hinterlands, which were accustomed to following their lead and whose speedy recovery for the language was deemed essential if the hinterlands themselves were not to be lost. This was true enough but it was a debasement of language to designate them *Fíor-Ghaeltacht*, which they plainly were not. Their inclusion could only cause wry cynicism in the truly Irish speaking districts which had to drop their Irish to shop in them, and caused even more cynicism in the no less (and no more) Irish districts which were left out, especially when grants and other benefits began to flow towards their undeserving neighbours.

Resentments were less evident on the outer edge of the Breac-Ghaeltacht, for although there were wide exclusions of districts which would have been admitted if the 1926 census had been used as a base, the fact that *breac* means speckled or spotted was unflattering and around the 25% mark there was little or no prestige for Irish, whether with grants or not. Note that census 'self-assessment' is not really such when it means parents as heads of households judging their own children's attainment in Irish. Wherever, as in the Breac-Ghaeltacht or the Galltacht, the parents themselves had little Irish, they were far more likely to assess their children's faltering progress at school as ability to speak it.

The 1926 census did attempt to distinguish native speakers of Irish from learners but was defeated by the utter incredibility of the returns and ended by counting both as simply Irish speakers. Native speakers were returned as 50% more numerous at ages 10–14 than at ages 5–9 (Census 1926, 1934). Hence the 1926 figures may be taken as absolute maxima of Irish strength when used as an independent check on the 1925 count of only eight months earlier.

The Gaeltacht of 1956

The period of 1926–45 was one of general economic stagnation in rural Ireland and diverted public attention from the problems of the Gaeltacht. Awareness of difficulties and anomalies brought about by its inappropriate boundaries increased as economic and social conditions improved around 1950 and was most intense in official circles which had to work with the anomalies. This time when redelimitation was considered it was decided to avoid a commission and public enquiries and instead

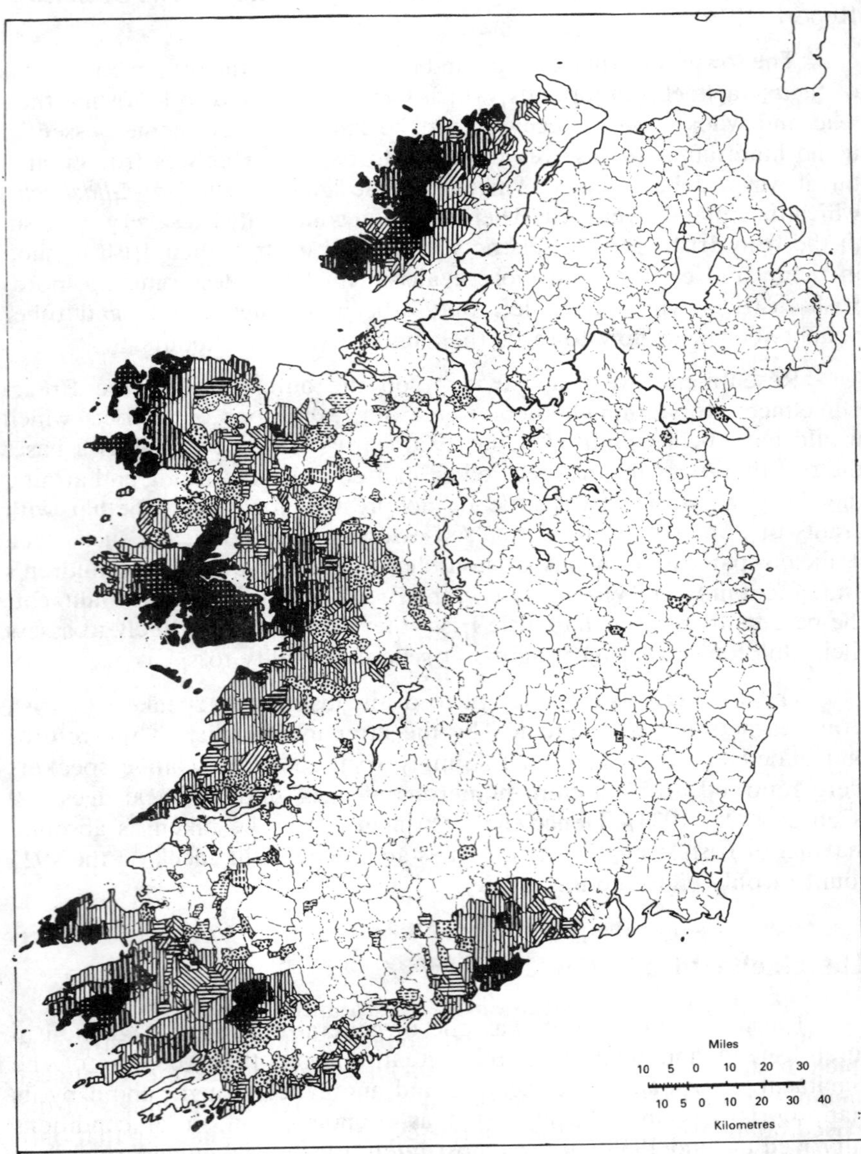

FIGURE 3.2 *Defining the Gaeltacht: Gaeltacht anomalies, 1926*

GAELTACHT ANOMALIES 1926

How the Gaeltacht Commission used its 1925 enumeration in designating the Fíor-Ghaeltacht and Breac-Ghaeltacht; and how far the 1926 Census confirmed or contradicted the Commission's designation.

The Commission specified that Fíor-Ghaeltacht (Irish-speaking) districts should have a minimum of 80.0% of Irish-speakers and that Breac-Gaeltacht (partly Irish-speaking) districts should have between 25.0% and 80.0% of Irish-speakers.

Fíor-Ghaeltacht

1. Both 1925 and 1926 above 80%
2. 1925 under 80%, 1926 above 80%
3. Both 1925 and 1926 under 80%
4. 1925 above 80%, 1926 under 80%

Breac-Ghaeltacht

5. 1925 above 80% (sic), 1926 under 80% but above 25%
6. Both 1925 and 1926 in range 25–80%
7. 1925 under 25%, 1926 above 25%
8. Both 1925 and 1926 under 25%
9. 1925 above 25%, 1926 under 25%

Galltacht (the rest: English-speaking only)

10. 1925 under 25% or not enumerated; 1926 above 25%
11. 1925 above 25%, 1926 under 25%
12. Both 1925 and 1926 above 25%
13. Both 1925 and 1926 under 25%

Eccentricities

14. Bundorragha (SW Mayo): designated Breac-Ghaeltacht despite 1925 83%; 1926 17%
15. Newcastle Rural (SW Limerick):excluded from Gaeltacht despite 1925 92%; 1926 19%

Town

All towns except Dingle are identifiable on the map by their shading. Dingle, the sole officially Fíor-Ghaeltacht town, fell into category 3 above, under 80% in both 1925 and 1926.

Note that six of the nine towns designated as Breac-Ghaeltacht towns were under 25% in both 1925 and 1926; only Galway City was above 25% in both enumerations.

to entrust revision to experts working in private free from the influence of pressure groups. Revision was finalised in 1956.

The 1958–63 Commission on the Restoration of the Irish Language was nevertheless already concerned about the inclusion of districts in which Irish was not the normally spoken language and the Gaeltacht Planning Studies (1971) all questioned the validity and usefulness of the revised boundaries for planning purposes, Ó Riagáin estimating that only 40–45% of the populations of the Gaeltachtaí could be regarded as Irish speakers. Mac Aodha suspected political 'influence' as the explanation, whereas Hanly and Ó Riagáin both avoided enquiring how the discrepancies had arisen. But the new Gaeltacht was intended to eliminate anomalies so those of us who wish to understand what went wrong this time do need to probe this question. It was obvious to the traveller in the Nua-Ghaeltacht in 1956 that the new boundaries were still too wide in terms of normal daily use of Irish and the author investigated the extent of the exaggeration and sought its origins.

First let it be said that the 1956 redelimitation was a marked improvement on the old one in its representation of linguistic realities. Compare Figures 3.2 and 3.3 which show that the new Gaeltacht excluded *all* the Breac-Ghaeltacht of 1926 (except two DEDs in Mayo) plus all the Fíor-Ghaeltacht districts which are shown on Figures 3.1 and 3.2 as dubiously categorised (again except in Mayo). This contraction reduced the official Gaeltacht from an area with an enumerated 181,375 Irish speakers (47.5% of its population) to one with 75,000 (77.4%) (Census 1961).

Redelimitation was conducted in full knowledge that the decennial census returns at face value were no guide to the distribution of the native and habitual Irish speaking population which the state desired to help. Even so, the aggregated age-grouped figures for each individual Gaeltacht in the census of 1946 fell as low as 2.2% among infants in the titular Fíor-Ghaeltacht of Clare and for all the Fíor-Ghaeltachtaí taken together was only 47%. For the entire Breac-Ghaeltacht 4.6% of pre-school infants were returned as Irish speakers. The census figures must thus have been helpful in enabling the state to discard the Breac-Ghaeltacht utterly and in pointing it critically towards the weaker Fíor-Ghaeltachtaí. Detailed local knowledge was nevertheless needed to determine accurate borders and all enquiry at the time made it clear that this had been entrusted to the three inspectors of schools responsible for the assessment of scholars for the deontas, the annual grant for native Irish speakers. I met all three and they were most helpful in specifying the margins of doubt in particular areas. All denied being subjected to political pressure, and having visited the entire Gaeltacht at that time I found no reason to doubt that assurance.

The human factor did, however, intervene to create what seemed anomalous inclusions. These chiefly related to school areas in which an excellent teacher of Irish was in charge, able to cajole some minimal support from parents and able to instil a semblance of native fluency into children during their first-year at school, at the *end* of which the qualifying inspection was normally conducted. In all these cases and at Claregalway where the priest was the decisive influence a superficial maintenance of

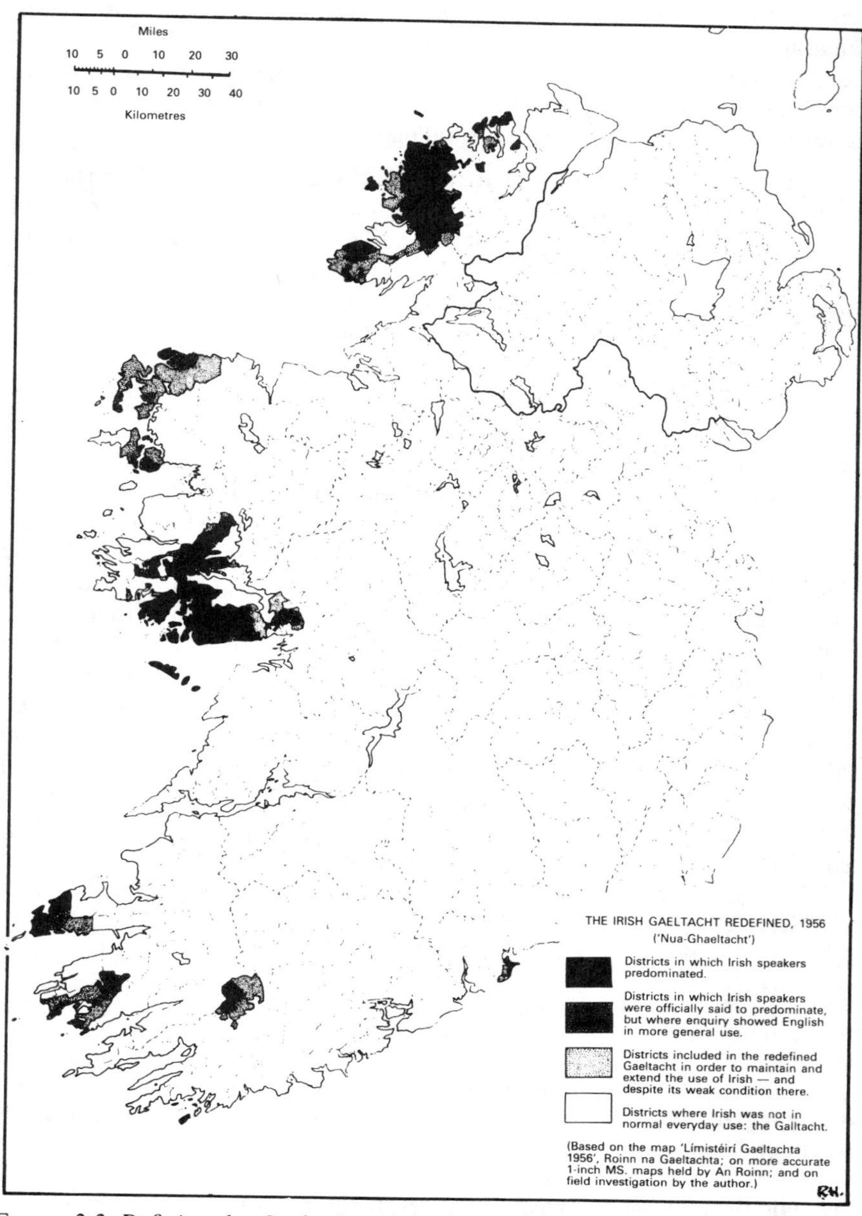

FIGURE 3.3 *Defining the Gaeltacht: The Gaeltacht redefined, 1956*

Irish occurred, masking increased use of English as the functional first language. Their little Gaeltachtaí were just sufficiently stronger than the neighbouring areas to warrant the benefit of the doubt in marginal decisions. Of course the inspectors made subjective errors on the side of generosity: but they were much smaller errors than were made in 1926.

It is not widely known that the truncated 1956 national census did include a special inquiry into the use and knowledge of Irish in all households in the (old) Gaeltacht areas. This was again entrusted to the Guards, whose results were evidently even more improbable than in 1925 and after careful checking were discarded unpublished (Central Statistics Office 1958, 1964). Thus one mistake of the Gaeltacht Commission was not repeated.

The area defined as Gaeltacht in 1956 is indicated on Figure 3.3, which also distinguishes the districts which I concluded as an outside observer to be too generously included. It was not necessarily that Irish was dead there but that English came naturally to the children at play or with strangers, and that it also came first to the adults among themselves for most public encounters. It cannot be argued that because I adjudged the distributions this way at the time and the language has died to most intents and purposes in these same areas since then, I was therefore right and the inspectors wrong. The situation was a fluid one of transitional bilingualism and my only advantage was that whenever the inspectors were in a district they were known as the men who tested the *deontas*, so people would 'put on' the Irish in their presence and children in school were shamelessly drilled to do so. Conversely, Gaeltacht people have long been criticised for 'putting on' English whenever a stranger was present; but because of my interest in Irish, unheard of from an Englishman, I was usually suspected of being a Dublin official and did get some inflated claims made for Irish in a few places where otherwise everyone was candid and willing to discuss the problem in depth and with all its nuances. The children I overheard at play made no pretences.

The question of political 'influence' arises legitimately when it comes to Figure 3.3's 'Districts included . . . in order to maintain and extend the use of Irish'. This summarises my translation of the key to the official map *Límistéirí Gaeltachta 1956*,[1] (Ordnance Survey (Ireland), 1956) which subdivided the new Gaeltacht into:

(a) Districts in which Irish speakers form a large proportion of the population;
(b) Neighbouring districts which in the opinion of the Government it is

appropriate to include in the Gaeltacht for the purpose of the use of Irish as the common language.

'Large proportion' was never defined but fairly clearly meant at least 'deontas-majority' in school. The non-Irish speaking districts added under (b) were equivalent to about a third of the total area of the new Gaeltacht. They were nothing to do with the inspectors but a matter of ministerial responsibility.

The map in Figure 3.3 shows that largest proportional additions to the predominantly Irish districts were in Erris (Mayo) and Iveragh (Kerry). There was in fact little in Mayo that was reliably Irish speaking and the usual guarded comment during 1950–60 was that the Minister for the Gaeltacht came from Mayo. The Ministry, Roinn na Gaeltachta, was itself created in 1956. Given the normal patronism and clientelism of Irish politics (see Parker, 1986) this was a tenable hypothesis and I tested it carefully. The leading authority on Irish in Erris affirmed that one person from actual experience could feel justified in saying Irish was the spoken language of practically all of it, while another's experience would lead to the conclusion that little was used. Few people depended on Irish alone and although a good percentage of children understood Irish at the age of five few spoke it fluently commensurately with their age. The position in Iveragh was broadly similar and a leading Gaeilgeoir[2] in the upper Inny valley confessed he had difficulty assessing the extent to which Irish was habitually spoken there, for all spoke Irish to him but many of the children were not so fluent when they entered school, which gave him doubts.

The 'rounding' of the Gaeltacht boundaries in Erris and the Rosses (NW Donegal) nevertheless contrasts so markedly with the fragmented pattern left unconsolidated in north Donegal and west Connemara that political pressure to spread the benefits as wide as possible in some areas and not in others of comparable weakness is plain. This may amount to no more than that if the minister was from Mayo and another decision-maker from NW Donegal and the schools inspectors gave them problems with fragmented distributions which did not make sense, logic and electoral advantage would readily persuade them that more rational boundaries were needed and would best be achieved by rounding *up*. But special Mayo influence is evinced by the inclusion of entirely anglicised Belmullet in the Erris Gaeltacht, whereas despite its centrality Waterville was omitted from Iveragh; and of hundreds of DEDs in the old Breac-Ghaeltacht, the only two to survive as Gaeltacht in 1956 were *both* in Mayo.

It should be mentioned here, though it made only small differences, that the 1956 demarcators had a flexibility missing 30 years earlier, for they were expected to subdivide DEDs which were linguistically heterogeneous and to take the townland[3] unit as the base where necessary. Unfortunately maps of them were not readily available in 1956 and while the inspectors knew well enough where their centres (or their people) were, neither they, Roinn na Gaeltachta, nor evidently the Ordnance Survey which produced the first maps knew where their legal boundaries lay, and they therefore mapped them with notable approximation. Roinn na Gaeltachta in 1958 let me copy its own working maps which superimposed what were thought to be correct boundaries on to 1 inch to 1 mile base-maps, but these did not agree in detail with more recent maps, especially in north Donegal and west Connemara where townland units were extensively used. This is worrying to those expecting maps to be accurate or conscious of discrepancies but it is of little consequence in practice because most of the discrepancies are in uninhabited areas (usually townland commons) so do not affect the apportionment of the *people* to Gaeltacht or Galltacht.

The failure of the Nua-Ghaeltacht to accord fully with the habitually Irish speaking areas would have mattered less if the decision had not quickly been taken to treat its core and periphery as *one* for the purposes of the new Ministry, and all later maps suppressed the initial distinction. This repeated the main mistake of the 1926–56 period, which was to treat the Fíor-Ghaeltacht and Breac-Ghaeltacht the same, except for education and a few other purposes.

The Gaeltacht enlarged, 1967–82

The official Gaeltacht today is substantially as delimited in 1956. The Meath 'colonies' (Land Commission, 1952) were added as an eastern outlier in 1967. A proportionately large addition was made in Corkaguiny (Kerry) in 1974, extending it massively and improbably into the old Breac-Ghaeltacht around and east of Cloghane, with smaller additions in Waterford near Ring. Most recently in 1982 more small additions were made in West Muskerry (Cork) and again in Meath. The reasons for these additions are contentious, except in the case of the colonies which were included after protests against their omission and a semi-recommendation in the report of the Commission on the Restoration of the Irish Language (1963). The same report asked the state to set up a public inquiry every five years to advise on desirable changes to the Gaeltacht boundaries but the ensuing White Paper (1965) merely agreed to do this 'from time to time', 'as experience suggests that revision is necessary'. No public enquiry accompanied the revisions which did take place.

So far as I can see the main reason for these little extensions has been benevolent, to encourage language efforts in non-Gaeltacht schools, and as several on the margins of the Gaeltacht were producing more and better Irish-speaking children than others within it their inclusion might seem just. It would also be politically more attractive than to admit failure and discourage local language workers by expelling the weakening districts: especially as that could mean conceding that in most cases they should never have been admitted in 1956. In a few cases changes in school catchment areas resulting from the closure of small rural schools combined Gaeltacht and non-Gaeltacht school catchment areas: but encouragement of successful language promotion by schools and local language workers was the main reason. This again is the sort of local detail it is vital to discover in order to understand otherwise incomprehensible Gaeltacht legislation.

Dilemmas and difficulties resulting from the Gaeltacht definitions of 1926 and 1956

Difficulties are inevitable when attempting to draw firm language boundaries through bilingual populations whose language preferences fluctuate with circumstances, sentiment and with perceptions of personal advantage. Ireland was emerging in 1925–6 from a long period in which people had come to be ashamed of the Irish language. Many mature observers had therefore grown up expecting the numbers of its speakers to be understated in the national census although by 1911 it was very clear that second language learners were producing an accretion of numbers which was unreal in terms of everyday use. Irish had become a major symbol of national identity and independence, and everyone *wanted* to believe the inflated figures which most of the Guards produced in 1925, except where they were obviously ridiculous.

Even reliable statistics cannot themselves decide what it is appropriate to class as 'Gaeltacht' or as Welsh speaking, Gaelic speaking, etc. What percentage of speakers to choose as diagnostic is a crucial problem for language planners and the bases selected for the distinction between Fíor-Gaeltacht and Breac-Ghaeltacht in 1926 were perfectly defensible at that time. It would have been impossible to administer the Breac-Ghaeltacht through Irish, yet foolish to hold back the re-Gaelicisation of the Fíor-

Ghaeltacht by maintaining a unitary Gaeltacht as was attempted after 1956. The primary fault lay not in the plan but in the greatly exaggerated extent accorded the Fíor-Ghaeltacht which (see Figures 3.1 and 3.2) meant that in practice it could not have been administered in Irish even if Irish-speaking officials, teachers and priests had been available. The Commission devised a sensible two-tier Gaeltacht and then ruined it by making much of both tiers indistinguishable in terms of their people's shared habitual preference for English. This made progress in such fields as the introduction of Irish as the medium of instruction in Fíor-Ghaeltacht schools both slow and acrimonious, as local people delayed as long as possible a change which was silly in relation to the normal language of the children but essential to the Department of Education under pressure from the Language Movement to make the Fíor-Ghaeltacht effective. Such problems would not have arisen if *Fíor*-Ghaeltacht had meant what it said, but made the Department of Education highly sensitive to local language realities, particularly when it came to paying out funds for language purposes.

Difficulties over the definition of the Fíor-Ghaeltacht came to a head for the Department of Education around 1930 over payment of a special bonus to teachers in schools in which Irish was the sole medium of instruction. The Department was unable to accept that Irish could in practice be the sole medium where a substantial number of children arrived at school ignorant of it or more at ease in English, and in 1931 confined the bonus to a Fíor-Ghaeltacht redefined for departmental purposes as those districts in which at least 50% of the children on first attending school spoke Irish only or Irish better than English. This definition was sharpened by the introduction in 1933–4 of a £2 *deontas* (bounty or grant) for every schoolchild aged six to twelve years where it could be certified by the parent, local school manager and principal teacher, and verified by inspection, that Irish was the habitual language of the child's home. This grant, now £10, has been a most potent force in encouraging a basic minimum of language maintenance in many Gaeltacht districts and especially because it gives access to much bigger housing grants. Its disbursement has often been criticised for unfairness in detail, but in this paper the crucial point is the contrast it presents to the 'blanket' provision of Gaeltacht benefits to non-Irish speakers under other acts.

The Department had also run into the problem of definition of both *Gaeltacht* and *native Irish speaker* when in 1926 it initiated a scheme of Coláistí Ullmhúcháin or Irish Preparatory Colleges, to stimulate recruitment of native Irish speaking Gaeltacht youngsters into the teaching profession. It was impossible to accept Gaeltacht residence as sufficient evidence of eligibility for scholarships.

It was a serious error that after the report of the Gaeltacht Commission no single government department was made responsible for co-ordinating language support policies in the Gaeltacht. So few were the funds available and so unrealistic the Gaeltacht borders that it may have been felt unnecessary to co-ordinate them and acceptable to let each department decide what to treat as Gaeltacht for its own purposes. Most, because they were involved at a much more superficial level than the Department of Education, were more liberal in the exercise of their discretion when applying language tests on giving aid. The following will serve to show the grotesque and confusing pattern of Gaeltachtaí that resulted. Most of this continued after 1956 and it was not before the White Paper of 1965 that several major departments were brought into line.

The provisions of the Local Appointments Act applied to the entire Gaeltacht as defined in 1926. The Gaeltacht Housing Acts of 1929–39 extended subsidies to parts of Cavan, Leitrim, Louth, Limerick and Roscommon and thus reinterpreted the Gaeltacht by applying the Commission's criteria to the 1926 census figures.

The School Meals (Gaeltacht) Act applied to most of the official Gaeltacht but omitted counties Clare and Waterford. The small parts of Sligo and Tipperary in the official Gaeltacht were also excluded, as they were also from the operations of the Vocational Education (Gaeltacht) Acts. The Garda Síochána (Guards) from 1934 treated the Gaeltacht as limited to the official Gaeltacht parts of only Donegal, Galway and Kerry. The Commission on the Restoration of the Irish Language (1963) exposed these anomalies, but only detailed them in the full (Irish) version of its report.

The various 'big' Gaeltacht definitions and interpretations all served to divert scarce funds and energies from the Irish-speaking core. The same objection did not apply to the 'dole', introduced in 1934 and available to all tenants of holdings with an annual valuation under £5, for this made no pretence of favouring Irish speakers and therefore involved none of the ill-feelings inevitable when so many 'Gaeltacht' grants were manifestly being swallowed by thoroughly anglicised communities and individuals. Indeed, by virtue of its valuation criteria the dole did especially benefit the Fíor-Ghaeltacht.

The great danger of expressly 'Gaeltacht' grants arose in the reactions of native speakers when anyone locally regarded as non-Irish speaking secured one: the basic aim of support schemes was to create conditions in which Irish could hope to survive and their over-generous extension could produce only the opposite result to that intended. Similarly, the confusing pattern of different Gaeltacht definitions for different purposes could only confuse and irritate.

People visiting the Gaeltacht would naturally expect to hear Irish spoken and it is a sensitive issue that many of the 'Irish colleges' and 'Irish summer colleges', some dating back to the early years of the Language Movement, are in areas where Irish is little used. There are manifest dangers in sending young Irish learners to perfect their Irish in a 'Gaeltacht' which really isn't there; just as there are dangers for a *weak* Gaeltacht in sending to it a stream of poorly motivated learners. Here is an extreme dilemma: sending learners to an effective non-Gaeltacht is no use to them but sending them to the real Gaeltacht, small and fragmented as it is, is sure to increase the anglicising impact unless they are rigorously selected (see Action Plan for Irish 1983–1986: Report 1984–1985).

One major dilemma in Gaeltacht support schemes compounded by faulty boundaries did not much arise before 1950. This was the problem of where exactly to locate new industry designed to employ the people in their home districts and so reduce or eliminate the need for English. Should these be put in existing peripheral anglicised towns and villages, or should the necessary infrastructure be developed where the real Irish speakers lived and industry be encouraged to go there? Until after 1950 the latter was impossible because of lack of funds and what 'Gaeltacht industries' existed before then were almost all inherited from the ex-British Congested Districts Board (CDB), and there were few complaints that they were too often centred in places which if nominally in the Fíor-Ghaeltacht were weak in use of Irish. The new Office for the Gaeltacht & the Congested Districts (1951) had little time or resources to do anything before it was replaced by Gaeltarra Eireann (1957) which undertook a major programme of economic development in the Gaeltacht until itself replaced by Údarás na Gaeltachta (the Gaeltacht Authority) in 1979.

Most early commentators were worried lest Gaeltacht industries in peripheral locations would merely intensify anglicising influences by drawing Irish speakers into work in English-speaking enterprises from which they would take English home to the true Gaeltacht every night. The Gaeltacht development studies around 1971 focused on this problem, mostly regretting that lack of infrastructure elsewhere made concentration in existing service centres almost inevitable.

In an unpublished analysis of the list of industries assisted by Gaeltarra in 1971 and Údarás in 1979 the author classified their locations according to language. (See Tables 3.1 and 3.2).

The distribution could be justified by equity and was a response to local initiatives which Gaeltarra rightly thought less likely to endanger the language than major new industries concentrated in a few localities. But the fact remains that the great majority were (and are) in places where Irish was weak or scarcely used. Non-Irish speakers must again have been seen collecting the bulk of the Gaeltacht grants 'for nothing', and although many would have qualified for state assistance on grounds other than language, helping them under Gaeltarra schemes could only discredit the Gaeltacht.

In the 1960s and 1970s much better targeting established major industrial estates of 'advance factory' type at Derrybeg in the NW Donegal heartland and at Carraroe in the centre of S Connemara. Similar developments took place at Furbogh and Spiddal on the eastern margins of Connemara. The latter were already so well within the Galway commuter belt that when as a result of agitation from the Gaeltacht the headquarters staff of Gaeltarra was transferred from Dublin to Furbogh cynicism was to be expected. Roinn na Gaeltachta set up its Gaeltacht headquarters there too. There is a double-edged argument here, the other side being that the

TABLE 3.1 *Gaeltarra Éireann: minor industries assisted in 1971*

Classified by language of their locations.

Gaeltacht	*Status of locality re use of Irish*					*Little or no Irish*		*Not known*	
	No. of enter-prises	*Mainly Irish speaking No.*	*%*	*Marginally Irish speaking No.*	*%*	*No.*	*%*	*No.*	*%*
Donegal	32	7	21.9	11	34.4	14	43.7	—	—
Mayo	7	—	—	—	—	7	100.0	—	—
Galway	28	11	39.3	4	14.3	10	35.7	3	10.7
Kerry	13	6	46.2	2	15.4	5	38.5	—	—
Cork	9	2	22.2	2	22.2	5	55.6	—	—
Waterford	—	—	—	—	—	—	—	—	—
Meath	1	—	—	1	100.0	—	—	—	—
Total	90	26	28.9	20	22.2	41	45.6	3	3.3

TABLE 3.2 *Údarás na Gaeltachta: industries assisted in 1985*

Classified by language of their locations. Enterprises classified by ownership, Údarás participation, and size.

Gaeltacht	*No. of enterprises*	*Status of locality re use of Irish*					
		Mainly Irish speaking		*Marginally Irish speaking*		*Little or no Irish*	
		No.	*%*	*No.*	*%*	*No.*	*%*
(a) *Subsidiary Companies (owned by Údarás) and Associate Companies (in which Údarás holds equity shares)*. Full-time employees 1,139.							
Donegal	7	3	42.9	—	—	4	57.1
Mayo	3	—	—	—	—	3	100.0
Galway	17	6½	38.2	5½	32.4	5	29.4
Kerry	6	3	50.0	—	—	3	50.0
Cork	1	—	—	—	—	1	100.0
Waterford	—	—	—	—	—	—	—
Meath	2	—	—	1	50.0	1	50.0
Total	36	12½	34.7	6½	18.1	17	47.2
Note: The ½ is a subsidiary company located in two places							
(b) *Major Companies assisted*. Full-time employees 1,844.							
Donegal	23	8	34.7	2	8.7	13	56.5
Mayo	8	—	—	—	—	8	100.0
Galway	25	13	52.0	7	28.0	5	20.0
Kerry	9	1	11.1	—	—	8	88.9
Cork	8	—	—	—	—	8	100.0
Waterford	1	—	—	1	100.0	—	—
Meath	—	—	—	—	—	—	—
Total	74	22	29.7	10	13.5	42	56.8

well-qualified professional Irish speaking staff of these authorities sometimes had wives and families who, living as hitherto in Dublin, were not as fluent in Irish as their husbands or fathers, and to deposit them in the real Gaeltacht would mean injecting an influential minority group which could shatter the already weakening adherence of the native population to Irish. The impact of Derrybeg and Carraroe was less predictable. (See Figure 3.4 for a depressing summary of the present state of survival of the Gaeltacht.)

The causes of this recent decline can be summarised briefly. The responsible bodies were fully alive to the dangers of commerical and industrial development and were careful to attract 'key' men who were

TABLE 3.2 *Continued*

Classified by language of their locations. Enterprises classified by ownership, Údarás participation, and size.

Gaeltacht		*Status of locality re use of Irish*					
	No. of enterprises	*Mainly Irish speaking* No.	%	*Marginally Irish speaking* No.	%	*Little or no Irish* No.	%
(c) *Minor Companies assisted.* Full-time employees 1,676.							
Donegal	89	24	26.9	3	3.4	62	69.7
Mayo	65	—	—	—	—	65	100.0
Galway	148	76	51.4	31	20.9	41	27.7
Kerry	54	14	25.9	—	—	40	74.1
Cork	12	—	—	4	33.3	8	66.7
Waterford	7	—	—	7	100.0	—	—
Meath	2	—	—	1	50.0	1	50.0
Total	377	114	30.2	46	12.2	217	57.6

Notes to both tables:
1. Locations are from Gaeltarra Éireann and Údarás na Gaeltachta. Attributions of language are the author's and include the following:
   Marginally or doubtfully Irish: Cornamona, Coolea, Crolly, Rathcarn, Spiddal.
   Little or no Irish: Annagary, Bangor Erris, Belmullet, Dingle, Downings, Dungloe, Falcarragh, all east of Galway, Gibstown, all Iveragh, all Mayo, and most of Muskerry.
2. I assessed Ballinskelligs (Iveragh) and Downings one class higher in 1971.
3. I have misgivings about classing as 'mainly Irish speaking' Fintown (two major and three minor companies) and Gortahork (four minor companies) in Donegal, and Kilkieran (two major and seven minor companies) in Galway. The people in each place certainly *can* speak Irish but it is doubtful if they use it as often as English, judging by their children's relative fluencies. They are nevertheless *less* marginally Irish than the localities so designated.

emigrants from the Gaeltacht to staff the new enterprises which grants and tax-exemptions attracted from the outside world. But there were inevitable difficulties in finding skilled technical staff within the Gaeltacht or among Gaeltacht emigrants keen to go home, so numbers of monoglot English speakers came in, willing to learn Irish but confronted by Gaeltacht workers fluent in English and anxious to demonstrate their modernity by using it. The returned emigrants also often brought English speaking wives and children. The Gaeltacht schools, largely 'Irish-medium', struggled to cope with the difficulties which resulted from the influx of incomers. The new factories themselves were of course aimed

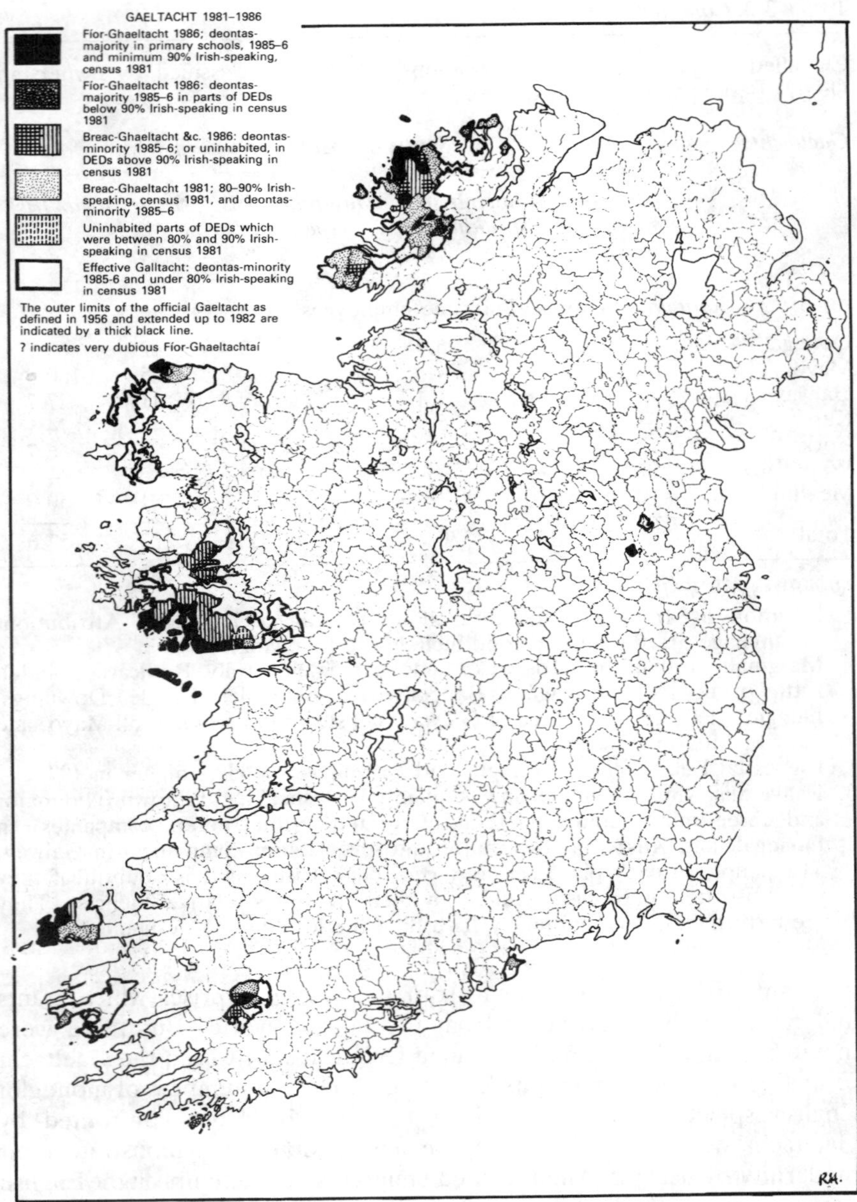

FIGURE 3.4 *Defining the Gaeltacht: Gaeltacht 1981–1986*

at outside markets, so the bulk of their correspondence and external telephone conversations would be in English. This highlights the great dilemma of Gaeltacht development. Neglect of development threatened to kill it slowly by emigration and the consciousness this gave of the need for English. Successful development threatened to immerse it in English by opening it to the horizontal and upward mobility and 'modernisation' which typifies Western urban-industrial society and which in Ireland functions exclusively through English.

That this massive industrialisation (by Gaeltacht standards) has been followed by serious Irish weakening may be coincidental, given that the period has also seen the universalisation of the motor car and *television* in the Gaeltacht. These are nevertheless inseparable from economic growth so the causal connection seems clear enough. It is also difficult to argue that if new industry had been excluded from the Gaeltacht heart it would have fared better. The *real* Gaeltacht had previously declined for want of employment within its bounds and although intensified decline coincided with the economic expansion which brought immense benefits after 1970, similar decline would surely have accompanied any 'conservationist' attempt to exclude it from those benefits.

It may be argued that the language loyalties of workers and managers in the new industries and commerical enterprises should have been monitored more thoroughly and benefits restricted to habitual Irish speakers who *merited* them by constant use of Irish. But how in a free and democratic country could this be monitored? Such monitoring is possible with young children in school but implies industrial espionage on language behaviour of adults at work and penalties such as dismissal of defaulters. Consideration of the implications will suffice to explain why the state has usually preferred to take the easy way, distributing aid after initial enquiries about language abilities and on receiving assurances about future language use, but avoiding invidious judgements of individual language loyalties once a grant was given. Aid on the individual principle may be far superior to territorially based support schemes, but is exceedingly difficult to apply and police. It has proved hard enough maintaining the new industries in the face of recession without threatening them further with language tests which could rid them of key staff in already difficult economic circumstances.

The Gaeltacht Colonies in Co. Meath (Land Commission, 1952) are a lingering side-effect of the erroneous delimitation of the Fíor-Ghaeltacht of 1926. Created as bases for the re-Gaelicisation of eastern Ireland, two of the three drew heavily for their settlers on Fíor-Ghaeltacht localities which were only shakily Irish-speaking, with inevitable results. The census of 1981 shows only 46% of their combined populations aged 65 and over as Irish speakers. These must be the original settlers or their survivors. The Land Commission has been criticised for faulty selection of the colonists but had no expertise in language affairs and was not in general concerned with them at all. It certainly cannot be blamed for not knowing that *most* of the Fíor-Ghaeltacht was not habitually Irish speaking when it was asked to select candidates for the prize of resettlement in Meath. Nor is it surprising that the English-inclined should have been prominent among those keen to improve themselves by migration from the Gaeltacht.

The Gaeltacht now: Conclusions

Again and again one is faced with basic questions which justify a 'big' Gaeltacht: How can Irish survive in a Gaeltacht without towns or major villages? How can the inner Gaeltacht survive without a protective fringe in which Irish is understood, if rarely spoken? How can the latter survive if discarded as a *Gall*tacht? The answer is now apparent and may be seen as negative evidence that the attempt at 'reconquest' had to be made. It has not proved possible to maintain Irish in a shrinking Gaeltacht which in reality *had* lost all its service centres by 1925 and pretending that they *were* Gaeltacht by hopefully designating them so merely disheartened real native speakers and discredited the Gaeltacht.

On the other hand the slowing of the rapid decline of the nineteenth century to a position where the true Gaeltacht core of 1926 was still reasonably intact in *area* by 1971–81 stands to the credit of those who long succeeded in convincing the people that the effort was being made to make their language respected and used throughout Ireland. They needed the assurance that the Breac-Ghaeltacht and the Galltacht were going to rejoin them in an Irish speaking Ireland, and the 'big' Gaeltacht was a token of the state's intentions, a recognition of what was needed but proved unattainable.

It was never politically practicable to jettison the residual native speakers of the marginal Gaeltachtaí when many of them were playing an admirable role in trying to stem the tide of English despite their neighbours' indifference, and it undoubtedly helped *their* morale by designating their areas Gaeltacht while the language died around them. It was not known in advance that once the children were lost they would not be regained. To revive a dying language needs supreme optimism to sustain the effort and to write off parts of the designated Gaeltacht would seem defeatism and a betrayal of basic nationalist principle. How could the state tell enthusiasts struggling to revive the language that it judged their efforts a definitive failure? It could only do this where the facts were incontrovertible, as with the old Breac-Ghaeltacht and pseudo-Fíor-Ghaeltacht by 1956 and even then it did not dare proceed by public inquiry.

It may therefore seem odd that the Nua-Ghaeltacht was also drawn too wide, with the added error of deliberately obscuring the distinction between its Irish core and anglicised periphery. This has been widely criticised and the perceptive *Gníomh don Ghaeltacht* (1971) recommended two-tier treatment with priority for Fíor-Ghaeltacht areas. Ó Riagáin's *Gaeltacht Studies* (Gaeltacht Planning Studies, 1971) said the same, recommending subdivision into the 'Gaeltacht proper' and a 'Gaeltacht Development Area', a sensible and honest description. This was never officially accepted but the centring of major industrial developments of the 1970s in the true Gaeltacht heartland shows that it did guide action.

Refusal by the state to admit publicly the divided character of the 1956 Gaeltacht may have reflected a realistic assessment of how tiny it was and how difficult it would be to institute and operate policies which could avoid affecting the whole of any of the demarcated pockets. It was nevertheless a major objection to the new boundaries that less than half its population spoke Irish among themselves or to their children. Fennell (1973; 1976) mapped the true Irish speaking parts in 1973 and 1976, and when in 1979 elections were held for the new Gaeltacht Authority (Údarás) one Donegal group (Cearta Gael) boycotted them because most of the electorate were habitual English speakers (Coakley, 1980). Fennell's maps however differ little (save in uninhabited areas) from my own detailed mapping during 1956–60 and Cearta's assertion was near true then because the marginal towns and villages had a bigger proportion of the population than they did of the area. Even so the population of the combined Gaeltachtaí was trivial, totalling 79,502 in 1981, in 20 geographically separate units scattered through seven different counties.[4] Figure 3.4 shows the official boundaries which were the basis for the elections.

The state had hitherto resisted pressures to use the Gaeltacht as a democratic unit of local government, considering that its component parts were too small and dispersed, having more in common with their anglicised neighbours than with each other. It is difficult to disagree, and the Committee on Irish Language Attitudes Research (1975) found that 82% of its (large) Gaeltacht sample had never visited another Gaeltacht area in a county other than its own, yet 48% had lived outside the Gaeltacht, over half of them in Britain. This serves as a potent reminder that no Gaeltacht boundaries, however devised, could serve to keep the people within them or to prevent constant contact with the English-speaking world. There were and are hardly any economic or social reasons to attract Gaeltacht people to other Gaeltachtaí compared with the pull of the English speaking towns, cities and countries overseas. Their problems are seldom specific to the Gaeltacht but are shared in common with neighbouring western Ireland.

Evans (1977) investigated the current Fíor-Ghaeltacht and Breac-Ghaeltacht in Munster and found national census returns of 90–100% diagnostic of those DEDs which were still substantially Irish in everyday speech and 80–90% indicative of marginal (Breac-Ghaeltacht) use of Irish alongside dominant English. This accords with my own impressions and Figure 3.4 is based on the application of these criteria to the most recent census figures for 1981, modified by use of the proportions of deontas awards for each Gaeltacht school in 1981–2 (Comhchoiste, 1985) and unpublished provisional figures for 1985–6. To add realism any large uninhabited areas of still strongly Irish districts have been omitted from the residual 'core'. A recent study-tour of almost the entire area leaves little doubt as to its validity, but such is the dominance of English everywhere compared with 30 years ago that it must be stated that *any* habitually Irish speaking area today is much less habitually so than it was then. The smaller pockets in particular could vanish in the next few years, as they amount to only one, two or three primary school areas.

I have tried to calculate the present Gaeltacht totals of habitual Irish speakers by using the 1981 Irish figures and 1985–6 deontas majority data. This produces an absolute maximum of 21,278. Evans' 90% base gives 21,665 for 1981. A more sceptical test assuming as habitually Irish only those DEDs with a minimum of 70% deontas recipients in 1985–6 leaves 6,547 persons in 12 DEDs. This may be understated because a number of strongly Irish schools had in them children present for a term to perfect their Irish but ineligible for the grant, but I recently visited Gaeltacht schools in which three-quarters of the infants were arriving with English as their first or sole language yet over 70% in the school received the deontas. The total population of the state was 3,444,405 in 1981.

What Údarás and Roinn na Gaeltachta with limited powers can do to save so atrophied a Gaeltacht is more than doubtful regardless of boundaries. The physical dimensions of its parts are puny. Including only deontas-majority areas as in 1985–6 they are as follows: NW Donegal 10 miles × 10, S Connemara 26 miles × 18 (26 × 2 for inhabited areas), W Corkaguiny 10 miles × 5. The rest are smaller.

If most of the Údarás electors are primarily English speakers, should the Gaeltacht be redrawn a second time? The 6,500 minimum may be assumed to be the real Irish speaking core of the Gaeltacht population and the 21,000 includes the usual addition which would be the Breac-Ghaeltacht of the revised 'rump'. Reduced to numbers of children, on whom the future depends, 4,018 (provisional figures) were adjudged to merit the deontas in 1985–6 and there were only 53 deontas-majority schools out of approximately 3,400 in the Republic.[5] Could such figures and the areas they represent form a viable language planning base for Údarás purposes? Against this loaded question is the equally weighted assertion of the Action Plan (Gníomh) of 1971:

> . . . at the risk of appearing obvious, we must stress that the only justification for devoting special attention to the Gaeltachtaí, rather than to other economically disadvantaged areas, is the national support for the Irish language . . . *If the selection of the Gaeltachtaí for special privileges fails to ensure the retention and expansion of Irish in them, the case for such privileges disappears.* (Gníomh don Ghaeltacht, 1971) (My italics)

The state has never felt confident enough about the future of the language to adopt this 'obvious' basis for its Gaeltacht schemes. It has felt able to use the carrot but rarely the stick. The Gaeltacht, because of its small population, insignificant and unorganised voting strength, economic weakness and general remoteness has rarely featured highly among the nation's priorities. Just as the language itself has become a symbol of the national heritage, so the Gaeltacht too has received episodic attention with a high 'tokenism' content with little regard for detailed inconsistencies and anomalies. But because it is also a symbol it has great emotive significance for all Gaeilgeoirí, who while a minority include many of the most dedicated and forceful people in Ireland. Their efforts are constantly thwarted by 'patterned evasion', which Streib (1974) found characterised the mass of the people in matters of language. It also characterises most Irish governments, except when they have nothing more pressing to worry about.

Cynics refer to the power of the Irish Revival 'industry' when asked about obvious anomalies in the Gaeltacht. Objectively this refers to the vested interests of teachers, state, semi-state and local government officials, (some) priests, doctors and other professional people whose careers have involved years mastering Irish and have blossomed around it. Some receive extra pay for their qualifications or for working through Irish in the Gaeltacht. Many regard their personal reputations as tied to the success of the Revival, so regard criticism of 'their' local Gaeltacht as a personal attack and its death as evidence of their own failure. Teachers are particularly prone to this feeling, no doubt as parents whose own neglect loses their children the deontas commonly blame the teacher: and if the deontas proportions fall below a certain level the teacher may lose the bonus for teaching 'through the medium'. A certain evasiveness on the realities of decline is therefore understandable.

In a relatively small country like Ireland, which with 3½ million people lacks the impersonal element of so much British bureaucracy, it is more than usually essential in politics to take note of personal feelings and not to disturb sectional interests which are doing little harm. The Gaeltacht is doing little harm, is only spending money which it deserves on non-linguistic economic and social grounds and even so is costing the country little compared with the agricultural subsidies. It is also emotive quite disproportionately to its importance and is a problem which is steadily removing itself. The entire population of Gaeltacht children from native Irish speaking homes would now fit into three or four British urban comprehensive schools.

Few now claim to know how best to save the Gaeltacht and there are immense dangers in hindsight when attempting to say what went wrong with the attempts to define and preserve it in the past. There were no precedents in 1925 for an attempt to revive a national language which had already become a minority one for its own nation. There were no precedents other than native reserves in the colonies for demarcating minority language areas in order to preserve their cultural identity — except when as at Versailles the minority was a majority elsewhere. There was little experience of the inadequacy of census enumeration of language ability as a guide to language use or genuine command. There was no awareness of such concepts as 'critical mass' below which a language could fall in numbers or proportions only at its extreme peril, nor of village and urban 'systems' command of at least one of which was essential for language survival. There had been no conceptual exploration of the territorial or individual alternatives in language planning strategies, nor indeed had much need been felt for language planning in the English speaking world to which all *Irish* speaking scholars belonged. Ireland pioneered the field and we learn from her experience.

The Irish language figures in the census enumerations and the

Gaeltacht Commission Report may seem a statistician's nightmare, showing an almost constant increase where there has been fairly steady decline, but they are a fine corrective to all superficial attempts to quantify social data on complex and sensitive issues, whilst at the same time they do reveal vital facets of the truth if interpreted with care and preferably with some independent check. It is also fair to ponder the words of the 1926 census, commenting on still earlier decline:

> From the regularity of the decline . . . it could be deduced that, were it not for the efforts which were made to save the language very few persons attaining the age of sixty in 1951 would be able to speak it. (Census 1926, 1934)

Whatever errors have been made in Gaeltacht planning, the death of Irish has been notably deferred, and comparison of the maps will show that the essential cores have survived remarkably well, considering their very weak position at the start.

It is now clear that the 'broad brush' Gaeltacht language policy has failed, that reliance on the schools has failed to halt Irish decline, and that accurately targeted major industrial investment in the real Irish-speaking cores of the two principal Gaeltachtaí has been accompanied by intensified decline. It may be said with confidence that much state aid for the Gaeltacht previously went to non-Irish speaking areas so was linguistically wasted; but we may now ask if better directed aid which would have benefited habitual Irish speakers earlier might have *speeded* the processes of decline. The question of geographic and numerical scale again arises, as no predominantly Irish speaking district as long ago as 1925 was more than 30 miles from end to end, not a single town or large village spoke Irish, and any material improvement in economic circumstances was bound to stimulate travel to anglicised places for goods, services and recreation not previously affordable.

Diffusing 'Gaeltacht' aid to such villages and towns included within its official bounds may have been an eccentric way of setting out to help true Irish speakers, but it was hoped so to win them back to the language. The paradox seems clear that the true Gaeltacht survived on neglect, on a bare self-sufficiency which exported the natural increase and all the discontented and left the residue of habitual native speakers too poor for frequent trips outside their townlands, insulated by poverty from the anglicising pressures which have accompanied prosperity or any 'improvement' in Ireland since the seventeenth century.

Now as the Gaeltacht withers the time approaches when it must be recognised that while Irish speakers are fairly numerous they are decreasingly found in the Gaeltacht; and if they are to be given special assistance or inducement it may be advisable to give it to them wherever they are in Ireland. It is a much wider question how far this would serve to maintain Irish as a normal living communicative language, the language of areally-identified communities as hitherto found in the Gaeltacht.

Notes

1. i.e. Gaeltacht territories.
2. Irish speaker; also used pejoratively of language workers.
3. The townland is the smallest traditional unit of agrarian organisation in Ireland. There are usually many of them in a DED and they are marked on 6-inches to 1 mile maps.
4. This is a fatal flaw in any case for 'strong' self-governing institutions for the Gaeltacht.
5. Figures kindly made available by Roinn na Gaeltachta. The Department of Education has also been very helpful.

References

Action Plan for Irish 1983–1986. Dublin: Bord na Gaeilge.
Report 1983–1984.
Report 1984–1985.
Report 1985–1986.

Census of Population, 1926 1934, Saorstát Éireann, 10, General Report. Dublin: Stationery Office.

Census of Population of Ireland 1946 1953, 8, Irish Language. Dublin: Stationery Office.

— 1961 1966, 9, Irish Language. Dublin: Stationery Office.

— 1981 1985, 6, Irish Language. Dublin: Stationery Office.

Central Statistics Office, Dublin 1958, 1964, unpublished manuscripts concerning abortive 1956 Gaeltacht Irish census.

Coakley, J. 1980, Self-government for Gaelic Ireland: the development of state language policy. *Europa Ethnica* 37 (3), 114–24.

Coimisiún na Gaeltachta: Report 1926. Dublin: Stationery Office. — Minutes of Evidence 1925. Dublin: Stationery Office; issued daily.

Coimisiún um Athbheochan na Gaeilge: Tuarascáil Dheiridh 1963, in Irish. Final Report of Commission on Restoration of Irish Language (pp. xvi + 486; cf. following.) Dublin: Stationery Office.

Comhchoiste um Oideachas sa Ghaeltacht: Tuarascáil 1985. In Irish. Report of Advisory Committee on Education in the Gaeltacht. Dublin: Stationery Office. (Includes schools 'deontas' figures for 1981–2).

Commission on the Restoration of the Irish Language 1963, Summary in English of Final Report. (pp. viii + 143. Skeletal compared with preceding version.) Dublin: Stationery Office.

Committee on Irish Language Attitudes Research: Report 1975. Dublin: Government Publications Office.

EVANS, W. S. H. 1977, The Irish speaking districts of Munster. A study of the economic and social geography of a relict speech area. Unpublished MA dissertation, University of Bradford Postgraduate School in Modern Languages & European Studies.

FENNELL, D 1973, *Sketches of the New Ireland*. Galway: Association for the Advancement of Self-Government.

— 1976, Léarscáil na Gaeltachta. In Irish. A map of the Gaeltacht. *Amárach* 21st May 1976 (2).

— 1977, Where it went wrong — the Irish Language Movement. *Planet* February/March, 3–13.

Gaeltacht Planning Studies 1971, The following were commissioned together so are bracketed here but are often known by the names of their individual directors or project leaders:

HANLY, D. P. 1971 *Planning report on the Galway Gaeltacht*. Dublin: An Foras Forbartha.

MAC AODHA, B. S. 1971, *The Galway Gaeltacht survey*. 2 vols. Galway: University College Social Sciences Research Centre.

Ó RIAGÁIN, P. 1971, *The Gaeltacht Studies*. Vol. 1: *A development plan for the Gaeltacht*. Dublin: An Foras Forbartha.

Gníomh don Ghaeltacht: an Action Programme for the Gaeltacht 1971. Report to the Minister for Finance and the Gaeltacht. Dublin: Gaeltarra/SFADCO.

Land Commission 1952, The Gaeltacht colonies in Co. Meath — a brief review. *Report of the Irish Land Commissioners 1951–1952* appendix A, (pp. 30–2). Dublin: Stationery Office.

Ordnance Survey (Ireland) 1956, *Límistéirí Gaeltachta*. In Irish. Map of Gaeltacht territories. Dublin: Ordnance Survey.

PARKER, A. J. 1986, Geography and the Irish electoral system. *Irish Geography* 18, 1–14.

Roinn na Gaeltachta, Na Forbacha 1987, provisional figures of primary schools 'deontas' awards, 1985–6. Unpublished.

STREIB, G. F. 1974, The restoration of the Irish language: behavioural and symbolic aspects. *Ethnicity* 1, 73–89.

White Paper: the Restoration of the Irish Language 1965. Dublin: Stationery Office.

See also the author's recent book:

HINDLEY, R. 1990, *The Death of the Irish Language: A Qualified Obituary*. London: Routledge.

4 The Geolinguistics of Breton

HUMPHREY LLOYD HUMPHREYS

Geographical Background

Brittany[1], a westward projection of French territory into the Atlantic, with an area of 34,024 km^2, forms a fairly massive peninsula whose general outine is regularly penetrated to a depth of 10–20 km by rias and more occasionally by larger indentations. It stretches over a distance of some 270 km and its extreme north-eastern corner is exactly halfway between Brest and Paris (255 km). Other spatial relationships which have been important in its past are the fact that it lies midway between Portugal and the Low Countries and — more immediately relevant to its linguistic development — the fact that the coasts of Cornwall and Devon are, at their nearest, only 156 km away.

The whole of Brittany lies within the Armorican Massif and its eastern boundary coincides with prominent physical features only along a bare sixth of its length — two areas of coastal marshland and a stretch of the Loire. Relief has an east-west orientation and is characterised by subdued skylines punctuated by valleys often quite dramatically incised. Land over 200 m is confined to north central peninsular Brittany, with the Monts d'Arrée, south of Morlaix, reaching a height of 387 m, forming the only uninhabited area of any size. Impermeable rocks, with only occasional concentrations of ores, are overlain by acidic, generally heavy, soils. The mild, humid climate has made it particularly suited to stock-farming, but this is associated with intensive arable production. There is of course internal variation reflecting altitude and more especially distance from the coast.

The distribution of population has always been dominated by a contrast between the interior (Argoad) with present densities generally between 30 and 50 per km^2 and the coastal belt (Arvor), with densities seldom dropping below 70 and frequently exceeding 160. In addition to a more favourable climate, the sea provided fish, fertilisers and commercial opportunities. The urban network confirms the importance of the sea — with the exception of Rennes (200,390) and Fougères (25,131), both on the eastern edge of Brittany, Pontivy (14,224) is the only town of the interior to have reached 10,000 before 1980. All other substantial towns are coastal or estuarine, the most important being Nantes (247,227), Saint-Nazaire (68,947), Saint-Brieuc (51,399), Saint-Malo (47,324) and, in the Breton-speaking part, Brest (160,355), Lorient (64,675), Quimper (60,162) and Vannes (45,397). As large-scale industrialisation never took place, the urban network is medieval except for the seventeenth-century towns of Brest and Lorient, and the nineteenth-century Saint-Nazaire. By 1600, the largest towns were Nantes (25,000) and Rennes (about 20, 000); in the Breton west, Quimper, Vannes and Morlaix each had about 9,000 inhabitants. In 1911, the rural population still accounted for three-quarters of the total and the 1968 census was the first to record an urban majority (53%).

Historical Background

Brittany's present distinctiveness goes back to large-scale immigrations of Britons between the fourth and eighth centuries. The older hypothesis (Loth, 1883), which is still quite widely repeated today, was that of a flight of refugees into a largely depopulated and completely Latinised Armorica. More recent authorities (Falc'hun, 1981; Fleuriot, 1980) see an organised plantation associated with a large-scale transfer of British legions into northern Gaul to counter the Barbarian threat. It is further presumed that cross-Channel communications had continued uninterrupted and that Gaulish was still spoken in Armorica. In this case, the Britons were settling in a country with which they were familiar and which spoke a dialect of the same language, for Brittonic could very well be labelled Insular Gaulish. It may further be surmised that the social status of the insular dialect was higher than that of Armorican, Latinisation being less advanced in Britain than in Gaul.

We are on firmer ground when we claim that Brittany has been a bi-ethnic unit since 850, when its kings extended their dominion well beyond the bounds of Breton settlement and deep into Romance-speaking territory. Their hold on most of this proved short-lived, yet the fact that Rennes and Nantes were permanently incorporated was to have profound consequences, for these two French-speaking cities would henceforth play

TABLE 4.1 *Basic population data on the Breton departments*

	Population 1982 000	*1954–82 %+*	*Density 1982 km²*	*Occupation structure 1982*			*Occupation structure 1954*		
				I	*II*	*III*	*I*	*II*	*III*
Finistère	828	12.7	123	22	29	49	50	27	23
Côtes-du-Nord*	539	8.4	78	28	26	46	58	20	28
Morbihan	591	11.7	87	24	31	45	56	23	21
Ille-et Vilaine	750	26.9	111	21	30	50	49	25	26
Loire-Atlantique	995	27.3	146	12	38	50	32	39	29
Brittany (total)	3,703	18.2	109						

* Officially renamed Côtes-d'Armor in 1990.

a dominant role. The Breton connections of the aristocracy were further weakened in the first third of the tenth century, when they sought refuge with French-speaking or English allies from a Viking occupation which also crippled the intellectual life of the Breton core by sacking the monasteries — from which the monks dispersed mainly up the Loire as far as Berry. Abundant Old Breton glosses (eighth to eleventh centuries) contain not a few abstract and technical words of native formation which point to a language used in scholarship and government, whereas Middle Breton (which is not abundantly attested until the fifteenth century) has in these areas of its vocabulary been deeply penetrated by French loanwords. The lexical transformation is entirely comparable with that which separates Middle English from Anglo-Saxon.

It seems almost irrelevant to mention the treaty of 1532, which united Brittany and France, for all it did was to convert a duchy of variable independence into a province which had a not inconsiderable degree of autonomy. Nothing happened to change the inferior social status of the language, for which no official function of any description is documented. Political recognition came with the Revolution: it was mildy positive in the federalist phase, during which Breton was used for printed proclamations; it was rabidly negative after the Jacobin triumph of 1793, which branded it as counter-revolutionary and incompatible with the *République une et indivisible*.

For most of the following century, the extirpation of Breton in the countryside could be only an ideal, for there was no instrument at hand with which to carry out the process. True, conscription, from which provincial Brittany had been largely exempt, did bring many men into contact with French and in the 1860s came the railways. It was in 1882, however, that machinery was set up which had as one of its central aims the establishment of linguistic uniformity over the whole of France; this took the form of a tight network of free, compulsory schools, dispensing education exclusively through the medium of French.[2] These provided a daily demonstration — whether by assertion or implication — of the inferiority of Breton and, more importantly perhaps, of the advantages which a knowledge of French conferred. The aspiration to learn French will be better understood if we bear in mind that the industrial revolution had led to the collapse of an important unmechanised textile industry and made an ever-growing population completely dependent on an agriculture that could barely support it: in 1872, over 7% of the population of Finistère and Côtes-du-Nord were beggars.

By 1914, a substantial majority of the first men to be called up had

had primary schooling and many of them would spend the next five years in a French-speaking environment. Although the war cemented solidarity with France and paralysed pro-Breton activities within Brittany, it also, by provoking reflection on the fate of stateless peoples, led to a new departure in Breton particularism. In the nineteenth century, this had taken the form of a romantic regionalism with numerous connections with a royalist aristocracy. In 1919, came the establishment of a more intellectual and more middle-class nationalism with more ambitious and more clearly defined aims. The Parti National Breton, although always claiming to be above the left–right dichtomy, lost its left wing and adopted a generally fascist ideology by 1930. A splinter of it actively collaborated with the Germans during the Occupation, a move which deepened existing splits within the wider Breton movement and brought discredit on it globally by association, antagonising the population as a whole and providing a restored French government with an excellent justification for hardening its traditional anti-Breton attitude. If many of the present weaknesses of the Breton movement owe much to these wartime events, differences in class and in attitudes to religion have always been important factors, while the linguistic particularism of the west has never necessarily coincided in its aims with the political particularism of the east.

Sociocultural Aspects of Breton

Religious themes dominated Breton writing down to the First World War, supplemented by a rich oral literature that only surfaced in print in the nineteenth century — to these, the popular periodicals added practical advice on household and farming matters. After the War the traditional reading public began to decline rapidly as the younger, bilingual generations turned to French for more varied, more up to date and more attractively produced reading material. A new trend is most strikingly represented by the nationalist literary quarterly *Gwalarn* (1925–44), which deliberately broke with these traditions and published more intellectual and personal literature aimed at an educated middle class. It was preoccupied with the task of creating a Breton-speaking élite and cultivated a language that was lexically puristic and as uniform as possible. It succeeded up to a point, but the resulting élite existed — and continues to exist — largely in a vacuum, for many of its members neither have nor desire any contact with the mass of traditional Breton speakers. The obsessive cohesion of this group often gives it the edge over the numerous, but less structured, group of language activists whose inspiration is more popular and whose methods are more pragmatic.

The present Breton-speaking population falls into two contrasting categories. The first is a residual, but still substantial mass of traditional speakers, which is generally rural and middle-aged to old. They are generally illiterate in Breton and tend to use French automatically with strangers, while not a few are even reluctant to speak Breton with friends in unfamiliar settings where French predominates. The second category consists of literate, activist speakers who use Breton over as wide a range of domains as circumstances permit. Their occupations are mainly intellectual or administrative and, as individuals or families, they are often isolated, dispersed as they are in French-speaking communities. It is impossible to give a reasoned estimate of the numerical strength of this category, though 10,000 is often given as an upper limit; a significant proportion did not have a Breton-speaking upbringing.

The only institution traditionally giving Breton a role, the Church, almost entirely abandoned it in the 1950s and the occasional services in the language are organised by an activist minority. In certain areas, however, Breton has made distinct advances. The state education system gave the language some recognition, temporarily during the Occupation, and definitively with the Loi Deixonne of 1951. This was a very modest move permitting an hour's Breton a week on a voluntary basis, with no back-up in the form of training or additional staff. Although the official position of the language has been grudgingly improved, especially since 1970, the provision made for it is skeletal. In 1984, only a little over 5% of all pupils had any instruction in Breton, of whom only a minority would have been brought up as active speakers. The teaching of Breton does seem to have made some impact on Breton publishing, for the editions of 500 current in the 1950s had grown to 1,500 and even 3,000 by 1983. Publications have also grown in numbers and in variety, but figures remain very low: 23 non-periodical titles of more than 50 pages in 1983. There were a dozen all-Breton periodicals, the largest number of subscribers being 915. Finally, broadcasting, which again made its debut under the Occupation, was resumed by the official regional station in 1946 at the rate of half-an-hour a week, rising to a full hour in the 1960s. The 1970s saw the inauguration of short daily programmes but the greatest changes came in 1982 with the establishment of Radio Bretagne Ouest. This station now broadcasts between 12 and 14 hours a week in Breton (of which five are also relayed throughout eastern Brittany) and there is also a local station in the centre which broadcasts over ten hours. In the nature of things, the programmes are amateur rather than fully professional in their standards and depend quite heavily on interviewing the public and playing records. They have an avid following of about

10% of Breton speakers and there are a further 20% who are regular listeners. Television broadcasts a hundred minutes a week, mainly on Sunday afternoon. Broadcasting is important as the only medium that can reach the traditional Breton speaker in any number.

Linguistic Boundaries

There has been a linguistic dichotomy in Brittany throughout its history, so the first task is to identify the territory of each language and establish the nature and position of the divide between them. In this section, this will be presented, in the main, as being linear, partly because most investigations have assumed it to be so, but largely because it is more convenient to take the simple generalisation as a starting point rather than the complex particulars.

As elsewhere, the reconstruction of past linguistic landscapes depends largely on place-name evidence, whose full complexities cannot be discussed here for lack of space. The ninth-century boundary of Breton (Figure 4.1) is in fact the line separating place-names in *-é* to the east from those in *-ac* to the west. These are strongly contrasting reflexes of a single originally Gaulish suffix (*-acum*) which was a tremendously productive element in the naming of Gallo-Roman estates. The *-é* (*-ay*) form came about as a result of the palatalisation and eventual effacement of '*c*' in this position, a characteristic of French; the area containing *-ac* place-names was therefore not French, or rather northern Gallo-Romance, between the seventh and the ninth centuries when this evolution was taking place. The twelfth century boundary is more general and encloses an area in which numerous Breton elements occur and the French *-ière* is absent. The unevenness of Breton place-names suggests a mixed population here and the northern end of this line pivots west to the vicinity of Saint-Brieuc by the fourteenth century, giving the linguistic boundary its modern outline. It seems to have crystallised in a zone of equilibrium between the main Roman road networks, that of Rennes and that of Carhaix, which were not superseded until the eighteenth century.

The mapping of the linguistic boundary has a respectable antiquity, for it appears in a number of seventeenth and eighteenth century atlases: a line separating *Haute-Bretagne* from *Basse-Bretagne*, 'low' here meaning the part furthest from the capital, Rennes, but in fact defined by its language, Breton. These maps unfortunately disagree among themselves, are sometimes marred by obvious errors, and give no indication of their sources — and this somewhat reduces their individual value. Coquebert

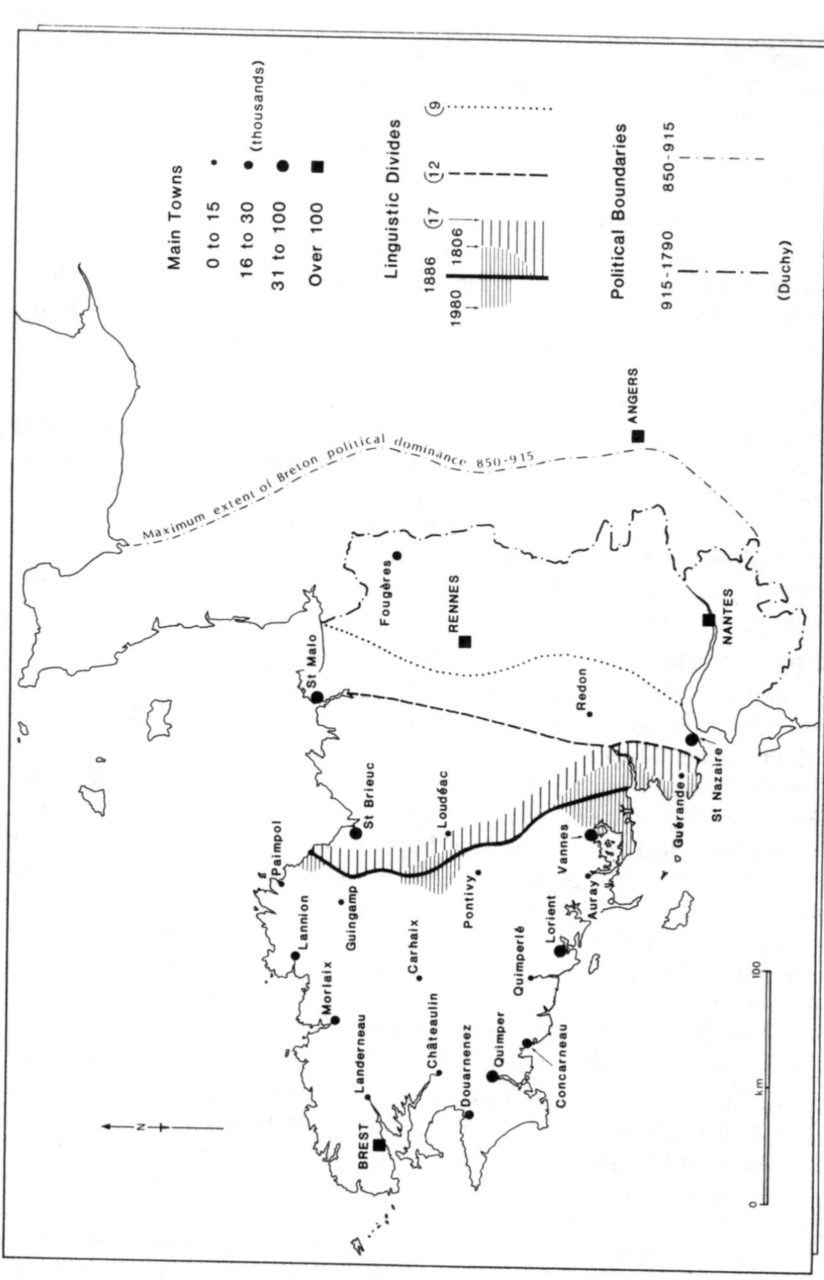

FIGURE 4.1 *Linguistic divides in Brittany.*

de Montbret's investigations gave very much more concrete results, for we know the year it refers to (1806) and we know the immediate source of his information (the *Préfectures* of Côtes-du-Nord and Morbihan) (Brunot, 1927: 536–40). Less satisfactory is the fact that his findings are almost exclusively on the level of the commune which is assumed to be either Breton or French.

Sébillot (1886) produced a much more detailed picture, defining the boundary in terms of the hamlets that lie next to it. It is based on reports received from six observers on the ground for Côtes-du-Nord and from a single correspondent in Morbihan. He seems to assume the static and linear nature of the boundary, although referring a number of times to mixed areas; he also neglects to give explicit criteria for defining the term *bretonnant* (Breton-speaking). Only in two cases does he refer to change: in Plouagat, there had been an increase in Breton-speaking since 1845 due to in-migration; in Batz, an enclave of Breton south of Guérande, where French was gaining ground rapidly, habitual speakers of Breton having declined from 400 to 200 in the previous ten years.[3] In addition to information on vernacular usage, Sébillot notes the language used for preaching; schools, of course, had not yet become a feature of the rural scene and there is no mention of them.

Panier's (1942) survey of the linguistic boundary was much more concerned with the dynamics of the situation for his main objective was to ascertain to what extent the Sébillot line had changed. He worked in the field, systematically interviewing *secrétaires de mairie* and parish priests, the people best fitted to act as informants in that their professional life required a detailed knowledge of their *commune* and its inhabitants. He also specifies that he considers Breton-speaking only those areas in which it was the spontaneous language of three generations, adding however, that aged speakers were to be found further east, often right up to the Sébillot line. Panier shows that there had been a moderate westward movement, with half the hamlets on the very edge of Breton territory in 1885 now French. This movement was almost imperceptible along some inland stretches and seldom more than 2 km elsewhere, except on the coast, where it reaches 5 km in Plouha in the north and 7 km in Ambon in the south (11 km, if we count the long peninsular commune of Damgan, just south-west of it). The Rhuys peninsula, south of Vannes is not mapped, neither is Mûr-de-Bretagne in the centre and its neighbours Caurel and Saint-Aignan; they are mentioned as being largely de-Bretonised, but considered as being enclaves. We may finish with two general remarks Panier makes on this frontier: firstly the strong tendency for Breton-speakers to use only French with their children;

secondly, the fact that the generalised knowledge of French facilitated marriages across it.

The most recent general survey of the boundary was carried out by Timm in 1976 (Timm, 1980); it gives far less precise information on both sources and locations than do the two surveys just described. This is no doubt a reflection of the fact that widespread abandonment of Breton *within* its traditional territory has made the linguistic divide far less noticeable, not only to outside observers, but also to the permanent population (Ambrose, 1980). Of 40 border 'communities' visited (presumably *communes*), only two, just north-east of Pontivy, could be considered Breton-speaking according to Panier's criteria, while in a further 28 Breton was used only by the oldest generation. Breton had completely disappeared from ten communities, mainly in the south-east, where the linguistic divide appears to have receded west of Vannes.

There is no doubt about the overall validity of the boundaries plotted by the above surveys and the convention of their linear representation is perfectly acceptable, provided the degree of generalisation inherent in it is not lost sight of. In concentrating on boundary displacement it is easy to overlook that far-reaching qualitative changes have taken place. Sébillot, who hardly discusses the actual significance of his frontier, lived at a time when monoglot Bretons were dominant in the rural areas, when the geographical transition from one language to the other was extremely sudden in most places. Panier found a frontier more clear-cut than he expected, though the population to the west of it was now largely bilingual; he notes that areas de-Bretonised from the nineteenth century on spoke a regional variety of standard French and not Gallo, the indigenous French dialect of eastern Brittany surviving as a rural vernacular. Timm (1980) characterises it as illusory, for Breton is in a state of advanced collapse throughout its traditional territory.

Variation Within the Breton Zone

Up to the nineteenth century, the social distribution of French would have been much more noticeable than its geographical distribution, for even in most of the towns in which they were concentrated, the habitually or exclusively French-speaking upper classes would have been a small minority. This urban habit has since spread through the urban hierarchy and finished by permeating the countryside as well. The de-Bretonisation of the larger towns presumably came earliest but neither the process nor the chronology are adequately documented. It is much easier to obtain information about the final stages of the transition, of which the essential step is the decision to bring up children in French rather than in Breton.[4] Anxiety to possess this passport to upward mobility or even to poorly remunerated employment was understandable in a region which could offer few alternatives to emigration to an over-abundant rural population. Raising children in French was already common in all but the smallest rural *bourgs*[5] in the 1930s and extended to the scattered rural population in the course of the 1950s. The first generation brought up in this way typically learnt Breton from monoglot grandmothers.

The earliest publication to provide systematically information on the linguistic situation throughout Brittany is the 1853 edition of Ogée. It merely states laconically whether Breton, French or both languages are spoken in each *commune*, only very occasionally adding further comment. There are errors and ommissions and the source and year of the information are not given. An article by Dauzat (1929) is the next milestone. This eminent French dialectologist spent several weeks in Brittany in the autumns of 1925 and 1926 enquiring and observing. He had no knowledge of Breton, but his work on rural vernaculars and his Auvergnat background lend acuteness to his analysis of social forces working in favour of French. Precise documentation is abundant — information on church usage is given for nearly a sixth of the *communes* — and the commentary is full.

The next important document is in many ways complementary to Dauzat's work, for it systematically collects information on the language used in preaching and catechising for every parish in Lower Brittany, though providing very little in the way of analysis or commentary. This survey was carried out by correspondence by the Breton-language quarterly *Gwalarn* in 1928–9, the respondents being mainly priests, sometimes schoolmasters or doctors. The results are presented as being incomplete and imprecise, replies having varied considerably in both scope and quality. They are nevertheless claimed to be useful in giving 'an approximate outline' of the real situation.

The criteria were appropriate in a country where the Catholic Church was an omnipresent institution with virtually no competition from any other religious organisation. Its actual hold on the population did in fact vary from the near absolute (in Léon in the north-west and in much of the Vannetais in the south-east) to the very slight in longstanding anti-clerical areas (the largest occupying all the east central part). However, although there would have been regional variations in attendance at mass, attendance at catechism classes was still well-nigh universal in 1928, the age-group involved being 8–12.

Information is given by parish, a unit which with very few exceptions corresponds exactly to the *commune*. Five categories of linguistic usage are distinguished, of which only the two extremes (Breton only, French only) have absolute values; the intermediate categories (mainly Breton, evenly mixed, mainly French) each cover a fairly wide range of gradations. Overall, the pattern of language use in the Church provides a fair reflection of the pattern in the community as a whole although there may well be exceptions. The absence of Breton preaching may, in some cases, simply mean that there were no monoglots left, while the absence of Breton catechism may reflect the desires of the parents rather than the actual practice of the children. However this may be, the disappearance of Breton from the only domain in which it had a formal public role involves the social demotion of the language. Discrepancies between *Gwalarn* and Dauzat are generally slight.

The language of preaching will be given precedence in this analysis (Figure 4.2) for chronological reasons. It catered for congregations born almost entirely before the First World War amongst whom only those under 40 had grown up in an age of universal schooling, free state elementary schools having been established in every *commune* between 1882 and 1887. Enforcement of attendance remained incomplete, in fact, until the War, especially in the more extensive *communes* of the interior. Sermons were exclusively in Breton over the greater part of the territory, generally the most rural and this is the background against which the following paragraphs will present the distribution of French.

Breton was often not used at all in the larger and medium-sized towns which, due to their commercial and administrative functions, had

TABLE 4.2 *Language of preaching and catechism 1928 — number of parishes in each category*

	F	*Fb*	*M*	*Bf*	*B*	*Total*
F	47	2	—	—	—	49
Fb	14	7	—	—	—	21
M	16	3	2	—	—	21
Bf	16	16	18	18	2	70
B	10	5	10	54	395	474
Total	103	33	30	72	397	635

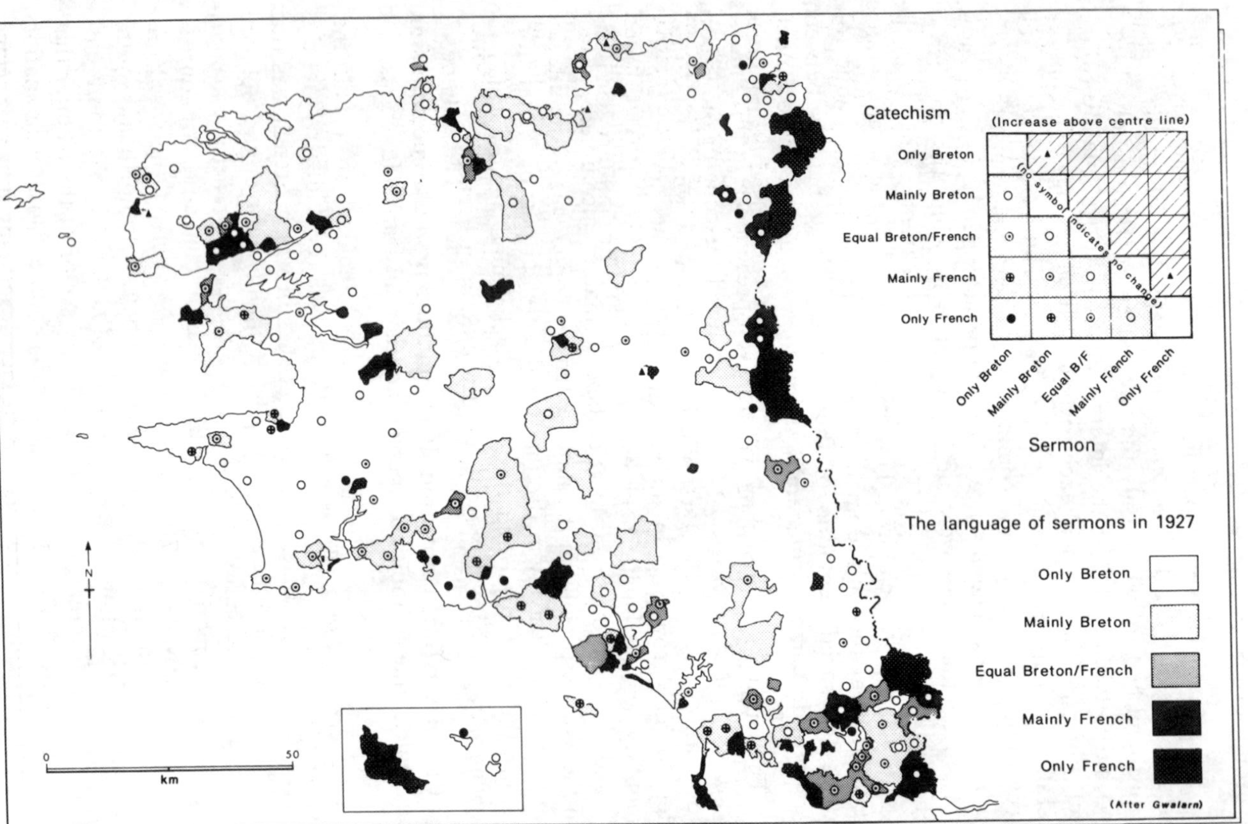

FIGURE 4.2 *The use of Breton in the Catechism compared with Sermons in 1927*

long contained an influential monoglot French element. The growth of the two largest towns was in fact specifically bound up with large influxes of non-Bretons from their foundation in the 1660s, when Brest became France's chief naval base and Lorient was built from scratch to serve as the base for the Compagnie des Indes. The urbanisation of the surrounding communes was very advanced, a situation contrasting strongly with that of Quimper (20,000). It is surprising to find Vannes with a similar population retaining some Breton preaching; this must reflect the fact that its municipal territory was far less completely urbanised than that of Quimper. The lack of Breton in Châteaulin (north of Quimper) is even more surprising for its population was under 3,000 and partly rural at that. Its status as *sous-préfecture* obviously enhanced its urban characteristics, but this cannot be the complete explanation, for the *sous-préfectures* of Pontivy and Guingamp, with two or three times the population and situated near the linguistic frontier, both retained some Breton preaching.

There are a number of coastal and insular communes where French has taken a strong hold. They include the largest, urbanised fishing ports (Concarneau, Douarnenez, Paimpol) but also smaller ones like Camaret, Ile-Tudy and Etel. Maritime contacts with French-speaking ports such as La Rochelle played an important role here in conjunction with the relative isolation from the rural interior. Two additional factors had contributed to the de-Bretonisation of the large island of Belle-Ile: military garrisons and the settlement of Acadian refugees in 1765. The influence of tourism was also becoming perceptible, though apparently only intense in the south-east, Carantec north of Morlaix, and Lampaul-Plouarzel west of Brest. Such resorts as Perros-Guirec north of Lannion and Bénodet south of Quimper, were still using more Breton than French. The volume of holiday-makers was of course much smaller than it would become after 1936 with the generalisation of paid holidays.

Along the frontier, Breton was clearly dominant over half the distance, while French was making inroads elsewhere — inroads that are a little exaggerated in that five of the parishes in which French was the only language of preaching were wholly or mainly east of the Sébillot line. Inland, the area most affected by the advance of French lay around Mûr-de-Bretagne, in the centre, a district whose cultivation of tourists went as far as advertising itself as *la Suisse bretonne*. Otherwise, this process was much more marked in the coastal belt, both north and south. At first glance, the whole of the large zone of collapse in the south-east suggests westward retreat, and that in the very sector of the frontier that had retreated most rapidly in the nineteenth century. Closer examination reveals that the Rhuys peninsula was in fact developing into an enclave and that the situation was quite complex. Isolation from the Breton heartland was particularly marked and contact with it would have taken place, on the whole, in the urban setting of Vannes.

Inland, there was a scatter of parishes where French had gained a foothold, sometimes even ousted Breton; they were, with two exceptions *chefs-lieux de cantons* whose nucleus grouped 1,000 to 3,000 inhabitants. Although not necessarily larger than the bourg of an ordinary commune, they possessed more urban attributes: a *gendarmerie*, a tax office, a judge, lawyers, doctors, more specialised shops and a weekly market. French was most strongly established where the municipal territory was small and completely built up, though Huelgoat, south of Morlaix is something of an exception. Here, the effect of tourism was probably emphasised by the fact that the rural population was both sparse and anti-clerical.

The examination of the language of catechism, viewed against the backdrop of the language of the sermon gives us a fair idea of the dynamics of the situation. Three-quarters of the parishes showed no change and four even showed greater use of Breton in the catechism. Elsewhere there was an increased use of French, usually gradual: in 89 cases there was a drop one step down the scale, while only in ten was there a complete changeover from Breton to French. The slight drop in outer Brest, Vannes, Guingamp and Carhaix meant of course the elimination of the Breton catechism. The most rapid changes were in a group of parishes on the south coast between Concarneau and Quimperlé which had sermons in Breton only and the catechism in French only; no explanation has been published and none springs to mind. The largest continuous area of decline was in the south-east where Breton had been eliminated from the catechism except in the Surzur-Theix block which was becoming a not very solid Breton enclave in French territory. A new feature is a northward extension of French in a belt which follows the frontier as far as Locminé. The increasing use of French around urban centres was general, Paimpol on the north-east coast providing a classic example while Lannion, 30 km to the west, was the most striking exception. In the most rural areas, signs of change were sporadic but commonest in the south-west.

It would have been particularly illuminating to have precise information on the basis on which the language of catechism was chosen in the mixed parishes and to what extent parental wishes were taken into account. Two types of segregation are well attested: segregation by sex and segregation by class. Loth mentions parishes in which the catechism was automatically French for girls and Breton for boys, attributing this to the particularly rigorous exclusion of Breton by nuns in Catholic schools — a procedure which had the general backing of parents. Class segregation could vary in the details of its application in that French catechism could be restricted to the leisured wealthy and professional classes or include also shopkeepers and the lesser *fonctionnaires* or employees of the State. This type of segregation took on a clear geographical dimension when, as generally happened, the French catechism was extended to all the children of the *bourg*, leaving only those from the scattered hamlets learning the Breton catechism.

Numerical estimates of Breton Speakers

No figures have yet been mentioned for the very good reason that no language statistics exist and it is important to remember that all figures given in this section, except for those referring to very small samples, are only estimates. We can begin with estimate-based estimates of at least 430,000 speakers in 1500 and 660,000 for 1685, assuming a third of the population of the whole of Brittany to be Breton-speaking. The nineteenth century brings census-based estimates: 967,000 in 1808 according to Coquebert de Montbret, and 1,320,000 in 1886 according to Sébillot, who further estimated that 51% of the population of Lower Brittany were monoglot Breton and only 5% monoglot French.

The best-informed and most meticulous estimate of the situation at the beginning of the present century is one by Broudic (1983) who collates census figures with information contained in detailed reports made by both civil and ecclesiastical authorities at the height of the conflict between Church and State, when there was strong pressure on the Church to enforce the French catechism as a practical step: contributing to the desired extirpation of Breton. For comparison, Table 4.3 includes

TABLE 4.3 *Estimated totals of Breton speakers, 1905 and 1952*

	c1905 (Broudic)		*c1952 (Gourvil)*	
Breton monoglots	900,000	60%	100,000	7%
Breton dominant (bilingual)	500,000	33%	700,000	47%
French dominant (bilingual)			300,000	20%
French monoglots	100,000	7%	400,000	27%
Total	1,500,000		1,500,000	

Gourvil's (1952) figures, whose precise basis, however is unknown.

I have myself worked out an estimate for the 1962 census combining experience of Welsh data with field experience in both Wales and Brittany. It assumes particular percentages for particular categories of *communes* as specified in Table 4.4.

This was perhaps the last census for which such a simple operation could have any meaning, for the following decade saw urbanisation penetrating into the deepest countryside as never before with the generalisation of the personal motor car. The total figure arrived at was 686,000 speakers, just over half the population of Lower Brittany, which is more or less in line with other estimates. Figure 4.3 summarises, by canton, the results of this estimate; it must be remembered that it is in fact a slightly modified map of rurality on the basis of the single criterion of dispersal of the habitat, a criterion with which Breton-speaking does correlate. Like Figure 4.2, it shows that proximity to French Brittany is secondary to the influence of the urban network. The block appearing in the north-eastern interior is universally acknowledged to be the most strongly Breton-speaking area; it is also, unfortunately, economically and demographically depressed like most of the centre, with an ageing population of only two-thirds of its 1936 total of 70,000.

Fieldwork has in recent years produced a small number of micro-censuses at the commune level and I give here simplified figures from one I carried out on the basis of the electoral register of Bothoa in 1982. This forms the northern half of the *commune* of Saint-Nicolas-du-Pélem (Côtes-du-Nord), halfway between Guingamp and Pontivy and 10 km west of the Sébillot line — and just outside the block mentioned in the previous paragraph. As its *bourg* is atrophied, Bothoa does not provide

TABLE 4.4 *Assumed percentages underlying Humphreys' estimate (1962)*

Communes		*Nucleated population*	*Scattered population*
Non cantons	< 5000	50%	80%
Cantons	< 5000	40%	80%
Rural	> 5000		
Urban	> 5000	30%	70%
Urban	> 10000	20%	50%

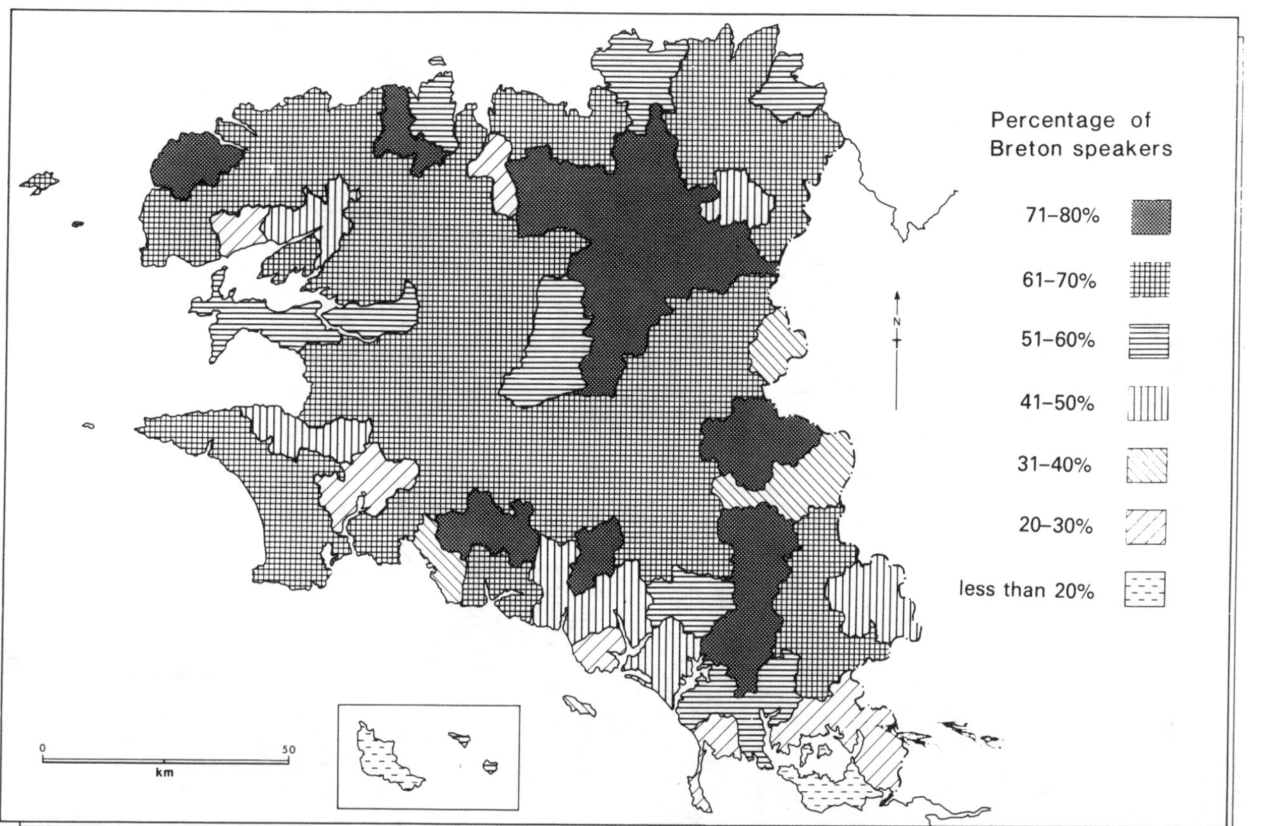

FIGURE 4.3 *The percentage of Breton speakers in 1962. (Source: Author's calculations from the 1962 census).*

an example of the contrast with the surrounding deep countryside that would be found in an autonomous *commune* — which seldom has such a low population total, incidentally. The population was only 56% of its 1946 level and 58.8% of the electors were male; the percentage of Breton-speakers would certainly have been lower were it not for the continuing emigration of young people.

There were no monoglot speakers of Breton; the last seem to have died about 1970 and were all women. The monoglot French over 40 were all incomers while the Breton-speaking included three — the children of temporary emigrants — born in Versailles and Rambouillet, south-west of Paris. It is conceivable that some of the persons in the 'uncertain' column have a fair passive knowledge of Breton but lack either the desire or the confidence to attempt to use it; such latent knowledge is now hardly likely to be activated by the necessity to communicate with a monglot. It is only in the youngest age group that there was a difference between the sexes: 15% of males under 30 were fluent Breton-speakers, but no females; females were 56% monoglot French, as against 37% of males, the proportion of semi-speakers being the same. These figures need to be approached with caution for several reasons: because the total figure is low (36), because of the imbalance between the sexes (75% male) and because of the high proportion of persons of uncertain status (25%). It was further discovered that of the 47 children of school age some half-dozen could speak Breton, though not to a high level of competence.

Dating from the same year is a questionnaire-based survey of

TABLE 4.5 *Ability to speak Breton among the voters of Bothoa*

Age	*Breton fluent*		*Breton semi.*		*Uncertain*		*French monoglot*		*Total*
	No.	*%*	*No.*	*%*	*No.*	*%*	*No.*	*%*	
80+	12	92.3	—	—	—	—	1	7.7	13
70–9	24	96.0	—	—	—	—	1	4.0	25
60–9	26	92.9	—	—	1	3.6	1	3.6	28
50–9	38	84.4	—	—	1	2.2	6	13.3	45
40–9	16	59.3	1	3.7	3	11.1	7	25.9	27
30–9	11	50.0	2	9.1	2	9.1	7	31.8	22
18–9	2	7.4	6	22.2	7	25.9	12	44.4	27
Total	129	69.0	9	4.8	14	7.5	35	18.7	187

Plouvien, 15 km north of Brest (Arzur, 1982). The 907 respondents must amount to a good half of the adult population, but the question of their representativity is nowhere discussed. Overall percentages are as follows: 60% spoke Breton, 26% understood Breton but could not speak it, 14% were completely ignorant of Breton. As in Bothoa, the contrast between the oldest and the youngest generations was a stark one: fluent Breton-speakers — 66+: 96%, 18–25: 14%; monoglot French — 66+; 1.4%, 18–25: 30%. The most sudden drop in the percentage of fluent Breton speakers was from 79% (41–50) to 33% (26–40).

The soundest basis for an overall assessment of the present situation is to be found in audience research carried out for Radio Bretagne Ouest in 1983, from which the language questions have been analysed in some detail by Broudic (1987). The socially representative sample of 999 is geographically biased in favour of Finistère, but its validity can reasonably be assumed to extend to the rest of Lower Brittany, excluding the de-Bretonised zone around Vannes. The population of this area in 1982 was 1,514,694, of which 1,189,035 were over 15; the projection of the 51.7% of the sample who claimed to speak Breton gives a total of 614,587 of which 40% were very frequent speakers and 40% occasional speakers. A further 12.6% claimed to understand Breton but not to speak it, which, projected gives 195,146. From now on, all data from this sample will be given only in the original percentages.

Table 4.6 confirms the steep fall in proficiency and practice from the oldest to the youngest generation. It is clear, too, that the potential for Breton is grossly under-realised. Not only do Breton speakers generally use French with strangers who may well themselves be Breton speakers, but many also use French with people they know to speak a Breton similar to their own.

Table 4.7 shows that both proficiency and practice are markedly less common among females — and this despite the fact that the knowledge of French became general much earlier among males, not

TABLE 4.6 *Percentage of Breton speakers by age group (RBO)*

Speak Breton	*15–24*	*25–34*	*35–49*	*50–65*	*65+*	*All ages*
Very often	1.0	4.7	18.7	37.6	41.1	20.9
Quite often	4.1	5.8	10.9	16.5	11.1	9.9
Sometimes	15.7	25.6	23.9	18.3	21.1	20.8
Total	20.8	36.0	53.5	72.5	73.3	51.7

TABLE 4.7 *Percentage of Breton speakers by sex (RBO)*

Speak Breton	*Very often*	*Quite often*	*Sometimes*	*Total*
Males	25.7	11.8	20.2	57.7
Females	16.6	8.3	20.5	45.4

least because of compulsory military service. It would be difficult to give dates, but to draw on personal experience in the early 1960s in the interior, I met only one man, aged 90, who was a pure monoglot, while I frequently came across women of the same category who were only in their 60s. In the most rural parishes, pure monoglots and semi-monoglots whose knowledge of French was completely passive would account for at least half the older women. Of those who are still alive today, many have subsequently learnt French from their grandchildren or great-grandchildren. Outside the towns, the use of French between Breton-speaking girls began after the First World War and had become common by the Second World War, the rapidity of this extension of French depending on the accessibility of the urban model, which was conditioned by social as well as geographical factors.

Table 4.8 confirms the correlation between Breton-speaking and rurality, though the inclusion of a substantial number of rural *communes* in the second column has probably toned down the urban–rural contrast. An example is Plogonnec, 10 km east of Douarnenez, only 622 of whose 2,709 inhabitants lived in the *bourg*. Incidentally only about an eighth of the *communes* have populations of below 500. The urban percentages will seem unexpectedly high to many, especially those in the final column, which refer to the single town of Brest. It is after all the naval capital of

TABLE 4.8 *Percentage of Breton speakers according to the size of the commune (RBO)*

	Population (000)			
	<2	*2–20*	*20–100*	*>100*
Very often	35.9	23.6	6.0	1.5
Quite often	12.8	9.9	8.0	6.8
Sometimes	20.3	21.6	26.0	17.6
Total	69.0	55.1	40.0	25.9

France and has the highest proportion of persons born outside Brittany, and were not its tram passengers once simultaneously forbidden in one curt sentence to spit and to speak Breton? The well-established perception of Brest as a completely French town developed first with reference to Brest *intra-muros*, dominated by monoglot French since the seventeenth century, which is only about one-fortieth of the area of the present municipality. The three communes which Brest annexed in 1946, although heavily urbanised, still had some Breton sermons in 1928 (see Figure 4.2). Like other towns, Brest has always drawn in population from the surrounding countryside and a very considerable number of urban Bretons are first-generation townsmen.

Table 4.9 confirms yet again the correlation with rurality, positively in the case of the farming population, negatively in the case of the professions, management and skilled workers. There is an interesting contrast between two categories which have the same potential for speaking Breton but whose practice differs: both management and trade recruit evenly from the whole of the population, yet while the former is strongly concentrated in an urban environment, the latter — covering shopkeepers and tradesmen — is dispersed throughout the whole inhabited space, both rural and urban, and, moreover, involves face to face interaction with a numerous clientele. The correlation with age is apparent in the percentages for students and also in the fact that 45% of Breton speakers are retired. Associated with these variations, but not easy to correlate directly with them on the information available, are variations in educational background, given in simplified form in Table 4.10.

TABLE 4.9 *Percentage of Breton speakers by occupation (RBO)*

	Speaks Breton			
	Very often	*Quite often*	*Sometimes*	*Total*
Farming	56.6	9.8	18.0	84.4
Management	2.9	14.7	35.3	52.9
Trade	18.2	9.1	25.5	52.8
Unskilled	10.2	11.1	21.3	42.6
Skilled	3.9	10.4	22.1	36.4
Professions	7.4	3.7	18.5	29.6
Students	1.4	1.4	12.7	15.5

TABLE 4.10 *Percentage of Breton speakers according to education (RBO)*

	Education			
	None	*Primary*	*Secondary*	*University*
Speaks Breton	66.7	75.2	43.2	26.7
Speaks Breton very often	66.7	44.8	10.5	2.3
Speaks Breton quite often	0.0	15.2	9.1	3.5

Conclusion

On a priori grounds, spatial relationships and the presence of the physical requirements for a solid agricultural economy might lead us to expect the unthreatened survival of Breton. Its decline, on the other hand, appears to result from a convergence of independent causes, many of them accidental and many of them belonging to a distant past. Some explicit reference to the Welsh situation, a comparison with which underlies the whole of the present chapter, may make this clearer. The establishment of Protestantism gave the language full official status in public worship, then brought about the generalisation of literacy and, finally, among nonconformists, brought training in the democratic process through the medium of Welsh. Secondly, industrialisation, although it was later to militate against the survival of the language, did in its earlier stages enrich the Welsh-speaking community, permitting the development of large-scale publishing and favouring adaptation to an urban life-style. Finally, Wales has not constituted a military or political threat to England since the fifteenth century and her language has never been unequivocally branded as an ideological threat to the British state. All these points contrast strongly with the Breton experience.

Notes

1. Brittany, in this chapter, is used for the historical province and not for the *région-programme*, from which Loire-Atlantique is excluded.
2. Catholic schools have an older, though not very fully documented tradition of teaching some Breton.
3. Breton finally disappeared here in the 1920s. Its survival was favoured by a virtually insular situation and by the fact that its inhabitants continued to peddle the salt they produced over much of Breton-speaking Brittany throughout the nineteenth century.

4. In-migration of non-Breton speakers has played a very minor role outside the coastal belt.
5. *Bourg* in Brittany — and in most regions of scattered population in France — means the administrative and commercial centre of a rural *commune*, normally clustered round the church. Many French dictionaries define it as a small market centre, the meaning it has in areas of nucleated settlement.

Bibliography

AMBROSE, J. 1980, Micro-scale language mapping: an experiment in Wales and Brittany. *Discussion Papers in Geolinguistics*, 2.

ARZUR, A.-M. 1982, Parle-t-on encore breton à Plouvien? Duplicated report.

BROUDIC, F. 1983, *Al Liberterien hag ar brezoneg — 'Brug': 1913–1914*. Brest: Brud Nevez.

— 1985, La production écrite de langue bretonne de 1973 à 1983: approche statistique. *Mémoires de la Société d'Histoire et d'Archéologie de Bretagne* 62, 441–68.

— 1987, 550.000 brezoneger a zo en Breiz-Izel, med piou int? *Brud Nevez* 104, 2–54.

BRUNOT, F. 1927, *Histoire de la langue française* 9–i (La Révolution et l'Empire). Paris: Armand Colin.

DAUZAT, A. 1929, La pénétration du français en Bretagne du XVIIIe siècle à nos jours. *Revue de philologie française* 41, 1–55.

DELUMEAU, J. (ed.) 1969, *Histoire de la Bretagne*. Toulouse: Privat.

FALC'HUN, F. 1958, Langue bretonne. *Orbis* 7–ii, 516–33.

— 1981, *Perspectives nouvelles sur l'histoire de la langue bretonne* (augmented edition of *Histoire de la langue bretonne d'après la géographie linguistique (1963)*. Paris: Union Générale d'Editions.

FLEURIOT, L. 1964, *Dictionnaire des gloses en vieux breton*. Paris: Klincksieck.

— 1980, *Les Origines de la Bretagne*. Paris: Payot.

GOURVIL, F. 1952, *Langue et littérature bretonnes*. Paris: PUF.

GWEGEN, J. 1975, *La Langue bretonne face à ses oppresseurs*. Quimper: Nature et Bretagne.

HEMON, R. (ed.) 1929, Enklask diwar-benn stad ar brezoneg e 1928. *Gwalarn* 19, 72–99.

— 1947, *La Langue bretonne et ses combats*. La Baule: Editions de Bretagne.

HUMPHREYS, H. Ll. 1979/80, *La Langue galloise: une présentation*. Brest: *Studi*, 13–14.

— 1985, Phonologie, morphosyntaxe et lexique du parler breton de Bothoa. Doctorat d'Etat, Brest.

LE DÛ, J. 1980, Sociolinguistique et diglossie: le cas du breton. Gardin, B, Marcellesi, J.-B. et GRECO Rouen. *Sociolinguistique: approches, théories, méthodes* 153–63.

LE MENN, G. 1975, Le breton et son enseignement. *Langue française* 25, 71–83.

— 1984, La littérature en moyen-breton de 1350 à 1650. *Actes du 107e Congrès national des Sociétés savantes (Brest, 1982*) 89–104.

LOTH, J. 1883, *L'Emigration bretonne en Armorique*. Paris: Champion.

MORVANNOU, F. 1980, *Le Breton, la jeunesse d'une vieille langue*. Brest: Presses populaires de Bretagne.

OGÉE 1853, *Dictionnaire historique et géographique de la province de Bretagne* (nouvelle édition revue et augmentée par A. MARTEVILLE et P. VARIN). Rennes.

PANIER, R. 1942, Les limites actuelles de la langue bretonne; leur évolution depuis 1886. *Le Français moderne* 10, 97–115.

PIETTE, J. R. F. 1973, *French Loanwords in Middle Breton*. Cardiff: University of Wales Press.

— 1978/80, *Istor ar yezhoù keltiek*, I and II. Lesneven: Hor Yezh.

SÉBILLOT, P. 1886, La langue bretonne: limites et statistique. *Revue d' ethnographie* 15, 1–29.

SKOL VREIZH 1976, Collective works: Morlaix: Skol Vreizh *Géographie de la Bretagne. Histoire de Bretagne et des pays celtiques.*

— 1983, I — *Des Mégalithes aux cathédrales.*

— 1973, II — *L'Etat breton (1341–1532).*

— 1978, III — *La Bretagne province (1532–1789).*

— 1980, IV — *La Bretagne au XIX*e siècle.

— 1983, V — *La Bretagne au XX*e siècle.

TANGUY, B. 1980, La limite linguistique dans la péninsule armoricaine à l'époque de l'émigration bretonne d'après les données toponymiques. *Annales de Bretagne* 87, 429–62.

TIMM, L. A. 1980, Bilingualism, diglossia and language shift in Brittany. *International Journal of the Sociology of Language* 25, 29–41.

— 1983, The shifting linguistic frontier in Brittany. In F. B. AGARD, G. KELLEY, A. MAKKAI and V. B. MAKKAI (eds) *Essays in Honor of Charles F. Hockett* (pp. 443–57). Leiden: Brill.

5 Language-Retreat and Regeneration in the Present-Day Scottish Gàidhealtachd

KENNETH MACKINNON

Questions on ability to speak Scottish Gaelic have been asked in the Scottish population census since 1881. Over this period of a century, the wording of the question has been substantially changed only twice. Originally in 1881, the question asked whether individuals over three years of age habitually used Gaelic. In 1891 this wording was altered to whether the individual was able to speak Gaelic and English, or Gaelic only. In 1971 additional questions were asked relating to abilities to read and write Gaelic, and in 1981 the question relating to ability to speak only Gaelic was dropped. After successive censuses these results have been presented in greater detail: firstly in terms of numbers per civil parish area; subsequently also in terms of local government authority area; since the beginning of the century also overall by age; and from 1921 by age and sex too. From 1951 separate Gaelic Reports have been published, and from 1971 age and sex tables of Gaelic abilities have been available in small area statistics. It is thus possible to present a recent historical account of the incidence of Gaelic abilities in Scotland in increasing detail both geographically and demographically.

The overall picture for Gaelic has been one of attrition. In 1881 'habitual' speakers of Gaelic numbered 231,594 out of a population aged over three years of 3,425,151 — or 6.76%. In 1981 the corresponding figures were 79,307 able to speak Gaelic out of 4,843,553 — or 1.64%. It will be seen though from Table 5.1, that on occasion numbers and proportions of Gaelic speakers have ostensibly increased. The position is

TABLE 5.1 *Numbers and proportions of Gaelic speakers at successive censuses*

Census (popln.	*Pop. 3+ present)*	*Numbers of Gaelic speakers:*			*% of Pop. 3+ speaking Gaelic:*		
		Bilingual	*Mono-lingual*	*Total*	*Bilingual*	*Mono-lingual*	*Total*
1881	3,425,151	(not separated)		231,594	(not separated)		6.76
1891	3,721,778	210,677	43,738	254,415	5.66	1.18	6.84
1901	4,146,733	202,700	28,106	230,806	4.89	0.68	5.57
1911	4,439,802	183,998	18,400	202,398	4.14	0.41	4.56
1921	4,573,471	148,950	9,829	158,779	3.26	0.21	3.47
1931	4,588,909	129,419	6,716	136,135	2.82	0.15	2.97
1951	4,826,814	93,269	2,178	95,447	1.93	0.05	1.98
1961	4,892,822	80,004	974	80,978	1.64	0.02	1.66
1971	4,967,108	88,415	477	88,892	1.78	0.01	1.79
(usually resident population)							
1971	4,926,339	(not separated)		84,601	(not separated)		1.72
1981	4,843,553	(Rdg,Wrtg,Spkg: 82,620)		79,307	(Rdg,Wrtg,Spkg: 1.71)		1.64

Sources: 1881 Gaelic Return, 1891 Census Part I, Table I, 1961–81 Gaelic Reports

also illustrated graphically in Figure 5.1.

The ostensible increase between 1881–91 is clearly due to the deletion of 'habitually' in the wording of the Gaelic question. However, the increase in Gaelic speakers between 1961–71 does require further explanation. It did occur on the occasion of another question change: namely, the addition of questions on Gaelic literacy. The increase occurred only in the Lowlands, as shown in Figures 5.2 and 5.3. The chief cause may be the greater numbers of migrant Gaels and learners claiming ability to speak Gaelic prompted by the new questions on literacy. (See MacKinnon, 1978.) Between 1961–71 attrition of Gaelic continued apace in the more strongly Gaelic areas — as it had during the ostensible increase of 1881–91. However, although by 1981 overall numbers and proportions of Gaelic speakers had again declined — to around the levels of 1961 — this decline masked actual increases for the first time ever in the more strongly Gaelic areas of the Western Isles and parts of Skye. It also masked increases amongst young people and in other specific areas. This chapter draws attention to these regenerative aspects and discusses the social and economic processes which are probably operant.

In the nineteenth century migration from the more strongly Gaelic

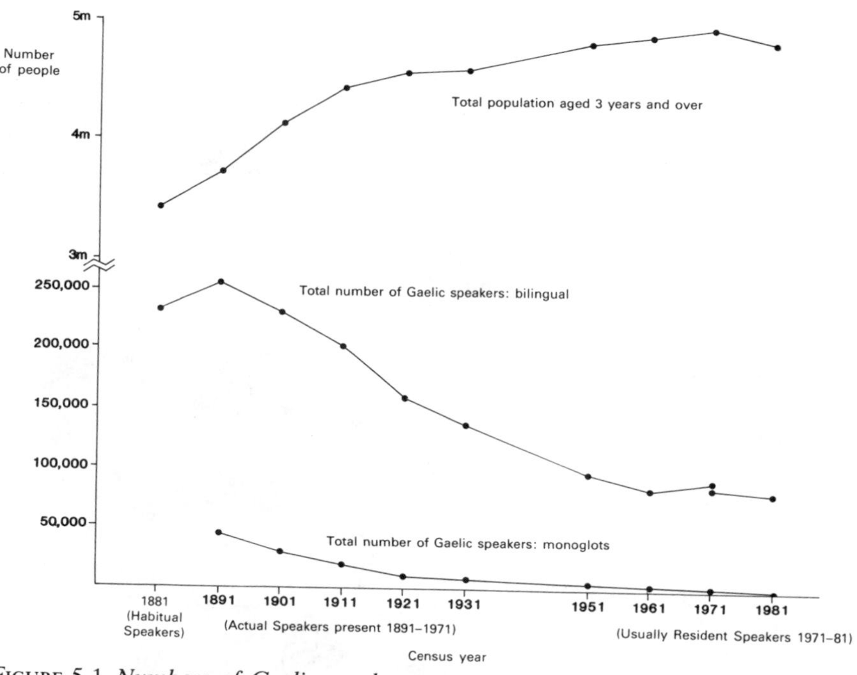

FIGURE 5.1 *Numbers of Gaelic speakers at successive censuses*

areas of the Highlands and Hebrides accelerated with industrialisation in the Lowland central belt. This can be illustrated by the changing size of the Gaelic-speaking populations of the 'Highland' and 'Lowland' counties, as in Figure 5.4. It is apparent that today the traditional Gàidhealtachd of the mainland Highlands and Hebrides only accounts for some 60% of Scotland's Gaelic-speakers. Some 40% dwell in an urban or a Lowland milieu. An even more discriminating picture can be drawn in terms of local areas such as civil parishes or enumeration districts. In Table 5.2 the levels of 75%, 50% and 25% local incidence of Gaelic speakers are taken as indicators of areas where Gaelic is still respectively the everyday speech of the local community, where it is still the speech of the majority, and where it is still essentially present amongst a noticeable local minority. The numbers of Gaelic speakers living in all areas above the national rate of incidence are also given. At civil parish level, historical comparison can be made for census returns over a century. (At enumeration district level, comparison can be made only between 1971 and 1981.)

Table 5.2 is illustrated graphically in Figure 5.5. Clearly economic

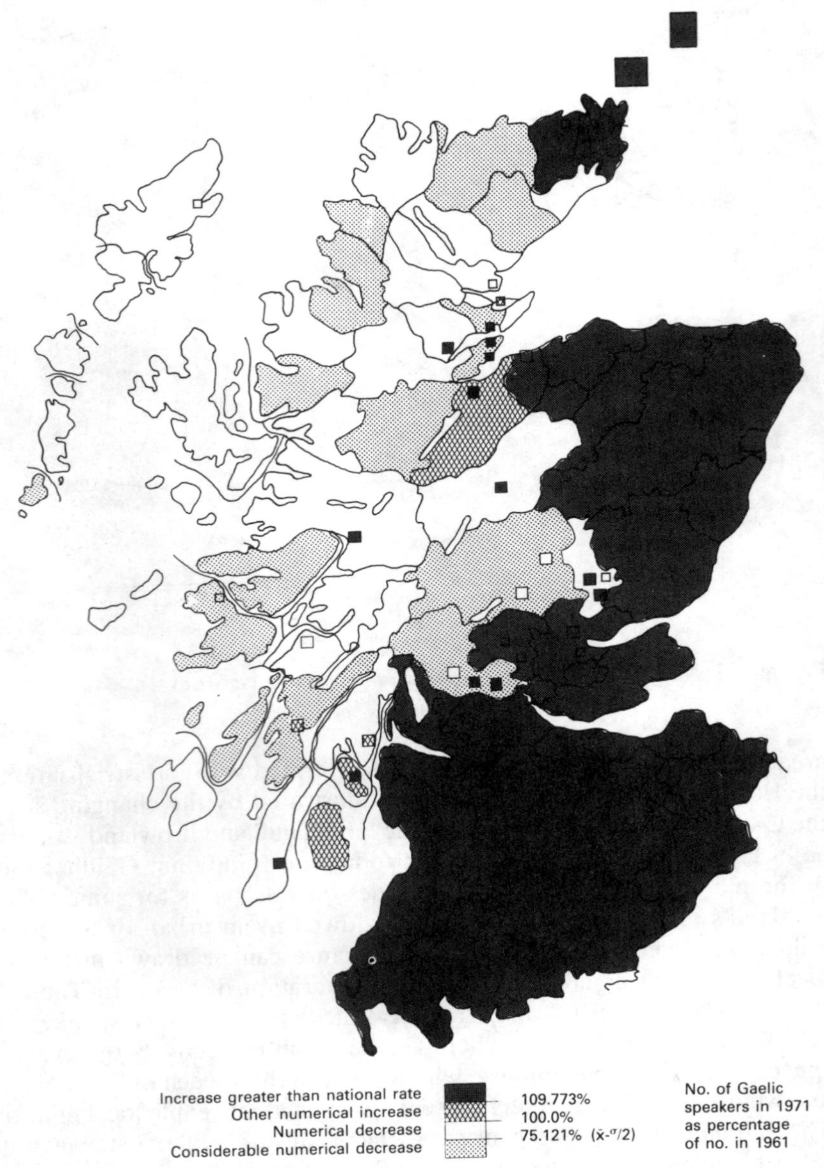

FIGURE 5.2 *Lowland counties and cities, Highland districts and burghs: numerical change in incidence of Gaelic speakers, 1961–71*

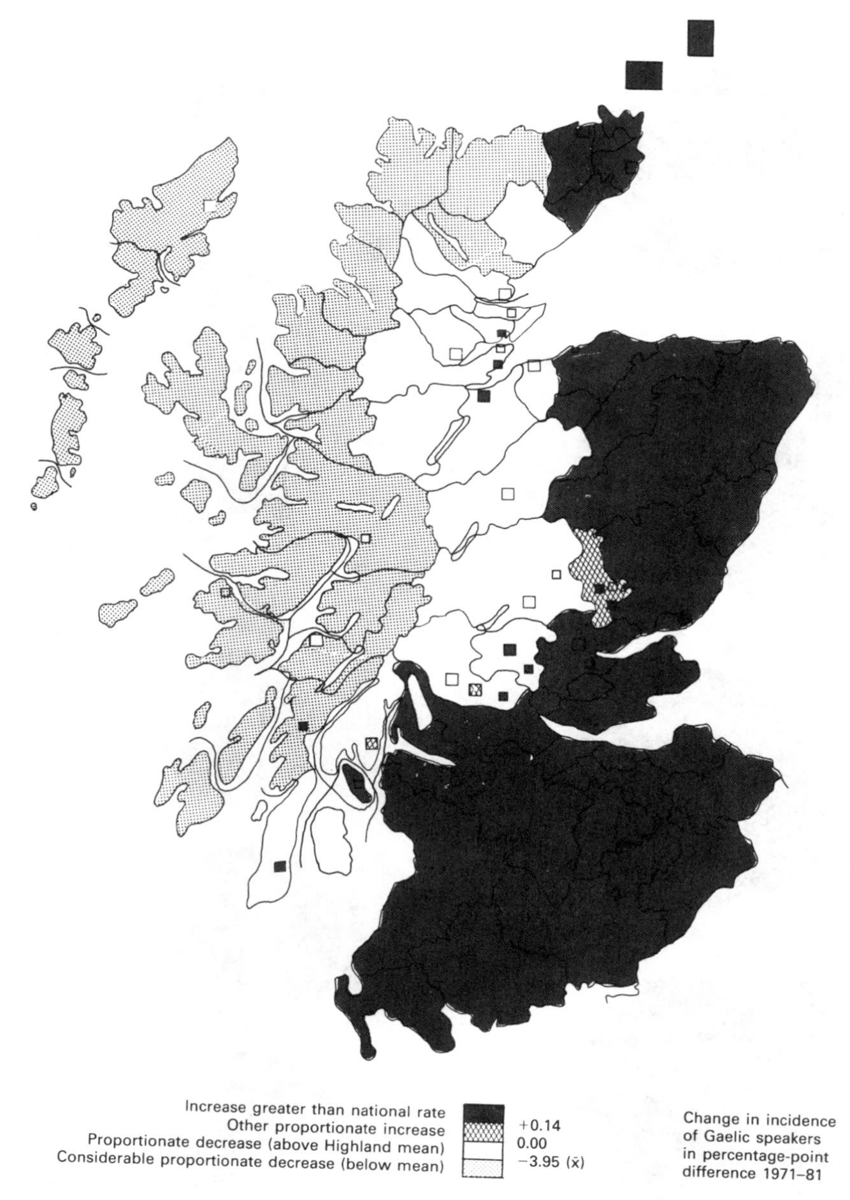

FIGURE 5.3 *Lowland counties and cities, Highland districts and burghs: proportionate change in incidence of Gaelic speakers, 1961–71*

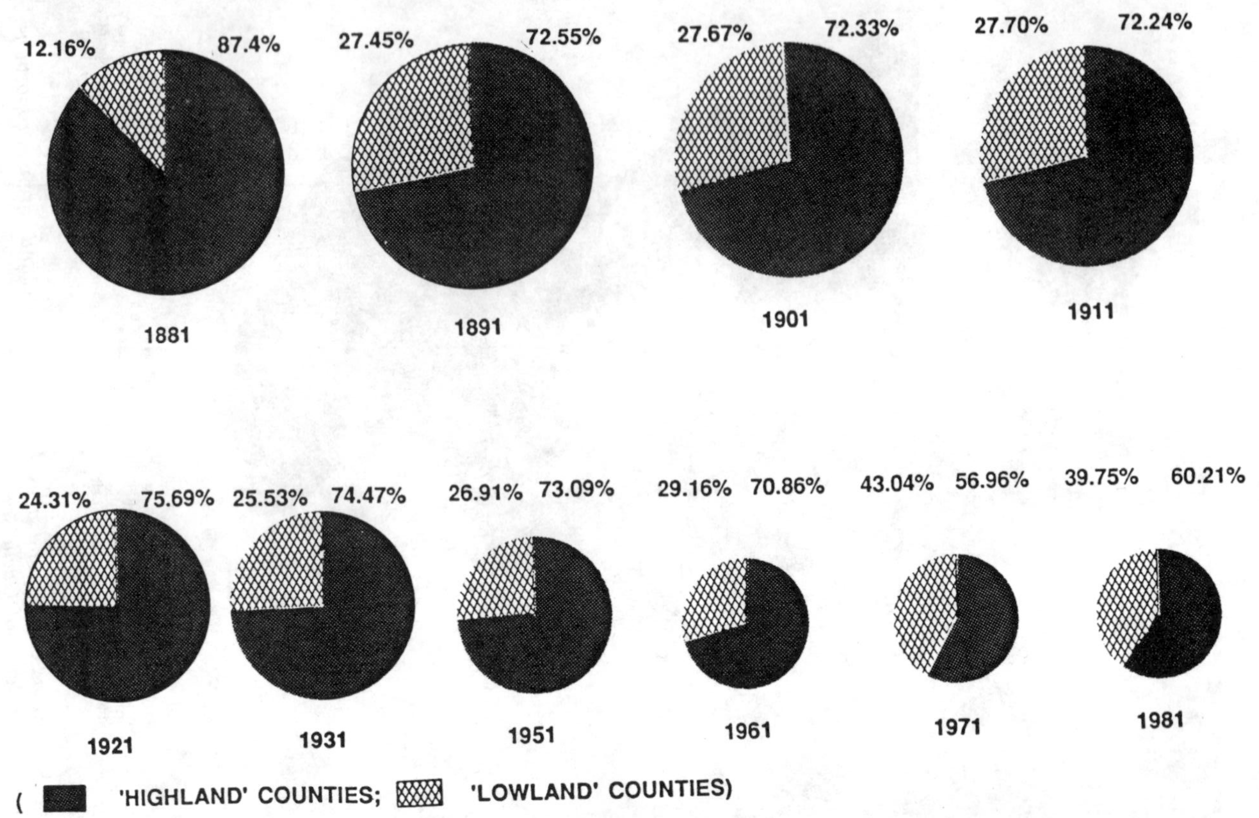

FIGURE 5.4 *Gaelic speakers in 'Highland' and 'Lowland' counties, 1881–1981*

TABLE 5.2 *Numbers of Gaelic speakers in areas of differing incidence 1881–1981*

Local Gaelic incidence	*1881 Census*		*1891 Census*		*1901 Census*		*1911 Census*		*1921 Census*	
	No.	*As %*	*No.*	*As %*	*No.*	*As %*	*No.*	*As %*	*No.*	*As %*
Over 75%	140,847	60.82	119,440	46.95	100,551	43.57	83,647	41.33	70,869	44.63
Over 50%	177,867	76.80	167,298	65.76	140,187	60.74	107,114	52.92	84,899	53.47
Over 25%	195,002	84.20	191,540	75.29	107,264	67.56	134,840	66.62	166,645	72.20
Over nat.	201,458	86.99	200,194	78.69	119,712	75.40	176,423	76.44	148,876	73.56
rate of incidence:		(6.76%)		(6.84%)		(3.47%)		(5.57%)		(4.56%)
Local Gaelic incidence	*1931 Census*		*1951 Census*		*1961 Census*		*1971 Census*		*1981 Census*	
	No.	*As %*	*No.*	*As %*	*No.*	*As %*	*No.*	*As %*	*No.*	*As %*
Over 75%	58,005	42.61	33,403	35.00	26,894	33.21	22,150	24.92	12,495	15.76
Over 50%	68,586	50.38	49,127	51.47	36,231	44.74	29,810	33.54	25,064	31.60
Over 25%	86,851	63.80	54,450	57.04	41,176	50.85	37,570	42.26	32,856	41.43
Over nat.	100,524	73.84	68,528	71.80	55,105	68.04	50,275	56.56	46,965	59.22
rate of incidence:		(2.97%)		(1.98%)		(1.66%)		(1.79%)		(1.64%)

(Percentages as proportions of all Gaelic speakers nationally)
Sources: 1881 Gaelic Return, 1891 Census Part I, Table I, 1961–81 Gaelic Reports.

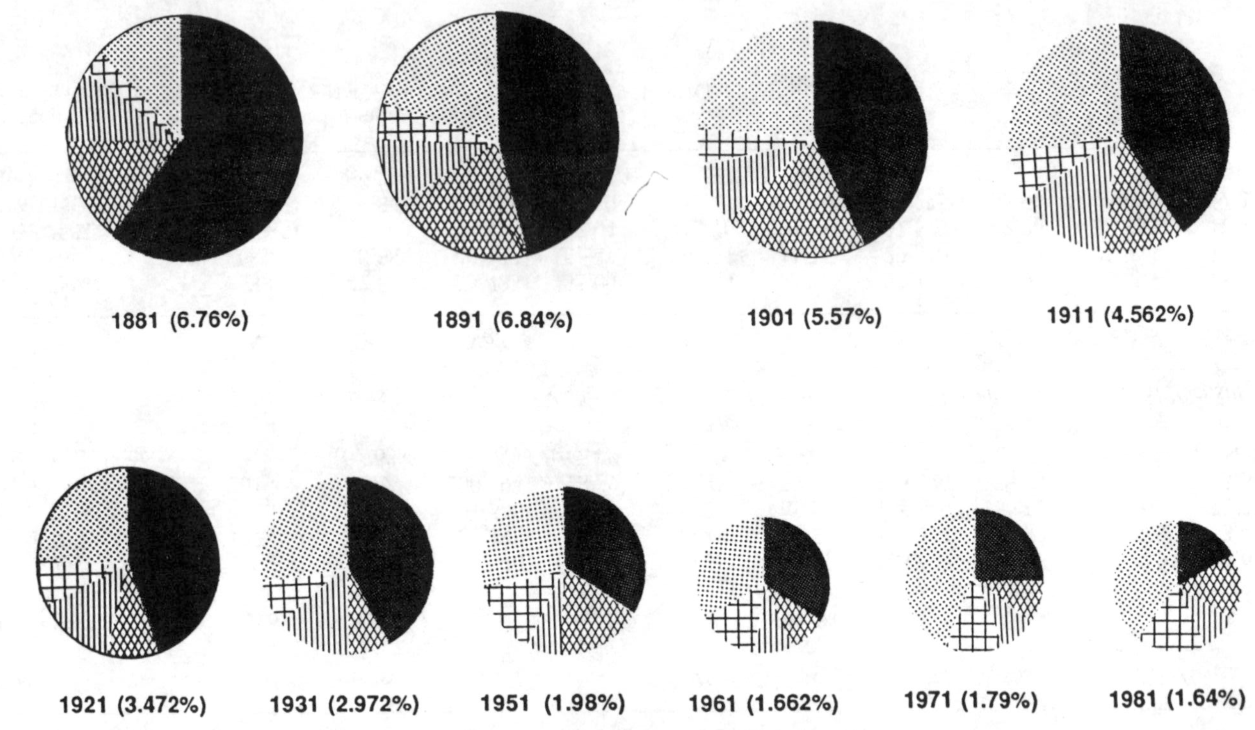

FIGURE 5.5 *Gaelic speakers in areas of differing incidence, 1881–1981. (In clockwise order: shading indicates areas of 75%+, 50%+, 25%+ and above national rate of incidence of Gaelic speakers)*

and social processes have changed the distribution of Scotland's Gaelic speakers over a century. Apart from the marked reduction in numbers, the location of the Gaelic population is noticeably altered. The most strongly Gaelic areas have shrunk north-westwards to Tiree, Skye and the Western Isles. In 1981 civil parishes where over 75% of the population could speak Gaelic contained only 15% of all Scotland's Gaelic speakers. In 1881 such areas contained over 60%. A century ago, the traditional Gàidhealtachd was home to almost nine out of ten of all Gaelic speakers, and is now home to only six out of ten. However, for enumeration districts, the situation is not quite so extreme. In 1981, enumeration districts which were over 75% Gaelic-speaking contained 20,345, or 25.65% of all Gaelic speakers, and those over 50% contained 27,816, or 35.07%.

A century ago, the Gaelic population was much more compactly distributed within its heartland, then not only the Western Isles and Inner Hebrides but also the Highland mainland, including sizeable populations in eastern areas such as Easter Ross, Loch Ness-side and Badenoch. (See Figure 5.6.) The 'centre of population' of Scotland's Gaelic speakers in 1891 may be estimated in the vicinity of Fort Augustus in the Great Glen. By 1981 this had moved south-westwards to a location west of Spean Bridge. (See Appendix for discussion of method and results.) The movement is definitely towards the general centre of population in the mid-Central Belt. Here the estimated centre of the Scottish population had moved only marginally a few km E by N-wards from a point between Cumbernauld and Airdrie to the vicinity of Slamannan, a movement away from Glasgow towards growing sub-centres of population in the east and north-east.

In 1981, not only did the Gaelic heartland contain far fewer Gaelic speakers, numerically and proportionately, it had itself contracted. (See Figure 5.7.) The Gaelic-speaking population was also more dispersed across the Highland area, and more concentrated in urban centres. These now account for rather more Gaelic speakers than the present-day Gaelic heartland areas of Skye and the Western Isles. (In 1981, 32,342 or 41% of all Gaelic speakers normally resided in Lowland Scotland; only 27,756 or 35% of all Gaelic speakers normally resided in Skye and the Western Isles.) Were the 'colonies' of Gaelic speakers in the Lowlands true communities, they would constitute a *Gaelic Archipelago* in a *Lowland Sea* of greater consequence than that of the Hebrides themselves.

Between 1961–81, the decrease of Gaelic seemed to reach some stability. This apparent stasis masks the fact that the numbers and proportions of Gaelic speakers continued to decrease in the Highland and Island areas in the period 1961–71, the ostensible increase occurring solely within the Lowlands, as has been noted already. However, in the period 1971–81, for the first time ever, the numbers and proportions of Gaelic speakers increased in a number of their heartland areas. (See Figures 5.8–5.11.)

These increases can be accounted for by a number of factors. Oil-related and other industrial developments had attracted Gaelic-speakers to settle in the Moray Firth and Cromarty Firth areas, Wester Ross, Caithness and the Northern Isles. The Arnish oil-rig fabrication and repair yard had attracted population back to Lewis. In a number of Highland and Island areas, the increase in numbers of Gaelic speakers is a feature of the age-groups of school attendance, and may be related to the development of Gaelic teaching schemes especially in primary education between 1971 and 1981. (See MacKinnon, 1984.) The numerical increase in Gaelic speakers in Highland Perthshire results specifically from this factor — but is also to be noted in some areas of Argyll.

The numerical increase in southern Skye was chiefly amongst schoolchildren and young adults, and may result from both of these factors. The increase in surburban areas around Glasgow (namely Bearsden & Milngavie, Strathkelvin, Cumbernauld & Kilsyth, Eastwood, and East Kilbride), may be accounted for by the movement of city Gaels: the result of concomitant upward social mobility and outward geographical mobility, and the relocation of inner-city population to new town and development areas.

Increases in Gaelic speakers amongst the school-aged population during 1971–81 have been more fully discussed elsewhere. (See MacKinnon, 1984; 1986.) This upturn amongst young people is noticeable nationally in both numerical and proportionate terms, but it can be shown to be an effect specific only to areas in which primary Gaelic teaching schemes had been in operation prior to 1981.

At this point between decennial censuses, it may be speculated whether the position for Gaelic in 1991 (if examined in a comparable manner in the next census) will be one of further and inexorable decline, or some measure of continued stability. In recent years there have been institutional improvements assisting the maintenance of Gaelic, notably developments in the location of new industry, in the media, in education and in the establishment of new Gaelic organisations such as *Acair* and *Comunn na Gàidhlig* (CnaG). These have encouraged the retention or return of vocationally skilled and professionally qualified young Gaels to the Gaelic areas. There has also been increased demand for Gaelic education.

Will such factors have any discernible future effect? The sudden collapse of new industries located in the Highlands — such as the Corpach pulpmill (which closed in 1980) or the Invergordon smelter (which closed in 1981) — may be the precursors of similar catastrophes in the oil-related sector, and by 1987 the Kishorn yard had finally closed. If the oil-related industries suddenly contract in the North of Scotland, there will be implications for the relocation of population generally, and in particular of Gaelic speakers who had moved from their home areas for work. Since 1981 there have been development programmes in small-scale agriculture and related activities (such as the Integrated Development Programme in the Western Isles) and the development of fish-farming in the more strongly Gaelic western areas. It will be interesting to ascertain whether these developments have had any marked bearing upon community language-conservation or language-shift.

As can be seen from Table 5.2, despite some increase in numbers and incidence of Gaelic speakers in some of the most strongly Gaelic areas during the period 1971–81, the numbers and proportion of the Gaelic population resident within civil parish areas of over 75% incidence continued to contract. This trend alone has the most important consequences for the maintenance of Gaelic as a community language. In 1961 one-third of all Gaelic speakers lived in parishes where three-quarters or more of the population spoke the language. In 1971 this proportion had fallen to one-quarter of all Gaels thus resident, and in 1981 to only 15%. Even in terms of areas of predominating Gaelic incidence (with 50% or more of their local populations speaking Gaelic), the proportions of the total Gaelic population located within these areas at these three censuses were only 45%, 34% and 32% respectively. At the present time there is concern to establish official policies for the Gaelic language by bodies such as local authorities and by *Comunn na Gàidhlig* (set up in 1985 with public funding). Unless attention is given to the means of securing the maintenance of economic health and social well-being of the Gaelic communities, there may well be no truly Gaelic communities left by the end of the century.

One of the most important conserving and stabilising factors for the Gaelic speech-community has been the maintenance of the crofting way of life. For more than a century the 1886 Crofters' Holdings Act has given security of tenure in the seven Highland and Island 'crofting

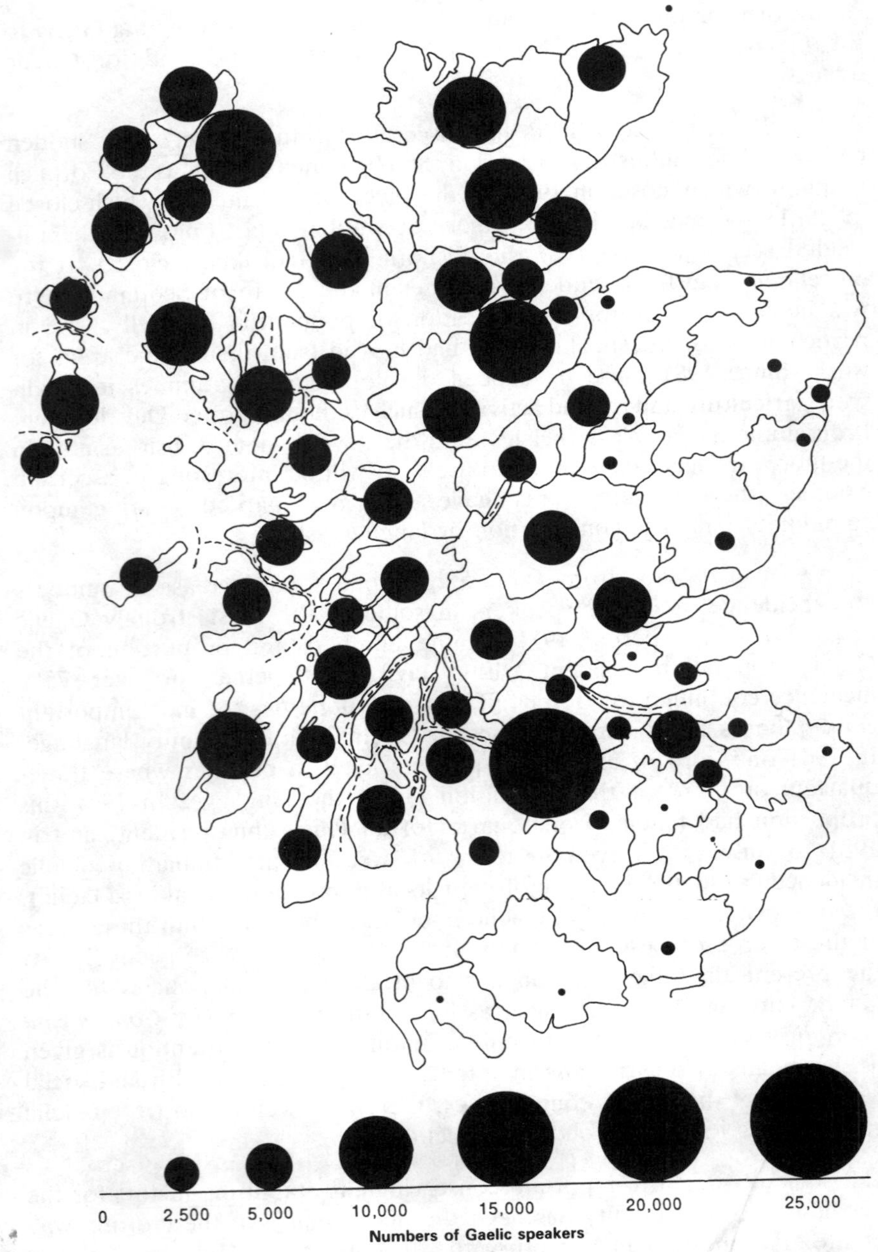

FIGURE 5.6 *Size and location of Gaelic populations: 1881 Census*

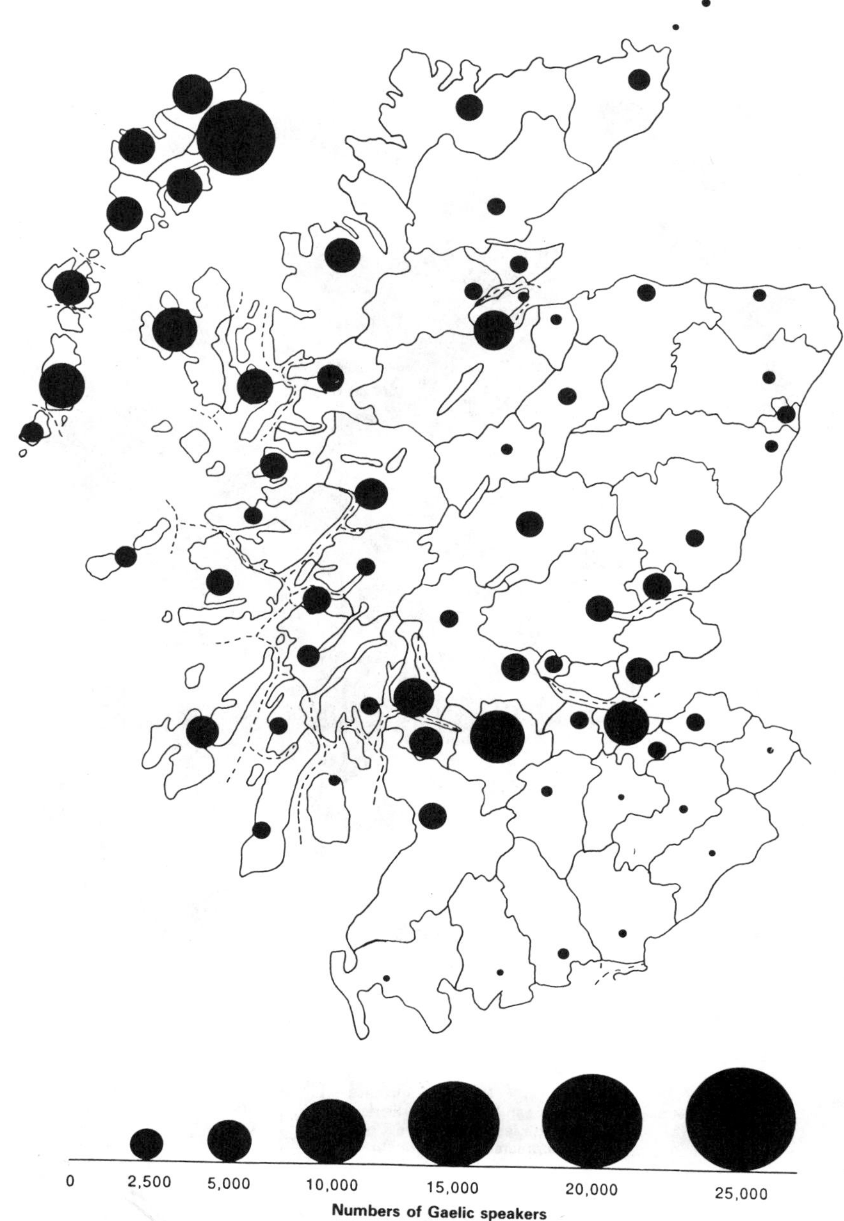

FIGURE 5.7 *Size and location of Gaelic populations: 1981 Census*

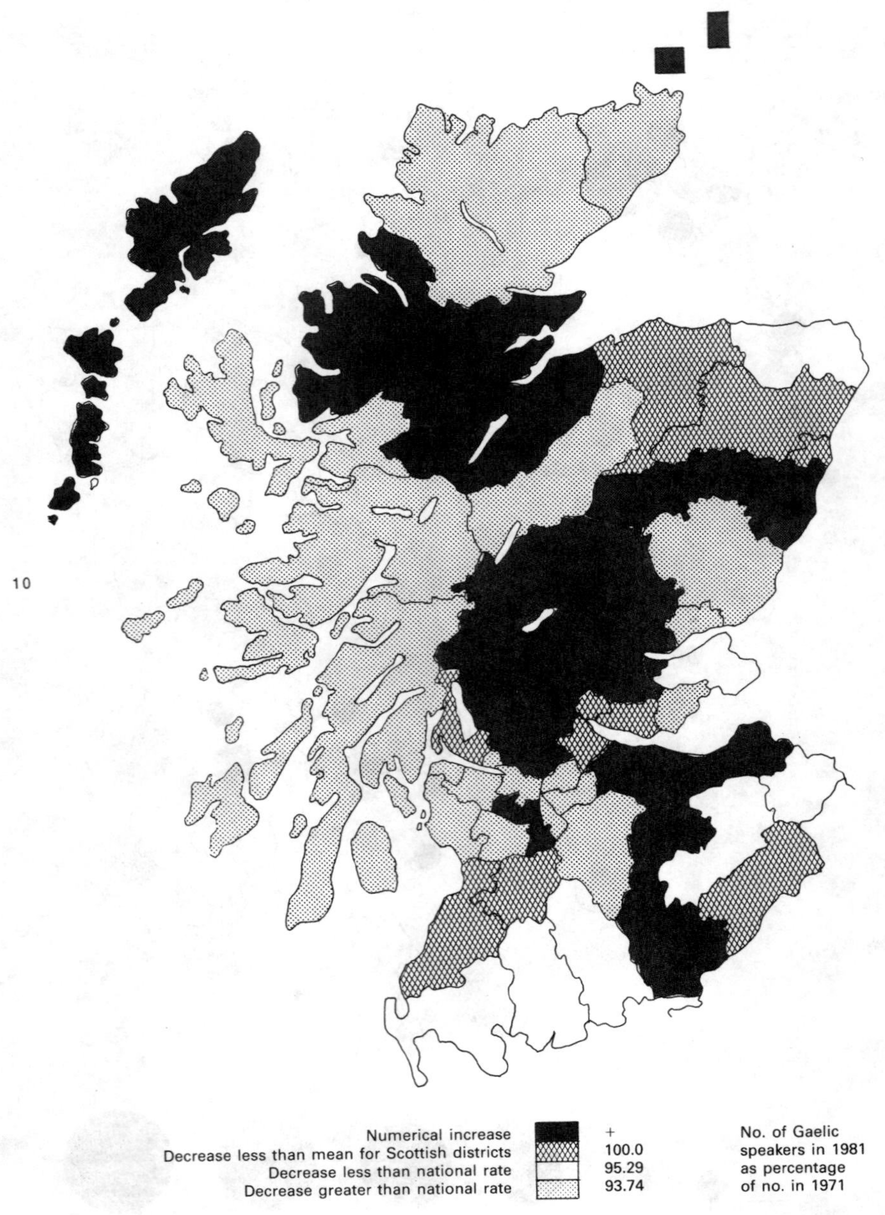

FIGURE 5.8 *Scottish districts and islands areas: numerical change in Gaelic speakers, 1971–81*

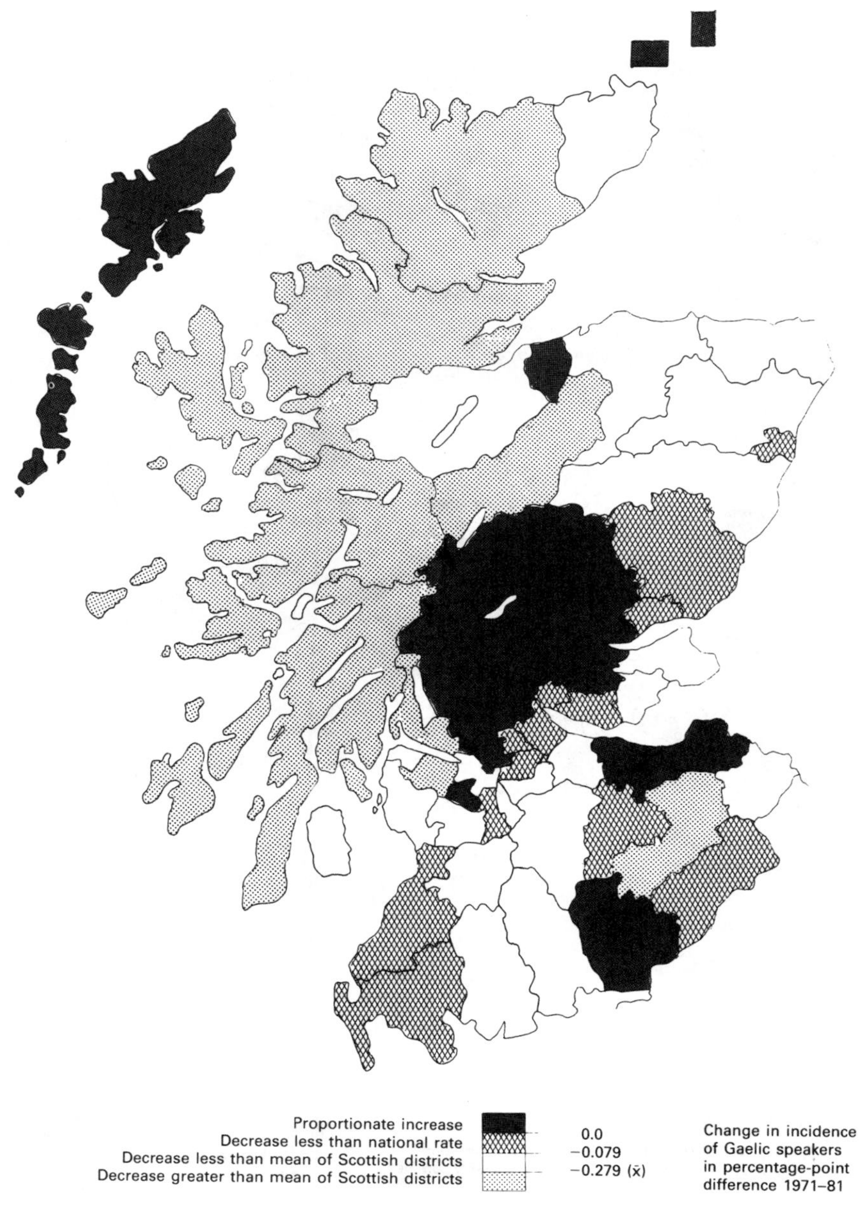

FIGURE 5.9 *Scottish districts and islands areas: proportionate change in incidence of Gaelic speakers, 1971–81*

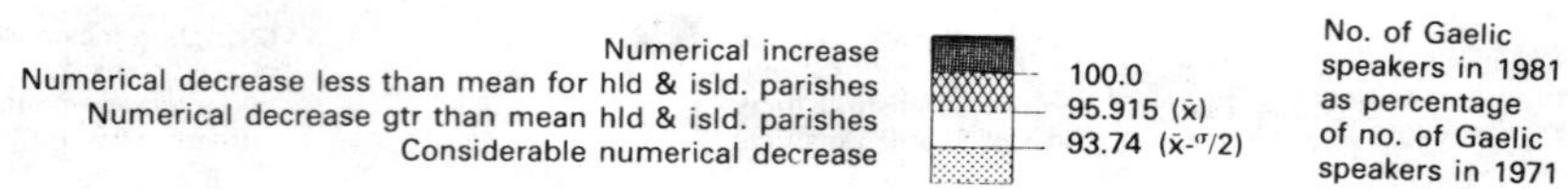

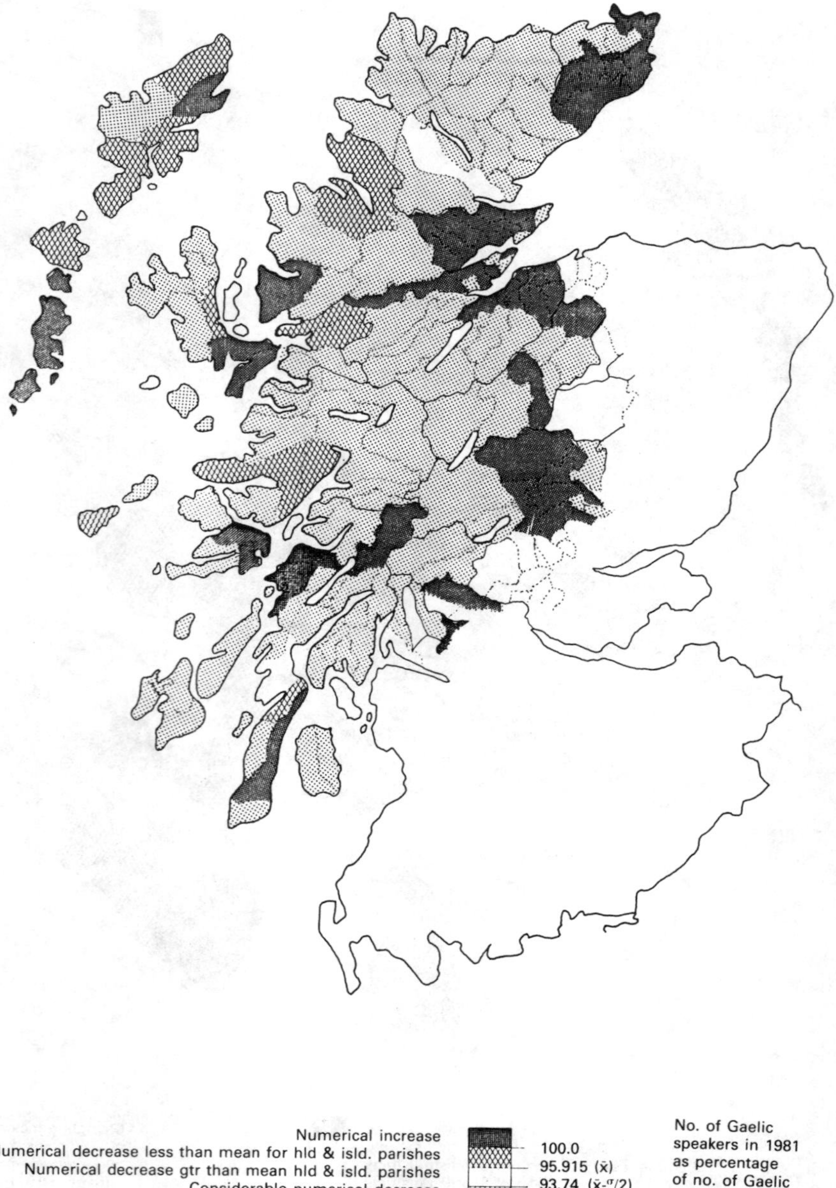

FIGURE 5.10 *Highlands and islands parishes: numerical change in incidence of Gaelic speakers, 1971–81*

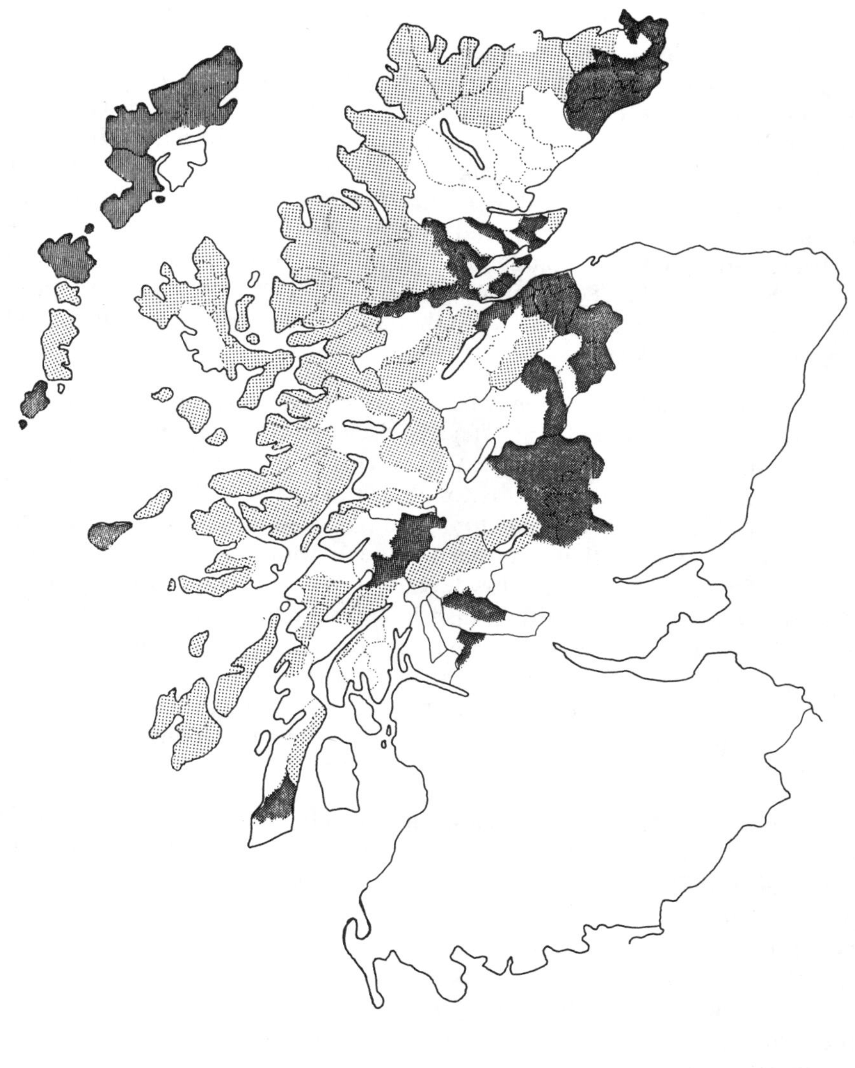

Proportionate increase
Proportionate decrease less than national rate — 0
Proportionate decrease less than mean of hld parishes — −0.079
Proportionate decrease gtr than mean of hld parishes — −2.264 ($\bar{x}$)

Change in incidence of Gaelic speakers in percentage-point difference 1971–81

FIGURE 5.11 *Highland parishes: proportionate change in incidence of Gaelic speakers, 1971–81*

counties' to the smallholders in this distinctively Gaelic form of communitarian small-scale subsistence agriculture. This is not to deny that crofters existed in other northern Scottish counties. They did — but the Act did not protect them, and neither the crofters nor the Gaelic language survive in them today. There is though a very pronounced relationship between the main Gaelic-speaking areas and those in which crofting is most strongly represented today. In fact the correlation between incidence of Gaelic-speakers and registered crofters in the civil parishes of the Hebrides and Highland mainland is overall of the order r = +0.723 (in Argyllshire r = +0.728, Inverness-shire r = +0.928, Ross & Cromarty r = +0.816, and Caithness & Sutherland r = +0.708 (all significant beyond the 0.001 level).

A further factor which may be associated with language-conservation is literacy. Colin Baker (1985: 21f.) has discussed the relationship between oracy and literacy in the context of Welsh language-conservation. He analyses the 1981 Census results for Welsh in terms of the 'gap' between oracy and literacy as a predictor of language-shift (Bowen & Carter, 1975). Baker suggests that in terms of a 'penumbral' belt of wards running through Dyfed, Powys and Clwyd, there is a conspicuous association of this 'oracy–literacy gap' with Welsh language-attrition (Baker, 1985: 28 Map 5). There are also more general weaknesses in Welsh literacy in Dyfed — which may spell further attrition for the language there. There is also a contrast between the Welsh heartland areas in which there are more 'younger' Welsh speakers than 'older', and the 'penumbral' areas in which the reverse is the case (Baker, 1985: 34, Map 6).

To some extent similar relationships can be demonstrated for Gaelic in Scotland. For example, if the proportions of Gaelic speakers literate in Gaelic in 1971 are correlated with Gaelic speakers in 1981 as proportions of the number in 1971, a significant although moderate relationship can be demonstrated in West Highland and Hebridean parishes (r = +0.295, sig. 0.01^{-08}, 50 d.f.). A complicating factor here is that traditionally Catholic Gaelic communities have had low levels of Gaelic literacy. Also, the number of Gaelic speakers in some parishes has increased owing to population movements engendered by oil-related and other industrial developments. Omitting these cases, however, makes very little difference to the correlation, which in any case, has low predictive value.

It was clear from the 1971 census that the highest levels of Gaelic literacy were associated with those areas in which Gaelic was the prevalent community language (with a local incidence of 75% or greater), and in which there were supportive local education authority policies, and adherence to Calvinistic Protestantism. (This was discussed more fully in chapter 3 of MacKinnon (1978) in terms of the 1971 census.) These areas have best maintained their Gaelic oracy at the 1981 census, although there has been a general and quite dramatic improvement in reported Gaelic literacy amongst Gaelic speakers in virtually every area in Scotland. The relationship between Gaelic oracy and literacy in Scottish districts is illustrated graphically in Figure 5.12. (There is a significant correlation of r = +0.576.) Similar relationships can be demonstrated in closer detail more locally. In Skye enumeration districts Gaelic oracy and literacy correlated positively and strongly: r = +0.586, as also in the Western Isles: r = +0.605.

As in the Welsh heartlands, the Gaelic heartlands can also furnish examples of local areas in which Gaelic is stronger amongst the age-groups of youth, than amongst the middle-aged or older population. There are thus some areas which can be said to support a viable Gaelic community on this measure. Those located in Skye and the Western Isles and are detailed in Table 5.3.

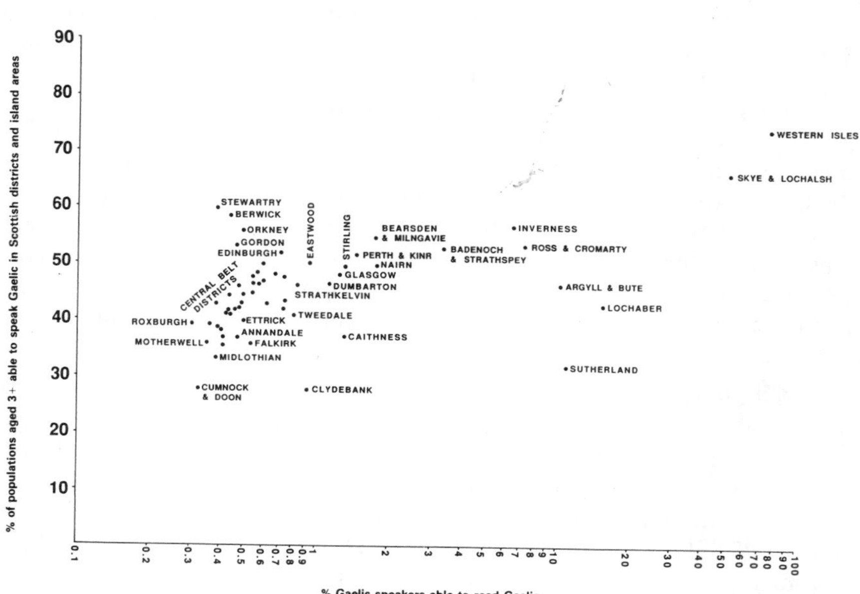

FIGURE 5.12 *Relationship between Gaelic oracy and literacy (reading ability) : Scottish districts and islands areas, 1981*
(Correlation: r = +0.576 sig > 0.00001, 54 d.f.)

The higher incidence of Gaelic speakers amongst children and young adults as compared with older adults may result from various typical causes. It may indicate a local speech-community adequately reproducing itself, or it may indicate a fairly strong Gaelic community into which middle-aged and older non-Gaelic-speakers have settled. This latter case would thus be one of a somewhat spurious viability. The reverse might be true in cases where the viability of a local Gaelic speech-community is masked by the fact that older Gaelic-speakers have moved in for employment or retirement purposes. In the above cases, the commercialised centres of Castelbay, Lochmaddy and Tarbert may be cases in point. In Skye the cases of Isle Ornsay and Camus Cross may result from younger Gaelic-speakers with young families moving in for employment purposes. It is difficult to identify viable Gaelic communities which are masked by the advent of older Gaelic-speakers, as their demographic profile is rendered 'top-heavy' — a shape which as readily results from loss of young people as the gain of older.

Conventionally, the viable reproduction of a community is *inter alia* a factor of birth rate. Together with in-migration, out-migration and death, this is a prime determinant of a community's ability to reproduce itself. In the case of a speech-community the position is not so straightforward. No one is born with power of speaking a particular language. This is acquired in early childhood or learned later in life. If an analogy of birth in so far as language is concerned is assumed, at the age of five years potential speakers will have become actual speakers. If in a local population, analysis is undertaken of the age-profile of the Gaelic speakers by themselves, some indication of viability can be derived by the proportion which Gaelic speakers in the 5–24 years age-group constitute within the total Gaelic population aged five and over. This measure also represents a 'potential', since usage habits may change during an individual's lifetime, or over time for the community as a whole.

A fully self-reproducing speech-community would have to produce new speakers in the age-group before family formation, e.g. amongst under-25s, in numbers to match loss from net out-migration and death. Ideally we should be looking for a proportion approaching one-half of the total of the local Gaelic speakers to be aged 5–24 years to be assured of clear viability for the local Gaelic speech-community. It is unlikely that local populations with fewer than one-third of their Gaelic speakers within this age-group will be able to demonstrate potential viability. These cases in Skye and the Western Isles are also detailed in Table 5.3.

The local Gaelic communities which demonstrate any form

TABLE 5.3 *Potentially viable Gaelic communities: Skye and the Western Isles*

Island/Civil Parish Enumeration District	*Number of Gaelic Speakers aged 5–24 as % of all Gaelic Speakers aged 5+*	*Intergenerational %-point increase of incidence of Gaelic in 5–24 age-group compared with over-25s*
Isle of Skye		
26 AE 01 Skulamus	19.6	+ 1.3
26 AF 02 Isle Ornsay	28.3	+ 5.9
26 AH 04 Camus Cross	22.0	+ 9.6
26 AH 01 Aird of Sleat	32.1	+ 1.0
26 AL 04 Torrin	32.5	+ 1.4
26 AN 10 Elishader	27.6	+ 2.0
26 AN 11 Staffin	39.2	+11.6
26 AN 12 Flodigarry	34.9	+ 2.2
26 AR 03 Borreraig	17.9	+ 7.2
26 AS 01 Ose	36.6	− 7.3
Isle of Barra		
56 AA 03 Vatersay	40.2	−14.9
56 AA 04 Tangusdale	39.9	+ 4.5
56 AA 05 Castlebay	39.6	+ 1.5
56 AA 06 Glen	36.4	− 6.4
56 AA 09 Eoligarray	42.6	− 0.1
56 AA 10 Ardveenish	28.0	+14.3
56 AA 11 Leanish	48.8	+ 5.5
Isle of South Uist		
56 AB 01 Eriskay	43.4	+10.0
56 AB 02 Kilbride	45.5	− 6.8
56 AB 03 North Boisdale	41.6	− 3.3
56 AB 04 Lochboisdale	46.6	− 8.8
56 AB 05 Daliburgh	37.0	+ 0.2
56 AB 06 Mingarry	44.4	− 7.7
56 AC 07 Stoneybridge	41.4	+ 1.9
56 AB 08 Stilligarry	36.5	+ 5.9
56 AC 09 Loch Carnan	51.5	+20.0
Isle of North Uist		
56 AC 05 Claddach Baleshare	33.3	+16.4
56 AC 06 Baleshare	42.9	+ 2.4
56 AC 09 Sollas	26.3	+ 4.8
56 AC 12 Trumisgarry	38.9	− 6.5
56 AC 13 Lochmaddy	36.3	+ 1.2

TABLE 5.3 *Continued*

Island/Civil Parish Enumeration District	*Number of Gaelic Speakers aged 5–24 as % of all Gaelic Speakers aged 5+*	*Intergenerational %-point increase of incidence of Gaelic in 5–24 age-group compared with over-25s*
Isle of Harris		
56 AD 04 Leverburgh	27.9	+ 5.2
56 AD 05 Northton	30.0	+22.2
56 AF 01 Tarbert	31.7	+ 4.5
56 AF 03 Scarasta	22.4	+ 9.6
56 AF 05 Borve	33.9	+ 5.8
56 AF 07 Seilebost	31.6	+ 1.5
56 AF 11 Carragrich	27.7	+10.9
Isle of Lewis (Lochs)		
56 AG 02 Leurbost (W)	32.9	+ 4.6
56 AG 03 Eishken	33.9	+25.6
56 AG 09 Laxay — Keose	31.0	+ 0.1
56 AG 11 Grimshader	31.3	+ 2.3
Isle of Lewis (Uig)		
56 AG 12 Callanish	40.2	+ 6.8
56 AG 13 Crulivig	35.9	− 2.0
56 AG 14 Gisla	26.2	+ 0.4
56 AG 15 Islivig	34.8	+12.8
56 AG 25 Carloway	20.6	+ 0.2
Isle of Lewis (Barvas)		
56 AG 20 Arnol	33.2	+ 3.6
56 AH 07 Barvas	34.7	− 2.8
56 AH 10 Lower Shader	36.6	− 5.7
Isle of Lewis (Stornoway)		
56 AH 12 Aird (Point)	41.4	+ 5.6
56 AH 16 Coll	36.4	+ 5.6
56 AH 29 North Tolsta	35.1	− 2.4
56 AH 30 New Tolsta	26.3	+ 0.3
56 AH 31 Tong (W)	33.8	− 7.2
56 AH 34 (Gress)	35.2	− 3.1
56 AJ 08 Laxdale	35.6	−15.0
Isle of Benbecula (South Uist)		
56 AK 03 Creagorry	37.1	− 6.6
56 AK 04 Torlum	49.0	+ 7.3

Source: Census (Scotland) 1981 Small Area Statistics, page 9. Table 40 Western Isles Island Area Enumeration Districts (courtesy Comhairle nan Eilean Department of Planning and Development)

of viability or language-maintenance may be identified by various characteristics. Many are remote and may be explained as retaining their Gaelic character through cultural lag. Others though, comprise the local communications centre and attract non-Gaelic incomers in the over-25 age-group, as for example Castlebay, Lochboisdale, Lochmaddy and Tarbert. It can be noted, though, that Gaelic speakers in the first three cases demonstrate a more youthful and viable demographic profile. In Skye, crofting has a particularly high profile in both Kilmuir and Sleat parishes. In fact, in 1981 Kilmuir had the highest proportion (35.2%) of its population registered as crofters of all parishes in the Highland crofting counties, and Sleat ranked third (with 33.3%). As the mean sizes of private households in these two parishes were 3.2 and 2.5 persons respectively, it can be appreciated that the crofting community comprised substantial proportions of the local population.

In two of the Sleat enumeration districts (Isle Ornsay and Camus Cross) the estate policies of Fearann Eilean Iarmain in employing younger Gaelic-speakers may also be shown as effective in promoting community language-maintenance. Other staple and stabilising occupations within the Gàidhealtachd include the Harris Tweed industry, fishing and fish-processing, and until recently seaweed for alginates. More recently, the establishment of the Arnish Yard (Lewis Offshore) just south of Stornoway brought some return of exiles and some population stabilisation to Lewis generally (Prattis, 1980). In all these cases some association with potential viability in the local Gaelic communities can be made. It is interesting that Benbecula and the north end of South Uist provide the strongest examples of potential community viability in the Western Isles, linked with positive and high rates of intergenerational Gaelic language maintenance in the Torlum and Loch Carnan enumeration districts — cheek-by-jowl with the anglicising influence of the defence establishments of Balivanich and the South Uist rocket range.

Attention has been focused in Wales upon eduction and environmental planning as the two most vital local-government policy fields which are crucially important for the maintenance of Welsh as a local community language (James, 1986; Osmond, 1987). The chief executive of Gwynedd County Council, speaking at a seminar on bilingualism convened by Highland Regional Council in Inverness in 1984, regarded the inclusion of language criteria within environmental planning legislation as essential for the maintenance of Welsh as a community language. The penetration of the remaining Scottish Gaidhealtachd by influx from elsewhere has not reached the proportions of the 'million in and million out' which Wales experienced in the 1980s. To some extent out-migration has abated in the Scottish Highlands and Islands, and the Gaelic homelands are too remote for weekend cottaging. Some degree of second homesteading is apparent in more accessible areas such as southern Skye and parts of the west coast. (On the occasion of the 1981 census there were 3,645 houshold units in Skye. Of these 336 were unoccupied, 237 households were absent and there were 85 vacant holiday units. SASPAC, page 4, Table 11.)

Yet attention has been drawn in Scotland to 'counter-urbanisation' or 'population turnaround' as affecting the Scottish Highlands generally, as the south-eastern English move directly from an overcrowded metropolitan core to an 'archetypal periphery — to Scotland, the UK and the EC' (Jones *et al.*, 1984). In 1981 9.5% of the Highland Region and 8.4% of the Islands Areas populations were English-born (Jones *et al.*, 1984: 79, Table 7.3). The authors of this paper identify a number of 'gatekeepers' and 'institutional barriers' which defend the cultural integrity of these areas: crofting and the Crofters' Commission, the Gaelic language in the Western Isles, estate owners and factors.

> Their powers of control are often absolute, and certainly in the case of estate management these powers are often arbitrarily and sometimes idiosyncratically applied. . . . Local authority planners too have an obvious gatekeeping function through development control. There is some evidence that a relatively relaxed policy exists in the region [in order to attract population to sparsely inhabited countryside].(Jones *et al.*, 1984: 81)

Another recent commentator observes that the 1976 Crofting Reform Act in enabling crofters to acquire ownership has facilitated decrofting and the creation of a land market which encourages the influx of 'white settlers' (Macinnes, 1987). The same author likens crofting administration to a custodial system maintaining Gaelic 'reservations' where 'ghetto mentalities' identify the survival of Gaelic with the survival of crofting. The 'inmates' are 'institutionalised', with the HIDB using the Crofters' Commission as a 'parole board'. These perspectives, alarming and amusing, may emphasise how precarious the present position for the Gaelic community has become.

Even at this advanced stage, the Gaelic community can be seen to possess some attributes of viability and capacity to regenerate. There are still localities in which the language is maintaining itself intergenerationally and which are still reproducing themselves as speech-communities. But these examples are, on the whole, scattered and interpenetrated. If they define the *fior-Ghàidhealtachd* today, this whole is rapidly becoming a discontinuous entity. There is a demonstrable demand for retention, enhancement and acquisition of the language amongst young people at school and amongst young parents. This is one of the most hopeful prospects for the language at the present time.

On the other hand, improving local work prospects which were regenerative in their effect during the 1970s, are now again parlous to say the least. As is being said clearly from Wales today, official bilingual policies are not going to save their language without vigorous educational policies and the teeth of effective environmental planning and development. In Scotland local authorities will not maintain their Gaelic populations without some form of positive discrimination, such as the provision of local industry tied to a policy of language-regeneration. (This may be to some extent 'artificial' — but then so are many of our present-day social and economic policies in both countryside and city.) Similar measures have been implemented in deprived inner-city areas with high concentrations of ethnic minorities by English local authorities. Similar policies have at least saved Irish in the surviving *Gaeltachtaí*, where Irish has been in an even more precarious position than has Gaelic in Scotland.

Ireland also has a couple of examples of 'counterdrift Gaeltachtai': *na Coilíneachtaí Gaeltachta*, in County Meath within 40 miles of Dublin. These represent a deliberate attempt to resettle Gaelic-speakers from the west in a more prosperous but yet Gaelic environment. Nothing like it was attempted in Scotland when Lewis haemorrhaged its surplus population in the 1920s — to the Canadian prairies. In the immediate post-war years some attempt was made at homesteading in Knoydart and Wester Ross — from the city into areas then still Gaelic in character, but without much intention of regaining the culture as well as the land. Little came of these — but as in mid-Wales some successful back-to-the land self-sufficiency communities are making it today, as at Scoraig in Wester Ross. In a sense these are even more anglicising than the piecemeal colonisation by 'white settlers'.

As yet there is no idea of doing something similar for Gaelic — much as the Jews did by establishing kibbutzim, first in Europe then in Israel, to restore Hebrew as a vernacular. Yet agencies such as the Crofters' Commission and the Highlands and Islands Development Board do have the means and powers to promote new forms of community resettlement with cultural as well as agricultural objectives. From time to time Highland estates come on to the market and are generally acquired by rich individuals or sporting syndicates from abroad. The Board has never yet used its powers to acquire such land. It could combine this with its initiatives in creating the *co-chomainn* (multi-purpose producer community co-operatives) in promoting new types of culturally regenerative community resettlement.

Such initiatives could gain recognition under crofting legislation and promote regrowth of the crofting community. The reports and records of the Crofters' Commission today chart the slow decline of the crofting community over the months and years. Rather than merely supervising this inexorable path to extinction, such agencies could harness the regenerative aspects still at work within Gaeldom to reverse the trend through the creation of *coimhearsnachdan ùra Gàidhealach* — new Gaelic communities.

Acknowledgements

The substance of this paper has arisen out of current work on the project Language-Maintenance and Viability in the Scottish Gaelic Speech-Community funded by the Economic and Social Research Council (personal research grant reference number GOO 23 23 28), which assistance and that of the Hatfield Polytechnic for secondment, media services and research support is gratefully acknowledged.

Permission to use Census Small Area Statistics (SAS 1981 and RSAS 1971) is acknowledged with thanks, in that material from Crown Copyright Records made available through the General Register Office (Scotland) and the ESRC Data Archive has been used by permission of the Controller of HM Stationery Office. The assistance of An Comunn Gáidhealach, Inverness and the Research and Consultancy Committee of the School of Business and Social Sciences, Hatfield Polytechnic, in the purchase of material is also gratefully acknowledged.

The assistance in making available census small area statistical material of ESRC Data Archive (per Dr N. Walford), Highland Regional Council Department of Planning (per M. Baldwin), Comhairle nan Eilean Department of Planning and Development (per R. MacKay and D. McKim) and the Highlands and Islands Development Board Library (per R. Ardern) are all gratefully acknowledged, as is the assistance of the Crofters' Commission for making available crofting registration statistics (per Mrs D. M. Urquhart).

References

BAKER, C. 1985, *Aspects of Bilingualism in Wales* (Multilingual Matters 19). Clevedon: Multilingual Matters.

BOWEN, E. G., and CARTER, H. 1975, The distribution of the Welsh language in 1971: An analysis. *Geography* 60 (1), 1–15.

JAMES, C. 1986, Planning for the language. *Planet* 55, February/March 1986 (Aberystwyth), 63–73.

JONES, H. R., CAIRD, J. B., BERRY, W. G., and FORD, N. J. 1984, Counter-urbanisation: English migration to the Scottish Highlands and Islands. In H. JONES (ed.) *Population Change in Contemporary Scotland* (Proceedings of 4th RSGS Symposium, May 1983). Norwich: Geo Books.

MACINNES, A. 1987, The Crofters' Holdings Act of 1886: A Hundred Year Sentence? *Radical Scotland* 25, February/March, 1987 (Edinburgh), 24–6.

MACKINNON, K. 1978, *Gaelic in Scotland 1971 — Some Sociological and Demographic Considerations of the Census Report for Gaelic.* Hatfield Polytechnic Social Science Research Reports Series No. SSR 11. Hatfield: Hertis Publications.

— 1984, Gaelic Language Regeneration Amongst Young people in Scotland 1971–1981 From Census Data, a paper given to the education workshop of the E.E.C.-sponsored conference, 'The Future of the Celtic Nations in the EEC' at Institut français de'Écosse/Heriot-Watt University, Edinburgh, 23 November 1984, Hatfield Polytechnic Social Science Reports Series No. SSR 15. Hatfield: Hertis Publications.

— 1986, Gender, Occupational and Educational Factors in Gaelic Language-Shift and Regeneration, a paper given at the Third International Minority Languages Conference, University College, Galway, 23rd June 1986. In G. MAC EOIN, A. AHLQVIST and D. ó HAODHA (eds) (1987) *Celtic Papers from the Third International Minority Languages Conference,* Clevedon: Multilingual Matters, and Hatfield Polytechnic Business and Social Sciences Occasional Papers Series No. BSS 14. Hatfield: Hertis Publications.

OSMOND, J. 1987, *A Million on the Move. Planet* 62, April/May 1987 (Aberystwyth), 114–18.

PRATTIS, J. I. 1980, Industrialisation and minority-language loyalty. In E. HAUGEN, J. D. MCCLURE, and D. S. THOMSON, (eds) *Minority Languages Today*, a selection from the papers read at the First International Conference on Minority Languages, Glasgow University 8th–13th September 1980. Edinburgh: University Press.

SASPAC Census (Scotland) 1981, *Small Area Statistics.* Edinburgh: General Register Office (Scotland).

UNWIN, D. J. 1981, *Introductory Spatial Analysis*. London: Methuen.

Appendix

Central tendency and dispersion of Scotland's Gaelic population

The computation of the centre of population for Scotland's Gaelic speakers was estimated from grouped data. For both censuses totals for the Gaelic speakers in all civil parishes with an incidence greater than the national rate were plotted within the 10 km national grid squares containing the main population centre of each parish, and similarly the totals for the four Scottish cities. For the 1891 census the totals and remainders of the then existing counties were allocated to the 10 km squares which contained the major centres of population, and similarly at the 1981 census on the basis of districts and islands areas. The results are thus only approximate, but may be reasonably indicative nevertheless. A more exact result would involve exhaustive research into the original enumeration books for 1891 and tedious computation. The 1981 data are more accessible and easier to have computed by OPCS, but the expense might not be justified.

The conventional method for assessing central tendency of a population is in terms of the mean centre. This enables a standard distance to be computed analagous to the standard deviation of a unidimensional distribution. Standard methods of significance testing can thus be undertaken. Following Unwin (1981: 40–5), the mean centre of the Gaelic population in 1891 was estimated at national grid reference 215 km E., 790 km N., (on the north flank of Geal Chàrn west of Loch Lochy). In 1981 the mean centre was estimated at GR 212 E., 786 N., (in Glen Mallie south of Loch Arkaig). The movement was only some 9 km south-westwards. Can this be said to be a significant change over time? Difference of means tests of the easting and the northing population plots yielded highly significant t-values of 8.388 and 19.327 respectively.

The standard distance of a population is a measure of its dispersal in areal terms. That for the Gaelic population in 1891 was 123.7 km, and in 1981 138.7 km, indicating that over time Gaelic speakers have become more dispersed throughout Scotland. An alternative measure of standard distance provides separate values for each axis (which may be used to define an ellipse rather than a circle about the mean centre). Significance of the change may be assessed by comparing these separate values over time. Difference in variance of the easting distributions between the two censuses yielded an F-value of 1.172, and for northing distributions F = 1.103 (both significant at about the 0.01 level).

An alternative method of assessing these data, could comprise an estimation of the median centre as a measure of central tendency, and the use of upper and lower quartile points to describe a measure of dispersion. These are easier to compute and plot, and provide greater contrast between the two points in time. They do not however enable significance to be readily assessed. The location of median centre for the

Gaelic population in 1891 was estimated at GR 227 E., 818 N., (south-west of Loch na Beinne Bàine), and in 1981 at GR 226 E., 799 N., (in Gleann Laogh south-west of Mandally) — a movement of 19 km south by westwards. The use of upper and lower quartile plots to define distribution of population is more sensitive to skewness in distribution than either standard distance or standard distance ellipse. Its application in this instance indicates both the increased dispersion of the Gaelic population between 1891 and 1981, and its increased skewness towards its chief centres of concentration in the Western Isles and Central Clydeside. Even in 1891 the central tendency lay in an area of depopulation and out-migration, and which is now only marginally Gaelic. With such bimodal distributions, measures of dispersion rather than central tendency are really the more meaningful.

6 An Essay in Historical Geolinguistics: Gaelic Speaking in Urban Lowland Scotland in 1891

C. W. J. WITHERS

Introduction

The geographical history of Gaelic in Scotland has two chapters. The first encompasses the retreat and decline of the language within the Highlands and Islands, a retreat of the Gaidhealtachd observable at parish level from the late seventeenth century and numerically assessible at ten-year intervals from 1881 using Census of Scotland statistics on Gaelic speaking (Campbell, 1945; Durkacz, 1983; MacKinnon, 1974; Withers, 1984). The second chapter involves what may be called Gaelic's 'urban Gaidhealtachd', resulting from the permanent presence in urban Lowland Scotland of large numbers of Gaelic-speaking migrants. By 1891, for example, when Scotland as a whole had an enumerated Gaelic-speaking population of 254,415 persons (including a registered 43,738 Gaelic-only speakers), Glasgow alone had a little over 7% of the national total. Whilst the numerical strength of Gaelic lay then in the Highland counties — Argyll, Inverness-shire, Ross & Cromarty and Sutherland having between them 69% of all Gaelic speakers — the three Lowland counties of Lanark, Renfrew, and Midlothian had a Gaelic-speaking population of 37,796 (14.9% of the national total), of which figure Glasgow had 17,978, Edinburgh had 4,781 Gaelic-speaking residents, and Greenock 3,191 (Census of Scotland, 1891, *P.P.*, XCIV: 136–53).

Whilst the numerical position of Gaelic in urban Lowland Scotland may be assessed from such census evidence, relatively little is known of the position of Gaelic in urban Scotland in the past — Gaelic's 'historical urban geolinguistics' — or of any differences by age or sex in proportions of the population speaking Gaelic within or between particular Lowland towns. Our understanding of what the census shows in regard to the numbers of persons speaking Gaelic in Lowland towns (as more generally in census evidence) has been reliant on the published, printed volumes, rather than on the more detailed but unpublished census enumerators' books. These enumerators' books permit identification of individuals and the place of residence of persons by detailed address and also allow, from 1851, assessment of place of birth at parish level. The 100-year restriction on access means no such information is yet available for the case of Welsh in the census.

What follows here is an essay in historical urban geolinguistics. Using the four towns of Aberdeen, Dundee, Perth and Stirling, as a case study, three themes are examined and discussed in what follows. First, the numbers of persons enumerated as being able to speak Gaelic according to the published census volumes and the unpublished enumerators' books. Second, consideration of where the Gaelic-speaking residents of urban Lowland Scotland were born — three distinctions may be made here: between the Highland-born Gaelic-speaking population; between persons who are Gaelic speakers born not in the Highlands but elsewhere in Scotland; and lastly, persons recorded as Gaelic-speaking but born outside of Scotland (of interest in this last respect are persons recorded as speaking Scottish Gaelic but born in Ireland). Third, an examination of differences by age and sex in the levels of Gaelic speaking in the four towns in question as evidenced by the unpublished census enumerators' books.

Gaelic in Urban Lowland Scotland and the 1891 Census

Questions on Gaelic in the Census of Scotland were first asked in 1881. The enumeration of Scotland's Gaelic-speaking population was then based on those who spoke Gaelic 'habitually'. Largely as a result of confusion over what this term meant in regard to language use, the recorded census totals (231,594 Gaelic-speakers in Scotland in 1881) under-enumerate the numbers speaking the language. Under-enumeration was by between 1% and 3% in the north-west Highlands and it is likely also that numbers of Gaelic speakers in the Lowlands were omitted (Fraser-Mackintosh, 1881: 438–41). For this reason the 1891 census is a more reliable guide to ability in language, not just because it recorded persons able to speak Gaelic only as well as numbers able to speak Gaelic and English, but because householders not enumerators were responsible for completion of forms (Census of Scotland, 1951: II, xlvii).

Three main points emerge from consideration of the geography of Gaelic for Scotland as a whole in 1891 (Figure 6.1): a distinction in relative proportions speaking Gaelic between the more strongly Gaelic north and west Highlands and the less strongly Gaelic-speaking south and east Highlands; the Gaelic-speaking Highland areas as a whole are areas of low population density; and most important in the context of this essay, large numbers of resident Gaelic speakers in Lowland towns are masked by the high population totals and densities in the largely non-Gaelic Lowlands.

What follows examines the Gaelic-speaking populations of the towns of Aberdeen, Dundee, Perth and Stirling. Each is considered in relation to the numbers speaking Gaelic according to the printed volumes and enumerators' books, the places of origin of the Gaelic population in the town, and the age and sex structure of the Gaelic-speaking population. Data is presented in a series of tables and maps for each town. The Highlands have been defined as the counties of Argyll, Ross & Cromarty, Inverness and Sutherland, together with those parishes in the counties of Bute, Nairn, Moray, Caithness, and Perthshire in which Gaelic was spoken by over 25% of the population in 1891 (Withers, 1985: 397; 1986b: 51). The Highlands thus defined may be seen in Figure 6.2.

Gaelic in Aberdeen in 1891

Aberdeen had a total Highland-born population in 1891 of 1,257 persons. This population was roughly equally divided between males and females. The majority of the Highland population were within the working age-ranges between 20–24 and 60–64 (Table 6.1). The Highland-born population in Aberdeen was mainly drawn from the north-east Highlands and the eastern coastal parishes of Inverness-shire, Ross & Cromarty and Sutherland. Relatively few migrants came from the far north and west, from Argyll or the Outer Hebrides.

Aberdeen had an enumerated resident total of 660 Gaelic speakers in 1891, a figure given in both the published census volume and the unpublished enumerators' books. Of these 660 persons, however, only 514 individuals were Highland-born as here defined; i.e. of Aberdeen's Highland-born population, only 514 (40.8%) were Gaelic-speakers. Assessment of the age and sex structure of Aberdeen's Highland-born Gaelic-speaking population suggests that, as a whole, more males were

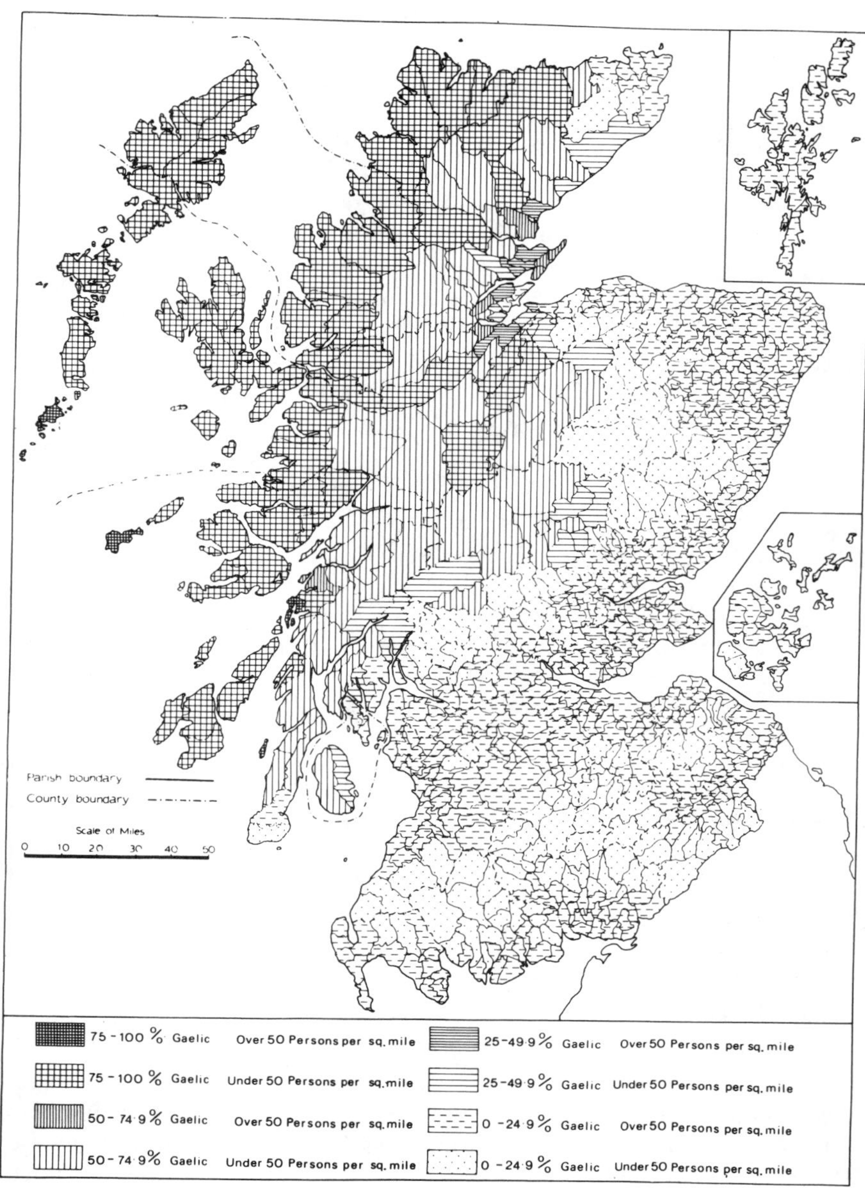

FIGURE 6.1 *The geography of Gaelic in Scotland, 1891 (by civil parish)*

FIGURE 6.2 *The Highland parishes*

enumerated as Gaelic speakers than females, but within certain age-ranges, more females than males spoke Gaelic. Table 6.2 shows numbers of Highland-born Gaelic-speaking persons in Aberdeen in 1891 by age cohort, and that number distinguished by sex expressed as a percentage of the total Gaelic-speaking population in the town. The right hand columns, again distinguished by sex, show the Gaelic-speaking population

TABLE 6.1 *Age and sex structure of the Highland-born population in Aberdeen, 1891*

Age cohort	*Males*		*Females*		
	No. in cohort	*Percentage of Highland male pop.*	*No. in cohort*	*Percentage of Highland female pop.*	*Total population in cohort*
0–4	11	1.76	15	2.32	26
5–9	29	4.68	25	3.92	54
10–14	25	4.01	32	5.02	57
15–19	43	6.90	30	4.73	73
20–24	55	8.83	56	8.83	111
25–29	41	6.58	56	8.83	97
30–34	49	7.86	53	8.81	102
35–39	55	8.83	56	8.83	111
40–44	37	5.96	50	7.84	87
45–49	52	8.34	50	7.84	102
50–54	45	7.22	47	7.40	92
55–59	35	5.61	45	7.09	80
60–64	46	7.39	34	5.26	80
65–69	41	6.58	36	5.64	77
70–74	27	4.33	25	3.94	52
75–79	18	2.88	15	2.32	33
80–84	12	1.92	4	0.63	16
85–89	2	0.32	3	0.44	5
90–94	—	—	2	0.31	2
95–99	—	—	—	—	—
100+	—	—	—	—	—
Totals	623	100.00	634	100.00	1,257

Source: *Census of Scotland*, 1891, and Census Enumerators' Books

in each age cohort as a percentage of the total Highland population in that cohort. There were, for example, 20 female Gaelic speakers in Aberdeen in the age cohort 45–49. These 20 women represented a little over 8% of the entire female Gaelic-speaking population in the town and exactly 40% of all Highland women in that age cohort. The 30 male Gaelic speakers aged 20–24 represented 10.9% of the male Gaelic-speaking population and 54% of all Highland-born males in the town. Only 44.14% of the male Highland-born population were Gaelic speakers. For females, the figure is 37.69%. There is no evidence to suggest that the older age ranges of the Highland-born population were more strongly Gaelic speaking than the younger members of the population. In only seven age ranges for Highland men and in only five age ranges for

TABLE 6.2 *Numbers of Gaelic speakers in Aberdeen, 1891 (Highland-born population only)*

Age cohort	*Numbers of Gaelic speakers in cohort*		*Percentage of Gaelic-speaking population*		*Percentage of total Highland population*	
	Male	*Female*	*Male*	*Female*	*Male*	*Female*
0–4	1	1	0.36	0.42	9.09	6.66
5–9	—	5	—	2.09	—	20.00
10–14	3	1	1.09	0.42	12.00	3.12
15–19	17	8	6.18	3.34	39.53	26.66
20–24	30	15	10.90	6.27	54.54	26.78
25–29	18	19	6.54	7.94	43.90	33.92
30–34	16	24	5.84	10.04	32.66	45.28
35–39	29	30	10.55	12.57	52.72	53.57
40–44	16	30	5.84	12.57	43.24	60.00
45–49	25	20	9.09	8.36	48.07	40.00
50–54	26	14	9.45	5.85	57.77	29.78
55–59	22	15	8.00	6.27	62.85	33.33
60–64	24	20	8.72	8.36	52.17	58.82
65–69	22	14	8.00	5.85	53.65	38.88
70–74	13	11	4.72	4.63	48.14	44.00
75–79	6	7	2.18	2.92	33.33	46.66
80–84	7	1	2.54	0.42	58.33	25.00
85–89	—	2	—	0.84	—	66.66
90–94	—	2	—	0.84	—	100.00
95–99	—	—	—	—	—	—
100+	—	—	—	—	—	—
Totals	275	239	100.0	100.0		

Source: *Census of Scotland*, Enumerators' books

Highland women was Gaelic spoken by more than 50% of the Highland-born population. There were no Gaelic-only speakers in Aberdeen in 1891.

Aberdeen had a non-Highland-born Gaelic-speaking population of 146 persons: 22.12% of the Gaelic population in the town. The majority of these non-Highland-born Gaelic speakers were born elsewhere in Scotland with only a handful born outside of Scotland (Table 6.3). We may infer several things from assessment of place of origin of the non-Highland-born Gaelic-speaking population (for Aberdeen and the other towns discussed here). Firstly, the totals given for towns such as Aberdeen itself in Table 6.3 most commonly represent the birthplace of children of Gaelic-speaking Highland-born parents whose out-movement from the

TABLE 6.3 *Place of origin and numbers of non-Highland-born Gaelic speakers in Aberdeen, 1891*

Elsewhere in Scotland					
Aberdeen	30	Edinburgh	4	Kirkmichael (Banff)	3
Aberdeenshire	1	Elgin	3	Lonmay	1
Abernethy (Moray)	1	Fife	1	Lybster	2
Alves	1	Forgue	1	Meikle Logie	1
Ardclach	5	Fraserburgh	1	Methlick	1
Ballater	2	Garlieston	1	Nairn	2
Ballindalloch	1	Garvock	1	New Machar	1
Banffshire	3	Glasgow	2	New Mills	1
Birse	1	Glenmuick, Tullich and Glengairn	2	Old Aberdeen	2
Caithness	1	Grange (Banff)	1	Old Machar	3
Cluny	1	Grantown	2	Ordiquhill	1
Corsiehill	1	Halkirk	4	Perth	2
Crathie & Braemar	14	Huntly	1	Pluscarden	1
Crimond	1	Inverallen	1	Port of Monteith	1
Cullen	1	Kildrummy	2	Stirling	2
Duthel	1	Kincardine O'Neil	1	Thurso	2
Dunnet	2	Kinloss	1	Tomintoul	3
Dyke	1			Wick	3
				Total	129
Not in Scotland					
America	1				
England	8				
Hull	2				
Ireland	6				
Total	17				

Source: *Census of Scotland*, Enumerators' books

Highlands parishes was marked by their moving between several places before settling in Aberdeen by 1891. These totals may thus indicate the transmission of Gaelic down the generations and within the family, from Gaelic-speaking Highland-born parents to their Lowland-born children, and to an extent may include, too, the adoption of Gaelic by the marriage partner of a Gaelic husband or wife. Secondly, the relatively large numbers of Gaelic-speaking persons from parishes like Crathie and Braemar is an indication of the in-movement into Aberdeen of persons from parishes still quite strongly Gaelic but whose total numbers speaking the language represented less than 25% of the total parish population and thus are not deemed Highland. The resident Gaelic population of

Aberdeen was thus made up in part of Gaelic speakers who had migrated from the Gaidhealtachd 'fringe' (cf. Figure 6.1). Thirdly, the presence of foreign-born (including English-born) Gaelic speakers most likely indicates the return to Scotland of children of earlier Gaelic-speaking emigrants. Lastly, enumeration of Irish-born persons as Gaelic speakers may indicate ability in Irish rather than Scottish Gaelic. This question of Irish-born speakers of Scottish Gaelic is discussed further below.

Gaelic in Dundee in 1891

Dundee had a Highland-born population in 1891 of 1,277 persons, 525 males, 752 females (Table 6.4). This imbalance may be accounted

TABLE 6.4 *Age and sex structure of the Highland-born population in Dundee, 1891*

Age cohort	*Males*		*Females*		
	No. in cohort	*Percentage of Highland male pop.*	*No. in cohort*	*Percentage of Highland female pop.*	*Total population in cohort*
0–4	7	1.30	11	1.40	18
5–9	11	2.10	12	1.50	23
10–14	19	3.60	21	2.73	40
15–19	25	4.70	42	5.50	67
20–24	47	8.90	45	5.91	92
25–29	39	7.40	83	11.03	122
30–34	46	8.70	77	10.20	123
35–39	43	8.11	68	9.04	111
40–44	52	9.91	66	8.70	118
45–49	44	8.32	74	9.80	118
50–54	45	8.40	71	9.40	116
55–59	39	7.40	50	6.60	89
60–64	42	8.00	42	5.51	84
65–69	28	5.30	31	4.13	59
70–74	18	3.40	32	4.20	50
75–79	9	1.70	20	2.60	29
80–84	9	1.70	4	0.50	13
85–89	1	0.19	3	0.40	4
90–94	1	0.19	—	—	1
95–99	—	—	—	—	—
100+	—	—	—	—	—
Totals	525	100.00	752	100.00	1,277

Source: *Census of Scotland*, Enumerators' books

for by the sexual division of labour within Dundee's textile industries in the nineteenth century. The great majority of Dundee's Highlanders came from Highland Perthshire, Inverness-shire, and Easter Ross, with few persons coming from the west Highlands and Islands, either from the Outer Isles, the north-west mainland or Argyll (Withers, 1986a).

The first difficulty arises in assessment of the numerical total for Dundee's Gaelic-speaking population. The published printed volumes give a figure of 733 persons (Census of Scotland, 1891, *P.P.*, 1892, XCIV: 141). The unpublished manuscript enumerators' books give a total of 760. There is no easy explanation to account for the difference. No boundary changes have occurred: the total of 760 was taken after detailed checking of all enumerators' books making up the city of Dundee. We must assume the enumerators' books to be accurate. There is no reason to suppose Dundee enumerators inefficient though the possibility remains that individuals have been considered as Gaelic speaking by enumerators yet not entered as such in the final printed returns. Whatever the *cause* of the difference, the fact of its existence cannot be doubted (see also below).

Of the total of 760 Gaelic-speakers 555 were Highland-born. This figure itself means that only 43.46% of the Highland-born population of Dundee were Gaelic speakers. Assessment by age and sex of the Highland-born Gaelic-speaking population reveals that Gaelic was more commonly spoken by (or, at least, was registered numerically as being more prevalent among) females than males (Table 6.5). Comparison with Table 6.4 thus suggests that of the 525 Highland-born males, 240 (45.7%) were registered as speaking Gaelic. For women, the 315 Highland-born Gaelic speakers represented 41.8% of the Highland-born female population. It is worth noting, however, that Gaelic was most commonly known by persons within the working age ranges, and was more commonly known by women than men within most individual age cohorts as well as in overall total. As for Aberdeen, there is no evidence to suggest an increasing prevalence in Gaelic towards the upper age ranges.

Dundee had a non-Highland-born Gaelic-speaking population in 1891 of 205 persons, 150 of whom were born elsewhere in Scotland (Table 6.6). As for Aberdeen (and for Perth and Stirling below), these figures include persons from Gaelic parishes which fall without the established criterion of definition; Gaelic-speaking children and other individuals born in the Lowlands of Highland parents; persons born in Canada — returning migrants or people from Gaelic districts in Canada such as Cape Breton — and, lastly, persons of Irish birth enumerated as Gaelic

TABLE 6.5 *Numbers of Gaelic speakers in Dundee, 1891 (Highland-born population only)*

Age cohort	*Number of Gaelic speakers in cohort*		*Percentage of Gaelic-speaking population*		*Percentage of total Highland population*	
	Male	*Female*	*Male*	*Female*	*Male*	*Female*
0–4	1	1	0.41	0.31	14.28	9.09
5–9	1	1	0.41	0.31	9.09	8.33
10–14	2	1	0.82	0.31	10.52	4.76
15–19	2	11	0.82	3.48	8.00	26.10
20–24	19	25	7.91	7.92	40.40	55.50
25–29	22	35	9.16	11.09	56.41	42.16
30–34	23	37	9.58	11.74	50.00	48.05
35–39	13	30	5.41	9.52	30.20	44.10
40–44	21	36	8.75	11.42	40.38	54.50
45–49	28	31	11.66	9.84	63.63	41.89
50–54	27	32	11.25	10.15	60.00	45.00
55–59	16	21	6.66	6.66	41.00	42.00
60–64	21	16	8.75	5.07	50.00	38.00
65–69	18	8	7.70	2.53	64.20	25.80
70–74	13	15	5.41	4.86	72.70	46.80
75–79	5	9	2.08	2.85	55.50	45.00
80–84	5	3	2.08	0.95	55.50	75.00
85–89	2	3	0.82	0.95	100.00	100.00
90–94	1	—	0.41	—	100.00	—
95–99	—	—	—	—	—	—
100+	—	—	—	—	—	—
Totals	240	315	100.00	100.00		

Source: *Census of Scotland*, Enumerators' books

speakers. It is probable also that the 16 persons for whom only 'Perthshire' is given as place of birth in the enumerators' books (Table 6.6), include individuals from Highland parishes but the imprecise description of birthplace makes this impossible to know with certainty.

Gaelic in Perth in 1891

Perth in 1891 had a Highland-born population of 1,117 persons, 469 males and 653 females (Table 6.7). The majority of Perth's Highland-born came from Highland Perthshire and the eastern parishes of Inverness-shire and Ross & Cromarty. Very few came from Argyll, the north-west mainland parishes or the Outer Isles (Devine, 1983; Gray, 1957; Withers, 1986a).

TABLE 6.6 *Place of origin and numbers of non-Highland-born Gaelic speakers in Dundee, 1891*

Elsewhere in Scotland					
Aberdeen	7	Dunning	1	Monifeith	1
Aberdeenshire	1	Edinburgh	4	Morayshire	1
Aberdour (Banff)	1	Forfar	1	Murroes	1
Alyth	2	Forres	3	Nairn	4
Amulree	1	Foyers	1	Newtyle	2
Arbroath	2	Glasgow	4	Perth	11
Auchterarder	1	Grantown	1	Perthshire	16
Auchtermuchty	1	Greenock	7	Redgorton	1
Auldearn	1	Halkirk	2	Renfrewshire	2
Bendochy	1	Kincardineshire	3	St Ninians	1
Blairgowrie	2	Kirkcaldy	1	Stonehaven	2
Boat of Garten	1	Kirkmichael (Banff)	6	Stonehouse	1
Caputh	2	Kirriemuir	1	Strathtummel	1
Claverhouse	1	Laurencekirk	1	Thurso	1
Carmichael	2	Longforgan	1	Tomintoul	7
Crathie & Braemar	4	Lundie	1	Wick	1
Dunbartonshire	1	Mains	2	Total	150
Dundee	25	Meigle	1		
Not in Scotland					
Canada	1	Manchester	1		
England	3	Montgomery	1		
Ireland	49	Total	55		

Source: *Census of Scotland*, Enumerators' books

As for Dundee, Perth's enumerated Gaelic-speaking population total in the published census volumes differs from that taken from assessment of the enumerators' books: the printed volumes give 800 (Census of Scotland 1891, *P.P.*, 1892, XCIV: 142), the enumerators' books a figure of 815. Of these 815 persons, 595 persons were Highland-born Gaelic speakers (53.26% of the total Highland-born population in the town). Of the total Highland-born Gaelic speakers, 240 were males (53.09% of the total male Highland-born population) and 355 females (54.36% of the total female Highland-born population). Across most individual age cohorts, Gaelic was spoken more by women than men, and as for Dundee and Aberdeen, the language was known (and presumably used more) by Highlanders within the working age ranges than in younger or older age cohorts (Table 6.8).

Perth's non-Highland-born Gaelic-speaking population totalled 220 persons, only 89 of whom were Scots-born Gaelic speakers (Table 6.9).

TABLE 6.7 *Age and sex structure of the Highland-born population in Perth, 1891*

Age cohort	*Males*		*Females*		
	No. in cohort	*Percentage of Highland male pop.*	*No. in cohort*	*Percentage of Highland female pop.*	*Total population in cohort*
0–4	6	1.32	9	1.37	15
5–9	15	3.30	22	3.36	37
10–14	23	5.06	20	3.06	43
15–19	43	9.47	32	4.90	75
20–24	28	6.16	43	6.58	71
25–29	37	8.14	59	9.03	96
30–34	40	8.81	59	9.03	99
35–39	42	9.25	60	9.18	102
40–44	36	7.92	64	9.80	100
45–49	35	7.70	53	8.11	88
50–54	38	8.37	49	7.50	87
55–59	27	5.95	31	4.47	58
60–64	34	7.40	40	6.12	74
65–69	15	3.30	37	5.66	52
70–74	14	3.08	38	5.70	52
75–79	16	3.52	24	3.67	40
80–84	3	0.66	10	1.53	13
85–89	2	0.44	1	0.15	3
90–94	—	—	2	0.30	2
95–99	—	—	—	—	—
100+	—	—	—	—	—
			—		
Total	454	100.00	653	100.00	1,107

Source: *Census of Scotland*, Enumerators' books

There were more Irish-born Gaelic speakers enumerated than for any other place. This total of 220 non-Highland-born Gaelic speakers represented 26.9% of the town's Gaelic population in 1891.

Gaelic in Stirling in 1891

Stirling had a Highland-born population of only 376 in 1891, of which total 155 were males, 221 females (Table 6.10). The majority of this quite small Highland-born population came from the north-west Highland Perthshire parishes. Stirling also drew proportionately greater numbers of Highlanders from Argyll. As for the other towns discussed

TABLE 6.8 *Numbers of Gaelic speakers in Perth, 1891 (Highland-born population only)*

Age cohort	*Number of Gaelic speakers in cohort*		*Percentage of Gaelic-speaking population*		*Percentage of total Highland population*	
	Male	*Female*	*Male*	*Female*	*Male*	*Female*
0–4	—	—	—	—	—	—
5–9	—	—	—	—	—	—
10–14	1	2	0.41	0.56	4.34	10.0
15–19	9	13	3.75	3.66	20.93	40.6
20–24	11	21	4.58	5.91	39.28	48.8
25–29	18	27	7.50	7.60	48.64	45.7
30–34	24	33	10.00	9.29	60.00	55.9
35–39	28	37	11.66	10.42	66.60	61.6
40–44	24	39	10.00	10.98	66.60	60.9
45–49	20	35	8.33	9.85	57.10	66.0
50–54	28	31	11.66	8.73	73.60	63.2
55–59	16	18	6.66	5.07	59.20	58.0
60–64	22	27	9.16	7.60	64.70	67.5
65–69	10	26	4.16	7.32	66.60	70.2
70–74	11	22	4.58	6.19	78.50	57.8
75–79	13	17	5.41	4.78	81.25	70.8
80–84	4	6	1.66	1.69	100.00	60.0
85–89	1	—	0.41	—	50.00	—
90–94	—	1	—	0.28	—	—
95–99	—	—	—	—	—	—
100+	—	—	—	—	—	—
Totals	240	355	100.00	100.00		

Source: *Census of Scotland*, Enumerators' books

here, relatively few Highlanders were drawn from the most distant north and west parishes (Osborne, 1958; Macdonald, 1937; Withers, 1985).

As for Dundee and Perth, there is for Stirling a difference between published volumes and enumerators' books in the given totals for Gaelic-speaking. In Stirling, however, the published volumes give the greater figure — 499 persons — as against the 482 derived from assessment of the enumerators' books.

Of the Highland-born population, 229 were Gaelic speakers (60.9% of the total Highland population). Of this total, 90 were males, 139 females (Table 6.11). In contrast to the other towns examined the non-Highland-born Gaelic-speaking population was larger than those Gaelic

TABLE 6.9 *Place of origin and numbers of non-Highland-born Gaelic speakers in Perth, 1891*

Elsewhere in Scotland					
Abernethy	1	Edinburgh	3	Nairn	1
Alyth	1	Forres	1	Perth	25
Auchtergaven	5	Glasgow	5	Perthshire	6
Bankfoot	1	Grantown	3	Pitcairngreen	1
Blairgowrie	1	Greenock	1	Rothes	1
Caithness	3	Kilspindie	1	Strathbraan	2
Cardross	1	Kincardineshire	1	Tannadice	1
Comrie	3	Kinfauns	2	Tealing	1
Coupar Angus	1	Kirkmichael (Banff)	1	Wick	1
Cowdenbeath	1	Leith	1	Total	89
Crathie & Braemar	1	Logiealmond	1		
Crieff	4	Methven	1		
Dalguise	1	Moneydie	2		
Dallas	1	Muthil	2		
Not in Scotland					
Canada	1				
Cape Breton	1				
Ireland	129				
Total	131				

Source: *Census of Scotland*, Enumerators' books

speakers claiming Highland birth (Table 6.12). As for Dundee, Perth, and Aberdeen, these were people either from partially-Gaelic parishes, from overseas, or were the Lowland-born children of Highland-born Gaelic-speakers. The large number of persons of Irish birth enumerated as Gaelic speakers is noteworthy. On the one hand, there is no reason to suppose on the evidence presented in the census and the question asked by enumerators that these people did not speak *Scottish* Gaelic; on the other hand, there is every reason to suppose that these individuals or a proportion of them did not speak Scottish Gaelic and were enumerated on facility in Irish. In several instances in Stirling (though not for the other towns) there is evidence of a Lowland-born Scottish wife, enumerated as a Gaelic speaker, married to an Irish-born Gaelic-speaker. This is not itself proof of their Gaelic being Scottish Gaelic or Irish nor does it illustrate how the language was used for various social purposes by such people, but what it may point to is the adoption of Gaelic by one marital partner with no other prior connections with the Highlands or Scottish Gaelic but with connections with 'Gaelic' through an Irish husband.

TABLE 6.10 *Age and sex structure of the Highland-born population in Stirling, 1891*

Age cohort	*Males*		*Females*		
	No. in cohort	*Percentage of Highland male pop.*	*No. in cohort*	*Percentage of Highland female pop.*	*Total population in cohort*
0–4	4	2.51	4	1.82	8
5–9	5	3.22	4	1.82	9
10–14	5	3.22	3	1.35	8
15–19	9	5.80	13	5.88	22
20–24	21	14.12	28	12.66	49
25–29	25	16.12	36	16.28	61
30–34	12	7.70	10	4.54	22
35–39	14	9.03	21	9.50	35
40–44	2	1.20	12	5.42	14
45–49	9	5.81	18	8.14	27
50–54	11	7.00	16	7.23	27
55–59	12	7.70	17	7.69	29
60–64	12	7.70	9	4.07	21
65–69	7	4.52	10	4.54	17
70–74	4	2.51	7	3.16	11
75–79	2	1.20	6	2.71	8
80–84	—	—	4	1.82	4
85–89	—	—	2	0.92	2
90–94	1	0.64	1	0.45	2
95–99	—	—	—	—	—
100+	—	—	—	—	—
Totals	155	100.00	221	100.00	376

Source: *Census of Scotland* and Census Enumerators' Books

Gaelic in Urban Lowland Scotland in 1891: The Evidence Assessed

In reviewing this evidence it should be remembered that the Census provides us only with numbers, not with any indication of how the language was used. It is dangerous to infer too much from statistics alone. Further, it is impossible to know with accuracy from the census the exact age at which unmarried persons or couples without children arrived in the city. The question of age at first arrival has implications for the issue of language maintenance within Gaelic-speaking populations in urban Lowland Scotland. If, for example, Gaelic-speaking Highland-born persons in the older age ranges had only recently migrated to a given

TABLE 6.11 *Number of Gaelic speakers in Stirling, 1891 (Highland-born population only)*

Age cohort	*Numbers of Gaelic speakers in cohort*		*Percentage Gaelic-speaking population*		*Percentage of total Highland population*	
	Male	*Female*	*Male*	*Female*	*Male*	*Female*
0–4	—	—	—	—	—	—
5–9	—	—	—	—	—	—
10–14	—	—	—	—	—	—
15–19	4	8	4.44	5.75	44.44	61.53
20–24	13	19	14.44	13.66	61.90	68.85
25–29	14	24	15.57	17.26	56.00	66.66
30–34	8	6	8.89	4.34	66.66	60.00
35–39	10	13	11.11	9.35	71.42	61.90
40–44	1	8	1.11	5.75	50.00	66.66
45–49	7	12	7.77	8.63	77.77	66.66
50–54	8	12	8.89	8.63	72.72	75.00
55–59	7	10	7.77	7.19	58.33	58.82
60–64	8	4	8.89	2.87	66.66	44.44
65–69	6	8	6.68	5.75	85.71	80.00
70–74	3	6	3.33	4.34	75.00	85.71
75–79	1	5	1.11	3.59	50.00	83.33
80–84	—	3	—	2.15	—	75.00
85–89	—	—	—	—	—	—
90–94	—	1	—	0.74	—	100.00
95–99	—	—	—	—	—	—
100+	—	—	—	—	—	—
Totals	90	139	100.0	100.0		

Source: *Census of Scotland*, Enumerators' books

town from strongly Gaelic parishes, it is reasonable to suppose they would keep their language and profess ability in it on enumerators' forms. If, on the other hand, large numbers of Gaelic-speaking Highlanders in the older age cohorts had been resident for a length of time in any particular town, it is legitimate to claim a degree of language maintenance amongst those people and to argue for both the maintenance of Gaelic amongst a section of the 'long stay' migrant population and for the reinforcement of the Gaelic population through the in-movement at any one movement of migrant Gaels.

One author has suggested in the context of temporary migration that persons in the older age ranges were more common in the later 1800s than earlier in the century when younger age groups predominated

TABLE 6.12 *Place of origin and numbers of non-Highland-born Gaelic speakers in Stirling, 1891*

Elsewhere in Scotland					
Aberfoyle	1	Drymen	1	Largs	1
Ardclach	1	Edinburgh	1	New Rattray	1
Auchterarder	1	Forfarshire	1	Perth	1
Ayr	1	Fyvie	1	Perthshire	2
Balfron	1	Gamrie	1	Port Glasgow	1
Bannockburn	1	Glasgow	3	Port of Menteith	1
Bridge of Turk	2	Glenalmond	1	Raploch	1
Buchanan	1	Govan	2	Rothiemay	1
Callander	5	Greenock	1	Stirling	21
Comrie	7	Grantown (Moray)	1	Tomintoul	1
Crieff	20	Halkirk	2	Wick	4
Culloden	1	Kilmadock	1	Total	97
Doune	3	Kinross	1		
Not in Scotland					
America	1	Ireland	150		
Canada	2	New Zealand	1		
England	2	Total	156		

Source: *Census of Scotland*, Enumerators' books

in seasonal movement (Devine, 1979). If we were to presume this pattern to hold for permanent movement, then we might argue for a hypothesis of continued (though fluctuating) 'language reinforcement' in urban Gaelic-speaking rather than one strictly of 'language maintenance' among a younger but ageing resident Gaelic population. Further, the census does not allow easy assessment of when an individual left his or her parish of birth; information useful to know given decline over time in Gaelic speaking throughout the Highlands. Persons having only recently moved to these towns from certain non-Highland parishes were in many cases coming from places in which perhaps one in four of the population spoke Gaelic in 1891: if, however, older Gaelic-speaking residents had migrated from such parishes in their youth, they would have been leaving parishes then much more strongly Gaelic than later, and, it might be claimed, would be more likely to know and speak Gaelic.

It is impossible to know the extent of what may be called 'language transmission' from census evidence; either the learning of Gaelic in any given town by persons not of Highland birth and with no prior connection with the language, or the probably more common transmission of Gaelic either from Highland-born parents to Lowland-born children or from a

Gaelic-speaking to a non-Gaelic marriage partner. Nevertheless, assessment of the evidence presented here for four towns serves as an important foundation to an understanding of Gaelic's historical urban geolinguistics. The principle facts discussed above may now be summarised below (Table 6.13).

The Numbers of Gaelic speakers in Aberdeen, Dundee, Perth, and Stirling 1891

For three of the four towns examined, there is a difference in total number of Gaelic-speaking persons between the published census volumes and the unpublished enumerators' books. The difference is not consistent,

TABLE 6.13 *Gaelic speaking in urban Lowland Scotland, 1891: the examples of Aberdeen, Dundee, Perth, and Stirling*

	Aberdeen	*Dundee*	*Perth*	*Stirling*
Total urban population	124,943	155,985	19,919	16,776
Total Highland-born population (as here defined) and as % of total population	1,257 (1.00%)	1,277 (0.81%)	1,107 (5.60%)	376 (2.24%)
Total Gaelic-speaking population, from (a): Published Census volumes (b): Enumerators' books (c): (b) as % of total urban population	(a) 660 (b) 660 (c) 0.52%	(a) 733 (b) 760 (c) 0.48%	(a) 800 (b) 815 (c) 4.09%	(a) 499 (b) 482 (c) 2.87%
Total Highland-born Gaelic-speaking population (from (b) above) and as % of total Highland-born	514 40.89%	555 43.46%	595 53.26%	229 60.90%
Total non-Highland-born Gaelic-speaking population and as % of total Gaelic-speaking population (from (b) above)	146 22.12%	205 26.97%	220 26.99%	253 52.48%
Male Gaelic-speakers as % of total male Highland-born	44.14%	45.17%	53.09%	58.06%
Female Gaelic-speakers as % of total female Highland-born	37.69%	41.88%	54.36%	62.89%

Source: *Census of Scotland* and Census enumerators' books

either in type or in degree. For Perth, for example, the 15 persons represent an over-enumeration of 1.88%; for Stirling, an under-enumeration of 3.40%. The fact and variable extent of these differences pose interesting questions on the Gaelic population of urban Scotland and the accuracy of census figures as a whole on numbers speaking Gaelic.

Given there were no boundary changes in the enumerated parishes here, explanation of the *cause* of error may lie either in the fallibility of the enumerators and other recording officers involved or in the head of household or family who filled in the form. As for 1861, 1871 and 1881, the 1891 census was conducted on a house-to-house basis. In the 1891 census, each enumerator 'left at each dwelling-house within his district a Schedule ... for the occupier or occupiers thereof, to be filled up by the same'. These schedules were collected by enumerators who 'copied all the particulars into the Enumeration Books, which, together with the schedules and other documents, were handed to the Local Registrars, who, after revising the work of the Enumerators, prepared Summaries of each District'. These summaries and the material on which they were based, were sent to the Sheriffs of the counties and to the chief magistrates of Scotland's eight principal towns 'and, after being examined and approved by them, were forwarded to the Registrar General in Edinburgh' (Census of Scotland, 1891, *P.P.*, 1892, XCIV: ix). Four stages exist here at which errors in numbers of Gaelic speakers may have occurred: at initial completion by the occupier; at the copying by the enumerator of collected schedules into enumerators' books; at the 'revising of the work' by local registrars; and at the final examination and approval of forms by sheriffs and magistrates. It is reasonable to suggest that errors are most likely to have been made in transcription at stages two and three, or in completion of the schedule. The schedules no longer survive so it is impossible to know for sure. It is possible, however, that the role and local knowledge of enumerators played an important part in the actual numbers included within any given qualitative category such as ability to speak Gaelic only or Gaelic and English.

Most Highland-born persons in these towns came from the more contiguous Highland parishes with each town drawing relatively few of its Highland population from the north and west mainland parishes or the Outer Isles. This general pattern supports for the later nineteenth century what has been discussed elsewhere of the patterns of Highland–Lowland migration for the mid-nineteenth century and earlier (Withers, 1985; 1986a). The Gaelic-speaking proportion of the Highland-born population varied between 40% (Aberdeen) and 60% (Stirling) (Table 6.13). It is possible that the relative numerical strength of Gaelic in each of the towns reflects the relative prevalence of Gaelic in the parishes of origin within the Gaidhealtachd (cf. Figure 6.1). But since it is likely also that many migrants arrived before 1891, we may assume, too, that the language was being maintained within given towns by persons who had earlier moved from parishes then more strongly Gaelic-speaking than in 1891. Explanation of the relative proportions speaking Gaelic within the Highland-born population also lies in the family structures of Gaelic-speaking families, in the attitudes of parents to retention and use of Gaelic and on the circumstances in which it was felt appropriate to use it. The census alone is of minimal use in these respects.

The Demographic Characteristics of the Highland-born Gaelic-speaking Population in Aberdeen, Dundee, Perth and Stirling, 1891

In Aberdeen and Dundee, the Highland-born male population was more strongly Gaelic than the Highland-born female population: the reverse was true for Perth and Stirling (Table 6.13). Within and between given age cohorts, Gaelic was spoken more by age groups within the working age range — from about 20–24 to 60–64 years of age — than by persons younger or older. Gaelic seems to have been more commonly spoken by males than females for given age cohorts of the Highland-born population (cf. Tables 6.2, 6.5, 6.8, 6.11). In very few age cohorts were all Highland-born individuals able to speak Gaelic. In each case, the numbers involved were small and the people involved elderly. The one Gaelic-only speaker enumerated here — a 91 year-old man in Dundee — was from Tomintoul, a non-Highland parish as here defined. In several cases here, the census enumerated entirely Gaelic-speaking Highland-born families. More common was the listing as Gaelic-speaking of both Highland-born parents or of one parent only, although both were Highland-born.

The Origins of Non-Highland-born Gaelic Speakers in Aberdeen, Dundee, Perth and Stirling, 1891

Two principal distinctions may be identified here: non-Highland-born, but Scottish, Gaelic speakers; and foreign-born Scottish Gaelic speakers in which category Irish-born Gaelic speakers represent the largest proportion from any given single place (cf. Tables 6.3, 6.6, 6.9, 6.12). The population included in the first category include persons born from parishes still quite strongly Gaelic but outwith the Highlands as here defined and children and relatives of Gaelic-speaking parents. In the second category, it is not easy to know the place of birth of the Irish-born since for the majority of Irish, enumerators' books record only 'Ireland' as birthplace. Many Irish in urban Scotland came from the north and north-west (Handley, 1945) — from Donegal, Tyrone, Antrim and County Down — with relatively few from southern Ireland (although Dundee had several Irish families from Queen's County). Irish was quite commonly spoken in parts of the north and north-west during the nineteenth century — between 50% and 80% of the population in parts of Donegal, for example, though by less than 10% in parts of County Antrim (Ó Cuív, 1971: 77–94) — but this is not itself clear proof that what the Irish-born Gaelic-speakers enumerated in these four towns were speaking or knew was Irish rather than Scottish Gaelic. Even so, the fact that so many Irish-born persons are enumerated as *Scottish* Gaelic speakers and that the proportion of such persons within the total-Gaelic speaking population of the four towns here considered increases as we move towards the principal receiving areas of Irish-born in Scotland — the west central Lowlands — may suggest that published census figures on Scottish Gaelic which have hitherto been taken as *accurate* totals of Scottish Gaelic speakers may not only not be accurate, but may also include numbers of persons with ability in Irish rather than *Scottish* Gaelic.

Conclusions

This paper has discussed Scotland's 'urban Gaidhealtachd' using the 1891 census figures on Gaelic. Bearing in mind the case study approach using four towns, several conclusions may be proposed. First, the census is not necessarily an accurate guide to numbers speaking Gaelic and is of little or no use in investigating how Gaelic was used, to whom, when, and why, or in exploring processes of language transmission. Second, assessment of enumerators' books reveals that the Gaelic population in urban Lowland Scotland was not drawn indiscriminately from a uniformly Gaelic Highland region, but from particular areas and districts within the Highlands not themselves necessarily highly Gaelic speaking and from parishes not in the Highlands proper. Third, important variations exist in the relative strength by age and sex in Gaelic speaking in urban Lowland Scotland, both within and between towns. Finally, although this essay has added in part to an understanding of Scotland's historical geolinguistics it has pointed, too, to the need for further exploration of

Gaelic in urban Lowland Scotland — on language in relation to occupation, for example, or within different family structures — as it has also hinted at the need for caution in use of census figures.

References

CAMPBELL, J. L. 1945, *Gaelic in Scottish Education and Life*. Edinburgh: Johnston.

Census of Scotland 1891, Parliamentary Papers. XCIV, 1892.

Census of Scotland 1951, Gaelic Report.

Census of Scotland 1981, Gaelic Report.

DEVINE, T. 1979, Temporary migration and the Scottish Highlands in the nineteenth century. *Econ. Hist. Rev*. XXXIII(3), 344–59.

— 1983, Highland migration to Lowland Scotland, 1760–1860. *Scott. Hist. Rev*. LXII(2): 137–149.

DURKACZ, V. E. 1983, *The Decline of the Celtic Languages*. Edinburgh: John Donald.

FLINN, M. (ed.) 1977, *Scottish Population History*. Cambridge: University Press.

FRASER-MACKINTOSH, C. 1881, The Gaelic census of the counties of Inverness, Ross, and Sutherland. *Celtic Magazine* VI, 438–41.

GRAY, M. 1957, *The Highland Economy, 1750–1850*. Edinburgh: Oliver and Boyd.

HANDLEY, J. E. 1945, *The Irish in Scotland, 1798–1845*. Cork: University Press.

MACDONALD, D. F. 1937, *Scotland's Shifting Population 1780–1850*. Glasgow: Jackson.

MACKINNON, K. 1974, *The Lion's Tongue*. Inverness: Club Leabhar.

Ó CUÍV, B. 1971, *Irish Dialects and Irish-Speaking Districts*. Dublin: Institute for Advanced Studies.

OSBORNE, R. H. 1958, The movements of people in Scotland 1851–1951. *Scott. Studs*. 2: 1–46.

WITHERS, C. W. J. 1984, *Gaelic in Scotland 1698–1981: The Geographical History of a Language*. Edinburgh: John Donald.

— 1985, Highland migration to Dundee, Perth and Stirling, 1753–1891. *Jour. Hist. Geog*., 11(4), 395–418.

— 1986a, *Highland Communities in Dundee and Perth 1781–1891*. Dundee: Abertay Historical Society.

— 1986b, Gaelic communities in Lowland Scotland, 1709–1891: explorations towards a social history. *Scott. Lang*. 5: 48–64.

7 What Future for Scotland's Gaelic-speaking Communities?

CLIVE JAMES

Introduction

This chapter examines the current extent of Scottish Gaelic-speaking communities in Scotland and to what extent their future survival is being planned. All reference to Gaelic/Gaels (etc.) are exclusively to Scottish Gaelic.

Following an examination using ennumeration district data from the 1981 Census of Scotland of the current location of Gaelic speaking communities, the activity (or lack of) of the main local government units, central government agencies and other relevant bodies in relation to the planning of Gaelic are examined. Prior to making conclusions a brief examination of the contemporary Faroe Islands situation is made. Throughout the chapter contemporary English versions of place names are regrettably used to avoid confusing the non-Gaelic reader.

Distribution of Gaelic-Speaking Communities in Scotland

In 1881 when knowledge of Gaelic was included as a question in the decennial census of Scotland for the first time, over a quarter of a million people aged three years or over could speak the language — 5% of the population of Scotland. Of these, 90% lived in the Highlands and Islands. One hundred years later, just less than 80,000 persons could speak the historic tongue of the Scottish nation — 1.7% of the population of Scotland. Today only 60% of the Gaelic speakers live in the Highlands

TABLE 7.1 *Gaelic-speaking communities in 1981*

Area (1981)	*No. of Gaelic speakers*	*% local population*	*% Scottish total*
Western Isles Island Council (WIIC)	23,447	80	30
Highland Region (HR)	16,632	9.5	21
Strathclyde Region (SR)	24,805	1	31

and Islands. A further 3,300 persons were able to read and/or write the language to give a maximum Gaelic community in Scotland in 1981 of 82,600 persons.

When the future of Gaelic-speaking communities is being examined the location of these speakers is critical. Table 7.1 shows this by local government areas. Over the traditional Highlands and Islands counties some 20% of the population can speak Gaelic. Within this area Lewis is the largest, single homogenous community of Gaelic speakers.

However, when the distribution of the Gaelic-speaking population is examined some striking facts emerge which are vital indicators for the survival of Gaelic-speaking communities for the future. There is general agreement that at least 70–80% of a community need to speak a language if it is to survive as a community language. Areas where more than three-quarters of the population speak Gaelic account for only one-quarter of the Gaelic speaking population. Even when the threshold is lowered to 50% only one-third of the total are included. Conversely some 50,000 Scottish Gaelic speakers (two-thirds of the total) live in areas where less than 50% of the total population speak Gaelic. Taking the 70% figure, the following Gaelic speaking communities emerge from the 1981 census:

WIIC: The entire island chain except the Balivanich and Stornoway areas;

HR: North Skye (Staffin, Flodigarry, Kilvaxter, Kensaleyre),

West Skye (Portnalong, Struan, Bracadale, Vaternish, Healaval),

South Skye (Elgol, north Sleat, Skulamus),

Canna;

SR: Tiree.

Over the remainder of the traditionally Gaelic-speaking Highlands and Islands the percentage is 60 or less — including most of Skye and all of Islay and Mull. On the mainland the highest percentages do not even exceed 50%. Only in remote Stoer, Achiltibuie, Inverasdale, Applecross and Inverinalate do they even approach that figure.

When thinking of future Gaelic-speaking communities the age structure of the population is important. The only communities in Scotland where there is a greater intensity of Gaelic amongst the younger generations than the older are:

WIIC: Most of north and west Lewis, Harris, Berneray, North Uist, South Uist, Barra;

HR: Parts of Skye (Duirinish West, Kilmur, Sconser, Sleat);

SR: Tiree.

If the trends 1961–71 and 1971–81 are briefly examined we see that: WIIC remains a static situation; HR has less decline on the islands, especially 1971–81; and SR has less decline on the islands, especially 1971–81, and there is the break up and virtual cessation of the Glasgow Gaelic community.

However, even in the strongest areas there has been a decline of the use of Gaelic in the shop, hall, school yard and around the sheepfold. While there is a more favourable parental attitude to Gaelic in schools, there are more linguistically mixed marriages. Surveys have shown continued loyalty to Gaelic (e.g. in Harris, North Skye, North Uist and Barra). Members of the Roman Catholic, Free and Free Presbyterian Churches have also been shown to possess a greater loyalty to the language than members of the established Church of Scotland.

In looking towards the future of Gaelic-speaking communities in Scotland the decennial census reports show how small the human resource for the future is and how the language is maintained over time. The pattern for younger persons during the period 1961–81 was fairly healthy with an increase in base numbers and language acquisition during subsequent decades. However, by 1981 the base figure had fallen drastically, (See Table 7.2).

Despite the numerical minority of Gaelic in Scottish society today an opinion poll has shown surprisingly high support for the language on

TABLE 7.2 *Gaelic speaking in Scotland 1961–91*

Census	*Age group*		
	3–4	*13–14*	*23–24*
1961	1,085	—	—
1971	1,227	1,756	—
1981	738	1,927	1,790
1991	—	?	?

an all-Scotland sample. Of those interviewed:

67% supported recognition of Gaelic;
64% supported promotion of Gaelic;
71% supported more Gaelic learners' programmes;
50% supported more Gaelic on radio and television;
68% supported bilingual signs and notices;
82% supported Gaelic being taught in all schools.

A survey in Barra and Harris saw the future of Gaelic being closely linked with more broadcasting, Gaelic in schools, summer schools for learners, Gaelic cultural centres and bilingual signs — in that order of importance. When the future of Gaelic-speaking communities is being discussed what is really under examination is the situation on some of the islands off the west coast of Scotland. The language may survive on other islands, on parts of the west coast and in urban centres elsewhere in Scotland. However, there it will be a language of restricted domains.

Strathclyde Region

Strathclyde Region is Scotland's most populous and wealthy local government unit. It's Gaelic-speaking population falls into two groups: (i) the traditional area of Argyll mainland and islands with over 6,000 Gaels; and (ii) the exiles' community in Glasgow with over 9,000 Gaelic speakers. The latter, which, when Glasgow was the factory of Scotland, once attracted a continual influx of Gaels in search of work who on arrival then reinforced the community which had arrived before them. However the economic decline of Glasgow has resulted in a more dispersed migration pattern. In the last 20 years the Glasgow Gaelic community which once reared Gaelic-speaking children (similar to the Liverpool Welsh and London Welsh) has largely ceased. This is most noticeable in the recent closure of several Gaelic churches in the city.

While Strathclyde Region has no formal policy towards Gaelic, it has become a partner in certain joint ventures such as *CnaG* and the publishing venture *Acair*. The Region has established a bilingual Gaelic–English primary school in Glasgow and several city high schools offer Gaelic on the curriculum. Two peripatetic teachers of Gaelic have been appointed to serve Argyll.

The vast territory of Argyll and Bute District Council covers what was traditionally almost entirely a Gaelic-speaking community. However, by 1981 very few enumeration districts had in excess of 70% Gaelic speakers and often the number of speakers involved was very small:

Tiree	Kilkenneth (93% — 143 speakers), Ruaig (86% — 86), Hynish (88% — 83) Balephetrish (70% — 76). (The two main settlements — Scarinish and Crossapol — were 60% Gaelic speaking.)
Coll	None.
Mull	Kilninian (90% — 9). (Laggan adjacent was 54% — 24.)
Islay	Lossit (83% — 25). (Portnahaven/Port Wemyss adjacent was 65% — 83.)
Jura	None.
Colonsay	None.

There are other remnants of Gaelic communities on all the islands above and the language is heard openly, especially on western Islay. Oban possesses a colony of exiles from all the western islands.

The Strathclyde Structure Plan cannot be said to consider the Gaelic tradition of Argyll except in wishing 'to counter depopulation'. Argyll and Bute District Council has produced local plans for 'Islay, Jura and Colonsay' and for 'Mull, Coll and Tiree'. The two plans are similar. Both contain an explanatory note in Gaelic covering a full page. In the context of Tiree the later plan notes that over 70% of the population of Tiree speak Gaelic (where it is acknowledged to be 'still in common use' as is 'still spoken in Mull and Coll but only by 27% and 28% of the population respectively' (Figure 7.1). While the population of Mull increased by 30% between 1971 and 1981 and Coll saw a minor increase, that of Tiree fell be almost 10%. One-quarter of Mull's population was born outside Scotland. Of Tiree's population of 750 some 30% is aged over 60 years and only 20% under 16. It is acknowledged that alternative employment to crofting is essential if Tiree is to retain its diminishing population. Lobster fishing is virtually the sole non-agricultural industry on the island, together with a small knitwear factory and local construction work. Holiday and second homes account for 28% of the dwelling stock. A gaelic 'image' to tourism on Tiree is beginning to emerge with some bilingual airfield, road and commercial signs and holding of language courses. This is lacking on Coll and Mull. Tiree also has an advantage over several islands in that it has a six year high school at Ard-Sgoil Thiriodh.

Whereas the local plans for the Argyll islands are competent, professional, technical documents, only the implementation of policies to retain the indigenous Gaelic-speaking population on Tiree will enable any form of Gaelic speaking community to remain in Argyll and Strathclyde into the next century.

Highland Region

The Highland Regional Council (*Roinn na Gaidhaeltachd)* established in 1975 and with its administrative headquarters in Inverness has the responsibility for over 16,000 Gaels — one-fifth of the Scottish total and one-tenth of its population. It has produced a 136 page *Guide to the Highland Region* (Highland Regional Council, 1985). The Convener's foreward says 'few areas in Europe are so rich in culture' without elaborating as to which culture (or language), although a few pages later a sentence reads 'The Gaelic influence was once predominant through most of the area and still is in the west and the islands'.Under 'Education' one can read of the bilingual education experiment in eleven primary schools on Skye and under 'Leisure' Gaelic drama is mentioned twice. In the lengthy sections rightly devoted to economic activity the close proven link between work and language survival is totally absent unless you wish to stay 'bed and breakfast with a Gaelic speaking family in Skye'. The climax is a full page about Gaelic in English followed by a Gaelic version of the same. While a fair picture is portrayed it leaves a rather old-fashioned image. However, the penultimate paragraph tells one that 'the Highlands and Islands Development Board ... is investigating projects which might link linguistic and community development'.

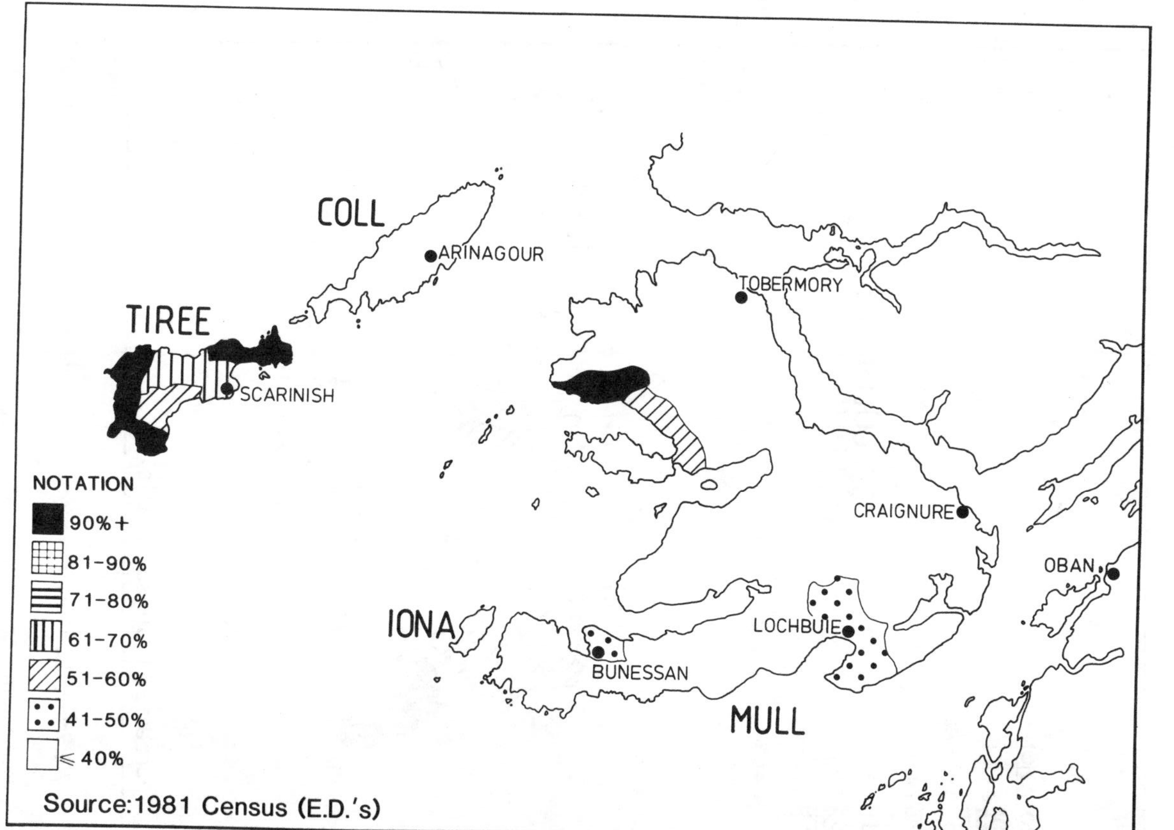

FIGURE 7.1 *Mull, Tiree and Coll — percentage of Gaelic speakers in 1981*

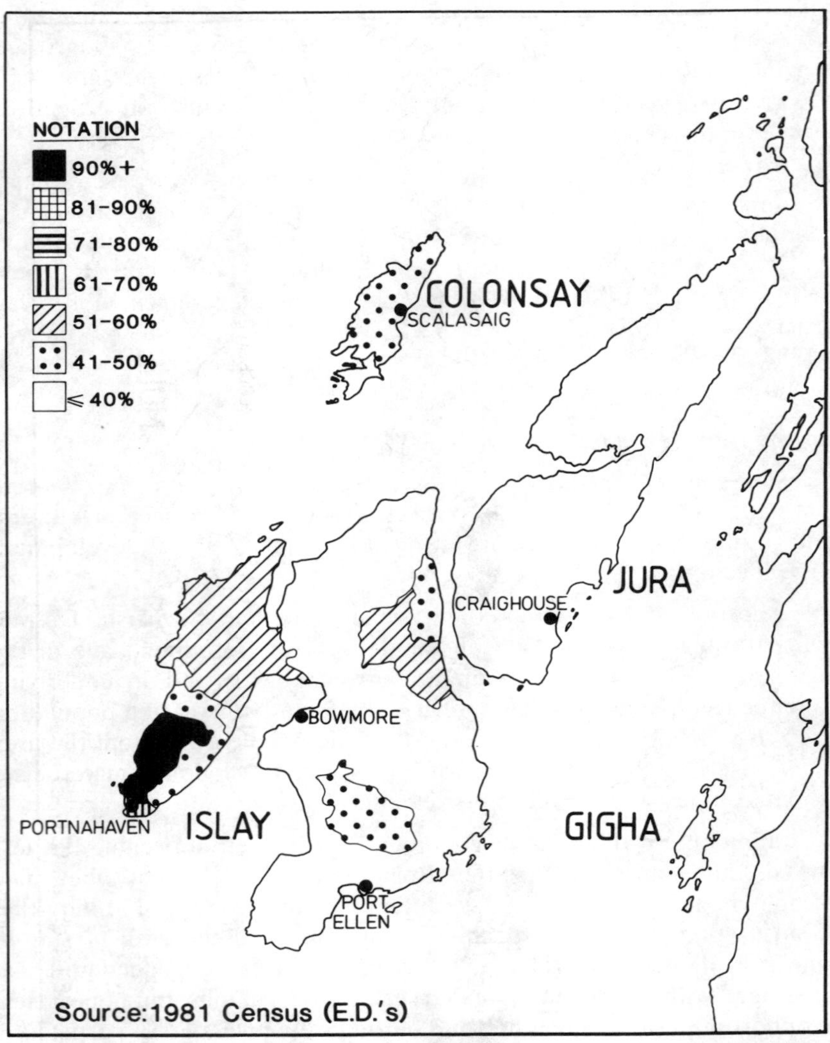

FIGURE 7.2 *Islay, Jura and Colonsay — percentage of Gaelic speakers in 1981*

Highland Region set up a Gaelic Sub-committee in 1977. One early benefit was the introduction of 12 travelling teachers of Gaelic in 1978. Out of the labours of the Gaelic Working Party in 1980 came some further offerings, notably bilingual signs at the regional boundary and bilingual directional signs in Skye and Lochalsh District, the latter with the Gaelic uppermost in green lettering with the English underneath in black lettering of the same size and script.

The Highland Structure Plan, approved by the Secretary of State with minor modifications in 1980, identifies as the key issue the scarsity of employment rather than land. Thirty per cent of the Region's Gaelic speakers (and the only remaining Gaelic communities excepting Canna) are in Skye and Lochalsh District. The Regional Council (1982) has prepared a local plan for this district, the first draft of which appeared in 1982. The entire Gaelic-related context in the 155-page document is as follows.

Extracts from Highland Region Local Plan

Skye and Lochalsh is also unique in the Region, in so far as more than half the population (54%) speak Gaelic. This aspect of cultural heritage plays an important part in the economic and social development of the locality.

Approximately 10,400 people live in Skye and Lochalsh. Despite having the highest proportion of population over retirement age in the Region (22.3%), deaths continuing to outweigh births, and the underlying economic trends, the area has shown a consistently increasing population in recent years. However, the drain of young people away from the area may reassert itself if a revival of the national economy materialises without compensating local improvements.

Population drift to larger communities has been noticeable but less marked than elsewhere in the Region as evidenced by the male unemployment rates. This may be due in part to the cultural affinity that prevails within the Gaelic-speaking community and the wish to stay at home to get local employment. This desire must be engendered and encouraged with a constant drive and search for local jobs, but nonetheless the opportunities remain limited and out-migration will persist particularly from small remote settlements.

The whole District forms an important tourist attraction based primarily upon romantic, historical association, the Gaelic culture and rugged scenery.

There has been much recent debate on the merits and demerits of bilingual roadsigns. This derives from local people's interest in promotion of the Gaelic language. In certain circumstances, such signs have been erected. They are of interest to tourists but their main function is to sustain the interests of the Gaelic language. However limited in such an objective, this step may be encouraged by the Council and accommodated where appropriate where there is no prejudice to standards of road safety. Place names, street names and other informational signs may therefore be bilingual; prescribed, directional traffic and road signs would remain unilingual.

Housing — Duirinish and Drumbuie

These attractive traditional crofting villages are listed by the Secretary of State as being of national importance for their architectural and historical interest. Any proposals for new infill development or modernisation of properties will need to take this into account in terms of siting, detailed design, scale and use of materials. It is important to protect the good agricultural land which lies between the two villages. Single-phase electricity supplies are a further development restraint. It is also important to note the Gaelic cultural interests still prevailing in small communities such as this. This must be protected indeed fostered not least by controlling the scale and phasing of new developments. Nowhere is the concept of incremental growth and change more important than in small settlements such as these and where there is evidence of a solid Gaelic cultural affinity.

The Gaelic College, *An Sabhal Mor*, has primarily a cultural function, but also economic, in terms of direct jobs. In the long term it contributes to the growing awareness of the cultural heritage and encourages the affinity of the people for their homeland. It is an important institution, therefore, and should be encouraged to thrive and prosper.

Portree is a tourist destination. It is a village of historic associations and charisma and the Gaelic language is sustained as much here as anywhere by everyday business and commerce. (Highland Regional Council, 1982)

A need for 350 additional jobs in Portree and north Skye are, correctly, seen to be 'promoted in ways which are self-sustaining, bring maximum benefit to local people and will maintain the integrity of the area'. At present 72% of all paid employment in Skye is in Services (including 21% in catering and 13% in construction), 10% in Primary Industries and 18% in Manufacturing Industry.

The surviving Gaelic speaking communities in north Skye are

insulated from the anglicising influence of Portree by the wild country beneath the Old Man of Storr (Figure 7.3). Along the A855 from Lealt through Staffin, Flodigarry, Kilmaluag, Kilvaxter and Linicro are a series of crofting townships before on the return road loop the more anglicised ferry and fishing port of Uig is reached. The resident population is about 750 persons and between 76% and 87% spoke Gaelic in 1981. At Staffin a community co-operative, Co Chomunn Stafainn, has been established which includes a community hall, shop, craft outlet and café. Most jobs in this area are based on crofting/fishing supplemented by local services and tourism.

In north-west Skye the Vaternish peninsula remains 76% Gaelic speaking, notably at Geary in a community of 110 inhabitants. The area north and east of Healaval Mhor was 71% Gaelic in a population of 190. On the west coast the Bracadale/Struan area was 72% Gaelic — 115 persons in the population altogether. The most Gaelic area on Skye is the Portnalong and Fiskavaig peninsula with 80% of a total population of almost 200.

Southern Skye contains few Gaelic communities. Remote Elgol is 74% Gaelic (105 total population) and north Sleat (Tokavaig, Torskavaig and Achnacloich) is also 74% (80 total population). Surprisingly, the Skulamus township adjacent to heavily anglicised Broadford is also 74% Gaelic (65 population in all). The Drumfearn/Isle Ornsay area falls below the 70% level by a mere 1% (as does the Boreraig township and Carbost in north west Skye).

Overall, with the exceptions quoted above, the Skye and Lochalsh District Plan could have been written for any part of rural Scotland. The adverse impact of certain types of development upon a linguistic community are not considered. Neither is the immigration to the area seen as a threat to the local society.

Highland Region is the local education authority for the largest proportion of the land area of the formerly Gaelic-speaking heartland. However whereas their own survey in 1978 showed that 81% of parents in Skye wished to see Gaelic taught in the primary schools, this policy is still not fully implemented. Teachers without the language are still being appointed to the island's primary schools. Conversely a Gaelic stream was set up in Portree in 1986. (The same year also saw the establishment of a Gaelic unit in Inverness.)

Much of the future of Skye is seen through further development of tourism. In 1977 the Scottish Tourist Board sponsored a study of tourism in Sleat. The population of 400 was found to be made up of 60% first

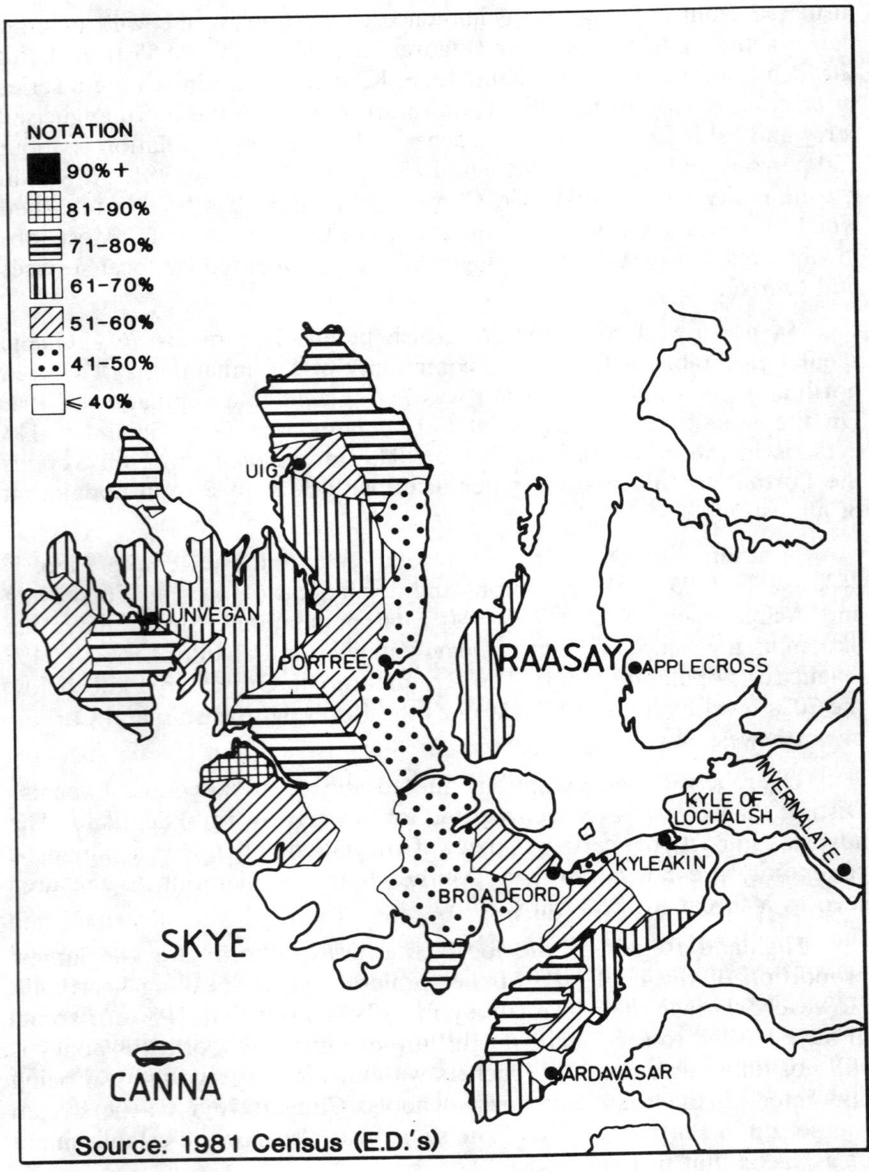

FIGURE 7.3 *Skye — percentage of Gaelic speakers in 1981*

TABLE 7.4 *Population of inhabited islands 1951–81*

	1951	*1961*	*1971*	*1981*
(a) *Southernmost Isles*				
Berneray	5	3	6	—
Vatersay	151	95	77	108
Barra	1,728	1,369	1,005	1,232
Eriksay	330	231	219	219
(b) *Dark Isle*				
South Uist	2,462	2,376	2,281	2,223
Benbecula	924	1,358	1,355	1,988
Grimsay (NU)	236	239	193	206
Flodday	17	14	19	9
Grimsay (SU)	22	13	4	12
Baleshare	75	59	64	66
North Uist	1,890	1,620	1,469	1,454
Eilean Na Cille	4	5	4	—
	5,630	5,684	5,389	5,958
(c) *Sound of Harris*				
Boreray (NU)	7	5	—	—
Killegray (H)	—	—	2	—
Leiravay (NU)	5	2	—	—
Pabbay (H)	2	2	4	—
Berneray	246	201	131	134
Scalpay (H)	541	470	483	461
Scarp (H)	74	46	12	2
Taransay (H)	5	5	5	—
(d) *Lewis and Harris*				
Harris	3,121	2,493	2,175	2,137
Lewis	23,344	21,614	20,047	21,253
Bernera	384	317	276	292
	26,849	24,424	22,498	23,682
(e) *Other uninhabited (1981) and military isles*				
Flannan Islands (L)	3	3	3	—
Ensay (H)	2	2	2	—
St Kilda	0	65	65	46
Kirkibost	6	—	—	—
Vallay	2	—	—	—
Sunamul	5	—	—	—
Western Isles total	35,591	32,607	29,891	31,842

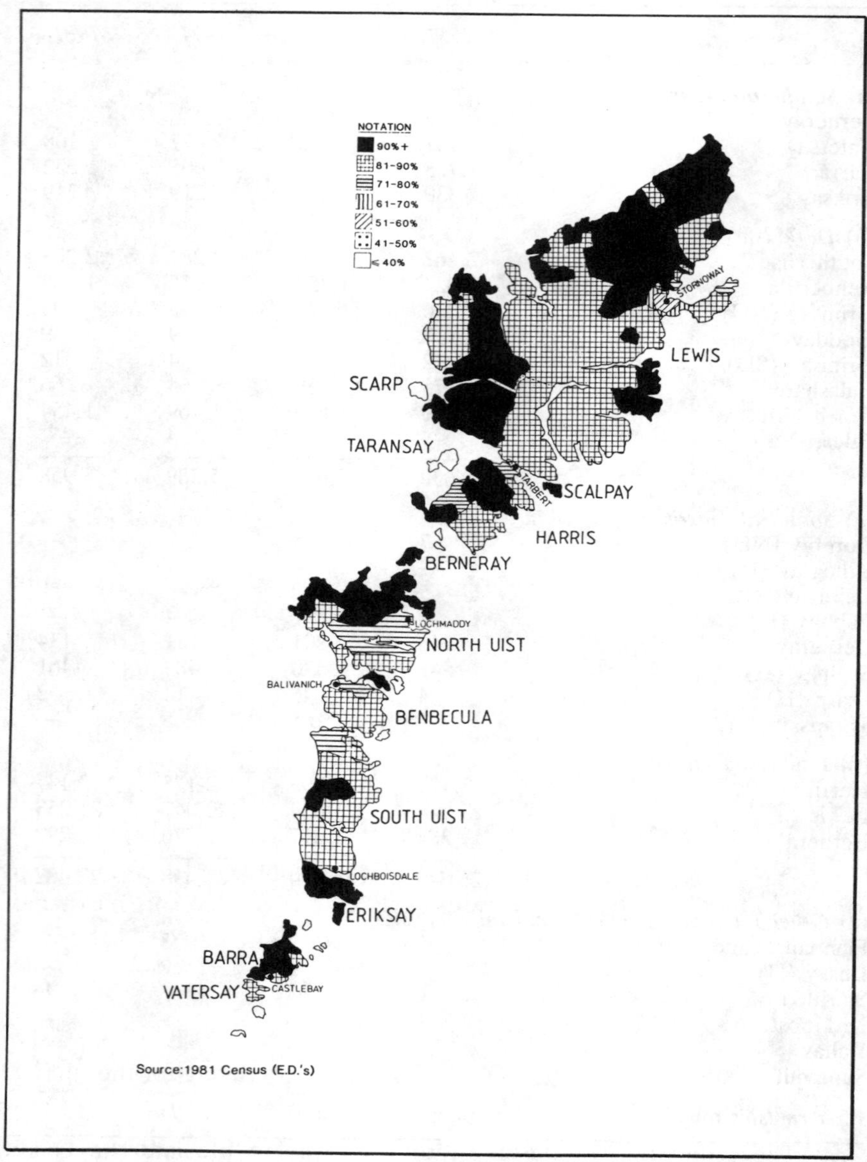

FIGURE 7.4 *Western Isles — percentage of Gaelic speakers in 1981*

TABLE 7.5 *Gaelic speakers in Western Isles enumeration districts 1981*

Percentage	*Total EDs*	*Cumulative total*	*Total speakers*[a]	*Cumulative percentage*
Over 90	53	53	10,356	44
81–90	38	91	6,547	72
71–80	14	105	1,969	81
61–70	13	118	2,744	92
51–60	8[b]	126	1,488	99
41–50	2[b]	128	102	99
Under 40	4[c]	132	161	100
			23,367	

[a] aged three years or older
[b] all near Stornoway
[c] all on north-west Benbecula

the population speak Gaelic (in Gwynedd only 55% of Welsh speakers live in similar situations).

Census statistics can be notoriously wrong in assessing the actual use of a language. Fortunately, in Lewis and Harris the results of a survey of language use in the context of the development of the Arnish steel fabrication yard are available. The sample was separated into six categories: (i) workers at the yard who previously were residents on the islands; (ii) workers who had returned to the islands to work at the yard; (iii) villagers living too far away to commute to Arnish; (iv) villagers living within commuting distance to Arnish; (v) townspeople in adjacent Stornoway; (vi) the management of the yard.

Questions were asked regarding: (1) ability of the sample to speak Gaelic; (2) the use of traditional Gaelic names and nicknames (patronymics); (3) use of Gaelic with friends and relatives; (4) use of Gaelic at work; (5) use of Gaelic at home; (6) use of Gaelic to older and younger people.

The results are shown in Table 7.6. Line 1(a) is similar that expected from the census. Taken overall the results are encouraging for the survival of the language.

The foundation of the Western Isles way of life and the Gaelic language is crofting. There are over 6,000 crofts registered with the Crofters Commission which form some 5,400 working units distributed among 250 crofting townships. Of these 94% are less than 100 'standard

TABLE 7.6 *Industrialisation and minority — language loyalty*

N =	*Resident workers (i) 109*	*Expatriate workers (ii) 75*	*Non-affected villages (iii) 100*	*Affected villages (iv) 105*	*Stornoway (v) 100*	*Yard management (vi) 25*
	%	%	%	%	%	%
1. Gaelic speakers in sample						
(a) Yes	66	80	95	91	50	16
(b) No	20	11	3	8	36	80
(c) Ltl.	14	9	2	1	14	4
2. Use of patronymics						
(a) Yes	34	43	49	53	21	8
3. Gaelic spoken with friends and neighbours						
(a) No	7	4	3	1	4	4
(b) Yes	55	75	93	88	43	16
(c) Occ.	16	13	2	5	16	4
(d) N/A	20	8	2	7	36	76
4. Gaelic spoken at work						
(a) No	12	7	2	9	12	4
(b) Yes	39	49	93	54	26	—
(c) Occ.	28	36	3	22	22	20
(d) N/A	20	8	2	12	38	76
5. Gaelic spoken at home						
(a) No	8	7	3	1	11	4
(b) Yes	61	68	93	88	40	16
(c) Occ.	11	17	2	5	12	4
(d) N/A	20	8	2	7	36	76
6. Gaelic spoken to older and younger people						
(a) Older	67	80	96	90	50	20
(b) Yngr.	40	60	88	58	12	4
(c) Dcrse.	−37	−20	−8	−32	−38	−16

Ltl. = Little Occ. = Occasionally N/A = Not Applicable

Yngr. = Younger Dcrse. = Decrease

man days' and provide less than two days work per week for their occupiers and are typical less than 5 ha. in area, averaging 3 ha. Nevertheless, they generate £2 million worth of agricultural production per annum. However, the islands are nowhere near self sufficient in food products — for example 90% of beef, 50% of sheep meat and 75% of milk is imported. Of the total land area 212,000 ha (77% of the total) is in crofting tenure, including 88,000 ha of common grazings. The recent legislation which enables crofts to be bought and sold may undermine this link between Gaelic and crofting.

Numbers in employment grew from 7,890 in 1974 to 9,130 in 1978 before declining to 8,900 in 1982. It was this growth in employment which led the in migration of the 1970s. Of the employees in 1982, 6,180 were on Lewis, of which 4,480 were in Stornoway itself. In fact, 50% of all employees are found in the Stornoway and Balivanich areas.

The main industries providing employment today (excluding self-employment) are agriculture and fishing (11%), textiles (13%), construction (9%), transport and communications (6%), distributive trades (9%) and professional and administrative services (46%).

After the land, the sea is the next most important physical resource in the Western Isles. Lobsters are the basis of the industry in the Uists, Benbecula, Eriksay and Barra, with herring also important at Eriksay and at Scalpay and Stornoway. Stornoway also fishes prawns and white fish in season. The catch annually is 25,000 tonne of whitefish worth £1 million and 2,500 tonne of shellfish worth £2.1 million. Herring accounts for 42% of landings by weight and shellfish 33%. About 60 boats are based at Stornoway, where 85% of landings in the islands are made, and 220 elsewhere, notably Castlebay, Eriksay, Lochboisdale, Grimsay and Scalpay. Fish processing is limited. Much of the shellfish harvest is exported by Wilsons of Holyhead, North Wales. Fish processing plants have been established at Stornoway, Kirkibost, Grimsay, Ardveenish (Barra) and Breasclete (Lewis) but several of these have had fluctuating fortunes. Exploitation of the sea's resources provides work for about 500 full-time and part-time fishermen and 120 full-time and 50 seasonal share based jobs. Seaweed is gathered for fertiliser. It is also gathered for conversion to alginate and taken either to the Keose co-operative plant on west Lewis or shipped to Oban for drying.

Manufacturing industry is very limited. Boat building and repairing is undertaken at Stornoway, South Uist, North Uist and Lewis. The Harris Tweed industry is very cyclical in production. After two bad years — 1975 and 1980 — the Harris Tweed industry experienced six relatively good years — 1980–6, but still below peak production. In 1986, 740 self-employed croft based weavers gained an income, nearly all on Lewis. About 350 mill workers are also employed, mostly in Stornoway with some in Shawbost and Garinin. Knitwear factories operate in Daliburgh and Stornoway. The other main element of the manufacturing sector is the steel fabrication yard at Arnish, just south of Stornoway. Here employment never rose to the promised 1,000 — a figure which would have resulted in large scale immigration of non-Gaelic speakers to the area. At the peak, some 500 were employed, while in 1987 it was down to 250. The lease agreement with the Stornoway Trust permits only essential maintenance work on Sundays in respect of the Presbyterian tradition of Lewis.

Within the services sector the main employers are: Ministry of Defence at Stornoway and Uists (435 service and 250 civil jobs); Comhairle nan Eilean (2,300 persons, half part-time, three-quarters of total on Lewis); Health Authority (550 full and part-time, most on Lewis).

Significantly, in terms of language survival, tourism is not nearly as important as on other Scottish islands but is the only growth income earner. Only 4% of visitors to the Highlands and Islands visit the Western Isles. Despite the *Gaelhols* scheme of the Western Isles Branch of *An Comunn Gaidhealach* the specific Gaelic element in Western Isles tourism is as natural as is the language of the community. The small scale of the industry can be judged from the total of only 24 hotels, 10 guest houses and 150 bed and breakfast establishments in the islands, together with 350 static caravans for hire. Hotels, bars and catering account for around 500 jobs throughout the islands.

It is more usual to talk in terms of 'development of tourism' than of 'tourism and community development'. The difference in emphasis is designed to stress the importance of seeing the benefit to the community first and to the tourist and the wider tourism industry second. Better roads may in fact reduce the local benefit of tourism as visitors are able to 'do' an area in less time (beware the suggested Skye bridge). Growth in domestic tourism is expected in specialist activities and pursuits — pony trekking, mountaineering, canoeing, orienteering, nature study, learning crafts, Gaelic lessons, working on a farm or croft (there are dude ranches in USA!), highland dancing, local history and legends, cookery, photography. Most communities in the Western Isles have the raw materials. They have real communities and real people. No new technology is required. Tourism is labour intensive and its revenue is widely spread among the community in terms of expenditure on accommodation, food, souvenirs, petrol, drink and meals, etc. Encouragement to local or community development of tourism would increase the likelihood of profits staying in the community and not filtering out. Community development can increase the chance of success, can identify the right persons to be involved, breed confidence in new projects, gain local and political acceptance and release local talent. Within the community there will be a product and accommodation. These need to be matched together and marketed.

Irrespective of how an income is earned in the Western Isles, it is likely to be a low income. In 1980, for example, the average weekly earnings for males in full time employment over 21 years was less than 80% of Aberdeen levels.

Registered unemployment in the Western Isles in December 1986 reached a total of 1,798 males (32.2% of the insured population) and 556 females (a figure deflated by the lack of employment for women, but who are entitled to claim benefit, and which decreases away from Stornoway and Balivanich). By island areas the figures were as shown in Table 7.7. The genuine unemployment figures are reckoned to be at least one-third higher than the official ones due to the numerous statistical devices which have been introduced to keep the numbers down.

Of those who left secondary school in the Western Isles in 1982: 17% found work in the islands; 7% found work outside the islands; 42% went on to further or higher education; 27% were on a government special programme; 7% were unemployed; 2% fell into other categories.

In 1976 Comhairle nan Eilean published its *Aithris na Roinne/ Regional Report* (entirely in English) — a planning document unique to Scotland within the United Kingdom context. It acknowledged that

> 'islanders, by having access to both Gaelic and English cultures have derived their own particular view of the world from comparing and contrasting aspects of these cultures. In particular the difference between native language of the Western Isles and that of most of mainland Britain has produced a strong stimulus for islanders to develop a distinct outlook and attitude to life as well as providing

TABLE 7.7 *Registered unemployment in the Western Isles, December 1986*

	Male	*Female*
Lewis	1,197	345
Harris	194	49
Uists and Benbecula	307	131
Barra	100	31
Totals	1,798	556

the basis for a feeling of community, in a broad sense, among Gaelic speakers within and outwith the area.'

It is most relevant to take note of what was said about community characteristics:

Extract from Regional Report — Community Characteristics

(i) The family unit can be viewed as still being strong throughout the area. Social control (and conformity) through community and extended family pressure is strong. Social evaluation is stressed as being a vital importance in child rearing practices. Family supports are still available in some measure but the implications of family rejection can be strong. This, together with the lack of anonymity inherent in small rural and especially island communities, may be a factor which encourages some young people to leave the islands.

(ii) The Church throughout the Western Isles is seen as being of major social importance and carries great authority (and control) over the outlook of the population. This involvement varies considerably in nature and emphasis between the Presbyterian middle and northern parts of the area and the Catholic southern part.

(iii) There is still a strong sense of community in rural villages, particularly with regard to township work and annual crofting and domestic activities. Communal sheep shearing and dipping, peat cutting, potato planting, etc. take place regularly. Traditional attitudes are still strong, making the introduction of new patterns of work/behaviour, in some cases, difficult.

(iv) Within the area there are differences in customs and ways of life between the islands and more noticeably between the rural crofting townships and urban Stornoway. (Comhairle nan Eilean, 1976)

The key issues to emerge from the analysis of the islands' council area were: continued population decline due to persistent and selective out-migration; unemployment, especially long term (30% is for over 12 months); dominance of employment in the tertiary sector; underdevelopment of the fishing sector; the importance of crofting; problem of livestock marketing; contracting of the Harris Tweed industry; underdeveloped nature of tourism; one-third of housing of below tolerable standard; the need for a six-year secondary school in the Uists; the role of bilingualism in formal education; the large number of small primary schools; the elderly population structure; very low level and uneven distribution of recreation provision; the need for an efficient inter and intra island communications system; high transport costs restrain development; 5,500 households lack main drainage; electricity supplies in rural areas are only capable of domestic loads; a very high landscape standard; a very high standard of flora and fauna.

Out of these issues developed the two main objectives of Comhairle nan Eilean: (1) the reversal of the trend of population decline due to persistent and selective out-migration from the area; (2) improvement in the situation of the people in terms of employment and the provision of public and other services.

These were to be achieved by action in five fields: (a) employment (development of indigenous activities; development of fisheries; promotion of development through provision of serviced sites and advance units; encouragement of non-agricultural activities supplementary to crofting; improvement of agricultural production); (b) housing (campaigning for a higher rate of improvement grant; greater grants and loans for crofters; encourage new houses for owner occupation; provision of housing for rent); (c) transport (press for Road Equipment Tariff on all ferries; co-ordinate all transport; finance social need transport; improve the main inter island link); (d) education (establishment of a six-year secondary in Benbecula); (e) infrastructure (extension of mains water supply; extension of mains drainage).

Proisect Muinntir nan Eilean — the Western Isles Community Education Project — was established in 1977 as a three year experiment with financial assistance from the Van Leer Foundation. The philosophy was

> that, basically, human life is indivisible and that, therefore, promotion of economics at the expense of social development, or social at the expense of cultural, is arbitary, artificial and, in the long run likely to be unsuccessful.

Thus the use of the Gaelic language was naturally an in-built element in all the activities undertaken.

It was hoped that through applying education resources the communities involved might see their problems more clearly and find ways of tackling them for themselves. Initially the project concentrated in three areas: Ness in Lewis, Harris and Iochdar in South Uist. From the start the need to understand local history as a stimulus to cultural awareness was considered central to the analysis of a community's social and economic reality. Out of this came the establishment of numerous local history societies now functioning in the Western Isles.

Out of the project have come certain conclusions towards the understanding of the factors crucial to long term community development:

a stable and cohesive social environment; an awareness of a sense of pride on the part of the community in its culture, including its language; a realistic and analytic awareness of the past and its part in shaping the attitudes of the present — liberating the past as force for, rather than against, progress; a conscious appreciation, on the part of developers, of the inter dependence of the social, cultural and economic domains in community life.

The WIIC subsequently adopted a 'development from within' philosophy strengthened by the new appreciation of the role of the Gaelic language and culture. This approach was encouraged by the outcome of the Van Leer project. In order to generate employment and retain its population many activities play a role: provision of premises (conversion of old, vacant buildings; conversion of empty property to offices; adaption of redundant schools; building of new units, as at Barvas); provision of land, as at Stornoway; finance (encouragement of participation in HIDB schemes); advice (the Council's own development officer compliments that of the HIDB, a local craft council has been set up); tourism (a large grant is paid to the Western Isles Tourism Council); training (through extensive participation in job creation programmes unemployment once fell below 7%, material and other non-labour costs were financed by HIDB 50%, WIIC 35%, and the sponsor 15%); Youth Opportunities Programme (there is no shortage of sponsors and there is a local Area Board); research and development into local and natural resources (aliginate, crabs, other shellfish, fish farming, peat); lobbying (against the proposed diesel areas electricity surcharge; continuance of the Arnish yard; establishment of consultative committees for crofting and fishing); transport (campaigning for a Road Equivalent Traffic on the ferries to the mainland — small vehicle ferries run by the Council run to RET rates).

In 1976 the Chairman of the HIDB visited Co. Donegal and was impressed by the success of local co-operatives. This led to the Board in 1977 establishing its Community Co-operative Scheme and the appointment in November 1977 of two Gaelic-speaking field officers in the Western Isles. When a co-operative (*co-chomunn*) is set up the Board matches local capital £1 for £1 on the condition that the co-operative is run on a one-member, one-vote principle. Normally an Establishment Grant is about £20,000. A 100% management grant of around £15,000 per annum is available for the first three years, followed by 50% for a further two years. In addition, *co-chomunn* is eligible for the usual 50% (occasionally 70%) HIDB assistance in grants or loans.

Every *co-chomunn* has a Gaelic identity and all but one in the

Western Isles a Gaelic name. Use of Gaelic by the field workers encouraged both confidence and trust. Gaelic at last has become a language of business, at least in less formal day-to-day administration. However, some of the managerial appointments have not been Gaelic speakers. In the Western Isles it is estimated that the *co-chomunn* have generated 28 full-time and 50 part-time equivalent jobs. The locations, employment and turnover in 1986 were as shown in Table 7.8.

At the present time, assistance to community co-operatives takes up about 2% of the Board's annual budget. Retailing in one form or another is the dominant activity. Other activities include salmon fishing, peat extraction, transport, catering, community hall management, knitwear, crafts, upholstery, tourism, building work, barwork, JCB operation, trout farming, horticulture, coal trading, fish processing and marketing, chandelry and DIY. Most co-operatives emerged out of some specific local development opportunity, for example the threatened closure of a village shop.

In October 1985 some 20 community enterprises in the HIDB area came together to form an association of their 3,500 individual members. The Association of Community Enterprises in the Highlands and Islands

TABLE 7.8 *Co-chomunn locations, employment and turnover in 1986*

Name	*All year*		*Seasonal*		*Out*		
	F	*P*	*FT*	*PT*	*workers*	*Trainees*	*Sales (£)*
Barra Community Co-op	2	1	1	0	0	0	133,000
Co Chomunn an Iochdair	3	2	0	1	0	0	201,000
Co Chomunn Bhatarsaidh	2	0	1	0	0	0	94,600
Co Chomunn Eirisgeidh	3	0	0	0	15	0	236,000
Co Chomunn na Hearadh	10	6	1	0	60	1	322,000
Co Chomunn na Pairc	6	0	0	0	60	0	102,800
Co Chomunn Scalpaidh	2	1	0	0	0	0	15,000
Totals	28	10	3	1	135	1	1,104,400

now produces its own magazine (which includes articles in Gaelic). Links are also maintained with Ireland.

The initial HIDB Community Enterprise programme was due to expire in 1986. It has, however, been extended for a further three years with £250,000 available per year in addition to normal grants and loans. The recognised positive and valuable features of community enterprises are: 94% of financial assistance goes to '*fragile areas*'; they are created and controlled by local people; they supply new or improved local services and exploit local resources; they are a reasonably cost effective method of creating employment; they have an educational and confidence raising effect; once created they can exploit new development opportunities; profits are retained locally.

To date one co-operative, Co Chomunn Nis in Lewis, has failed and has gone into voluntary liquidation. A pioneer Co Chomunn established in November 1979, its main trade was in agriculture requisits. Following its demise in February 1986 the Association is looking for guidelines to prevent similar occurrences. Not listed above is the Keose Co-operative who took over an alginate plant and who collect, dry and grind seaweed. Sixteen full time real jobs have been generated and an annual turnover of £300,000. Diversification into salmon farming and mussel cultivation has since taken place.

Besides a potential long term economic impact, the *co-chomunn* have great potential for strengthening the social and cultural fabric of community life. From its natural community base Gaelic has been discreetly introduced into a minor business domain where previously English was the norm.

The largest single public investment in the Western Isles in recent years has been the £57 million Integrated Development Programme. This has been funded 60% by the Department of Agriculture Scotland (DAFS) and 40% by the European Economic Community (EEC) and commenced in September 1982, for a five-year period. There is a steering committee comprising representatives of DAFS, WIIC, HIDB, the Scottish Economic Development Department, the North of Scotland College of Acriculture and the Crofters Commission. The overall economic and social objectives were set as: to increase income and employment opportunities; to maintain the indigenous population, to preserve the islands' communities and to build up a reservoir of skilled persons; to add value to Western Isles products, to encourage greater economic self-sufficiency and to maximise investment within the Isles; to promote a level of infrastructure on services necessary for economic and social needs; to encourage and support community effort, self reliance, identity and culture; to maintain a proper balance between human needs and the environment.

Grants paid to December 1986 amounted to £14.8 million, in the following categories: land improvement schemes (£8.4 million); building and machinery (£2.4 million); livestock improvement scheme (£1.7 million); livestock marketing (£0.6 million); fish farming (£3.3 million); fish processing and marketing (£1.4 million); miscellaneous (£0.3 million). Grant aid was at 75% for land improvements, 75% for buildings and marketing and 50% for machinery.

The 6,000 crofts in the Western Isles have 24,000 ha of in-bye land and it was hoped to improve 13,000 ha over five years at a cost of £1.6 million, although by December 1986 some £7.3 million had been spent, hence increasing grazing and reducing the need for feed substitutes. At present the lack of winter fodder and the cost of imported feed results in livestock being sold off in the autumn. An estimated 10,000 acres of common land was to be improved at a cost of £1 million to lengthen the grazing season and improve stock condition, in fact £1.4 million was spent. One-fifth of the coastal machair was scheduled for re-seeding and draining, a total of 1,000 ha. Here, there is a serious clash with conservation interests (Grade I National Nature Reserves and Sites of Special Scientific Interest (SSSIs) cover 13% of the Western Isles and 40% of the land area) although expenditure here was only £50,000 compared with an estimated £300,000. National Scenic Areas cover 40% of the land area as well. The machair is the habitat for 40% of Britains corncrakes, 14% of the plovers, 19% of the dunlins and 50% of the greylags. The herb rich sward contains over 60 different species. However, except in financial extent the agricultural measures are scarely different from the pattern of support over the past 20 to 30 years.

One of the traditional weaknesses of Western Isles agriculture has been marketing. The formation of the Highlands and Islands Livestock Limited (HILL) has provided a marketing body for west coast and island crofters. It represents 1,000 producers, including 450 in Lewis. Each area has a 'fieldsman' who is trained in the grading of lambs. HILL's job is to sell the stock, co-ordinate transport, gather in money and pay it out again. Crofts gain convenience and stability of prices. A new mart has been provided at Lochmaddy and another is proposed at Lochboisdale. Lochmaddy slaughterhouse has been upgraded and new ones built at Tarbert and on Barra to supplement the existing Stornoway abattoir. The HIDB is investigating the feasibility of a small-scale sheep meat processing plant on Lewis.

Social funds from the EC will enable a further £35.6 million of expenditure. This will mainly go on roads, piers and ferries. It will however, include: tourism (£2.7 million); exploitation of seaweed resources (£0.8 million); promotion of Harris Tweed Industry (£0.8 million); mineral exploitation (£1.0 million). Under the IDP the development of berthing and landing sites has been approved at Kallin (Grimsay), Griminish (N. Uist), Scalpay, Kirkibost, Poll na Cran (Benbecula), Berneray, Orosay (S. Uist) and Tong (Uist). Other slipway priorities required include Petersport, Loch Ceann Dibig and Cheesebay, followed by Carloway, Leverburgh, Skigersta, Miavaig, Scalpay and Breasclete.

Despite its intent of being an 'Integrated Development Programme', there was little revolutionary about its content. An 'Agricultural Development Programme' might have been a better title with such a high proportion of the funding going towards agriculture, notably land improvement and fencing. However, the project did concentrate on development of the islands' natural resources and not importing external 'solutions' to essentially local problems.

The Report of Survey for the Western Isles Structure Plan was published in November 1983. The tone of the entire report is set in the 'Background' section:

> The Western Isles in common with many other parts of the Highlands and Islands has, over the past 250 years, experienced social and economic changes which, in many instances have been severe and which have contributed significantly to the formation of the 'character' of the area today. It is necessay, in addition to appreciating the social and economic changes which have taken (and are taking) place, to consider two further elements which have been, and still are, important to the formation of the 'way of life' and 'character' of the area. The geography (location, form, physiography) of the area, and the existence of a language different from that of the country as a whole must be recognised as being basic to an understanding of the area, its history and its development.
>
> Many of the planning and development problems and opportunities which the Structure Plan must tackle have their origins or background in the historical/geographical/linguistic context. It is important therefore to view the remaining chapters of the Report of Survey against this background. (Comhairle nan Eilean, 1983)

Contrary to popular expectations the population of the Western Isles is quite urbanised. Of the 30,700 resident population in 1981 (an increase of 7% over 1971) 40% live in and around Stornoway in the

Broadbay area. By island areas the total population is distributed: Lewis — 66%; Harris — 9%; Uists and Benbecula — 20%, and Barra — 5%. Relative to Scotland, the Western Isles has more young people, less working age people and more elderly and the very old. Between 1971 and 1981 population growth occurred in the Barra, Benbecula and Broadbay area. Net in-migration 1971–81 was in contrast to the selective out-migration of past decades which gave rise to the current unbalanced age structure. It is envisaged that overall the population will stabilise with small scale growth or decline in certain areas. In economic terms crofting and pluralism dominate the work pattern.

The draft Written Statement for the Western Isles Structure Plan was issued in November 1986. It mainly addressed three key issues: (1) the lack of job opportunities throughout the area, in particular outwith Stornoway and Balivanich; (2) the provision and maintenance of an efficient communications network both within the islands and between the islands and the mainland which does not penalise the users as a result of the insular nature of the area; (3) the provision and maintenance of service and facilities appropriate to the needs of the dispersed settlement pattern of the Western Isles. Among the aims is included 'to safeguard and promote the unique cultural and linguistic attributes of the area'. This aim is to be achieved through a series of 22 objectives. Promotion of economic development in the islands is seen as a greater importance than resolving land use conflict. Thus a policy area/strategic network approach is adopted which involves: (1) identification of parts of the Isles where similar policies may be applied to similar problems, concentrating on dynamic principles and a common direction; (2) identification of a strategic network of settlements or groups of crofting townships which is superimposed on to the policy areas. This *de facto* acknowledges selective action in the future in determining priorities for expenditure both in locational and chronological terms.

Settlements in the Western Isles can be categorised into six levels: (1) Stornoway — the main industrial, commercial, service and administrative centre; (2) local administrative, educational, transport, housing, health centres, etc. — Tarbert, Balivanich, Daliburgh, Castlebay; (3) more localised centres than (2) e.g. Ness, Shawbost, Carloway, Back, Bayble, Leurbost, Balallan, Leverburgh, Scalpay, Lochmaddy, Bayhead, Iochdar, Lochboisdale; (4) settlements with a primary school and other service functions; (5) townships with only minimal facilities; (6) very small settlements with no facilities.

After identifying the various facilities of the settlements a broad geographical/functional analysis of the Western Isles showed four main zones: (1) areas dependent upon or directly related to Stornoway — an inner commuter area of Stornoway and its environs, a traditional area where commuting and traditional activities co-exist, and an outer area where traditional activities dominate but with some commuting; (2) areas of more productive agriculture on the machair land (3) remote and/or hilly areas where traditional activities dominate, but few settlements and poor roads; (4) the populous small islands of Vatersay, Eriksay, Berneray and Scalpay.

Out of this classification emerges four policy areas: (1) *Central Policy Areas* — Stornoway and Balivanich — with a concentration of employment and population; (2) *Intermediate Policy Areas* within commuting distance of Stornoway and Balivanich but mainly dependent on traditional activities and with local services; (3) *Peripheral Policy Areas* which are remote, sparsely populated and have poor communications — both isolated parts of the 'mainland' or offshore islands; (4) *Moorland Policy Areas*, which are virtually uninhabited and used for extensive grazing and game.

The Written Statement contains detailed Strategic Land Use Policies which can be implemented by *Comhairle nan Eilean,* Supporting Policies which it is considered desirable to include in the Plan as they contribute to the implementation of the land use aspects and Proposals for implementing both sets of policies by the Council and other bodies. These policies concern the topics of: general economic development; agriculture; fishing; minerals; industry and commerce; transport and communications; settlements and services. The emphasis throughout is on development based on the evolution of local resources, both physical and human, but recognising the dominant role of Stornoway and Balivanich as centres of paid employment and services. Proposals for specific projects are dispersed throughout the isles. In addition there is an element of positive discrimination in favour of the Peripheral Policy Areas on the 'mainland' and inhabited off-isles. These mainly involve investment in infrastructure, economic development and roads.

The Central Policy Areas include the two areas with the lowest incidence of Gaelic speaking: (1) Stornoway/Broadbay extending to and including Back, Eye Peninsula, Leurbost/Crossbost/Ranish and Achmore where the percentage of Gaelic speakers increases outwards from 57% in Stornoway town to an inner band of 65–70% and then increases to 78–94% in the crofting townships; (2) North-west Benbecula and North-west South Uist, including Balivanich, Creagorry and Iochdar — outside

Balivanich with ED figures of 4–35%, the remainder of the area is in the range of 78–89%. Looking through past censuses the range of figures has been very similar with only slight percentage decreases over the decades.

'The Peripheral Policy Areas' on the mainland are: west Uig beyond Gisla power station (84–95%); north Pairc west of Balallan (82–96%); Rhenigidale — a roadless township on the Harris mainland (100%); north Harris along the B887 (99%); southern Bays of Harris (86%); with Scalpay (95%); Berneray (91%); Eriksay (97%); Vatersay (90%) on the off-isles. Except on the off-isles where the revival of fishing has brought young people back to the islands (although sometimes with non-Gaelic-speaking wives and children) most of the Peripheral Policy Areas have an aged population structure.

The Highlands and Islands Development Board

The HIDB was established by Parliament in 1965 as a radical answer to the needs of a neglected area affected by economic decline, social fragmentation and steady depopulation. Within its area of remit dwell over 46,000 Gaelic speakers who comprise 20% of the population of the Board's area and who are 57% of all Scotland's Gaels.

To spur the development process the Board was given wider powers and more scope for initiative than any other United Kingdom development agency. They can: make grants, loans, or packages of both, meeting up to 50% — or exceptionally 70% — of the cost of any private development; buy shares and appoint directors in any enterprise; provide specialist business advice and support services such as job training; acquire, sell and manage land, and construct building, for let or sale for industrial or other use; assist social development projects; sponsor publicity and marketing for the area, or for local companies; set up and run businesses at their own hand; undertake strategic planning with other public and private organisations, and commission research and feasibility studies.

In the ten years to December 1983 the HIDB approved assistance totalling £175 million (at 1983 prices), creating or retaining an estimated 23,500 jobs in 7,000 enterprises. Three-quarters of all grants and loans have been made to applicants from within the Highlands and Islands. Responsibility for promoting commercial projects is divided between four functional divisions: fisheries; industries development and marketing; rural land development (including farming and forestry), and tourism.

The Board has seen three phases of operation. The early period between 1965 and 1970 saw the development of policies. The Western Isles were not among the Board's growth centres, perhaps thankfully so if it avoided encouraging in-migration on a large scale. Of relevance to the Gaelic west coast and islands was the Fisheries Development Scheme with grants and loans for new and second-hand boats. Tourism, was also an important factor in these early years, receiving 45% of grants.

The period 1971–5 was the oil years. There was also the continued development of fisheries, especially fish processing. However, Lewis lagged behind in fishing and in 1974/75 fish prices fell. Growth in tourism contined.

Since 1976 adjustments have been made in the light of local government reorganisation. The Board lost its regional planning role in Highland Region and showed new interest in the west coast and islands. It has also been an era of decentralisation. Since 1977 there has been a permanent office in Stornoway. In 1976–8 tourism consumed over a third of the annual budgets. Lewis saw the development of onshore fishing related industry such as the Breasclete fishing processing plant which was intended to dry ling and blue whiting for export to Scandinavia and West Africa. Much of the literature of the Board extols the potential of the Highlands and Islands by external industrial interests through large grants for incomers. Scorn and mistrust has grown up with the Board's area over the refusal of small grants to extend local businesses.

The initial Board in 1965 did not contain a single Gaelic speaker. Of the current Consultative Committee of 31 members only two are Gaelic speakers. In its early years the Board did directly sponsor certain Gaelic language projects such as the *Club Leabhar* book club and a Gaelic Learners' LP course in 1966. However, a 1969 study on the problems of the Galway *Gaeltacht* in Western Ireland felt that the HIDB had 'no interest in Gaelic'. In 1977 a seminar on bilingualism was convened and the *Cliath* primary school book project received a £6,000 grant. The year 1978 saw a report produced on Gaelic broadcasting.

The Board's Gaelic conscience then awoke and a working party was set up which produced the report *Cor na Gaidhlig* in November 1982. This lead to the establishment in 1986 of *Comunn na Gaidhlig (CnaG)* in partnership with the WIIC, HR, SR, and *An Comunn Gaidhealach*. Subsequent Gaelic projects funded include a forum on Gaelic and youth in 1983, the funding of the adult learners body 'CLI' for three years 1983–6 and £1,500 in 1986 to subsidise three drama weeks at *An Sabhal Mor Ostaig*. Rarely has a specific Gaelic project not been funded. In the Board's first 17 years of existence very few applications were made. In the following two years grants in excess of the previous total were paid out. Much of this increase stems from ideas recommended in the report of the Working Group into the language.

The Board's budget in 1984/5 was £41 million. Almost half (£18 million) was spent on grants and loans, 80% of all applications coming from within the area. Of the cases approved 53% are for sums less than £5,000, 75% are for sums less than £10,000, 89% are for sums less than £25,000.

In 1983 it cost the Board £4,409 for every job created. In the same year the Board assisted 450 firms at a cost of £6,215 million — an average of £13,000 per firm. In addition, 54 social cases were approved at a total cost of £144,000 — £1,600 each in average.

Many of the HIDB's activities duplicate the work of the WIIC in the Western Isles. Between 1976 and 1980 the HIDB supported 315 projects on the Western Isles. Grants of £2,785 million was paid out and loans of £5,940 million. It is estimated that this created 770 new jobs and retained a further 560. The Board has developed industrial sites at Parkend in Stornoway and Barvas in Lewis.

Recently the contents of the Board's Structure Plan for 1986–91 became known. The aim is to increase the ratio of private to public investment to a level of 7 : 2. This will penalise development promoted by local people without much access to capital. The Western Isles and Skye and Lodalsh are now regarded as 'fragile' and in need of 'special attention and a high level of assistance'. The proportion of spending on factory building is to increase at the expense of that on training 'to reflect lower demand for company training and a reduction of the commitment to supporting MSC Community Programme'. Fish farming is seen as a growth sector, especially in salmon, with diversification into other species such as halibut.

For the Western Isles the Board's priorities are: positive discrimination across the Board's full range of programmes — areas of particular high need include Harris, Barra and Vatersay; strengthening of crofting communities by encouraging diversification and co-operation; maintenance of the momentum in sectors assisted under the Integrated Development Programme; promotion of the Gaelic language and culture, integrated with economic initiatives where appropriate. For Skye and Lochalsh the priorities are: promotion of more intensive levels of agricultural and other activity in crofting townships; encouragement for self-help and co-operative initiatives in all sectors of the local economy; promotion of the Gaelic language and culture. In 1987 the Board is to fund a £250,000 industrial estate at Broadford on Skye.

Unless the provision of sufficient private capital is unavailable in these areas these new priorities give greater hope for holistic community development in the future.

Comunn na Gaidhlig

Comunn na Gaidhlig resulted from a report prepared for the HIDB in November 1982 and began to function in 1984. Section 5 of the report entitled *Language, Community and Development: the Gaelic Situation*, examines the connections between '*Language and Development*'.

Extract from Section 5 of the report: Language, Community and Development: the Gaelic Situation (1982)

It begins by saying:

Throughout history there is considerable evidence of co-incidence between the linguistic decay and the social and economic disintegration of communities. In the case of Gaeldom the linguistic decline of the past two hundred years has co-incided with periods of intense hardship and a general economic decline. If that economic decline has been stemmed to some extent in recent years, it should also been noted that this has coincided with a period of heightened linguistic awareness. Since an increasing number of bodies take pragmatic decisions based on such co-incidence, and since it is increasingly becoming a matter for international research and thus offers potentially beneficial global linkages, it is a matter which should increasingly exercise development authorities in the Highlands.

and continues:

There is ample recent evidence of the Gael returning to the Gaelic communal ambience when given the opportunity, and this participating in and adding to the economic development of the area. Numerous well-attested examples have been noted in the oil-related construction yards at Arnish and Kishorn: a few years ago the fishing industry in islands like Scalpay, Eriskay, Vatersay and Barra produced examples of similar phenomenon. We have already noted that the creation of Comhairle nan Eilean has added a new and welcome dimension to the Gaelic intelligentsia, while Fearann Eilean Iarmain has also persuaded young Gaels to return home.

A new and interesting example of this tendency is beginning to emerge. The extension of Gaelic education in Highland primary schools seems to be playing a role in influencing Gaelic parents to return to an area where their children may have the benefits of a bilingual education. Thus the children bring back with them parents who, having gained new skills and perspectives elsewhere, are still young enough to bring constructive elements back to a community from which they have not become too distanced by time.

An examination of a range of development projects in the indigenous Gaelic areas of the Highlands over the past fifteen years suggests that many of them have been linguistically and culturally erosive. The fact that they have not been recognised as being so would seem to depend on two factors — the cultural dimension had as yet hardly entered into the developmental equation in Scotland, and such development as has taken place in the Gaelic areas has tended to be diffuse and on a relatively small scale.

But though individual development projects in the Gaelic areas have tended to be small and scattered, the cumulative effect of development strategy has undoubtedly been to dilute both language and culture.

The tourist industry is probably the development sector which has done most to undermine the viability of the Gaelic language and culture within its native environment, not through the large but ephemeral annual influx of visitors, but through the very considerable influx of new residents who have come to service the industry. Why the industry should have this apparent imbalance of incomers as opposed to local people involved in it is no real mystery. If one accepts that only a certain proportion of any population will have the necessary skill, incentive and access to financial resources to make a go of tourism, then clearly the actual number of people who have these particular attributes within the Gaelic community is infinitesimally small compared with the numbers outside. But the Highlands generally, and the Gaelic areas within them, are one of Britain's main tourist assets in terms of scenery and environment, and can support a tourist industry on a scale far beyond the resources of the local people to service on their own. Hence a major anglicising influence permeates the whole area, and its high public profile tends to further diminish the status of the Gaelic language.

The grievance has frequently been heard in the Highlands and Islands that development policies actively favour the incomer at the expense of the local person. There does not seem to be much evidence to support an accusation of deliberate bias in this respect on the part of the development authorities, though several circumstances may conspire to give such a grievance a semblance of credibility. The Highlands, after all, are under-populated and under-developed and, given the financial aid available for development, are a natural target area for talented entrepreneurs from the more populous parts of Britain which may be short on development opportunities, as, indeed, we have just noted in regard to the tourist industry. Such incomers may also come from a background which allows them to approach and speak to development agencies with an ease and confidence which history and communal experience have eroded in many local people of equal skill and talent. But what really matters is that a niggling irritation at being forced to accept cultural change imposed from without still lingers under the surface in many Highland, and particularly Gaelic, localities; and such irritation is as likely to lead to apathy as it is to positive assertion, and is thus likely to be counter-productive to any kind of development.

To the extent that development strategies in the highlands have hitherto omitted to take account of a linguistic and cultural dimension it does seem that the local grievance of receiving inequitable treatment has some basis in fact. Certainly most developments that have taken place have contained within them factors which have been both supportive and inimical to Gaelic language and culture; supportive to the extent that they provide employment which retains Gaelic-speaking families in their indigenous area, inimical in the sense that they attract non-Gaelic speakers into an already fragile linguistic and cultural arena; and most developments seem to contain within them these contradictory factors at one and the same time. The Irish experience shows how difficult it is to neutralise this inherent tension even when linguistic and cultural dimensions have an explicit role in regional and communal development; when such dimensions are ignored it follows that development strategies can be accused of being blindly and needlessly destructive of the local cultural base and local cultural aspirations.

If this is true, not only are development policies guilty of destroying a large and important part of the persona and identity of the area and community they set out to regenerate, but they are also guilty of eroding part of the potential basis for wider future development and of negating the effort and resources devoted to a more holistic approach to the development question by other agencies in the field. Thus the operation of a bilingual school, for instance, might be brought to nought by thoughtlessly placing beside it a major development heavily dependent on incoming population. This is not to argue that such a development ought not to take place, but that the linguistic and cultural factors should be considered as part of the wider development equation, and that all steps be taken to strengthen the cultural make-up of the community so that it could hope to absorb such a development if it was found on balance that it should go ahead. . . . From *Language, Community and Development: the Gaelic Situation* (1982)

A conscious appreciation on the part of developers of the interdependence of the social, cultural and economic domains in community life is one of the crucial factors in long-term community development. A healthy linguistic situation can be a considerable source of community strength. There is a need for a holistic approach to development following initiatives taken along linguistic and cultural channels within the Gaelic community.

> It now seems clear that to think of development largely in terms of attracting massive industrial investment to the area is futile, and a look back over the experience of the last twenty years shows that it never was an option of real significance in the more fragile crofting areas of the west. Highland Region's current attachment to the slogan 'Small is beautiful' would seem to be a realistic assessment of the situation from the local perspective. Thus, the western seaboard and island communities are largely going to be thrown back on a process of regeneration from within their own resources. And one of the basic resources of these communities — as much part of their communal make-up as their response to the sea and the land — is their language and culture.

How might holistic development take place? In the field of tourist-related initiatives several ideas have been mooted; for example: establishment of a *Bureau Fiosrachaidh Gaidhlig*/Gaelic Information Bureau in Edinburgh to deal with all Gaelic related tourist matters (festivals, Gaelic week-ends, Gaelic Hotels/B&B — this would develop the smaller-scale initiatives already began by the Western Isles Tourist Board through their *Gaelhols* scheme and by *An Sabhal Mor Ostaig*; promotion of indigenous foods in Gaelic speaking areas; provision and distribution of source materials in Gaelic for interpretative centres, museums, accommodation. One of the major sources of funding for Gaelic related initiatives in the Gaelic-speaking communities has been and is likely to continue to the HIDB. It was recommended that the Board: displays a Gaelic face to the Gaelic community through a greater degree of bilingualism; appoints Gaelic speakers to posts in the Gaelic-speaking areas and in other parts where there is a large degree of contact with the Gaelic community; examines its development policies and strategies to ensure that they include the cultural and linguistic dimension, including the definition of a 'Gaelic factor' which could be routinely brought into play at an early stage in the consideration of individual developments and projects.

The national policy for Gaelic, in *Comunn na Gaidhlig's* opinion, should recognise the principle that community development has social and cultural (including linguistic) dimensions as well as purely economic ones. In practice this has two main implications; that economic development can be either highly supportive of or inimical to linguistic development. All other government agencies involved in the development of the Gaelic communities, e.g. the Industry Department for Scotland, Department of Agriculture and Fisheries for Scotland, the Scottish Development Department and the HIDB, should give active recognition to the principle of the interdependence of the social, cultural and economic domains in community life as this relates to Gaelic.

In their submission to the review of the Highland Regional Council's Structure Plan *Comunn na Gaidhlig* made the following comments:

- the development of indigenous resources should be central to the strategy
- natural resources — the land and the sea
- human resources — the potential and culture of the people;
- that the Gaelic influence is an integral part of the heritage of the whole of the Highland Region;
- past mistakes where economic development initiatives have offered economic advancement at the expense of the language and culture of the people and a more negative than positive effect in terms of community development should be seen as such;
- people who receive mixed messages about their linguistic and cultural identity and personal worth are not likely to be motivated to participate actively and enthusiastically in development initiatives;
- conversely, communities whose language and culture are valued by the powers that be are most likely to have the self-confidence to become involved in the process of development;
- recognition of the linguistic and cultural identity of the Gaelic-speaking peoples for the area should be one of the basic factors in the development strategy for the Highland Region. This is particularly true for the areas in which the language is strongest, but the dynamics of linguistics and cultural interaction are such that any coherent strategy must make appropriate provision for the language and culture in all areas in which it exists.

The Gaelic presence in the Highland Region was categorised by *CnaG* into three groups: (1) areas where the language is the language of the community, e.g. in parts of Skye such as Staffin and Sleat; (2) areas where there are large concentrations of native Gaelic speakers in a mainly English mileu, e.g. Inverness and Fort William; (3) areas where the language is weaker but still with residual pockets of native Gaelic speakers and a number of learners. In planning for social and economic development, authorities should have regard to the implications of their strategies for the cultural environment and should seek to identify opportunities to strengthen the cultural and linguistic fabric of the community. For example, new council housing should be provided in crofting townships rather than in growth centres such as Portree or Broadford. Development of tourism should be seen in terms of benefit to the community and not the visitor. Museum and interpretative services should be based on the principle of validation of the language and culture of the area. In the field of Nature Conservation a balance is seen to be needed between the development of a flourishing rural economy through greater educational and interpretative facilities and through staffing policies. Relevant educational and training facilities in the coastal areas could provide the younger indigenous population with the skills needed to develop the fisheries industry — catching, handling, processing and marketing.

The 1986/7 work programme of *CnaG* consists of six areas: (1) community development — linking of language with social and economic development; (2) work with parents, young persons and children; (3) education; (4) language development research and planning; (5) language promotion; (6) establishment of a national policy framework. The four aims of *CnaG* include 'to confirm the integral position of the Gaelic language in the economic, social, moral and cultural development of the Gaelic speaking community' (CnaG, 1986).

The Montgomery Report (1984)

In their evidence to the Montgomery Committee on the powers and functions of the unitary islands councils in Scotland, the Western Isles Islands Council believed that if the islands were to progress in the economic field the people in the islands will require strengthened confidence through the preservation of their cultural background. Economic prosperity is interrelated with cultural activities. However, in order to restore and develop community confidence the Council needed additional finance. This was necessary to further develop the Gaelic element of bilingualism in the primary schools, to increase the degree of Gaelic teaching in secondary schools and for other visible aspects of bilingualism such as road signs and the public face of the islands council. *Comhairle nan Eilean* also wanted to take over some of the economic development functions of the HIDB (and health authority functions and airports). They claimed that reorganisation in 1975 had been a success and wanted to build on it. The Wheatley Report had earlier stated that 'local government should be regarded as the first choice for the assignment of public services to be provided on a local basis'. *Ad hoc* boards were to be avoided. In this context it should be noted that 83% of HIDB funding to industry and business is less than £25,000 per project, the average in 1983 being just over £17,000 per enterprise.

The Faroese Situation

In contrast to the Western Isles there is a ring of confidence radiating from the Faroe Islands. This group of 18 inhabited islands and a few uninhabited islets with a total area of about 1,400 sq. km. (540 sq. miles) lie isolated in the North Atlantic in latitude 62 degrees about midway between the Shetland Islands and Iceland. Faroese is the main language of the islanders. The population today is around 44,000 and with the exception of about 3,000 foreigners (mainly Danish) all speak Faroese fluently. In addition there are about 10,000 Faroese speakers living outside the islands, mainly in Denmark.

Since the Home Rule Act of 1948 settled the legal position and rights for the Faroese language both the linguistic, cultural and economic situation has been revolutionised. In the first two years up to the age of nine years of school only Faroese is taught. From then on Danish is introduced and later on English. Secondary education has been decentralised with 69 lower schools providing the first seven years of education with 97% of pupils living at home. Eighteen of these schools are also lower secondary and cater for the next three years of education. Afterwards there are seven upper secondary schools throughout the islands. Then there is a choice of navigation, technical, business, nursing and teaching training colleges in the islands and the Faroese Academy provides the first two years of university education in certain subjects.

Seven newspapers are published in the islands, one of which is in both Danish and Faroese and six entirely Faroese. Twenty magazines are published in the language. About 40 book titles are published annually, half educational and half poetry, novels and stories. Three towns have specialist bookshops. Established in 1957 the islands' radio station broadcasts 50 hours per week, nearly all in Faroese. Television commenced transmission in 1984 and broadcasts three hours per day. About 18% of television programmes are in Faroese (62% of which are news, current affairs or religious) and 82% in other languages. There is a semi-professional theatre company and several amateur companies. Both the biggest religious sects, the Plymouth Bretheren and the Danish National Church (Lutheran), now use Faroese almost entirely. In 1952 the Faroese Academy of Science was founded. There has been a lectureship in Faroese at the University of Copenhagen since 1936 (which was upgraded to a chair in 1953). Since 1975 the islands have issued their own stamps, passports and bank notes. Postage stamps create an income of £2.5 million and provide 50 jobs. No wonder that many Faroese would like to dispense with Danish altogether!

Along with cultural prosperity there has been economic prosperity. The backbone of the economy is fishing with 45% of the catch coming from the 200 miles exclusive fishing zone. Some 300 boats totalling 40,000 tons catch around 300,000 tons of fish each year. This generates 98% of the islands' exports, 28% of the Gross National Product and 25% of the employment. Numbers of fishermen, however, fell from 4,300 in 1960 to 3,200 in 1970. The sales organisation *Foroya Fiskasola*, established in 1948, controls between 80% and 90% of fish exports. Its 20 filleting factories and two fish meal plants produce over 200 fish derived products. In recent years fish farming for salmon and trout has grown in importance.

Only 34 sq. miles of land, 6% of the total, is cultivated. Agriculture accounts for 1.6% of the workforce and 3.5% of the Gross National Product. The islands are self sufficient in milk, but their 80,000 sheep do not enable self sufficiency in sheep products. In fact 60% of food is imported.

From the needs of the fishing industry two modern shipyards employing 300 men have developed. Other local industries include cord and rope manufacture, brewing, paints, detergents, ceramics, toilet and kitchen products, knitwear, clothing, building industry components, plastics and soap. Some 63% of all exports go to Denmark, but only 15% of exports come from that country. Tourism, based on scenery and rod fishing, is a growing industry. Sixteen hotels throughout the islands have 820 beds and four youth hostels accommodate 235 persons. In addition, bed and breakfast accommodation is available and three camp sites provide for the hardiest visitors.

Since 1948 internal transport has been revolutionised. Two pairs of islands have been linked by bridges. New roads run along cliffs, through mountains and across sounds. The small tidal range assists the operation of the good internal car ferry service and regular passenger ferries serve all other inhabited islands. Bus services link all the main settlements. In 1954 a large new hydro-electric power station was opened at Stromo. Together with small water powered and diesel stations all settlements are now supplied with mains electricity. Locally produced coal provides two-thirds of house fuel.

The islands have two banks, three saving banks and an insurance company. Fifty communes, ranging from Torshavn with 14,000 inhabitants to the smallest with just 26 people, provide local services financed by local income tax. There are three doctors and 1.5 dentists per 1,000 population. The three main hospitals have 340 beds between them. Faroese central income tax provide 55% of government expenditure, the remaining 45% being funded by a block grant from Denmark. However, the foreign debt now exceeds £70 million.

Despite a growing population and cultural and economic prosperity, between 1961 and 1965 some quarter of the natural population growth emigrated in search of work and employment. In 1970 an Investment Fund was set up to promote diversification through 90% loans at less than market rates and a wide range of incentives are available. There is no shortage of entrepreneurs, especially from Faroese previously working in Denmark and elsewhere. In order to diversify the economy away from fishing the following courses are being followed: further development of fish processing to increase the value added and reduce transport costs; fish farming of trout and salmon; development of knitwear as an export industry; processing of alginate; development of the merchant shipping, including new ferry links with Scotland and Scandinavia; exporting of technical advice in shipping.

Conclusions

The cardinal issue is to maintain the economic viability of the area where there is still substantial Gaelic communities and to give the language and the literature the prestige they deserve. There is a subtle connection between a pride in a language and the distinctive life-style it conveys and the social morale needed to maintain and develop a community. This has been observed in many places (such as the Faroese Islands). It would therefore need to be an integral part of statesmanship concerned with the rehabilitation of outlying areas to encourage Gaels in Gaeldom.

The preceeding sections have demonstrated that there are few Gaelic speaking communities remaining in Scotland. Despite the anglicising influence of Stornoway and Balivanich only the Western Isles can be thought of as a predominantly Gaelic area, with 80% of its population able to speak Gaelic in the 1981 Census. The responsibility upon *Comhairle nan Eilean* is therefore great. In the absence of an influential Lord of the Isles, *Comhairle nan Eilean* must lead Gaeldom. This is true for educational matters (and very wise policy decisions will have to be taken in terms of location of educational establishments and the role and status of Gaelic in the current review of the provision of primary and secondary education in the Western Isles) and economic matters. *Comhairle nan Eilean* must have wisdom, finance and power. Good Christians are wise people. Only the Scottish Office can supply adequate financial resources. There is a substantive case for strengthening the powers of *Comhairle nan Eilean* (and the Orkney and Shetland Isles Islands Councils) to include much of the powers of the HIDB. Additional responsibilities should include the ownership and management of airports and harbours currently vested in other public bodies. Further education linked to economic development of the islands' resources needs to be developed. Newspapers, radio and television in Gaelic must be expanded. The three great natural resources of the area — the land, the sea and the people — must be developed in harmony and import substition industries encouraged behind the tariff of freight charges. Inter-island links must be strengthened further, particularly Barra to South Uist and North Uist to Harris. A credit union could revitalise the financial sector.

The draft Structure Plan for the Western Isles — *Dreach Aithisg Sgriobhte Comhairle nan Eilean* — provides a sound basis for the survival of Gaelic in the Western Isles through its recognition of the uniqueness of the area, and the need for jobs, improved internal communications and retention and provision of services on a dispersed pattern in accordance to the distribution of the population. (It is the Gaelic speaking population that is most dispersed.) The Aims, Objectives, Strategic Land Use Policies and, especially, the Supporting Policies of the draft Plan based on the three types of Policy Areas and Strategic Settlement Network interpret the problems and suggest ways forward to a future for the islands. What is in fact proposed is holistic development which respects and builds upon the pluralistic nature of the islands' economy. It is to be hoped that the Secretary of State when he is asked to approve the final Plan will not insist on standardising the Plan to fit the mainland model.

From a strong base on the Western Isles there can then be the potential of supplying the other Gaelic speaking communities on the islands of Skye, Raasay and Canna with external assistance on their constant battle against local sources of anglicisation. Both groups of communities can then assist the survival of vestige Gaelic communities on the other islands and the mainland and provide a linguistic homeland for exiles and learners in the cities and other parts of Scotland.

There is a future for Gaelic-speaking communities in Scotland if the correct steps are taken now.

Bibliography — Scotland

ADAMS, B. 1983, Conflict in the Western Isles. *Geographical Magazine* July 1983.

Argyll & Bute District Council 1984a, *Islay, Jura and Colonsay Local Plan*. Lochgilphead: Argyll & Bute District Council.

— 1984b, *Mull, Coll & Tiree Local Plan*. Lochgilphead: Argyll & Bute District Council.

ARMSTRONG, A. 1982, The failure of planning in the Highlands. *Town and Country Planning* April 1982.

BLACKBURN, S. 1983, *Human Case for Isles*. Planning 512, 1 April. Gloucester: Imbit Publications.

BROADY, M. (ed.) 1973, *Marginal Regions — Essays on Social Planning*. London: Bedford Square Press.

BROWNING, Dr M. 1981, The rural co-operative — an economist's viewpoint. *The Planner*.

BROWNRIGG, M. and GREIG, M. A. 1974, *The Economic Impact of Tourist Spending in Skye*. HIDB Special Report 13. Inverness: HIDB.

CAUFIELD, C. 1982, Friends the Hebrides can do without. *New Scientist* 24 June 1982.

Comunn na Gaidhlig 1985, Outline Submission to Highland Regional Council Structure Plan Review: Issues paper. Inverness: CnaG.

— 1986 *Towards a National Policy for Gaelic*. Inverness: CnaG.

Comhairle nan Eilean 1976, *Regional Report*. Stornoway:Comhairle nan Eilean.

— 1977, *The Bilingual Policy — a consultative document*. Stornoway: Comhairle nan Eilean.

— 1982, *Bilingual Policy*. Stornoway: Comhairle nan Eilean.

— 1983, *Western Isles Structure Plan — Report of Survey*. Stornoway: Comhairle nan Eilean.

— 1986a, *Western Isles Structure Plan — Draft Written Statement*. Stornoway: Comhairle nan Eilean.

— 1986b, *Review of Educational Provision in the Western Isles — a consultative document*. Stornoway: Comhairle nan Eilean.

ENNEW, J. 1981, Gaelic and the Language of Industrial Relations. In E. HAUGEN, J. D. MCCLURE and D. THOMPSON, (eds) *Minority Languages Today*. Edinburgh: Edinburgh University Press.

GEDDES, A. 1955, The Isle of Harris and Lewis — a study in British Community. *Scottish Geographical Magazine*. Edinburgh.

Highlands and Islands Development Board 1979, Interview: Alistair Hetherington. *North 7* March/April 1979. Inverness: HIDB.

— 1981a, Why Comhairle nan Eilean is the envy of local authorities. *North 7*

January/February 1981. Inverness: HIDB.
— 1981b, Uncovering the roots of co-operation. *North 7* March/April 1981.
— 1982, *Cor na Gaidhlig: Language, Community and Development: The Gaelic Situation*. Inverness: HIDB.
Highland Regional Council 1982, *Skye and Lochalsh Local Plan — Draft Written Statement*. Inverness: Highland Regional Council.
— 1985, *Guide to the Highland Region* (2nd edition). Inverness: Highland Regional Council.
HOUSTON, G. 1987, *An Interim Assessment of the IDP for Agriculture and Fish-farming in the Western Isles*. Inverness: Highlands and Islands Development Board.
HUNTER, J. 1979, How food prices inflate rural cost of living. *North 7*.
MACCALLUM, J. D. and ADAMS, J. G. L. 1981, Employment and unemployment statistics for rural areas. *Town Planning Review* June 1981.
MACGREGOR, B. 1979 Regional Planning in a remote area — the Highlands and Islands Development Board. *Town and Country Planning Summer School, 8–19 September, University of York*. London: RTPI.
MACKINNON, K. 1984, Scottish Gaelic and English in the Highlands. In P. TRUDGILL (ed.) *Language in the British Isles*, Cambridge: Cambridge University Press.
MACLEAN, D. and MURRAY, R. 1978, Economic development in the Western Isles. Paper given at a Conference on Regional Development and Language Planning, Regional Studies Association, Galway.
MACTHOMAIS, F. 1984, Gaelic and Economic Development, CARN, Summer 1984.
MONTGOMERY, L. 1984, *Report of the Committee of Inquiry into the Functions and Powers of the Islands Councils of Scotland*. Cmnd 9216. Edinburgh: HMSO.
New Edinburgh Review 1976, Gaelic — a time to survive. New Edinburgh Review 33.
Planning Exchange, The 1980, *Development in Remote Rural Areas* Proceeding of a Stornoway Conference. Glasgow: The Planning Exchange.
PRATTIS, J. I. 1981, Industrialisation and Minority Language Loyality. In E. HAUGEN, J. D. MCCLURE and D. THOMSON, (eds) *Minority Languages Today*. Edinburgh: Edinburgh University Press.
Registrar General, Scotland 1985, *Census 1981: Scottish Gaelic*. Edinburgh: HMSO.
Scottish Tourist Board 1977, *The Social and Cultural Impact of Tourism; A Case Study of Sleat, Isle of Skye*. Edinburgh: Scottish Tourist Board.
SMITH, I. C. 1977, Scottish Gaelic. *Planet* Feb/March 1977, 36.
Social Work Today 1983, Blemishes Idyll, *Social Work Today*, 14(27), 15th March 1983.
THOMSON, D. 1981, Gaelic in Scotland, Assessment and Prognosis. In E. HAUGEN, J. D. MCCLURE and D. THOMSON, (eds) *Minority Languages Today*. Edinburgh: Edinburgh University Press.
Welsh Books Council 1984, Publishing in Scottish Gaelic, *Llais Llyfrau*, Spring 1984.
WHEATLEY, LORD 1969, *Royal Commission of Local Government in Scotland: Report*. Cmnd 4150. Edinburgh: HMSO.
WHITELEGG, J. 1981, Folk who live in the Isles. *Geographical Magazine*, April 1981.

Bibliography — Faroe Islands

COULL, J. R. 1975, Faroese fish for prosperity. *Geographical Magazine* January 1975.

GREEN, D. 1981, The Atlantic Group: Neo-Celtic and Faroese. In E. HAUGEN, J. D. MCCLURE and D. THOMSON, (eds) *Minority Languages Today*. Edinburgh: Edinburgh University Press.

HEATHERINGTON, P. 1981, A Force Ten from the Faroes. *Guardian Week-end*. Saturday 8th August 1981.

Highlands and Islands Development Board 1978, Confidence — Secret behind the success of the Faroe Islands. *North 7* September/October 1978.

JACOLOSON, J. F. 1965, *The Farthest Shore*. Copenhagen: Royal Danish Ministry of Foreign Affairs.

MERRETT, J. 1982, Islands of prosperity in the North Atlantic. *Geographical Magazine* March 1982.

POULSON, J. H. W. 1981, The Faroese language situation. In E. HAUGEN, J. D. MCCLURE and D. THOMSON, (eds) *Minority Languages Today*. Edinburgh: Edinburgh University Press.

ROSIE, S. 1985, Faroe — our remarkable northern neighbour. *An Baner Kernewek* February 1985.

Royal Danish Ministry of Foreign Affairs 1959, *The Faroe Islands*. Copenhagen: Royal Danish Ministry of Foreign Affairs.

— 1971, *The Faroe Islands* — Special Edition of *The Danish Journal*. Copenhagen: Royal Danish Ministry of Foreign Affairs.

— 1983, *Fact Sheet Denmark — The Faroe Islands*. Copenhagen: Royal Danish Ministry of Foreign Affairs.

STEPHENS, M. 1974, The Faroe Islands. *Planet 26/27* Winter 1974.

8 Bicultural Conflict in the Context of the Core-Periphery Model

DON CARTWRIGHT

Introduction

The core-periphery model and its utility, or futility, in the analyses of ethnic resurgence and movements toward self-determination in plural societies has been discussed by scholars from several disciplines. (Some of these are to be found in: Williams, 1982; Kliot & Waterman, 1983; Gottman, 1980; Laponce, 1987.) In this application of the model, emphasis will be placed upon sociocultural developments within minority communities that share peripheral situations, with secondary attention to core area policies and programmes as they relate to these groups. These developments will be assessed through analyses of language usage and language-related census data for ethnic groups. Language usage is one element of cultural identity that can be measured, and it provides a reliable indicator of ethnic survival.

Peripheral areas are considered in the context of a New World model and an Old World/African model of core-periphery. In the New World model, peripheral ethnic regions may evolve into cultural transition zones between distinctive cultural realms. Here the peripheries of two nations, or cultural groups, become a zone of ethnic contact and interaction with a potential for cultural linkages between the two realms. Within the cultural transition zone, the resident ethnic groups will each enjoy access to social, cultural, economic and business domains in which the use of the mother tongue is traditional. Proximity to respective culture cores is a significant element in this cultural commitment. Ideally, this domain usage should not contribute to a two-solitude pattern — areally and culturally — in the zone, whereby, because of exclusiveness, contact and interaction between members of the two groups rarely occurs. If competence in the second language is common for both populations, domains should also develop in which association will take place in both languages. This association will involve both formal and informal networks. Biculturalism becomes prevalent and social and cognitive distances between constituent groups is minimal. Policies and programmes that are directed toward the zone, perhaps inadvertently, can have a negative impact upon this bicultural harmony, and will be condemned by members from *both* groups. It is this dual reaction within the periphery that can also help to keep social and cognitive distances between cultural realms to a minimum. If the bicultural distinctiveness of the zone erodes, through internal procesess and/or core area programmes and policies, the ability of this geographical region to enhance relations between adjoining cultural realms will be lost. Social and cognitive distances between the realms will develop with increases in misunderstandings, suspicions and declining empathy the potential by-products. This intepretation of the geopolitical significance of cultural transition zones may be applied internationally and intranationally.

In the Old World/African model, social and cognitive distances between members of a peripheral, ethnic minority and core-area representatives of the majority may grow if the latter misinterpret sociocultural processes on the margins and fail to satisfy the aspirations of the inhabitants (Williams, 1982b). Within such a plural society, social, economic and political cleavages become a constant risk for the state. In their geographical analysis of the Northern Ireland problem, Boal & Douglas (1982) focus upon these cleavages between constituent communities and demonstrate the manner in which they produce a plural society that is racked by division rather than one enhanced by integration.

A Paradigm of Cultural Interaction in Transition Zones

The model of the development of cultural contact in geographical transition zones, illustrated in Figure 8.1, is applicable to a New World environment where European nations established their spheres of interest. Usually boundaries that were established between expanding colonial territories were antecedent in that they preceded settlement and an expanding communications/transportation network. Even if the frontier regions were inhabited by indigenous populations, as in southern United States, the model applies since these people were usually treated as a nuisance factor and, once neutralised, were herded on to reservations with boundaries that not only restricted their interaction with the now-dominant cultural group but also inhibited integration.

With the expansion of settlement from the respective ecumenes into the frontiers, improved communications and transportation technology facilitated growth of core-area influence (phase 2). Various policies and programmes associated with these growth processes were often influential beyond the boundary of areal jurisdiction and features of one cultural

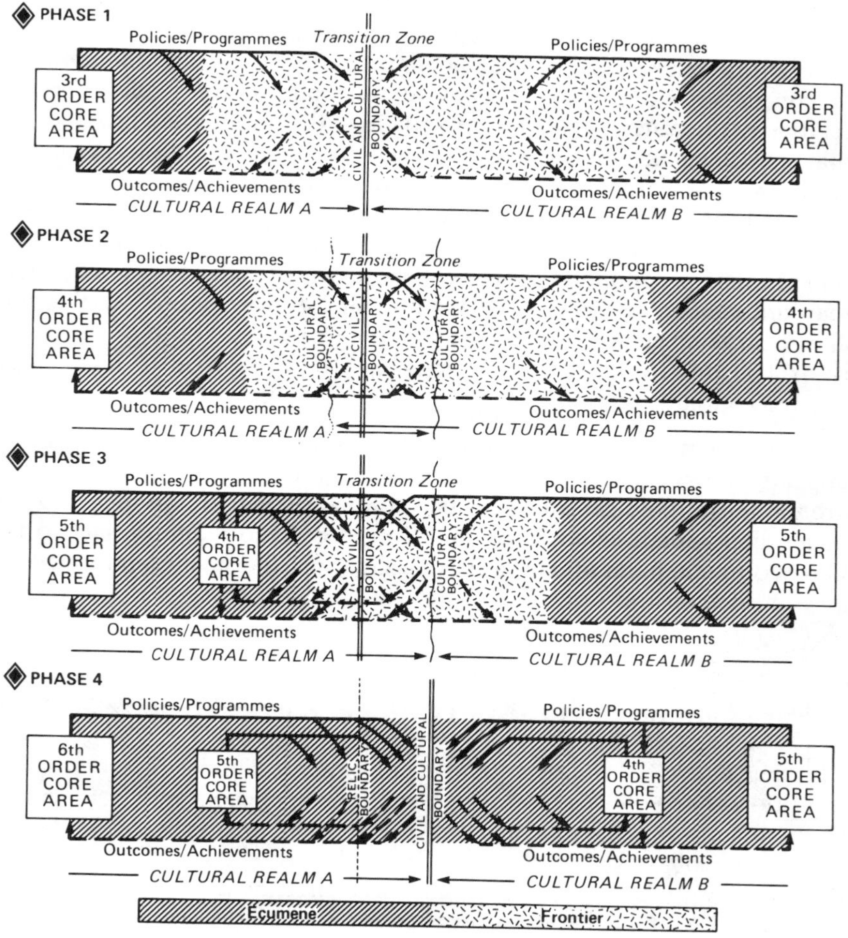

FIGURE 8.1 *A paradigm of the development of cultural contact in geographical transition zones*
(New World Model)

realm began to mix with the other. In time a true cultural transition zone emerged with the characteristics of a plural society: different preferences for building styles, land, agricultural activities, language and perhaps institutions. Minorities within the periphery will be culturally subordinate to the centre because they lack political influence and a dependency situation arises. The centre in the model is considered to be the political centre as well as the cultural hearth for the majority population. It may lack or lose major economic, financial and judicial aspects of centrality to other urban places, but because it keeps administrative control it is vital to this model. This geographical situation may prevail for several generations (phase 3) with little or no pressure to relocate the boundary to concur with perceived changes to the limits of one cultural realm relative to the other (phase 4). Nevertheless, the policies and programmes that are developed in an administrative core area for these peripheral lands may exacerbate a potentially volatile relationship between and among those who inhabit the region or generate conflict where a spirit of accommodation had evolved. The assessment of success or failure of policies and programmes, again by those who reside in the core-area, may not concur with the social realities of the frontier/boundary region and local conflict may evolve. If policy-makers see a loss of territorial control in this region, strong policies may be developed to re-establish control and authority.

A variation of the model of cultural interaction in transition zones appears in Figure 8.2. The processes of expansion for two cultural realms are similar to those described for the New World model, but the existence of an intermediate cultural realm is considered more appropriate to the Old World and parts of Africa. In this situation, the smaller, intermediate

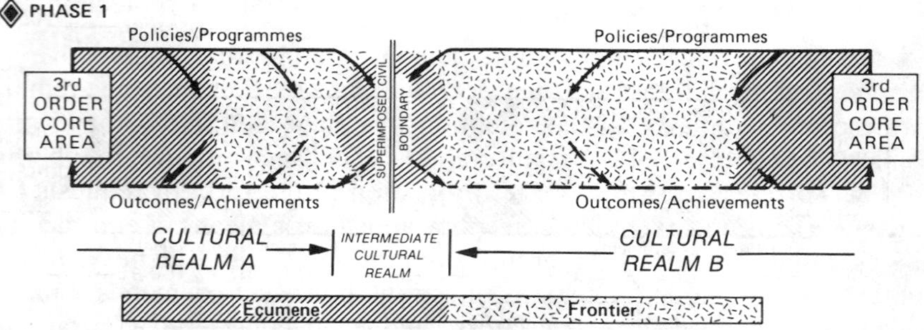

FIGURE 8.2 *A paradigm of the development of cultural contact in geographical transition zones*
(Old World/African Model)

cultural realm is first absorbed into the respective spheres of interest of the neighbouring realms. If unable to defend or exert its territorial integrity, this realm must eventually endure a superimposed boundary which is delimited to settle territorial competition between realms A and B. This line is usually established without regard for the settlement patterns of the intermediate cultural realm which becomes areally and politically divided by the new boundary. Again policies and programmes are devised, usually in core-area administrative centres, to incorporate border territories into the functional and formal organisation of the state. The outcomes of these are assessed and new policies or programmes devised normally to defuse centrifugal tendencies among the peripheral, residual population of the formerly intermediate cultural realm. Since the progression between phases involves a time dimension, subsequent phases, as in Figure 8.1, can presage the erosion and possible demise of this geographically peripheral cultural region.

Another dimension to the model, and the major emphasis in this chapter, involves the erosion of the intermediate and cultural transition zone that can develop because of internal processes. Changing migration and journey-to-work patterns can alter daily routines of human contact and interaction which will eventually be reflected in changing domains of mother tongue and second language usage. Increasing association and involvement with members of the other ethnic group can also increase the incidents of exogamy. One outcome of these internal processes, particularly if reinforced by core area policies and programmes, can be the evolution of a phase 4 situation in which the intermediate or cultural transition zone has disappeared. Only relic features of the landscape remain to remind one of the zone's existence, and a cultural/political boundary now dominates the area. Before this occurs, however, one should anticipate demands from the minority for cultural protection.

In spite of institutional and domain sharing that can evolve in peripheral/cultural transition zones, certain exclusive domains must remain as these are significant to the retention of ethnic identity. If these vital domains begin to erode, the cultural space between ethnic groups also erodes. To re-establish this space, protection in the form of requests for language rights and extended usage may appear as a means of entrenching one essential element of the group's diminishing cultural identity. In the context of the model, one may illustrate how such demands can be misinterpreted by central legislators, and even considered contrary to established policies and programmes, particularly in the realm of status language planning. These have been developed by core-area legislators most of whom represent the numerically dominant cultural group. A few examples may illustrate the utility of the model in focusing upon the periphery.

Cultural Transition Zones in the United States, Belgium, Spain and Canada

The southern United States, from Florida to California, exhibits cultural features of the landscape that reflect the Hispanic and Anglo zone of contact and interaction. Alvarez (1984) has analysed the transitional character of the United States/Mexico 'border belt' and revealed the existence of a true social system conditioned by historical, sociocultural and economic factors. In this context, he maintains that the transition zone ('border communities') is not only a conjunction between two social spheres, but has its own organised social dynamic, based upon these factors, since they influence, and have influenced, human movement and interaction throughout the border zone. As one element in this social dynamic, the Spanish language has become well entrenched particularly in urban centres within the transition zone. Spanish is perceived by some legislators, however, to be penetrating the American south at the expense of English. This is considered to be divisive, and, therefore, a centrifugal element to national unity. A recent resolution in the United States that proposes to amend the Constitution to proclaim English as the official language of the country (Senate Joint Resolution 167, 9th December 1983) may be interpreted as an attempt to re-establish control over the international boundary.

Those who promote this resolution also encourage official status for English at the state level. Several states have declared this status but must wait for ratification by the legislature. California achieved this through a referendum held in 1986, and Colorado and Florida used the same procedure to establish official status for English in 1988. Not only has areal expansion of the transition zone been moderated by these state-level measures, but a message has been sent to the non-anglophone population in the transition zone that biculturalism will be accommodated only on terms set by the majority. The attitude in the United States is, apparently, that any accommodation to the plural realities of the cultural transition zone will only weaken the political fibre of the nation, and any value in cultural contact with Mexico and Central America through the zone is secondary to this. In this context their treatment of the zone is more in harmony with the Belgian situation, albeit for different reasons.

In Belgium, the Flemish in the north and Walloons in the south are highly homogeneous and functionally unilingual. Between these realms whatever cultural transition zone that did exist has been replaced by a well-defined linguistic boundary. McRae (1986) has analysed the evolution of this division and demonstrates that the size and location of linguistic minorities in the respective ethnic areas have been relatively small over time, and, those that do exist, are not strongly concentrated along the linguistic boundary. Legislation in the 1930s gave political reality to the linguistic division between Flanders and Wallonia, but also provided flexible territorial limits. This flexibility was intended to accommodate ethnic interaction, consequently the cultural boundary remained permeable. This changed in the 1960s, however, when legislation entrenched ethnic territory through the transfer of administrative units to respective unilingual zones according to local language preference. This legislation was an outcome of intense Flemish efforts to create a fully unilingual cultural realm in the north and was the culmination of the social, cultural, economic and political tensions that dominated relations between the two groups for over a century. Flemish nationalists became as intransigent as the Walloons who had traditionally opposed Flemish minority rights in the south. This separation was fortified through the development, and official sanction, of institutional unilingualism. The state government tried to maintain cultural linkages between Flanders and Wallonia, but McRae (1986) discovered that these linkages have become weaker since the cultural trends of the 1960s and 1970s. Language contacts have diminished as the Flemish, who traditionally carried the burden of two languages, have pursued cultural and administrative autonomy. They have become less willing to accommodate a situation of unbalanced bilingualism. Whatever potential there was for a cultural transition zone in Belgium to enhance a spirit of empathy and to foster ethnic interaction, it has been lost.

If the objective of politicians, in the formulation of policies and programmes to enhance national unity, is to maximise the processes identified with co-operation and to reduce those associated with conflict and competition, then the policy of autonomy for the peripheral ethnic communities in Spain will probably be assessed in Madrid as positive. Local reactions against programmes associated with this policy may be confusing or intimidating to legislators in the administrative core area. After all, the use of other languages is guaranteed since they have official status in their respective autonomous communities. Argemi i Roca (1986) points out, however, that the Constitutional Tribunal, the body that must adjudicate conflicts between the legislation and its local application, has been required to intervene on numerous occasions, thereby demonstrating that local practices may be considered as contravening the legal situation established in Madrid. The Constitution of 1978 recognised the multilingual structure of the country, but confusion and ambiguity has evolved over the procedure to protect and recognise the usage of local languages (vernaculars). This can contribute to the erosion of domain language usage in regular patterns of human contact and interaction. In the face of this, Cobarrubias (1986:4) has discussed the significance of normalisation processes to the use of vernaculars '... in functions they had never been used in before, such as the media, higher education, public administration and the like' and cautions that 'language spread' should be considered an essential part of this process. He points out that normalisation processes in Spain involve not only the gradual recovery of formal functions that have eroded for a language, but also the use of language in functions that have never been used before. Institutionalised bilingualism in Spain has not had the outcome that was expected. Because of the nationwide, official status of Castilian and the proviso that all Spaniards have the duty to know and the right to use Castilian, Alvarez (1986) believes that Euskara has been reduced to the status of a 'minority' language even within the peripheral Basque Country. Consequently, he considers that aspect of the cultural heritage to be in a critical stage. If this assessment is accurate, local processes associated with human contact and interaction must counteract this potentially erosive situation or this stage will indeed be critical.

Canada's cultural transition zone, first identified by Richard Joy (1972) as the 'bilingual belt of Canada', extends through three provinces: from eastern and northern New Brunswick, through southern Quebec adjacent to the United States border, metropolitan Montreal, and into the Ottawa Valley and eastern and northern Ontario (Figure 8.3). The processes of penetration into the zone beyond respective core areas were varied throughout but certain features were common. Each enjoyed early, local isolation that allowed the entrenchment of cultural characteristics and the development of culturally supportive institutions (Gaffield, 1987). Furthermore, in many parts of the zone, current minorities are the descendents of pioneer settlers and this has provided a local sense of legitimacy both to their pride of heritage and in earned minority rights.

The portion of Canada's cultural transition zone that is situated within Quebec has been the focus of policies generated by provincial legislators to protect the cultural integrity of that province against anglo incursions. For generations Anglo-Quebecers, who are concentrated in this part of the province, functioned as if they were an extension of the

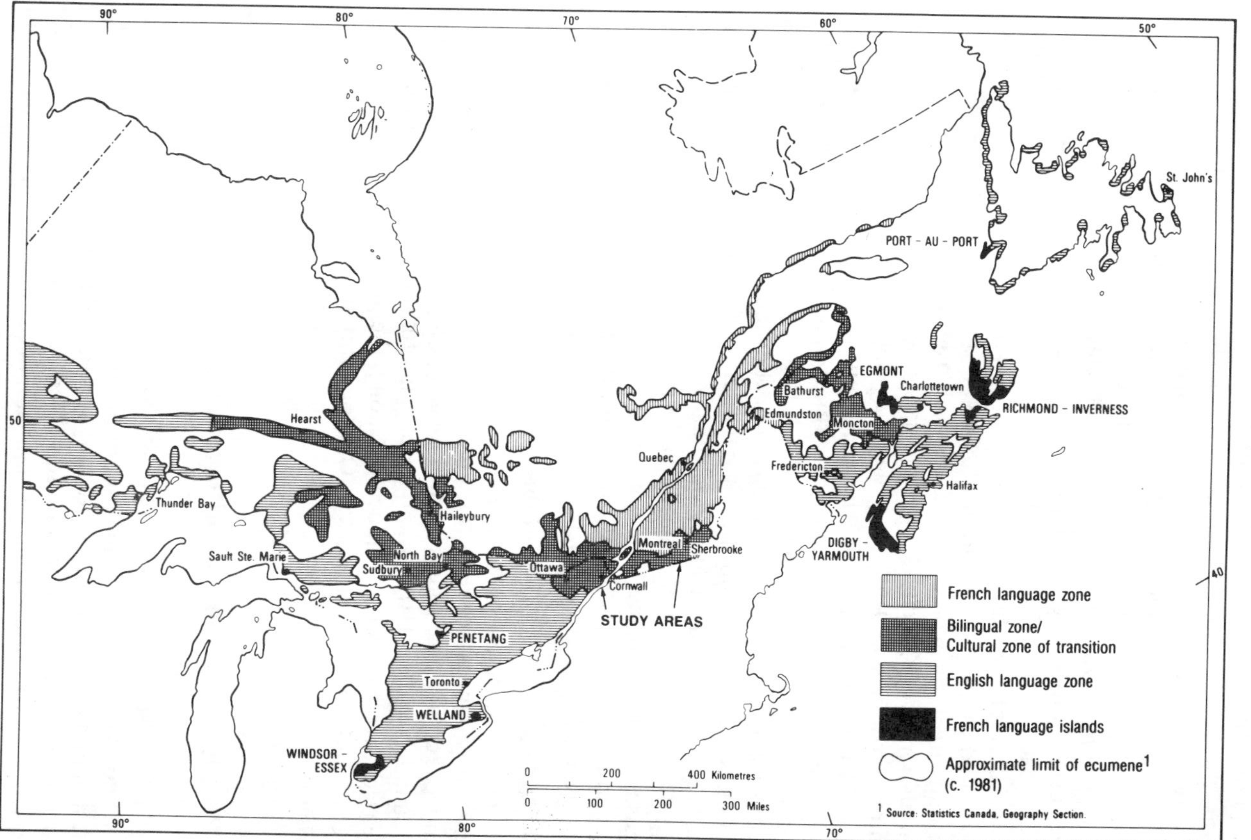

FIGURE 8.3 *Language zones in central and eastern Canada, 1981*

anglophone majority of Canada rather than a minority within Quebec. It was the francophone who accommodated to the language of the minority anglophones, and was expected to do so. Over the years this produced a situation where English penetrated the francophone cultural realm to a much greater degree than French into the anglophone cultural realm. In the 1970s, the government of Quebec passed two laws that were designed to strengthen the French language of that province against the encroachment of English. These language laws helped to make the provincial boundary less permeable to the English language but also contributed to the out-migration of many anglophones from Quebec. The resultant areal shrinkage of the cultural transition zone prompted the Commissioner of Official Languages in Ottawa to caution that further cultural erosion will lead to a national division of the two founding groups; an ethnic separation whereby French will be spoken in Quebec and English in the rest of Canada. He referred to this process as 'linguistic territorialisation on the Belgian model' (Canada, 1985). It is interesting to contrast the perceptions of this zone between legislators in Ottawa and Quebec City. To the former, it is the setting for a linguistic partnership and, hence, a geographical region that will contribute to national unity; a significant isthmus, symbolically and functionally, between French and English Canada. To the latter, it could once again become the salience of anglo-cultural invasion and, therefore, a region in which the outcomes of provincial policies and programmes must be so monitored.

To illustrate the theme of this chapter that bicultural accommodation within cultural transition zones/peripheries may serve to lessen social and cognitive distances between cultural realms, and thereby enhance rather than weaken national unity, we will focus upon processes within a portion of Canada's cultural transition zone. The following is an overview of research that has been conducted among the minority anglophones in Quebec and the francophones in Ontario who are located in the cultural transition zone.

A Profile of Canada's Cultural Transition Zone

In Canada, we are fortunate to have access to data that have been collected from language-related questions in the census. Preliminary investigation of these data can identify trends and help to expose processes that influence areal patterns of settlement and ethnic interaction within the cultural transition zone. These are necessary antedecents to field research. To illustrate, analyses have been conducted on migration and language-related questions for two areas within the cultural transition zone, one in eastern Ontario and the other in eastern Quebec.

Migration

A significant process in any specified geographical area is the change in population composition that is associated with migration. Certain economic advantages will attract people to a region or, relative to the perceived advantages of another region, will fail to hold people in the area under consideration. In a cultural transition zone, this process is significant beyond the immediate impact upon the human resource base since it can alter the ethnic composition and eventually affect the language domains of the constituent cultural groups. If one group declines in numbers, it will be difficult to sustain religious, educational, business and cultural institutions which add to its cultural vitality. When these begin to decline, another push factor is added to the out-migration, particularly for the smaller cultural group. As the composition of the plural society shifts away from a balanced, or near balanced, situation the opportunities for exogamy increase. When in-migration becomes the main factor in population growth for a region, because of a declining birthrate, it takes only a few generations before only a small percentage of the population can trace ancestry to original settlers. The rest are in-migrants and the descendents of in-migrants. The historical processes that contributed so much to current patterns of settlement and human interaction can, thereby, become less significant to the heritage of the present population, or forgotten altogether.

Throughout the 1960s and 1970s the proportion of the francophone population to total has declined in that portion of the cultural transition zone that is beyond Quebec. This reduction is due, in part, to assimilation, out-migration from economically deprived areas within the zone and the encroachment of anglophones into those areas that are within commuting distance of Ottawa and Montreal. Within Quebec, the anglophone minority has steadily lost in proportion to total population since the zenith in the 1860s. During the census period 1971 to 1981, for example, the English mother-tongue population of Quebec dropped by almost 11%.

Migration data were obtained from Statistics Canada for three censal/intercensal periods: 1966 to 1971, 1971 to 1976 and 1976 to 1981, for specified regions within the cultural transition zone and beyond. By grouping census divisions into specified regions, the effect of changes to the boundaries of these divisions over time can be minimised. The tabulations were structured to establish the origins and destinations of in-migrants and out-migrants by the mother tongue of the migrants. The origins of in-migrants were considered significant since those who enter a cultural transition zone from a unilingual, or homogeneous, region are less likely to empathise with the accommodative features of this plural society than those who have left an area which is culturally similar to the destination. Destinations for out-migrants are also important for one may hypothesise on the potential loss of cultural characteristics according to the new place of residence. Francophones who leave one area in the cultural transition zone, for example, are in less danger of experiencing language shift if they move to another area within the zone, than if they move to an area within the unilingual anglophone region of Canada (Cartwright, 1987). It is also possible to assess the stability of a cultural transition zone itself when one has origins and destinations of migrants which can then be compared with changes in the size of ethnic populations relative to the total population.

Net migrations for francophones and anglophones in eastern Ontario and eastern Quebec are illustrated in Figure 8.4. According to the tabulations obtained from Statistics Canada, certain areas are dominant source/destination regions for the migrants of eastern Ontario and eastern Quebec. These are the Montreal census metropolitan area, the Ottawa metropolitan area and the rest of Canada for the former. For eastern Quebec, the major source/destination regions are Montreal, Quebec (excluding the cultural transition zone) and the rest of Canada. Over the censal/intercensal periods covered, the net migration for francophones versus anglophones for eastern Ontario, from and to the Ottawa metropolitan area, is negative for the former. The magnitude of this loss is even greater for the francophones when one tabulates the source/destination of the Montreal CMA for eastern Ontario. The in-migration of anglophones from this metropolitan area far outnumber the francophone in-migrants. Many of the former are able to commute to jobs in Montreal from eastern Ontario, thereby avoiding any perceived restrictions brought about by Quebec's Official Language Charter and higher provincial taxes. It has been calculated that the majority of anglophones who left Quebec after 1974 were unilingual (Cartwright, 1985a), and if some of these selected eastern Ontario they may not be sympathetic to the cultural aspirations of Franco-Ontarians.

Largely an agriculturally based economy, eastern Ontario has, over the past two decades experienced a decline in farm population but a growth in those classified as rural, non-farm. These people are located

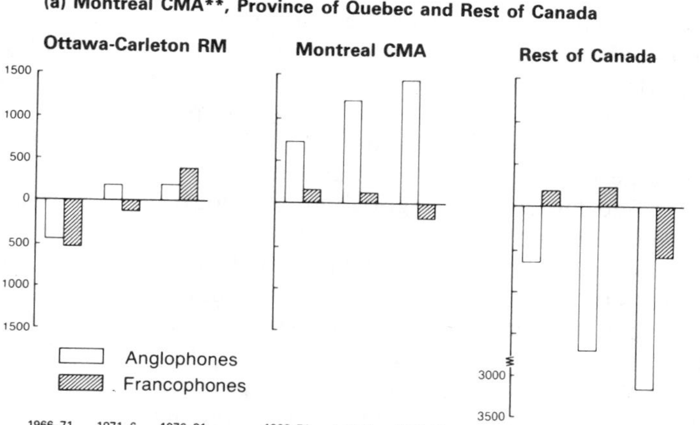

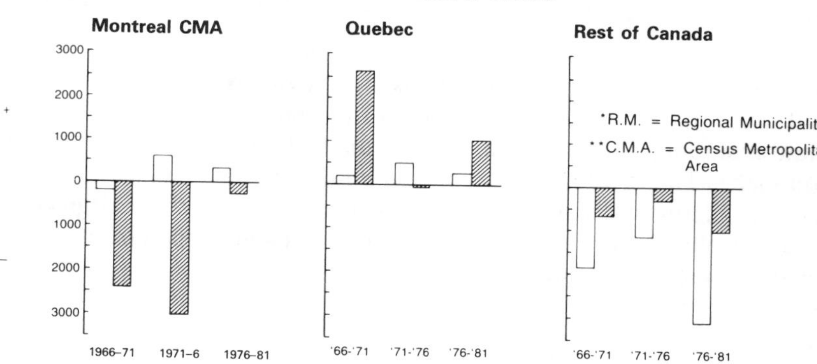

Source: Statistics Canada, special

***RM = Regional Municipality**
****CMA = Census Metropolitan Area**

FIGURE 8.4 *Net migration for eastern Ontario with major source/destination regions — 1966 to 1981*
(< 5 years of age excluded)

in a rural environment but make the largest portion of their incomes elsewhere, mostly in urban centres such as Ottawa and west Montreal. A shift in the composition of the population and a reduction in the number of farms and in farm population has developed from this migration process. In this section of the zone of transition, the French mother tongue population was about 69,000 in 1961 and constituted 55% of the total population. By 1981, this number had declined to about 65,000 which represented 48% of the total.

Eastern Quebec has lost francophones to the Montreal metropolitan area and to the rest of Canada, beyond Quebec and the transition zone, and although the area has attracted people of French mother tongue from other parts of Quebec, there has been a net loss for the census periods 1966 to 1981 (Figure 8.4). While some anglophones have, in declining numbers, been attracted to this part of the zone, these have been negated by the large out-migration to the rest of Canada. The economy of this area is based largely upon agriculture and tourism supported by small-scale industrial capacity in the largest urban centre, Sherbrooke. Since 1966, these activities have been unable to absorb the labour force. Much of the western area, however, functions as a dormitory for Montreal, and it is this that accounted for a recent increase in total population. In spite of this, the anglophone population in this region dropped by 6.0% from 1971 to 1981, while the francophone population increased by 10.5%. Once a majority throughout the region, the anglophones are now a minority in each of the census divisions that make up this part of the study area.

Not only has there been a shift in the ethnic composition of the population in these two study areas, the areal extent of the respective minorities in eastern Quebec and eastern Ontario has also waned, so that the transitional nature of this area seems to be giving way to a linguistic boundary. This could become areally similar to the Belgian situation of a sharp linguistic division between the two founding cultural groups. To help identify this trend we may now turn to data developed from language-related questions on the census.

Language-Related, Census Data

A useful index that can help to identify the patterns of language penetration and ethnic interaction throughout the cultural transition zone is the index of language intensity. This index utilises two census populations that are derived from language-related data obtained through the Census of Canada. Canadians are asked to declare their mother tongue (the language first learned as a child and still understood) but must also state which of Canada's official languages they can speak (English only, French only, Both, Neither) and the language that the respondents speak most often in the home. The index is calculated from the census responses to home language and official languages: unilingual, and is based upon the assumption that people will function throughout their community in a language that is similar to, or different from, the home language depending upon the strength and pervation of the second official language (Cartwright, 1987). Those who must switch to a second language to function outside the home will register low on the index, while those who use their mother tongue in *and* beyond the home will have high values.[1]

By focusing upon representative regions within the transition zone it is possible to demonstrate the trends that are presented through the analysis of census data. The index of language intensity for the French and English languages presented in Table 8.1, relative to the size of the respective populations, demonstrates the pervasiveness of English even in census divisions in which anglophones are a minority. In some census divisions in which the indices are high for *both* groups, we have an example of the two-solitudes concept where, as along the linguistic boundary in Belgium, many people from the two ethnic communities are unable to interact.

Further refinement in the application of the index of language intensity will reveal whether a measure obtained for a census division is truly representative for all age groups in that ethnic population. The graphs in Figure 8.5 provide a visual impression of the index for French and English by specified age cohorts for eastern Ontario and eastern Quebec. The graphs are derived from data obtained from Statistics Canada. For the two census years, data were assembled for francophones and anglophones by mother tongue, by home language, by official languages and by sex for specified age cohorts. These were run at the scale of the census sub-division with data then aggregated for the census division. Profiles in Figure 8.5 were derived from the census divisions within each study area. To facilitate comparison, Statistics Canada was requested to make the 1971 data compatible with 1981 census boundaries, thereby overcoming changes in the limits of geostatistical units between the two censuses. This is a very costly process, therefore it was done only for those units considered to be within the cultural transition zone. The selected age cohorts did not include those below the age of five years because the range of interaction for these pre-school children is normally limited to the home. Furthermore, Statistics Canada classifies their ability with the official languages according to the declared home language of the parents. Beyond this age, children begin to attend school and their range of interactions alters accordingly. The remaining age cohorts are intended to isolate groups entering the labour force, the youthful mobile element of the labour force, the entrenched and the retired.

In eastern Ontario the index of language intensity for French for the youngest, labour-force cohorts (15–24 years and 25–44 years) is well below the index for the entire census division. There is rapid

TABLE 8.1 *Mother tongue populations and index of language intensity, French and English, for regions and census divisions within the cultural zone of transition, Ontario and Quebec, 1981*

Region & census division	*English mother tongue*		*French mother tongue*	
	% of total population	*LI* index*	*% of total population*	*LI index*
Eastern Ontario				
Prescott	21	0.70	77	0.39
Russell	23	0.80	75	0.37
Ottawa/Carleton	70	0.91	19	0.15
Glengarry	58	0.82	38	0.21
Stormont	66	0.86	30	0.15
Northern Ontario				
Cochrane	44	1.03	47	0.26
Nipissing	66	0.95	28	0.17
Sudbury	61	0.93	36	0.18
Sudbury RM	59	1.07	29	0.12
Timiskaming	68	0.96	26	0.25
Gaspesie, Quebec	13	0.67	85	0.79
Eastern Townships/ L'Estrie				
Compton	18	0.60	81	0.74
Richmond	10	0.41	90	0.78
Sherbrooke	9	0.47	90	0.65
Stanstead	19	0.61	80	0.67
Brome	45	0.59	51	0.57
Missisquoi	19	0.49	79	0.62
Greater Montreal	20	0.49	67	0.58
Ottawa Valley	17	0.53	78	0.60

*LI = language intensity index
Source: Statistics Canada, Special Tabulation Catalogue CA1 BS95, C901–904 (1981).

accommodation to English among the francophones in these age groups. A similar profile constructed for the anglophone population illustrated a small accommodation to French for the younger age groups, but it was not as marked as for the francophones to English (Cartwright, 1985b). The increase in the index for the older cohorts possibly represents a

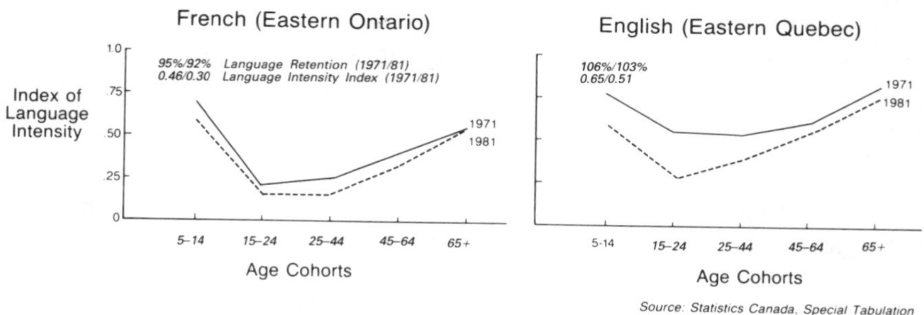

FIGURE 8.5 *Index of language intensity by age cohorts for French in eastern Ontario and English in eastern Quebec, 1971 and 1981*

residual population from those who have been assimilated and/or those who have used their skills in two languages to obtain employment elsewhere. Those beyond the age of retirement have a lower range of contact and interaction, and may have lost the ability and necessity to function in the second language.

The age groups among the minority anglophone population in eastern Quebec have a higher register on the index of language intensity than the francophones in eastern Ontario. Nevertheless, there has been a drop in this value for the former, particularly for younger anglophones since 1971. This is probably indicative of the out-migration of unilingual anglophones from the province during the 1970s leaving a residual minority population that is better equipped to function in a province that now has one official language. The older anglophones illustrate an entrenchment that, because of commitments to career, friends and property investments, makes them less mobile than the younger.

The profiles of the index of language intensity suggests that the younger age cohorts among the anglophone minority in eastern Quebec are accommodating the majority language of that province, but are well short of the degree of accommodation among the young francophones to English in eastern Ontario. Since these data can provide only indications of trends toward accommodation or division within a plural society, it is desirable to seek corroborative evidence through field research. To this end such research has been conducted within the eastern Townships/L'Estrie in eastern Quebec and in eastern Ontario.[2] Questionnaires were designed so that information could be obtained on early and current language usage among francophones and anglophones in various domains. Personal and parental attitudes toward second-language acquisition were also acquired. Since our purpose here is to compare the trends found among the minority populations within the cultural transition zone toward domain exclusiveness or mutality, specific findings have been selected for presentation. The respondents have been grouped into four cohorts to conform to those illustrated in the profiles of the index of language intensity (Figure 8.5).

Preliminary analyses were done for abilities in the second language, for attitudes toward second language acquisition, and language usage at work and among friends. Comparisons of responses have been made between francophones and anglophones in eastern Quebec, and for those in eastern Ontario, and preliminary results presented elsewhere (Cartwright, 1985b). Since we are now comparing minorities on both sides of the provincial boundary, these early results will be summarised and added to current analysis of language usage when respondents obtain specified community services, select newspapers and magazines and choose television programmes. Comparisons for the attitudes expressed and for domain usage will be made for the anglophones in eastern Quebec and the francophones in eastern Ontario (Franco-Ontarians).

Within the research area of eastern Quebec, there is a progressive development among the anglophone respondents, from oldest to youngest, in their ability to speak French. Only 7% among the youngest indicated that they could not speak the second-language at all compared to 26% among those over 65 years of age (Table 8.2). Among the francophones in eastern Ontario there was no significant difference statistically in the responses among the four age groups. Very few responded that they were unable to speak English; none among the youngest. The attitudes toward acquisition of the second language was generally positive on both sides of the boundary. This should not be surprising if the supposition that the majority of the anglophones who departed Quebec were unilingual is correct. The attraction of English, as measured through the index of language intensity on the Ontario side of the zone, has affected all the francophone respondents.

Tables 8.3 and 8.4 provide data on language usage among friends and at work. An encouraging feature among these responses is the progressive involvement by the younger anglophones in using French within eastern Quebec. This helps to substantiate their positive attitude toward the acquisition of the language. Franco-Ontarians, however, use the second language in these domains more frequently than the minority in Quebec. Relatively few use 'always French' compared to anglophones in eastern Quebec who responded 'always English'.

TABLE 8.2 *Ability to speak the second official languge by anglophones in eastern Quebec and francophones in eastern Ontario, 1985*

Age group	*Not at all* %	*Not very well* %	*Fairly well* %	*Very well* %
Anglophones in Quebec n = 435				
65+	26	45	28	1
45–64	16	43	31	10
25–44	8	43	36	13
< 25	7	34	44	15
Francophones in Ontario n = 335				
65+	—	9	55	36
45–64	6	13	43	38
25–44	4	12	41	43
< 25	—	8	40	52

TABLE 8.3 *Language usage with friends outside the home for anglophones in eastern Quebec and francophones in eastern Ontario, 1985*

Age group	*Always English* %	*Often or occasionally French* %	*French > English* %
Anglophones in Quebec n = 435			
65+	61.5	37.5	1.0
45–64	58.1	40.0	1.9
25–44	49.2	46.2	4.6
< 25	35.8	60.4	3.8
Francophones in Ontario n = 332			
65+	31.6	52.6	15.8
45–64	25.0	63.3	11.7
25–44	19.0	73.0	8.0
< 25	18.8	68.0	13.2

A greater percentage of anglophones in eastern Quebec use both official languages to obtain governmental, professional and personal services than anglophones in eastern Ontario (Table 8.5). This situation, as one might expect, is reversed for the francophone population within the Ontario/Quebec transition zone which demonstrates the attraction of

TABLE 8.4 *Language usage at work for anglophones in eastern Quebec and francophones in eastern Ontario, 1985*

Age group	*Always English* %	*Often or occasionally French* %	*French > English* %
Anglophones in Quebec n = 405			
65+	46.7	46.7	6.6
45–64	25.0	58.8	16.2
25–44	22.3	60.2	17.5
< 25	29.8	64.8	5.4
Francophones in Ontario n = 302			
65+	5.0	75.0	20.0
45–64	6.3	71.8	21.9
25–44	9.2	72.4	18.4
< 25	8.1	67.6	24.3

TABLE 8.5 *Percentage of English and French mother-tongue populations in eastern Quebec and in eastern Ontario using both or the other official language to obtain specified services, 1985*

Specified services	*English mother tongue*		*French mother tongue*	
	Other language Que./Ont.	*Both Que./Ont.*	*Other language Que./Ont.*	*Both Que./Ont.*
	% %	% %	% %	% %
Municipal	8.8/2.6	34.9/19.2	7.9/10.3	31.5/43.0
Church	2.3/6.3	6.2/ 2.9	6.7/ 6.4	15.0/18.2
Social Club	3.7/3.7	12.9/11.1	7.2/ 6.4	24.3/28.9
Bank/CP	7.1/7.9	30.3/17.6	5.0/ 6.4	28.1/33.6
Bus./Pro. Club	2.5/2.6	11.2/ 7.1	6.1/ 4.3	27.0/25.1
Doctor	3.7/1.7	11.5/10.1	13.0/25.4	22.2/23.3
Dentist	6.0/5.1	15.3/ 8.0	7.3/16.2	19.4/19.2
Lawyer	3.1/2.9	12.0/ 8.2	5.0/10.6	18.5/24.2
Ins. Agent	4.7/4.1	14.3/10.5	4.9/ 9.8	20.5/22.6
Real Estate	2.2/1.1	11.6/ 7.2	4.3/ 5.4	19.7/23.4

CP = Caisse Populaire, a credit union.

the official language in the respective provinces. What may be surprising, however, are the differences in the percentages of anglophones who use both languages or French to obtain services in Quebec when compared with the francophones in Ontario who use both languages or English for specified services. Francophones within this portion of the cultural transition zone gravitate more to the English language when seeking various services beyond the home than do the anglophones to French. A strong majority of the latter still function in their mother tongue for the services specified in Table 8.5. Of all those listed, the Church still seems to sustain a linguistic affiliation in the mother tongue. This may be so because religious services are offered in French and English at separate times in the same church, or perhaps religion for these respondents is still an important domain for ethnic identification.

A significant indicator of the accommodation to the second language is illustrated in the minorities responses to television viewing habits (Figure 8.6). It is here that the involvement of young anglophones in the milieu of Quebec begins to wane. More than half of the respondents, in all age groups, watch television only in English. On the other hand, the francophones in eastern Ontario are strongly addicted to English-language programmes. The younger francophones watch these programmes more frequently than the older respondents. Very few Franco-Ontarians in the study area watch French programmes only. Within the transition zone there are many programmes that are available in both languages, and this was reflected by the respondents in the two study areas, the majority of whom stated that selections of programmes in the mother tongue were adequate.

In their preference for newspapers and magazines, the Franco-Ontarians have greater attraction to publications in their mother tongue than to television programmes (Figures 8.7 and 8.8). When one contrasts the respondents from the two study areas, however, many more Anglo-Quebecers are attracted to the written media in their mother tongue. While the majority of Franco-Ontarians in all age groups reported that they read newspapers and magazines often or exclusively in English, only a very small percentage of anglophones had a similar preference or experience in French in eastern Quebec.

Discussion

'Mere possession of a language is meaningless unless it is used. Language does not exist when it is not used' (E. Annamalai, 1986: 2).

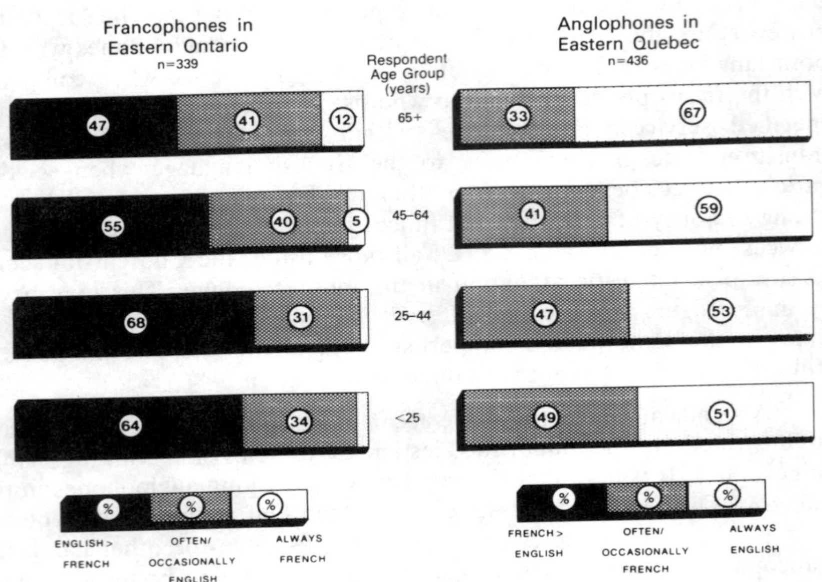

FIGURE 8.6 *Television viewing habits by language of programmes for anglophones in eastern Quebec and francophones in eastern Ontario, 1983*

To a core area administrator this statement may be used to justify denial of official-language status to a minority population, or even a programme to extend domain usage of the language. This will be based on the perception that beyond the home, the minority language is 'used' less and less. Members of this cultural group are observed using the language of the majority at work, to obtain services, and in many social situations. To the minority population, however, this statement validates their efforts to extend language rights and to receive official sanction so that usage can be promoted beyond the narrow confines of home and school.

We know that mass media promotes homogenisation within a population in contrast to, and perhaps in conflict with, interpersonal communications which foster differentiation (Abler, 1975). For the anglophones within Canada's cultural transition zone, mass media preferences and most interpersonal communications are linguistically complementary. For the minority francophones in the Ontario portion of the zone, however, there is some conflict between the two. The risk is

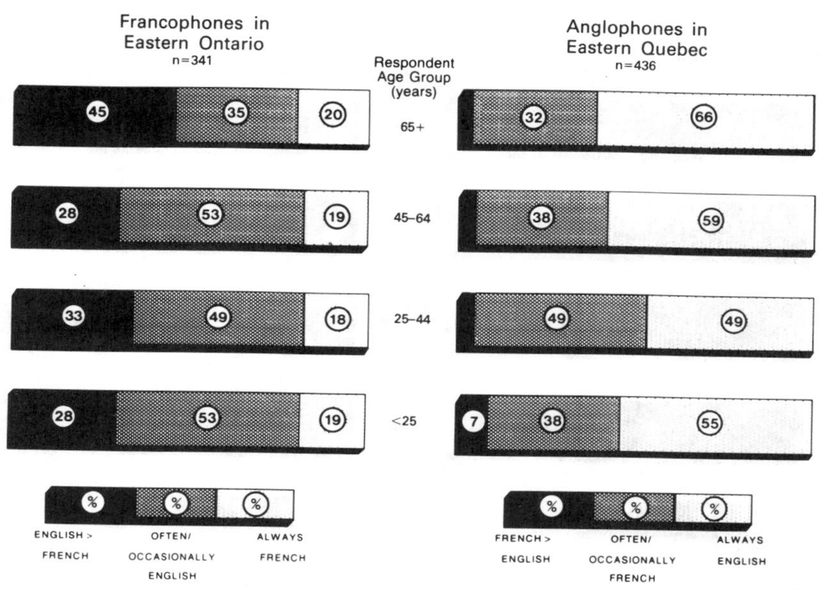

FIGURE 8.7 *Newspaper reading habits by language for anglophones in eastern Quebec and francophones in eastern Ontario, 1985*

that the trend toward English mass media will erode the integrative force of interpersonal communications. The Franco-Ontarians in the study area, as a cultural group, have decreased in numbers, have decennial growth rates that are well below provincial levels and language retention rates that have also declined. In some parts of the cultural transition zone, they are experiencing a diminution in geographic concentration as improved transportation networks facilitate encroachment of the urban shadow. Add to this the tendency for gravitation toward cultural domains of the majority anglo community '. . . and the stage is set for the use of language as a boundary-maintaining device' (Veltman, 1977: 51).

Veltman hypothesised that since ethnicity continues to be an important element of self-identification, and as cultural space that separates ethnic groups begins to erode, language may emerge as an ethnic boundary of greater significance. We have observed the erosion of cultural space among the Franco-Ontarians through association with the numerically dominant anglophone group at work and in social situations, in preferences for English-language television, newspapers and

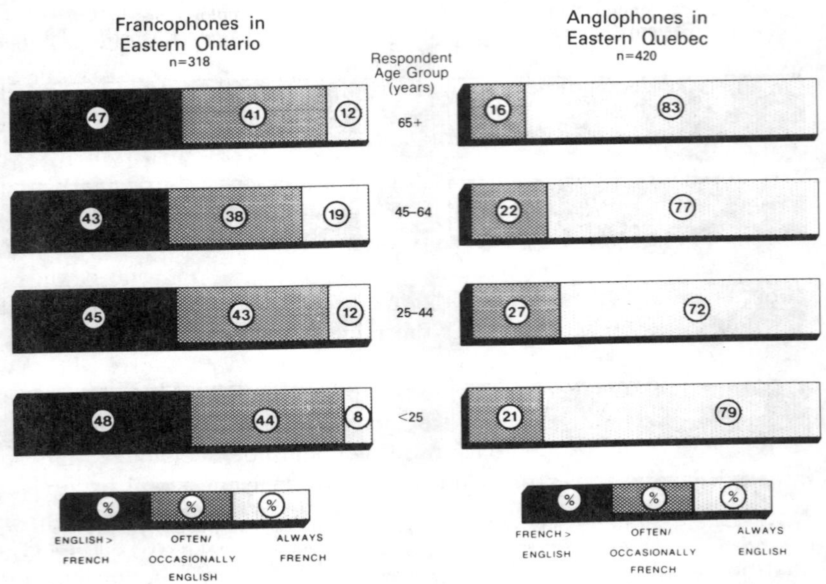

FIGURE 8.8 *Magazine reading habits by language for anglophones in eastern Quebec and francophones in eastern Ontario, 1985*

magazines and for various services within and beyond their community, therefore we should expect demands for the preservation of language to arise more frequently. Veltman also points out that such a revitalised ethnic boundary can also function as a unifying factor for a fragmented minority. A lack of empathy for the significance of language to a 'critical' stage for Franco-Ontarians in the zone may generate conflict which could negate some of the positive outcomes of status language planning that have been forthcoming in the anglo-dominant core area of Ontario. Franco-Ontarians are offered provincial government services through a functional organisation of territory. That is, rather than declaring French an official language of the province, the government of Ontario has opted for services in education and the courts according to individual demand and for other government services in designated areas, which include the transition zone. For many in Ontario, this provision of services is considered adequate for the Franco-Ontarians. Suggestions that French be granted official status anywhere in the province are treated gingerly by the provincial government because of the fear of a backlash from the majority. If legislators do not believe that a viable, bicultural transition zone can help to reduce social and cognitive distances between French and English Canada, this preoccupation with backlash will prevail.

Language legislation that was promulgated in Quebec during the 1970s has provided security for the French language and has probably encouraged young anglophones to develop their involvement with francophone society, but it has also contributed to the exodus of many non-francophones and to uncertainty for future employment opportunities among those who remain. The legislation will be a negative for Quebec and for Canada if the Quebec portion of the transition zone is allowed to erode further. A survey conducted in Quebec among anglophones found that the young members of the minority felt uncertain about their future in Quebec (CROP, 1983). If this is true for those who have demonstrated a stronger accommodation to the French language than older people, they may leave the province thereby reducing the proportion who are best suited to break the 'two solitudes' element that has dominated parts of the zone, and domain exclusiveness will be revived. Many of these young, Quebec anglophones have recently taken up the cause of minority francophones beyond Quebec. There has been a revelation of kindred souls. The potential of this as a contributor to national unity should not be overlooked. Its demise accompanying an eroded zone, would be a severe setback.

It is within the cultural transition zone that regular programmes are developed to promote integration between the two ethnic communities without respective loss of ethnic identity. Schools have been established in which the two groups follow independent curricula in the mother tongue but in the same building. They socialise and participate in sports activities in both languages. A church will provide service in both languages simultaneously. Some parallel business and service clubs have given way to single institutions in which the two ethnic groups interact in each other's language. These are traits that must be preserved. This geographical region is the one location in the nation where these activities can develop, flourish and contribute to the demise of ethnic social and cognitive distances that have become endemic in Belgium and in Northern Ireland. An example is provided for the rest of the nation that two solitudes need not be the legacy for Canada, linguistic territorialisation, with its negative connotations, need not be inevitable and empathy between French and English Canada can be attained in time.

A similar comparison may be made for the cultural transition zone within the United States. For those who focus on growing or diminishing numbers only within a minority population, knowledge of patterns of distribution and interaction will be considered irrelevant. Similarly, the reactions in Mexico and Central America to policies and programmes directed at the Hispanic population in the American portion of the transition zone will be irrelevant since a consuming view of national unity must take precedent. To provide thrust to their argument for unity, those who promote official status for English only look northward to Canada and lament a drift toward the 'Canadian situation of bilingualism' in the United States. They will not look southward to observe the impact that their lack of empathy has in Mexico and Central America, and the resultant negative attitudes that develop toward the United States.

In the Old World/African model, efforts to accommodate a peripheral ethnic minority, that is struggling with similar erosive processes, will do more to promote national unity than the palliatives that are regarded by the recipients as half-hearted and even delusive. If the model has relevance, it will help us to promote the importance of the periphery and the cultural transition zone to enlightened national unity and as a significant link, symbolically and functionally, between cultural realms.

Notes

1. If we can assume that people who encounter no pressure to learn a second language in their community will remain unilingual, we should anticipate a similarity in size between a home-language population and a unilingual population. Thus, to provide an indicator of the potential for language usage beyond the home, it was decided to use the unilingual population — those who replied 'English only' or 'French only' to the official languages question — in a cross-tabulation with responses to the home-language question. The former must be considered the least subjective of the language-related questions in the census, and while the latter can be confusing to respondents who were raised in a home where more than one language was used, it does provide a measure of those who are still able to speak their mother tongue. We are also comparing two census populations that have current time frames. Thus, when the unilingual French/English population is cross-tabulated with the home-language (French/English) population we can establish an index that will range from 1.00 to 0.00. By comparing these two census populations for any census division or subdivision the index may be expressed in the following form:

$$\frac{\text{official-language population} \left\{\begin{array}{l}\text{French}\\ \text{English}\end{array}\right. \text{only}}{\text{home-language population} \left\{\begin{array}{l}\text{French}\\ \text{English}\end{array}\right.} = \begin{array}{l}\text{index of}\\ \text{language}\\ \text{intensity}\end{array}$$

Any community that has an index close to 1.00 may be considered one in which people can function well in their mother tongue during a daily pattern of contact and human interaction. When the index approaches 0.00 the opposite occurs: people must switch to the other official language for most services, to function at work, and for many daily contacts. Hence, the index becomes a measure of the intensity with which a particular language permeates the area.

2. This field research was supported by a grant from the Social Science and Humanities Research Council, Ottawa.

References

ABLER, R. 1975, Monoculture or miniculture? The impact of communications media on culture in space. In R. ABLER, D. JANELLE, A. PHILBRICK and J. SOMMER (eds) *Human Geography in a Shrinking World*. Massachusetts: Duxbury Press.

ALVAREZ, R. 1984, The border as social system: the California case. *New Scholar* 9, 119–33.

ALVAREZ, J. 1986, Euskara: the Basque language. *Contact Bulletin, European Bureau for Lesser Used Languages*, 2 (3), 4.

ANNAMALAI, E. 1986, Language rights and language planning. *New Language Planning Newsletter*, Central Institute of Indian Languages, 1 (2), 1–3.

ARGEMI I ROCA, AURELI 1986, Multilingualism in the Spanish State. *Contact Bulletin, European Bureau for Lesser Used Languages*, 2 (3), 1.

BOAL, F. W. and DOUGLAS, J. N. H. (eds) 1982, *Integration and Division: Geographical Perspectives on the Northern Ireland Problem*. London: Academic Press.

Canada: Office of the Commissioner of Official Languages 1985, *Annual Report*. Ottawa, Ontario: Ministry of Supply and Service.

CARTWRIGHT, D. 1985a, The impact of minority on language policy and the impact of language policy on minority in Quebec. In J. COBARRUBIAS (ed.) *Language Policy in Canada: Current Issues* (pp. 37–59). Quebec: International Center for Research on Bilingualism, Laval University.

— 1985b, An official languages policy for Ontario. *Canadian Public Policy* 11, 561–77.

CARTWRIGHT, D. 1987, Accommodation among the anglophone minority in Quebec to official language policy: a shift in traditional patterns of language contact. *Journal of Multilingual and Multicultural Development* 8, 85–103.

COBARRUBIAS, J. 1986, Language policy and language planning efforts in Spain. Paper presented at the Conference on Language Planning, Ottawa, Canada.

CROP (Centre de Recherch sur l'Opinion Publique) 1983, *Etude des communautés francophones hors de Québec des communautés anglophones au Québec des francophones au Quebec et des anglophones hors Québec* vol. 2. Ottawa: Ministry for Secretary of State.

GAFFIELD, C. 1987, *Language, Schooling and Cultural Conflict: The Origins of the French-Language Controversy in Ontario*. Montreal: McGill-Queen's University Press.

GOTTMAN, J. (ed.) 1980, *Centre and Periphery: Spatial Variation in Politics*. Beverly Hills: Sage Publications.

JOY, R. 1972, *Languages in Conflict: The Canadian Experience*. Toronto: McClelland and Stewart.

KLIOT, N. and WATERMAN, S. (eds) 1983, *Pluralism and Political Geography*. London: Croom Helm.

LAPONCE, J. A. 1987, *Languages and Their Territories*. Toronto: University of Toronto Press.

MCRAE, K. 1986, *Conflict and Compromise in Multilingual Societies: Belgium*. Waterloo, Canada: Wilfrid Laurier University Press.

VELTMAN, C. 1977, The evolution of ethno-linguistic frontiers in the United States and Canada. *The Social Science Journal* 14 (1), 47–58.

WILLIAMS, C. H. (ed.) 1982a, *National Separatism*. Vancouver: University of British Columbia Press.

— 1982b, Separatism and the mobilization of Welsh national identity. In C. H. WILLIAMS (ed.) *National Separatism* (pp. 145–201). Vancouver: University of British Columbia Press.

9 The Spatial Organisation of Language in Canada, 1981[1]

JOHN DE VRIES

Introduction

Earlier work on Canada's language situation has demonstrated the existence of rather durable spatial patterns. Such analyses, traditionally based on Census data, show the persistence of concentration by mother tongue, ethnic origin or the ability to speak English or French from the beginning of the twentieth century through to 1971 or 1976 (details may be found in Joy, 1972; Lachapelle & Henripin, 1982; Lieberson, 1970; Maheu, 1970; Vallee & de Vries, 1978; de Vries & Vallee, 1980).

This analysis updates that work through 1981, on the basis of the 1981 Census. In particular, changes which occurred in the decade 1971–81 will be analysed in somewhat more detail. In this chapter, provinces are used as units of analysis.

The Distribution of Mother Tongue Categories

For the sake of simplicity, I have divided the responses to the question on mother tongue into three categories: English, French and Other. The last category, thus, includes all of the 'non official' languages, those of Native Canadians as well as those associated with immigrants. At this stage, these 'other' languages are given least emphasis. Eventually, more detailed work will have to be done on the largest language groups included in the category 'other'.

In 1981, a little over 61% of the population had English as mother tongue, about 26% French, while the remaining 13% had a mother tongue other than French or English.

Overall this shows very little change from 1971, when corresponding percentages were 60, 27 and 13. The intercensal decade showed a slight increase in the proportion with English as mother tongue, a slight decrease in the French category, while the 'other' mother tongue category maintained roughly the same proportion in the Canadian population. Such marginal processes of change are extremely slow, as they have been for the entire period for which comparable data are available. Not surprisingly, then, much of what will be written about the 1981 language patterns will be a virtual repetition of what has been written about the 1971 patterns. In what follows, the 1971 information will be used as a baseline from which the more recent data may be evaluated and analysed.

When we consider the spatial segregation between the three mother tongue categories we find, again, that little has changed between 1971 and 1981. See Table 9.1. The segregation index, used in the table (also known as the index of dissimilarity, or 'delta') has a range from 0 (no segregation) to 1.00 (maximal segregation). Values may be interpreted as 'the proportion of one group which would have to be redistributed for the two percentage distributions to be identical'. To illustrate: the segregation between English and French mother tongue groups in 1981 had an index value of 0.81. In other words, 81% of either group would have to move to another province for the percentage distributions of the English and French mother tongue groups by province to be identical. See de Vries & Vallee, (1980: 74) for further details. A detailed discussion of segregation indices is provided in James & Taeuber (1982).

The decade 1971–1981 showed, again, very little change: the French and English mother tongue categories were already highly segregated in 1971 and became even more so by 1981. The segregation between French

TABLE 9.1 *Segregation indexes between mother tongue categories, Canada, 1971 and 1981*

	English	*French*	*Other*
English	—	0.810	0.137
French	0.785	—	0.750
Other	0.158	0.744	—

Segregation indexes are based on the distribution of the population by province. Upper triangle gives values for 1981, lower triangle for 1971.

and 'other' mother tongues, also high in 1971, increased by a tiny amount, while the segregation between English and 'other' decreased somewhat. Even at the relatively crude level of provinces, the data show the slightly increased tendency towards the 'two solitudes', with the French mother tongue population increasingly concentrated in Quebec and New Brunswick (these two provinces contained 87.7% of the French mother tongue population in 1971, 88.8% in 1981) and the English mother tongue population increasingly concentrated in the rest of the country (Quebec and New Brunswick together contained 9.2% of the English mother tongue population in 1971, but only 7.8% in 1981). Despite these observable changes, we again notice the slow rate of change in these patterns. As we shall see, the percentage distribution of mother tongue by province for 1971 gives a good description of the patterns for 1981. Tables 9.2 and 9.3 give these distributions for 1971 and 1981 respectively. We see the slight decline in the share having French as mother tongue, a small increase in the proportion with English as mother tongue, and virtually no change in the segment with an 'other' mother tongue.

While the marginal frequencies did not show much change between 1971 and 1981, the distributions by province did show, in a number of places, somewhat larger differences. We note, in particular, the increasing proportions of the English mother tongue population in Alberta and British Columbia, compared with decreases in Quebec and all of the

TABLE 9.2 *Percentage distribution of mother tongue, by province, Canada, 1971*

	English %	*French* %	*Other* %	*Total* %
Newfoundland	3.97	0.06	0.14	2.42
Prince Edward Island	0.79	0.13	0.04	0.52
Nova Scotia	5.65	0.68	0.57	3.66
New Brunswick	3.16	3.72	0.30	2.94
Quebec	6.08	84.01	13.26	27.95
Ontario	46.03	8.32	44.61	35.72
Manitoba	5.11	1.04	9.46	4.58
Saskatchewan	5.29	0.55	7.45	4.29
Alberta	9.74	0.80	11.33	7.55
British Columbia	13.93	0.66	12.12	10.13
Yukon	0.12	0.01	0.09	0.08
Northwest Territories	0.13	0.02	0.62	0.16
Total	100.00	100.00	100.00	100.00
Per cent of Total	60.15	26.86	12.99	100.00

TABLE 9.3 *Percentage distribution of mother tongue, by province, Canada, 1981*

	English %	*French* %	*Other* %	*Total* %
Newfoundland	3.78	0.04	0.13	2.34
Prince Edward Island	0.77	0.10	0.04	0.50
Nova Scotia	5.33	0.58	0.57	3.49
New Brunswick	3.04	3.75	0.27	2.86
Quebec	4.71	84.98	13.49	26.45
Ontario	44.74	7.58	46.49	35.44
Manitoba	4.93	0.84	7.43	4.21
Saskatchewan	5.17	0.41	5.35	3.97
Alberta	12.17	0.99	11.34	9.19
British Columbia	15.06	0.71	14.20	11.27
Yukon	0.14	0.01	0.08	0.10
Northwest Territories	0.17	0.02	0.62	0.19
Total	100.01	100.01	100.01	100.01
Per cent of Total	61.25	25.64	13.11	100.00

Atlantic provinces. For the population of French mother tongue, we note especially the increased concentration in the province of Quebec. For the third segment, that of 'other' mother tongues, we see slight increases of the shares in Ontario and British Columbia.

A difficulty with the values in Tables 9.2 and 9.3 is that they add up to 100% in every column; as such, columns pertaining to a particular mother tongue segment may be compared. It is, however, *not* the case that populations have remained stationary during this intercensal decade. The total Canadian population increased, as a result of births exceeding deaths and immigration exceeding emigration. To obtain a more detailed view of the change, I calculated the percentage change, for each cell in Tables 9.2 and 9.3, based on the measured group size. The results are given in Table 9.4. The bottom line shows that the total Canadian population increased by 11.77% between 1971 and 1981. This overall increase did not, however, apply equally to the three mother tongue segments separately: rates of increase range from 6.6% for the population of French mother tongue to 12.7% for those of other mother tongues. These intercensal changes are the results of several demographic processes:

(a) natural increase, i.e. the difference between births and deaths;
(b) net international migration, i.e. the difference between immigration and emigration;

TABLE 9.4 *Percentage change for the period 1971–81, by mother tongue and province, Canada*

	English %	*French* %	*Other* %	*Total* %
Newfoundland	8.08	−26.10	4.57	7.98
Prince Edward Island	10.25	−19.70	11.02	8.58
Nova Scotia	7.15	−9.25	12.57	6.44
New Brunswick	9.38	7.52	1.36	8.64
Quebec	−11.95	7.83	14.64	5.66
Ontario	10.51	−2.94	17.45	10.79
Manitoba	9.72	−14.13	−11.49	2.58
Saskatchewan	11.11	−19.87	−19.05	3.26
Alberta	42.01	30.97	12.73	35.98
British Columbia	22.94	14.88	32.07	24.21
Yukon	31.41	15.56	−8.27	25.49
Northwest Territories	51.13	6.01	13.35	30.82
Total	11.91	6.60	12.71	11.77

(c) net language shifts, in this case manifested by a change in the classification of persons by mother tongue (e.g. someone who in 1971 was classified as having an 'other' mother tongue and in 1981 as English would have manifested mother tongue shift).

We know that overall natural increase in Canada, during the period 1971–81, amounted to about 8.3 per thousand (cf. de Vries, 1982: 22). While we do not know anything about the magnitude of the other processes, we could entertain some simple hypotheses. We might assume that the overall change for the population of French mother tongue is almost entirely due to natural increase. Thus, we would have to deduce that, for this group, net migration and mother tongue shift would be close to zero. By a similar argument — if we assume that rates of natural increase for the two remaining segments were contributing around 8% to their intercensal increase — we may postulate that their growth was also attributable to net migration and net mother tongue shift. It is likely that net international migration was the more important factor for those of other mother tongues; for those of English mother tongue, language shift may also have contributed.

When we look at the detailed figures in Table 9.4, we see that the overall growth rate of 11.9% for the English mother tongue category masks rather large variations by province. Quite high rates of increase are, again, registered by Alberta, British Columbia, the Yukon and the

Northwest Territories. If it is indeed the case that these provinces and territories gained substantially through net migration, it appears that migrants were predominantly of English mother tongue. In all these cases, except British Columbia, growth rates for the English mother tongue segment exceeded total provincial growth rates. It should be noted that such a net differential could have been caused by a combination of several processes: higher probabilities of immigration for persons of English mother tongue, and higher probabilities of out-migration for others ('out-migration' may not be easily distinguished from mother tongue shift).

At the other end of the range, we find that the English mother tongue segment in Quebec *decreased* by about 12%. Such a decrease could be the result of a negative migration balance, or of net shift to French mother tongue or both. The remaining provinces had intercensal growth rates at or above those we might expect on the basis of natural increase. This suggests that, for example, Manitoba or Saskatchewan (both of which had very low total intercensal growth rates) may well have had net migration losses for all mother tongue categories, combined with net language shift towards English mother tongue from persons of French or other mother tongue.

Such inferences are further supported by the growth rates for the provincial French mother tongue populations. The overall growth rate of 6.6% is exceeded in Alberta, British Columbia, the Yukon, Quebec and New Brunswick. Virtually all of the other values are negative, indicating a decline in the *size* of these groups. For the first three provinces, the high growth rates are probably the result of net migration (one would be best not to put much weight on the rate of increase for the Yukon, where frequencies were quite small). Since growth rates are smaller than the corresponding provincial total rates, it may be that persons of French mother tongue were underrepresented in the migration flows into these provinces, or overrepresented in the flows from them. Alternatively, it may be that a positive net migration balance was partly offset by losses through mother tongue shift. In Quebec and New Brunswick, the French mother tongue groups may have had positive net migration balances. In addition, mother tongue shift to French may have been zero or small positive in Quebec; it was probably negative but small for New Brunswick. For the remaining provinces, the declines in the size of the French mother tongue population may have been the result of negative migration balances, or the effect of mother tongue shift towards English, or both.

The 'other' mother tongue category had considerably less variation across provinces than did those of English and French mother tongue. Above average rates for British Columbia (of 32%) contrasted with decrease in size for Manitoba, Saskatchewan and the Yukon. Net shift towards English may well have been a significant factor in these last three cases. The relatively high rates of increase for Quebec and Ontario probably reflect international migration, which has traditionally favoured these two central provinces.

The detailed analysis of growth rates by mother tongue and provinces revealed some changes which were hidden by the high degree of stability in the marginal distributions. The excursus into the provincial growth rates suggests that we should pay particular attention to the English mother tongue group in Quebec and to the French mother tongue groups in all provinces except Quebec and New Brunswick. Particularly interesting may be the changes in Manitoba and Saskatchewan, which were not all that obvious when we dealt with the marginal changes by mother tongue.

Readers who have followed the demographic, political and social developments in Canada since the early 1970s are likely to say, at this point, that we have spent considerable energy in 'revealing' something which was already known. We 'know' that the English population of Quebec has declined; we also 'are aware' of the vulnerable position of the French minorities outside Quebec and New Brunswick. The rather methodical development of the analysis so far has two functions: first of all, a pedagogical one. I have tried to demonstrate that somewhat subtle changes may be masked by overall marginal stability. If we were considering comparable data for another society, say Finland or Switzerland, we might not a priori 'know' about such regional shifts. A naive analyst might be tempted to stop if marginal distributions showed very little change, and would thus miss the lower-level changes.

The second purpose was methodological as well as pedagogical: the gradual 'unfolding' of the analysis has produced a nice fit between what we 'know' from the mass media (or other sources) and the census data. This should give us some faith in the descriptive potential of the census data.

It may be educative to consider the intercensal change in even further detail. One way to do this is by means of a method of analysis developed by Theil (1972), generally called statistical decomposition analysis. To show the association between a person's province of residence and mother tongue, I calculated values of *mutual information* (Theil, 1972: 125). That is, when we have a distribution p_{ij} (where i = province, j = mother tongue and p_{ij} is the proportion of the total population in province i with mother tongue j) and marginal distributions $p_{i.}$ and $p_{.j}$ (for province and mother tongue, respectively), the mutual information is given as

$$\ln\left[\frac{p_{ij}}{P_{i}.P._{j}}\right].$$

Obviously, when there is statistical independence between the two characteristics, we will find that $p_{ij} = p_{i.}p_{.j}$ for all i,j and that thus the mutual information will be 0. If the two characteristics are not independent, not all values for p_{ij} will be 0. Positive values indicate overrepresentation (that is, more persons in cell {i,j} than one would expect under conditions of statistical independence). Similarly, negative values indicate underrepresentation. The magnitude of the mutual information for a given cell {i,j} is associated with the degree of overrepresentation or underrepresentation.

The data for 1971 and 1981 are given in Tables 9.5 and 9.6.

We see that the *overall* association between province of residence and mother tongue did not change all that much. (We would not have expected this either, given the preceding analyses.) The median value (across provinces) for English mother tongue changed from 0.254 in 1971 to 0.272 in 1981; corresponding values were from −1.873 to −2.015 for French mother tongue and from 0.131 to −0.010 for Other mother tongue. The data for English mother tongue show the well-known negative

TABLE 9.5 *Mutual information for the cross-classification of province of residence by mother tongue, Canada, 1971*

	English	*French*	*Other*
Newfoundland	0.494	−3.644	−2.860
Prince Edward Island	0.430	−1.407	−2.597
Nova Scotia	0.435	−1.686	−1.846
New Brunswick	0.073	0.235	−2.284
Quebec	−1.525	1.101	−0.746
Ontario	0.254	−1.457	0.222
Manitoba	0.109	−1.477	0.725
Saskatchewan	0.208	−2.060	0.551
Alberta	0.255	−2.239	0.407
British Columbia	0.319	−2.738	0.179
Yukon	0.328	−2.435	0.084
Northwest Territories	−0.242	−2.158	1.342

TABLE 9.6 *Mutual information for the cross-classification of province of residence by mother tongue, Canada, 1981*

	English	*French*	*Other*
Newfoundland	0.478	−4.00	−2.893
Prince Edward Island	0.429	−1.641	−2.579
Nova Scotia	0.424	−1.799	−1.807
New Brunswick	0.061	0.271	−2.344
Quebec	−1.725	1.167	−0.673
Ontario	0.233	−1.542	0.271
Manitoba	0.158	−1.609	0.568
Saskatchewan	0.263	−2.272	0.299
Alberta	0.281	−2.232	0.210
British Columbia	0.290	−2.770	0.231
Yukon	0.357	−2.510	−0.230
Northwest Territories	−0.127	−2.271	1.197

association with Quebec residence, which became somewhat stronger between 1971 and 1981. The westward movement of the population of English mother tongue between 1971 and 1981 can be seen clearly in these data: values increased for Manitoba, Saskatchewan and Alberta, and decreased for Ontario and all of the provinces to the east. Finally, these values on mutual information for the English mother tongue demonstrate the persistent 'ecology of language' in Canada; the further one moves either east or west from Quebec, the stronger the association between province and English mother tongue (the exception is Ontario, where the degree of overrepresentation is not as large as we would expect, given the values for Quebec and Manitoba).

Similar patterns, though of opposite signs, are shown by the values of French mother tongue. They show a maximum for Quebec and relatively steady declines as one moves west or east. Whereas the values for the English mother tongue segment suggested a westward drift between 1971 and 1981, those for French mother tongue indicate increased concentration in Quebec and New Brunswick. Only Alberta was an exception to this overall pattern. As I suggested earlier, Alberta appears to have had a positive migration balance for the population of French mother tongue.

Following the statistical decomposition methodology, I then analysed to what degree the observed changes in the *marginal* distributions (by province and by mother tongue) could explain the changes in the joint distribution. Quite obviously, if we find that the population of Alberta (to take one example) increased rapidly, we might hypothesise that all of the groups in that population have grown rapidly (the null hypothesis would be, in this case, that all three of Alberta's mother tongue categories had the same intercensal growth rate). Such a phenomenon could, by itself, explain the above average rate of increase for the English mother tongue segment in the total Canadian population (given its overrepresentation in Alberta) and the below average growth rate for the French mother tongue population (given its underrepresentation), as long as differential provincial rates of increase were not *completely* the result of internal migration. By similar arguments we could hypothesise that the above average growth rate for those of English mother tongue could 'explain' the high growth rates for Alberta and British Columbia, as well as the low growth for Quebec (again based on the observed associations reflected in Tables 9.5 and 9.6). Such simple-minded explanations would not help us at all in explaining the low growth rates for Manitoba and Saskatchewan, however. In any case, it is clearly not true that changes in the joint distribution can be entirely attributed to differential rates of increase for the categories of one marginal distribution only. Obviously, if we observe rather pronounced differences in the growth rates for categories of *both* of the marginal variables, the resulting joint distribution may well be the product of the initial joint distribution and changes in the two marginal distributions only. (This line of analysis is analogous to that followed in the study of occupational mobility, where some part — structural mobility — is attributable to changes in the marginal distributions, while the remainder — exchange mobility — indicates additional moves between marginal categories.)

We can calculate the expected joint distribution which would result if intercensal changes were due *only* to the marginal changes. Table 9.7 gives these expected values, as well as the observed values for 1971 and 1981. When we compare the expected values with the observed values for 1981, we see that the method of 'marginal adjustments' in general provides reasonably good estimates of the values after a decade of change. The overall change can be measured, following Theil, by a summary measured called *information inaccuracy*. This measure is calculated as:

$$\sum_{i=1}^{m} \sum_{j=1}^{n} q_{ij} \ln \frac{q_{ij}}{P_{ij}}$$

where p_{ij} represents the joint distribution in 1971 and q_{ij} represents the joint distribution in 1981. A quick inspection of the above formula shows that we are measuring the degree to which the *initial* distribution (p_{ij})

'predicts' the final distribution (q_{ij}). If there were *no* changes, for any combination of i and j, all the m × n components of the information inaccuracy would be zero (as would their sum). Under all other conditions, the sum of these m × n components will be larger than zero. Greater deviations from zero indicate greater inaccuracy in 'predicting' q_{ij} on the basis of p_{ij}.

The *total* information inaccuracy yielded a value of 0.00498. We can now calculate a similar measure, using the *expected* distribution as our starting point. That is, we are assessing the degree to which the 'marginally adjusted' joint proportions predict the observed proportions. This yields a value for the information inaccuracy of 0.00194. We may view these information inaccuracies as measures of 'spread' or 'dispersion' (i.e. measures comparable to variances or chi-squares). Thus, we can say that the overall information inaccuracy of 0.00498 has been reduced to 0.00194 due to the marginal adjustments, or by 61% of its initial value.

Careful inspection of the data in Table 9.7 shows that the estimates are relatively close to the observed 1981 values, except in the following cases: English mother tongue in Quebec; French mother tongue in Ontario, Manitoba and Saskatchewan; Other mother tongue in Manitoba and Saskatchewan. In all these cases, the data show relatively large declines between 1971 and 1981, of which only a small component is picked up by the estimation technique. For example, the English mother tongue population in Quebec declined from 3.7% of Canada's population in 1971 to 2.9% in 1981, but the estimate is 3.5%. In other words, only one-quarter of the actual decline is signalled by the marginal adjustment procedure. The procedure appears to have a tendency to underestimate the magnitude of relatively large changes.

In sum, we may conclude that a large share of the intercensal changes in the mother tongue distribution by province may be attributed to relatively high rates of increase for Alberta, British Columbia and the Northwest Territories, and relatively low growth rates for Manitoba, Saskatchewan and Quebec. In addition, there were minor effects due to differential growth rates by mother tongue.

The Distribution of Official Language Categories

To shed further light on these intercensal changes in the spatial patterning of language in Canada, I also considered the distribution of the population by 'official language(s) spoken': English only, French only, Both and Neither. Tables 9.8 and 9.9 give the distribution of official

TABLE 9.7 *Observed (1971 and 1981) and expected proportions, joint distribution of province by mother tongue, Canada, 1971–1981*

	English			*French*			*Other*		
	Observed 1971	*Observed 1981*	*Expected 1981*	*Observed 1971*	*Observed 1981*	*Expected 1981*	*Observed 1971*	*Observed 1981*	*Expected 1981*
Newfoundland	0.0239	0.0231	0.0231	0.0002	0.0001	0.0002	0.0002	0.0002	0.0002
Prince Edward Island	0.0048	0.0047	0.0047	0.0003	0.0003	0.0003	0.0000	0.0000	0.0000
Nova Scotia	0.0340	0.0326	0.0324	0.0018	0.0015	0.0017	0.0008	0.0008	0.0007
New Brunswick	0.0190	0.0186	0.0185	0.0100	0.0096	0.0097	0.0004	0.0004	0.0004
Quebec	0.0366	0.0289	0.0346	0.2257	0.2179	0.2137	0.0172	0.0177	0.0162
Ontario	0.2769	0.2740	0.2749	0.0224	0.0194	0.0222	0.0579	0.0609	0.0572
Manitoba	0.0307	0.0302	0.0283	0.0028	0.0022	0.0026	0.0123	0.0097	0.0122
Saskatchewan	0.0318	0.0316	0.0294	0.0015	0.0010	0.0014	0.0097	0.0070	0.0089
Alberta	0.0586	0.0745	0.0715	0.0022	0.0025	0.0026	0.0147	0.0149	0.0178
British Columbia	0.0838	0.0922	0.0933	0.0018	0.0018	0.0020	0.0157	0.0186	0.0174
Yukon	0.0007	0.0008	0.0008	0.0000	0.0000	0.0000	0.0001	0.0001	0.0001
Northwest Territories	0.0008	0.0010	0.0009	0.0000	0.0000	0.0000	0.0008	0.0008	0.0009

language by province, for 1971 and 1981.

In the marginal distributions, we see a slight decline in the proportion speaking English only, somewhat larger declines in the group which speaks French only and those speaking neither official language, and a fairly strong increase in the proportion able to speak English and French.

Segregation between official language categories, based on the provincial distributions, is summarised in Table 9.10. We note quite high levels of segregation between those able to speak French only and those who can speak English only, which even increased between 1971 and 1981. Overall, French monolinguals appear to be highly segregated from those unable to speak English or French, while their segregation from those able to speak both of the official languages was at a much lower level. French monolinguals became more segregated from all three other categories during the period 1971–81. Other values were considerably lower, but they too increased, with the exception of the segregation between English monolinguals and those unable to speak either official language, where a slight decline was noted. Inspection of the Lorenz-curves (not included in this manuscript) reveals that all pairwise comparisons except 'English only–Neither' satisfy the Lorenz-criterion.

TABLE 9.8 *Percentage distribution of official language by province, Canada, 1971*

	English only %	*French only* %	*Both* %	*Neither* %	*Total* %
Newfoundland	3.54	0.01	0.32	0.20	2.42
Prince Edward Island	0.70	0.02	0.31	0.01	0.52
Nova Scotia	5.05	0.11	1.83	0.32	3.66
New Brunswick	2.74	2.60	4.69	0.19	2.94
Quebec	4.37	94.55	57.37	19.86	27.94
Ontario	46.47	2.39	24.69	53.26	35.71
Manitoba	6.09	0.13	2.79	6.45	4.58
Saskatchewan	5.99	0.05	1.59	3.48	4.29
Alberta	10.54	0.09	2.79	5.63	7.55
British Columbia	14.20	0.05	3.50	8.37	10.13
Yukon	0.12	0.00	0.04	0.01	0.09
Northwest Territories	0.18	0.00	0.07	2.22	0.16
Total	100.00	100.00	100.00	100.00	100.00
Per cent of Total	67.09	17.99	13.45	1.48	100.01

TABLE 9.9 *Percentage distribution of official language by province, Canada, 1981*

	English only %	*French only* %	*Both* %	*Neither* %	*Total* %
Newfoundland	3.41	0.00	0.35	0.15	2.34
Prince Edward Island	0.69	0.01	0.27	0.01	0.50
Nova Scotia	4.81	0.05	1.69	0.28	3.49
New Brunswick	2.59	2.24	4.96	0.16	2.86
Quebec	2.64	95.97	56.09	17.54	26.45
Ontario	45.90	1.52	25.11	50.85	35.44
Manitoba	5.68	0.07	2.17	5.26	4.21
Saskatchewan	5.61	0.02	1.19	2.47	3.97
Alberta	12.68	0.09	3.87	7.70	9.19
British Columbia	15.62	0.04	4.19	13.40	11.27
Yukon	0.13	0.00	0.05	0.02	0.10
Northwest Territories	0.23	0.00	0.07	2.18	0.19
Total	100.00	100.00	100.00	100.00	100.00
Per cent of Total	66.95	16.56	15.29	1.21	100.05

TABLE 9.10 *Segregation indexes between official language categories, Canada, 1971 and 1981*

	English only	*French only*	*Both*	*Neither*
English only	—	0.933	0.558	0.218
French only	0.902	—	0.399	0.805
Both	0.550	0.372	—	0.453
Neither	0.247	0.771	0.440	—

Notes: Segregation indexes are based on the distribution of the population by province.
Upper triangle gives values for 1981, lower triangle for 1971.

That is, when we superimpose the Lorenz-curve for 1981 on the one for 1971 (for the same pair of official language categories), the two curves do not cross. For the 'English only–Neither' comparison, the curves cross at two points. We can therefore state unambiguously that segregation increased for all combinations of official language categories, except the 'English only–Neither' case, where we are unable to say whether it increased or decreased (see James & Taeuber, 1982: 24).

In the preceding section, we noted the increased concentration of the French mother tongue population in Quebec. The data by official language shed further light on this: the proportion of French monolinguals living in Quebec increased from 94.6% in 1971 to 96% in 1981. A similar concentration was *not* evident for those able to speak both official languages: the percentage living in Quebec decreased from 57.4% in 1971 to 56.1% in 1981. The concentration in New Brunswick and Ontario increased somewhat during the same period, so that the percentage of Canada's bilinguals living in these three provinces only declined from 86.9% to 86.1%. Thus, the increased concentration of the French mother tongue population in Quebec appears to be primarily associated with French monolingualism. Bilingualism — in the 'official' variety — appears to have remained a feature of the provinces of New Brunswick, Quebec and Ontario.

The westward drift which we noted for the population of English mother tongue is equally observable for the English monolinguals. The percentage living in the provinces west of Quebec increased from 83.3% in 1971 to 85.5% in 1981.

As with the analysis of the patterns by mother tongue, we may consider intercensal growth rates by official language category and province. Consider Table 9.11. The English monolingual category increased by 11.4%, or just a little under the total rate of increase. Recall that the growth rate for the English mother tongue category was 11.9% (Table 9.4). Thus, it appears that the English mother tongue population increased its share of the total population through net migration, language shift or differential natural increase, but that some group changed from being monolingual English in 1971 to being bilingual in 1981.

This contrast is much more marked from the French segments: the French mother tongue segment grew by 6.6%, but French monolinguals increased only by 2.8% (well below what we might expect on the basis of natural increase). It appears that there was considerable movement from French monolingualism to bilingualism. Given the concentration of French monolinguals in Quebec (where they increased at a little less than the provincial growth rate), it is likely that this shift took place largely outside Quebec. Bilinguals increased by 27%, well above the growth rates for the other groups. It is likely that much of this growth may be attributed to second-language acquisition during the intercensal period (rather than higher net migration balances, or lower death rates among bilinguals). Much of this increase may have come from the various official language minorities.

The group speaking neither official language decreased by 8.8%.

TABLE 9.11 *Percentage change for the period 1971–81, by categories of official language and province, Canada*

	English only %	*French only* %	*Both* %	*Neither* %	*Total* %
Newfoundland	7.57	−72.55	37.33	−31.20	7.98
Prince Edward Island	9.21	−70.59	7.35	(16.67)	8.58
Nova Scotia	6.03	−55.13	11.56	−21.84	6.44
New Brunswick	5.08	−11.53	34.12	−24.17	8.64
Quebec	−32.61	4.32	24.12	−19.42	5.66
Ontario	10.07	−34.80	29.11	−12.88	10.79
Manitoba	3.86	−47.91	−1.16	−25.48	2.58
Saskatchewan	4.33	−61.48	−5.08	−35.36	3.26
Alberta	34.05	12.10	75.87	24.62	35.98
British Columbia	22.60	−18.59	51.99	46.06	24.21
Yukon	23.76	(−50.00)	50.41	(28.57)	25.49
Northwest Territories	42.67	(−40.00)	29.95	−10.44	30.82
Total	11.43	2.78	26.96	−8.76	11.77

Note: Figures in parentheses are based on 1971 frequencies of less than 100.

We saw, earlier, that the Other mother tongue category increased by 12% during the same period. Given that those speaking neither English nor French are almost all from the Other mother tongue category, it is clear that there must have been a considerable rate of acquisition of English, or French, or both, during the period 1971–81.

If we look at the rates of change by province, we will get a clearer picture of what may have happened. Let us take the data column by column. The category speaking English only increased with rates roughly equal to the total provincial growth rates — somewhat higher in Prince Edward Island, Manitoba, Saskatchewan and the Northwest Territories. Markedly lower growth rates were attained for English monolinguals in New Brunswick, while the group registered an absolute decline of about one third in Quebec. In general, rates of increase for the English monolinguals were lower than those for English mother tongue, compared province by province. Such a pattern might point to several processes: shifts from French mother tongue or Other mother tongue to English mother tongue, and/or from speaking English only to speaking both English and French. For Quebec, it is safe to hypothesise that the propensity to migrate out of the province, already high for people with English as mother tongue, is substantially higher for those unable to speak French. Note that part of the contrast in rates of decline for the

English groups in Quebec may also be due to the acquisition of French by those people who in 1971 resided in Quebec, had English as mother tongue but were then unable to speak French.

For the segment able to speak French only, we see negative growth rates in all provinces except Quebec (with an increase of 4.3%) and Alberta (12.1%). Declines in the other provinces ranged from 11.5% in New Brunswick to over 70% for Newfoundland and Prince Edward Island. In these last two provinces, these declines were considerably larger than the corresponding losses to the French mother tongue segment. It appears that we observe the symptoms of relatively rapid language shift, partly intergenerational (shift in mother tongue), partly through the acquisition of English. Such an acquisition of English is indeed hinted at by the high rate of increase in the numbers able to speak both English and French in Newfoundland (over 37%). In Prince Edward Island, the process of minority decline may well have progressed to the stage where acquisition of English is partly offset by a decline in the ability to speak French.

Official bilingualism increased in *all* provinces except Manitoba and Saskatchewan. For the remainder, increases ranged from 7.4% in Prince Edward Island to 76%in Alberta. The most likely scenario, then, seems to be that French mother tongue minorities outside Quebec are continuing to lose ground to English. This shift appears to be most advanced in Manitoba and Saskatchewan (where the French mother tongue population decreased in absolute numbers, where the number able to speak French only was cut roughly in half, and where even the ability to speak both English and French declined between 1971 and 1981). Even in New Brunswick — generally considered the province where the French minority was stable — the drift towards English appears to have started: the population of French mother tongue increased by 7.5%, but French monolingualism declined by 11.5% and bilingualism increased by 34%. In this province, however, the hypothesised move towards bilingualism for the population of French mother tongue may have had an English counterpart; the population of English mother tongue increased by 9.4%, but the population speaking English grew only by 6%.

The population able to speak neither official language declined by over 10% in all provinces except Manitoba and British Columbia (note that data for Prince Edward Island and the Yukon were based on very small frequencies in 1971). In general, the data suggest relatively high rates of acquisition of English (or French, or both) for persons of Other mother tongue; for most provinces, the number of persons with Other mother tongues increased, while the number speaking neither French nor English decreased. The exceptions were Alberta and British Columbia; in these two provinces, the pattern may well be due to the immigration of persons unable to speak either official language.

I calculated values of the mutual information for official language categories by province, for 1971 and 1981. These data are shown in Tables 9.12 and 9.13. We find the by now familiar association between province of residence and language characteristics: increasing association between distance from Quebec and English monolingualism (with maxima in the east for Newfoundland, in the west for Saskatchewan), increasing negative association between distance from Quebec and French monolingualism (largest negative values found for Newfoundland and British Columbia) and a comparable association for official bilingualism (largest negative values found for Newfoundland and British Columbia in 1971, Saskatchewan in 1981). The inability to speak either official language seems to be associated with residence in Ontario, Manitoba, British Columbia and the Northwest Territories.

A detailed comparison between Tables 9.12 and 9.13 shows that the mutual information of province and official language did not change all that much from 1971 to 1981. Most notable were the changes in mutual information for those speaking French only; an increase in an already positive value for Quebec, combined with decreases in negative values for the other provinces. Here again, we find indications of the

TABLE 9.12 *Mutual information for the cross-classification of province of residence by official language, Canada, 1971*

	English only	*French only*	*Both*	*Neither*
Newfoundland	0.379	−5.216	−2.016	−2.515
Prince Edward Island	0.307	−3.385	−0.500	−4.009
Nova Scotia	0.322	−3.522	−0.693	−2.428
New Brunswick	−0.070	−0.122	0.467	−2.751
Quebec	−1.855	1.219	0.719	−0.341
Ontario	0.263	−2.703	−0.369	0.400
Manitoba	0.285	−3.567	−0.496	0.341
Saskatchewan	0.333	−4.511	−0.996	−0.210
Alberta	0.334	−4.484	−0.994	−0.292
British Columbia	0.338	−5.400	−1.063	−0.191
Yukon	0.328	−6.494	−0.715	−2.051
Northwest Territories	0.088	−4.137	−0.792	2.621

TABLE 9.13 *Mutual information for the cross-classification of province of residence by official language, Canada, 1981*

	English	*French*	*Both*	*Neither*
Newfoundland	0.377	−6.502	−1.904	−2.764
Prince Edward Island	0.315	−4.609	−0.639	−3.736
Nova Scotia	0.321	−4.304	−0.722	−2.536
New Brunswick	−0.101	−0.245	0.549	−2.909
Quebec	−2.303	1.289	0.752	−0.410
Ontario	0.259	−3.150	−0.344	0.361
Manitoba	0.300	−4.162	−0.661	0.224
Saskatchewan	0.346	−5.414	−1.209	−0.477
Alberta	0.322	−4.594	−0.865	−0.178
British Columbia	0.327	−5.470	−0.990	0.173
Yukon	0.316	−5.946	−0.662	−1.825
Northwest Territories	0.177	−4.834	−0.927	2.444

increased concentration of French monolingualism in Quebec. Note, furthermore, the relatively large changes in mutual information for bilinguals in Prince Edward Island, Manitoba, Saskatchewan and the Northwest Territories (becoming increasingly negative) and New Brunswick (becoming larger positive), as well as the value for Alberta which 'goes against the grain' by becoming less negative. Median values across provinces remain virtually constant for English only (from 0.315 to 0.316) and for bilinguals (from −0.704 to −0.692), increase (negatively) for French only (from −3.852 to −4.602) and for those able to speak neither official language (from −0.317 to −0.444).

Following the line of analysis used on the mother tongue data, I also constructed the matrix of joint proportions we would expect if the internal changes were entirely due to the changes in marginal distributions. Table 9.14 gives the comparison between the *observed* proportions in 1981 with the *expected* values. As with the analysis for the mother tongue data, the marginal adjustment procedure explains most of the intercensal change in the spatial pattern by official language. The total information inaccuracy (that is, the 'error' we would make if we postulated that the joint distribution for 1971 described that for 1981 correctly) was 0.00835. The marginally adjusted values reduce the total information inaccuracy to 0.00282, a reduction of about 66%. Recall that we may interpret this to mean that, of the total intercensal change for 1971–81, about two-thirds may be explained by changes in the marginal distributions by province and by categories of official languages spoken. Particularly

TABLE 9.14 *Observed and expected proportions, joint distribution of province by official language, Canada, 1981*

	English only		*French only*		*Both*		*Neither*	
	Observed	*Expected*	*Observed*	*Expected*	*Observed*	*Expected*	*Observed*	*Expected*
Newfoundland	0.0228	0.0228	0.0000	0.0000	0.0005	0.0005	0.0000	0.0000
Prince Edward Island	0.0046	0.0045	0.0000	0.0000	0.0004	0.0005	0.0000	0.0000
Nova Scotia	0.0322	0.0317	0.0001	0.0002	0.0026	0.0029	0.0000	0.0000
New Brunswick	0.0173	0.0168	0.0037	0.0046	0.0076	0.0072	0.0000	0.0000
Quebec	0.0177	0.0250	0.1589	0.1557	0.0858	0.0825	0.0021	0.0021
Ontario	0.3073	0.3025	0.0025	0.0045	0.0384	0.0403	0.0062	0.0065
Manitoba	0.0380	0.0368	0.0001	0.0002	0.0033	0.0042	0.0006	0.0007
Saskatchewan	0.0376	0.0367	0.0000	0.0001	0.0018	0.0024	0.0003	0.0004
Alberta	0.0849	0.0850	0.0002	0.0002	0.0059	0.0057	0.0009	0.0008
British Columbia	0.1046	0.1048	0.0001	0.0001	0.0064	0.0065	0.0016	0.0012
Yukon	0.0009	0.0009	0.0000	0.0000	0.0001	0.0001	0.0000	0.0000
Northwest Territories	0.0015	0.0014	0.0000	0.0000	0.0001	0.0002	0.0003	0.0003

bad estimates are produced for several now familiar groups: English monolinguals in Quebec (where the decline was much larger than expected), French monolinguals in Nova Scotia, New Brunswick, Ontario, Manitoba and Saskatchewan (where the procedure estimated little or no change, while the observed declines were fairly substantial), bilinguals in Manitoba and Saskatchewan (estimated increases, but observed decreases) and those speaking neither official language in British Columbia (observed increase, but an expected decrease).

Summary

So far we have analysed the distribution of the population by mother tongue and by official languages spoken, by province, for the period 1971–81. We have seen that general patterns (the 'ecology of language') changed very little at that level of spatial detail. Overall trends showed slight relative losses for the population of French mother tongue, for those speaking French only and for those speaking neither English or French. Relative gains were most pronounced for the population speaking both English and French. These broadly constant distributions masked, to some degree, relatively intensive processes of change affecting several provincial linguistic minorities rather strongly. We noted the decline of the English mother tongue population in Quebec, in particular where this was associated with the *inability* to speak French. Moreover, we noted hints of continuing erosion for the French minorities outside Quebec, most clearly for Manitoba, Saskatchewan, Newfoundland and Prince Edward Island, but also tangible for Ontario and New Brunswick. It appears that the French-language minorities in Alberta and British Columbia were given temporary reprieves in the process of decline, by rather high levels of net immigration.

The analyses conducted have yielded a few answers, but many more additional questions. While the more sophisticated techniques suggested that much of the intercensal change may be 'explained' by changes in marginal distributions, such explanations are only statistical in nature. In other words, to state that Manitoba and Saskatchewan had declining percentages of the total Canadian population leads to further questions about population change; to what degree was this phenomenon attributable to differential rates of natural increase, to what degree was it associated with internal or external migration? In a similar vein, the partial explanation based on high rates of increase for bilinguals begs a whole sequence of further questions regarding the underlying processes. Was the increase in bilingualism due to higher rates of natural increase, or to the effects of international migration or to the acquisition of the second official language by persons who in 1971 were able to speak one (only) or neither of the official languages?

Moreover, the isolated deviations from these overall rather stable conditions invite further analysis. On the one hand, we would like to move some of the spatial analyses to lower levels of aggregation, say counties and census divisions. On the other hand, we will need to check out to what degree the various hunches about minority language maintenance and shift are borne out by the data.

Notes

1. Much of this paper was written during my tenure as Visiting Researcher in the Social and Economic Studies Division of Statistics Canada. I would like to acknowledge, in particular, the comments made by Rejean Lachapelle and Brian Harrison. Responsibility for this version is, of course, mine only.

References

JAMES, D. R. and TAEUBER, K. E. 1982, *Measures of Segregation*. Madison: University of Wisconsin, Center for Demography and Ecology (working papers 82–16).

JOY, R. J. 1972, *Languages in Conflict*. Toronto: McClelland and Stewart.

LACHAPELLE, R. and HENRIPIN, J. 1982, *The Demolinguistic Situation in Canada*. Montreal: Institute for Research on Public Policy.

LIEBERSON, S. 1970, *Language and Ethnic Relations in Canada*. New York: Wiley.

MAHEU, R. 1970, *Les francophones du Canada, 1941–1991*. Montréal: Editions Parti-Pris.

THEIL, H. 1972, *Statistical Decomposition Analysis*. New York: Elsevier.

VALLEE, F. G. and DE VRIES, J. 1978, Trends in bilingualism in Canada. In J. A. FISHMAN, (ed.) *Advances in the Study of Societal Multilingualism* (pp. 761–92). The Hague: Mouton.

DE VRIES, J. 1982, Canada's population: selected aspects of structure and change. In D. P. FORCESE and S. RICHER (eds) *Social Issues: Sociological Views of Canada* (pp. 15–40). Scarborough, Ontario: Prentice-Hall Canada Inc.

DE VRIES, J. and VALLEE, F. G. 1980, *Language Use in Canada*. Ottawa: Statistics Canada.

10 Gaelic in Nova Scotia

JOHN EDWARDS

Issues of language and group identity take on special significance when a language is at some risk because of a powerful neighbour. Thus, situations of contact between minority and majority groups are often worth close attention on psychological, sociolinguistic and sociological grounds. A recent discussion (Edwards, 1985) has clarified two points of relevance here. The first is that continuation of an original language is not essential for ethnic group continuity. What seems to be central here is that group boundaries continue to be perceived, even with radical alterations in the cultural content within them (see Barth, 1969). This boundary continuity can survive the loss of any given objective marker of groupness (like language), and the only essential element is a continuing sense of groupness — this can be supported by shared objective characteristics, or by more subjective or symbolic contributions (see Gans, 1979).

The second point, however, is that language is still commonly taken to be *the* central pillar of ethnic identity. This is understandable because language is, after all, a visible and objective group marker which can have both communicative and symbolic value. The modern association between language and group identity dates to the German romanticism of the early nineteenth century. Thus, Herder observed that language represents the 'collective treasure' of national groups (Barnard, 1969), and von Humboldt noted that language was the 'spiritual exhalation' of the nation (Cowan, 1963). Smith (1971: 182) summarises things quite neatly here when he states that 'the notion that nations are really language groups, and therefore that nationalism is a linguistic movement, derives from Herder's influence'. Indeed, we can trace this language-group relationship from the time of the German romantics, through the Celtic and other nationalistic movements of the last century, and on into this century — emerging wherever language and group manifestations have found apologists (see Fishman, 1972).

Among other language situations, useful work has been done on the surviving Celtic languages, all of which are now endangered species. Manx and Cornish are no longer the maternal languages of anyone, Irish, Welsh and Scots Gaelic are threatened by English, and Breton must contend with French. Yet in all these cases, efforts have been (and, in some quarters, continue to be) made to stem the decline. A summary of these situations is given in Edwards (1985), and a number of important and possibly generalisable points have emerged from this:

(1) Languages in decline typically have a predominance of middle-aged or elderly speakers; there is a lack of transmission to the younger generation.
(2) Weakening languages are often confined to rural areas, and associations are often made between the language and poverty, isolation and lack of sophistication of its speakers.
(3) Bilingualism in the declining language and its powerful linguistic neighbour is often only a temporary phenomenon, to be ultimately replaced with dominant-language monolingualism.
(4) Language decline can be understood properly only as a *symptom* of minority–majority contact; it is thus extremely unlikely that efforts directed towards language preservation alone will be successful.
(5) *Active* desires to stem the decline of threatened languages are usually operative only for a minority within a minority group. Indeed, revivalists are sometimes *non*-group members who have become apologists for language maintenance.
(6) There are important and obvious differences, for the ultimate fate of a language, between native speakers and those who study and learn the language on a more self-conscious basis.
(7) Cultural activities and symbolic manifestations of ethnicity often continue long after group language declines. They support a continuing sense of groupness yet do not hinder successful movement in the mainstream.
(8) The media are two-edged swords for declining languages. It is, on the one hand, desirable that minority languages be represented in them; on the other hand, however, the media act to channel dominant-language influence to the minority group.
(9) Language change, rather than stasis, is the historical pattern and ordinary people are largely motivated by practical necessity in linguistic matters.
(10) It is important to realise that there can exist a distinction between communicative and symbolic aspects of a language. For majority

speakers of majority languages, both aspects generally co-exist, but they can become separated; minority-group speakers who no longer use the original language for ordinary, communicative purposes often retain an attachment which involves the language as group symbol.

In the study of language-group relationships, it is clear that we need more information from ordinary group members (Dorian, 1982; Edwards, 1985). The points listed above derive largely from examination of the historical record rather than from direct sociolinguistic investigation, and further confirmation and elaboration of them would be useful. As well, the study of language contact situations is often of intrinsic interest on both linguistic and social grounds.

The present study is an attempt to provide further data relating to the points outlined, while at the same time illuminating a particular language situation of considerable inherent interest — as a transplanted variety, as one part of the larger Canadian linguistic pattern, and as a language in the gravest danger from a linguistic neighbour. Scots Gaelic in Nova Scotia was once the most flourishing of all transplanted Celtic languages (and MacKinnon (1985b) has described Cape Breton Island and eastern Nova Scotia generally as still the most populous Celtic speech community in the new world). Yet, as will be seen below, it has received little systematic attention. There is, indeed, some urgency to study here since Gaelic in Canada is a fast-shrinking language and could well become extinct — so far as ordinary native speakers are concerned — in a relatively short time.

In general, then, the study of Gaelic in Canada can add to our knowledge of minority–majority linguistic group contact settings, and can thus help our understanding of the relationship between language and the continuity of group identity. For Gaelic in Canada a popular motto — familiar in many other language contexts — is *sluagh gun chanain, sluagh gun anam* (a people without its language is a people without its soul). It is of some interest to attempt to find out how applicable this may be. Before turning to the present study itself, however, it is necessary to provide some background on the Gaelic language and its speakers in Nova Scotia.

Historical Background

The major settlement of Nova Scotia by Scots began in the 1770s. The emigrants, mostly Highlanders, came voluntarily during the eighteenth century (Bumsted, 1981, 1982; Withers, 1984); after 1800, however, most came as victims of the Scottish clearances. Thus, Bumsted (1982: xi) notes that 'the case for landlord heartlessness is much stronger after 1815 than before'. Campbell & MacLean (1974) and MacLean (1978) have suggested that there were four main waves of emigration, as follows:

(1) *From the beginning until 1803*. The beginning, for Nova Scotia, came with the 1773 voyage of the *Hector*. Leaving Ullapool with some 200 people on board, the ship arrived in Pictou after a terrible — and, unfortunately, typical — crossing (see also Bumsted, 1981, 1982; Prebble, 1969). Although emigration was checked for a time because of the American Revolution, Prebble has estimated that 10,000 Highlanders left for Nova Scotia and Upper Canada between 1800 and 1803 — though we must bear in mind Withers' (1984) caution that no accurate figures are available for early emigration to North America. Before 1802, it can be noted, there was no direct emigration to Cape Breton Island and most went first to Pictou and Antigonish counties and then on to Cape Breton (Millward, 1980). In 1803 a Passenger Act was passed, intended to ensure better conditions of passage; these, however, hardly improved.
(2) *1803–1815*. During this period settlement continued in Pictou, Antigonish and, to some extent, western Cape Breton. Emigration declined with the need for men during the Napoleonic wars.
(3) *1815–1821*. It is estimated that about 20,000 Scots left for British North America during this period. Sinclair (1950–1) notes that large-scale emigration to Cape Breton Island began in 1817, and it is this wave which determined the Highland character of the island.
(4) *Late 1830s to early 1850s*. Perhaps 15,000 came to Nova Scotia during this time. By 1830 large numbers of Highlanders had moved east from Pictou towards Cape Breton (Campbell, 1948) and, also by this time, the Scots had become the largest ethnic group in Nova Scotia. British government policy now encouraged emigration and Prebble (1969) observes, for example, that 58,000 left for Canada in 1831 and 66,000 in 1832. Anderson (1973) notes, relatedly, that during the 1820s to 1840s, waves of Gaelic-speaking Highlanders came to western and central Ontario.

For Nova Scotia, the majority of emigration occurred between 1790 and 1830 (MacLeod, 1958). The Scottish influence was strongest in Antigonish, Victoria, Inverness and Cape Breton counties. Cape Breton Island as a whole was settled later and remained the firmest bastion of Scottish culture (Dunn, 1974; MacLean, 1978) — aided in this by its rurality and physical isolation. Population estimates for the island during the major emigration period are 8,000 (1817), 18,000 (1827) and 38,000 (1838). For those readers unfamiliar with the area, the map in Figure 10.1 may be of some use. It should be noted that Cape Breton Island, now joined to the mainland by a causeway, is part of the province of Nova Scotia. There is, furthermore, a Cape Breton *county* (one of four on the island).

The Gaelic Language

Shaw (1977) has estimated that, in 1880, the number of Gaelic speakers in Cape Breton Island was close to the number of Gaelic speakers in Scotland today (some 88,000 according to the 1971 census). Relatedly, Stephens (1976) reports that in 1890, in a House of Commons speech about making Gaelic an official language in Canada, a member claimed that three-quarters of the total Cape Breton population of 100,000 spoke Gaelic.

By this time, however, the language was already weakening. In the middle of the nineteenth century complaints were being heard about the younger generation's lack of interest in the language (Anderson, 1973), but there is also evidence that parents *wanted* their children to learn English, and punished them for speaking Gaelic (Kelly, 1980; MacInnes, 1977–8; Sinclair, 1950–1). Gaelic was also primarily an oral language in Nova Scotia (Campbell & MacLean, 1974) and Kelly notes that Gaelic literacy was rare in Cape Breton. Indeed, as Anderson (1973) points out, most immigrants were illiterate in both Gaelic and English. This meant, among other things, that Gaelic newspapers and even newspaper columns were generally short-lived. Sinclair (1950–1) does refer, however, to *Mac Talla* (The Echo), an all-Gaelic, four-page weekly printed in Sydney between 1892 and 1904. Even the advertisements were in Gaelic in *Mac Talla*, which had at its height some 1,400 subscribers. Campbell & MacLean (1974) observe that no other Gaelic paper in the world survived as long, and an editorial in the paper itself (1902 — cited by Campbell, 1948) claimed that it was the only Gaelic paper in the world.

Out-migration from Cape Breton to other parts of Canada and to the 'Boston States' was also a factor in the decline of Gaelic, as was the decrease in isolation brought about by improvements in road and rail links. Gaelic became a stigmatised variety, associated with backwardness and rurality (Anderson, 1973; Campbell & MacLean, 1974; MacInnes 1977–8). Campbell (1948) observes that Gaelic was seen as a social liability, particularly for one's children. It became the language of 'toil,

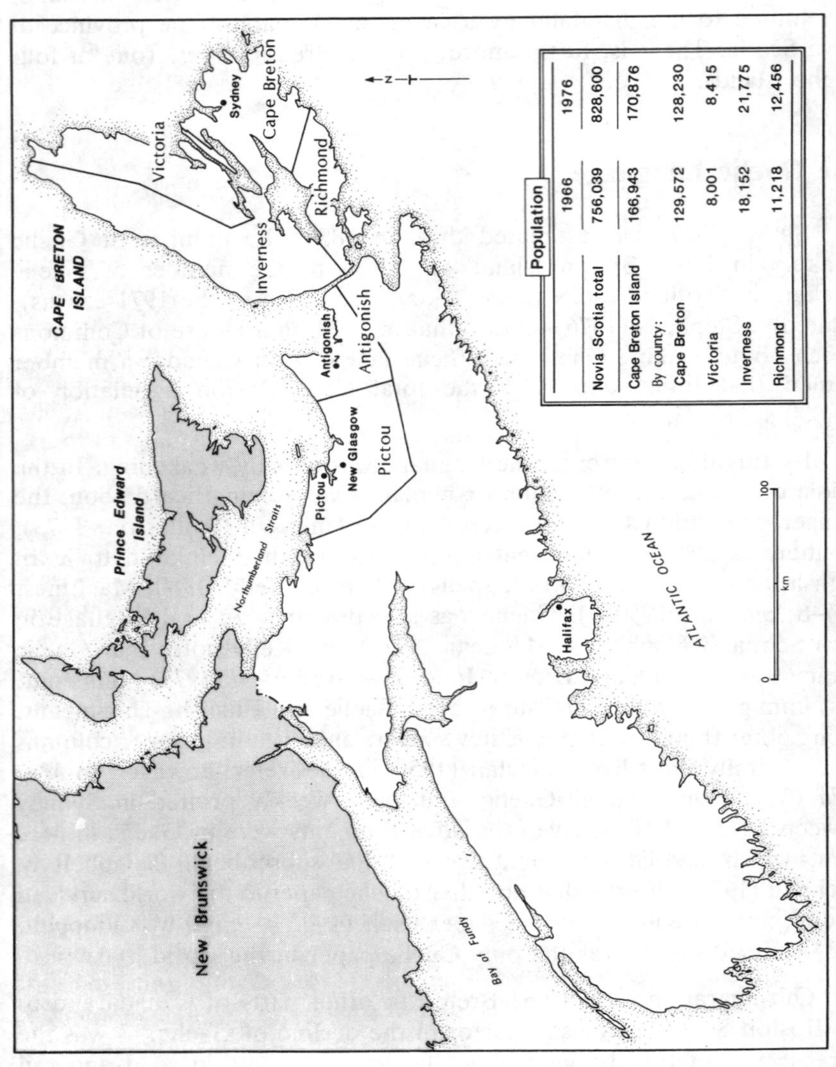

	1966	1976
Novia Scotia total	756,039	828,600
Cape Breton Island	166,943	170,876
By county:		
Cape Breton	129,572	128,230
Victoria	8,001	8,415
Inverness	18,152	21,775
Richmond	11,218	12,456

FIGURE 10.1 *Selected locations in Nova Scotia*

hardship and scarcity' while English was the language of 'refinement and culture' (Dunn, 1974: 134). These factors led Campbell & MacLean (1974) to estimate that, after 1830, Gaelic only rarely had complete domination within a community.

With regard to Gaelic at school, the Nova Scotia Education Act of 1841 permitted the language as a medium of instruction, if a school district so desired. However, in all but a few cases, the Scots made little effort to take advantage of this legislation (Campbell & MacLean, 1974; see also MacKinnon, 1985b). As already noted, English and not Gaelic was seen as the key to advancement. Campbell (1948: 70) points out that the settlers 'carried with them the idea that education was coincident with a knowledge of English'. When state schools were established in 1864 there was no provision for Gaelic (Campbell, 1948; MacEachen, 1977). Both teachers and parents were by this time often hostile to Gaelic, and children could be punished for speaking it at school (MacEachen, 1977). In 1879, the Nova Scotia government made it clear that no funds were available for Gaelic instruction (Anderson, 1973). Only in 1921, with the language well in decline, was it admitted as an optional subject if the majority of students demanded it; of course, by this time there was little such demand (Anderson, 1973). As well, there were now very real difficulties in finding suitable teachers (Dunn, 1974).

MacLean (1978) claims that Gaelic has decreased by about 50% every ten years since 1921, and the estimates of others would seem to bear this out — although precision is difficult since, until 1931, Gaelic was classified with English for census purposes (Campbell & MacLean, 1974; see Mertz (1989) on the rapid shift to English during the 1930s and 1940s). Also, census data are often not very reliable on language matters. For example, Foster (1983) refers to under-reporting of Gaelic competence in Nova Scotia. He cites a study by MacInnes who claims that the denial of competence is an effort to ward off outside intervention from the 'impertinent, the inquisitive and the romantic' (Foster, 1983: 183) and to avoid possible stigmatisation (see also Dorian, 1986). Another difficulty is revealed in Canadian census data which showed, amazingly, that those claiming Gaelic-language mother tongue increased from about 7,500 in 1961 to about 21,400 in 1971. This, as MacKinnon (1979a) has pointed out, is largely due to coding procedures which, for the latter census, included Celtic languages other than Welsh with Gaelic.

MacLeod (1958) estimates that there were some 30,000 Gaelic speakers in Cape Breton Island in 1931 and Campbell (1948), on the basis of a survey of Cape Breton Gaelic, estimated 25,000. He noted, too, that the strongest preserve of the language was in Inverness county, and that nearly all the Gaelic speakers were bilingual. In 1941 there were about 10,000 speakers (Dunn, 1974), in 1951 about 7,000 (MacLeod, 1958), and in 1961 about 3,400 — these figures all refer to Cape Breton Island. A visiting Scottish scholar estimated in 1985 that about 1,000 people could understand Gaelic in Cape Breton, but fewer than 100 were 'very fluent speakers' (MacLean, 1985).

The actual census figures — for Canada as a whole, and for Nova Scotia separately — are as follows (from MacKinnon, 1979a; figures are rounded off, and indicate those with Gaelic mother tongue): 1931 — Canada: 32,000; Nova Scotia: 25,000; 1941 — Canada: 32,700; Nova Scotia 12,000; 1951 — Canada: 14,000; Nova Scotia: 6,800; 1961 — Canada: 7,500; Nova Scotia: 3,700; 1971 — Canada: 21,400 (clearly an error of coding, see above); Nova Scotia: 1,420 (this figure for 'Gaelic' in Nova Scotia is probably a reasonably accurate reflection of Scots Gaelic speakers) (Anderson (1973) notes that, of the 1,420 total, 965 were in Cape Breton Island); 1976 — Canada: 1,620; Nova Scotia: 540. Finally, MacKinnon (1985b) notes that the 1981 census reports 1,200 speakers of *all* Celtic languages in Nova Scotia. Mac-Kinnon has also (in a personal communication, 1986) agreed that there is under-reporting of Gaelic competence in Cape Breton Island (see above), and that census estimates may thus be too low; also, he has noted that Canadian census procedure may have an overly rigorous definition of 'Gaelic speaker' (see below).

Currently, the state of Gaelic in Cape Breton Island is a precarious one. As a bastion of the language it now may have fewer speakers than are found elsewhere in the country. Anderson (1973) notes, for example, that there are now more Gaelic speakers in Toronto than in Nova Scotia (see also MacPherson, 1985). A very generous recent estimate put the number of Gaelic speakers in Cape Breton at 5,000 (Shaw, 1977); however, even allowing for under-reporting of linguistic competence, and even if we were to apply it to Gaelic speakers throughout the country, this is clearly an optimistic figure (see census figures above; see also Stephens, 1976).

Now, as MacKinnon (1979a) observes, Nova Scotia is the most English of the mainland provinces, with the 1971 census showing 93% as English mother-tongue speakers. As well, in this same census, only about 140,000 claimed Scottish origins (about 18% of the total population; this dropped to 15% in 1981). The fact here is that, over the period 1871–1971, the Scots in Nova Scotia have declined, 'being overtaken by the English from 1901 onwards' (MacKinnon, 1979a: 1; see also MacKinnon, 1985b).

MacKinnon (1979a) also usefully summarises some 1971 census data which indicate that of those claiming Gaelic as a mother tongue in Nova Scotia, 88.5% reported English as the language used most often in the home.

One is forced to conclude, with Campbell & MacLean (1974) that Gaelic in Nova Scotia, and particularly in Cape Breton Island, is now in the gravest danger. It is found mainly in rural areas; Dunn (1974) thus observed that the language was preserved in the country and forgotten in the town. As well, it is spoken mainly by older people. Inverness county, its strongest centre, has lost many to out-migration prompted by poor economic prospects at home. Those who now support Gaelic (whether fluent speakers or not), those who are members of Gaelic organisations, and even those who are students of the language are largely middle-aged or over (Campbell & MacLean, 1974).

General efforts in support of Scottish culture tend, in the eyes of some at least, to be superficial, even distasteful (MacDonnell, 1981); this seems particularly so when culture is allied to tourism drives (see Taylor (1986), who refers to a $500,000 promotion of things Scottish to attract foreign tourists; see also the useful recent paper by MacDonald (1987), on Scottish stereotypes and tourism). The romanticism over a Scottish past which Anderson (1973) discusses is demonstrated by children in full regalia singing songs they do not understand, and by the alliance between Scottishness and commercial interests. As Shaw (1977) aptly points out, people praise Gaelic in English, and it is perhaps telling that the major Gaelic society in Cape Breton holds its meetings in English.

Nonetheless, despite these features, there is no doubt that the Scottish ancestry of many in Nova Scotia is a valued aspect of life, even if their ethnicity is now mainly of a symbolic kind (Gans, 1979). Only for a very small number does the Gaelic language — in its ordinary communicative role — figure as an element of Scottish ethnicity. Most public displays (e.g. the annual Highland Games in Antigonish) are events open to all, and some others (a kilted golf tournament, for example) appear as mere curiosities. However, one should not downplay the significance and endurance of symbolic ethnicity which, attacked by some as merely representing 'ethnic residue', remains precisely because it is not stigmatising, does not visibly differentiate people for the large part of their day-to-day life and, in minority–majority contact situations, does not interfere with success and advancement in the social mainstream. MacKinnon (1979a) presents some examples of the remaining public use of the Gaelic language and, interestingly, mentions the exaggeration in some circles in Scotland of the Scottishness of Nova Scotia. Language, as a visible ethnic marker, is often a casualty of social interaction but, despite the view expressed by some — in the present Gaelic context, for example, by MacDonald (1982) and MacPherson (1985) — it is not an essential condition of Scottish ethnic continuity (for a general discussion, see Edwards, 1985).

Scots Gaelic revivalists, as those elsewhere, often paint a romantic picture of present and past which may not always accord with reality. As an example, one can consider the following expression, cited in Campbell & MacLean (1974: 178):

> The one who is taught Gaelic acquires knowledge of wisdom and an understanding of truth and honour which will guide his steps along the paths of righteousness, and will stay with him for the rest of his life. The Gaelic is a powerful, spiritual language; and Gaels who are indifferent to it are slighting their forefathers and kinsmen.

Campbell & MacLean feel that the revivalists have been over-optimistic, and that there is no evidence that their efforts have had much effect. Gaelic, for these authors, is now in 'the realm of the exotic' (Campbell & MacLean, 1974: 180). In fact there has been very little organised revivalist sentiment in Nova Scotia and it is hard to deny that what little there *has* been has bypassed two essential groups — the shrinking pool of older Gaelic speakers, and young children (Shaw, 1977; see MacInnes (1977–8) on the revivalist aims of the Scottish Catholic Society of Canada, a rather élitist organisation which existed between 1919 and 1949). This is despite the fact that, as in other contexts, the school has often been singled out as a major agent of linguistic revitalisation — even though it has been argued that schools acting in isolation from extra-academic forces cannot significantly influence language dynamics (Edwards, 1985). In the Nova Scotia context, Dunn (1974), for example, notes that the 'obvious' solution to the decline of the language is to teach Gaelic in the schools; he goes on, however, to qualify his remarks by stating that schools must attend to practicalities rather than to 'abstract ideals', and admits that parents have not generally seen Gaelic instruction as practical.

Kelly, clearly a supporter of Gaelic, makes the more general and probably more realistic comment that:

> One occasionally hears the opinion expressed that only by official recognition and support will the language be saved from extinction. But surely the will to survive must be there in the first place,

> otherwise what does survive will likely be no more than the superficial trappings (Kelly, 1980: 62).

While 'superficial trappings' may reflect that symbolic ethnicity which can be quite enduring (see above), one understands what Kelly is referring to here. There must be a collective will for a language to survive, and this will must be grounded in daily necessities and desires (Edwards, 1985). The usual course — when mundane necessity no longer provides practical language domains — is for a transition to bilingualism, and then to monolingualism in the larger language. Dunn (1974) thus notes that Gaelic–English bilingualism is a stepping-stone on the road to English monolingualism. On this point, Greene (1981: 2) cites the view of the eminent Irish dialectologist, O'Rahilly, who observed in 1932 that 'when a language surrenders itself to foreign idiom, and when all its speakers become bilingual, the penalty is death'. This is a harsh judgement, yet the fact remains that people will not indefinitely maintain two languages when one will serve across domains.

Recent news on the Gaelic educational front in Cape Breton was that classes in the language in Inverness had been discontinued after a ten-year experimental programme. While voices have been heard protesting at this, no concerted effort has been mounted to save the classes, which had been seen by some as of only peripheral importance in any event — MacKinnon (1979a), for example, noted that such classes can hardly save the day for Gaelic. Also, the Gaelic College on the island (founded in 1939; see MacKinnon, 1979a) closed its doors in the autumn of 1985 due to financial difficulties; some of the staff tried to block the closure which was temporary but which indicates something of the disarray among apologists for Gaelic culture in the area (MacKinnon (1979a) reported management difficulties at the College — i.e. eight years ago). A Scot now living and teaching in Cape Breton has said that while Gaelic is a living language in Nova Scotia, 'young people have not been learning it in recent years' (cited in Wilson, 1982), and this summarises the recent state of affairs.

Finally, we can note that there have been few systematic/experimental studies of Gaelic undertaken in Nova Scotia. Campbell (1948) visited Cape Breton Island in 1932 and sent a questionnaire to all clergymen, of various denominations, to discover the number of Gaelic speakers, their distribution and the general condition of the language. He found, as noted above, that almost all of those speaking Gaelic were bilingual. Campbell's survey is further discussed by Sinclair (1950–1) who notes that Campbell's questions included 'Do the children speak English or

Gaelic, or both?' and 'Is Gaelic declining in your parish?'. The results revealed that the language was used less and less by children, and was declining among the older adults. Although Campbell himself mistakenly observed that the 'proportion of Gaelic speakers does not decrease in the younger age groups' (Campbell, 1948: 69; see MacKinnon, 1979a), Sinclair cites Campbell as stating that 'on the whole it cannot be denied that Gaelic in the Maritimes is a dying language' (Sinclair, 1950–1: 258–9).

The most recent, and most important, investigation of Gaelic in Nova Scotia is that of MacKinnon; his findings, based upon fieldwork undertaken during 1976–8, are reported in a series of papers (MacKinnon, 1979a, 1979b, 1982, 1985a, 1985b), and represent study of two rural Cape Breton communities. One of these was mainly Catholic (99 respondents, 96 of them Catholic), the other largely Protestant (112 respondents, 84 of them Protestant). Among the first, Catholic group 44 respondents (44%) claimed Gaelic as their mother tongue; among the second, Protestant group, 33 (29%) did so. MacKinnon (1979b) observes, however, that the 1976 Canadian census showed only 540 Gaelic speakers for *all* of Nova Scotia (see above). Therefore, either his sample overestimates or else the census underestimates the incidence of Gaelic speaking. MacKinnon points out that the Canadian census is rigorous, in so far as it lists Gaelic only for those who are native speakers and who can still understand it (level of comprehension unspecified). He compares this with the Scottish practice in which recorded Gaelic speakers are simply those having some degree (again, level unspecified) of linguistic ability.

To summarise MacKinnon's major findings of relevance here, we can note first that older people are more fluent in Gaelic than are younger ones, and use it more often; it is thus rare to find native speakers who are less than middle-aged. Such speakers also, unsurprisingly, exhibit the highest levels of 'language loyalty' (i.e. have the most positive attitudes towards Gaelic). MacKinnon (1979a: 8) reported that there were still a few Gaelic monolinguals left by 1975–6 — 'a handful of women in their 80s and 90s'; he also observed at this time a few families raising children through the medium of Gaelic (later, MacKinnon (1985a) noted that at the end of the 1970s he found only two cases of active transmission of Gaelic to children). Generally, young people are not using Gaelic, and young women were found to be the least language loyal of all, and to use the least Gaelic.

Language loyalty generally is low, but the highest levels of it are found among those who are most fluent (unsurprisingly), among Catholics, and among the semi-skilled. This last group constitutes what MacKinnon calls the ethnic 'core' — fishing, farming and forestry being the main occupations — who, as well as having the most favourable attitudes towards Gaelic are also the leaders in language maintenance. Language loyalty also correlates with relatively low levels of formal education; this in turn correlates with the age factor (see above). A more general *cultural* loyalty is more evident than is language loyalty alone, and is less restricted to a particular group.

On the religious dimension, MacKinnon found Catholics to be slightly more language loyal than Protestants, more fluent and stronger in terms of language maintenance. This may be due to a closer knit and more embracing culture associated with Catholicism, but MacKinnon also notes that it may reflect a simple difference in physical isolation — Catholics being more isolated. Gaelic literacy, however, was found to be higher among Protestants (particularly Presbyterians), reflecting perhaps their emphasis upon home bible study and reading.

In general, MacKinnon notes the precarious state of the language, observing that it is too late to save Gaelic as a general communicative medium. However, although the language shift is 'acute and advanced', commitment to Gaelic and, more generally, to the Scottish culture is expressed in 'various ways' (MacKinnon, 1985a: 4). Relatedly, MacKinnon (1982: 26) asks if Gaelic might be enshrined 'as a "cultural" if not a community language'.

> May there still be a 'cultural' role for Gaelic in the transatlantic diaspora? Probably most Scots Canadians . . . are of Highland rather than Lowland origin. It is pitiful to see their descendants adopt a Lowland cultural identity — one which was never that of their actual forebears . . . There is still a very lively and very Gaelic culture in eastern Canada at any rate. This and the language could yet reinforce one another . . . (MacKinnon, 1985a: 18)

Kelly's (1980) unpublished dissertation also provides some data of sociolinguistic interest, although the number of respondents was small. He documents the (by now) familiar features of the decline of Gaelic and makes some particularly interesting remarks about the changing fortunes of the language in education.

Method

Subjects

There are three groups of subjects in the present study. The first comprises Gaelic speakers (hereafter referred to as group 'G') who had been studied already in a Gaelic folklore project undertaken by the Celtic Studies Department of St Francis Xavier University. With the advice and assistance of those running this project, a list of 89 potential respondents was drawn up. Of these, 17 were unable to complete the questionnaire used in the present study (see below) for various reasons, and 22 more failed to return the form. There are, thus, 50 completed questionnaires from this group.

The second group (hereafter referred to as group 'GS' — for 'Gaelic Society') includes Gaelic speakers as well as those with an interest in the language and in Scottish heritage. All respondents here were members of the Cape Breton Gaelic Society, founded in Sydney in 1969. Drawing upon membership lists and upon meeting attendance registers for the last five years, a total of 251 names was assembled. Of this number, 30 proved impossible to contact and 132 failed to return the questionnaire; therefore, 89 completed questionnaires were obtained for this group.

The third group is drawn from the New Glasgow and Antigonish Highland Societies, and comprises persons who are actively studying Gaelic (hereafter called the 'GL' group — for 'Gaelic Learners'). The number of people in group GL was 20.

Materials

A questionnaire was drawn up in which the following topics were covered: demographic information and Gaelic background, Gaelic competence and use, evaluations of Gaelic, the current status, transmission and survival of Gaelic, and (for the GL group) information dealing with the learning of the language. Respondents were encouraged to add comments, either of a general nature or relating to specific questions. While it might be argued that such comments are not 'objective' in the sense that they do not conform to predetermined categories of response, they nevertheless can inform and illuminate other data. Indeed, as will be seen from the examples presented below, the spontaneous comments — sometimes covering a number of pages — were unusually rich and varied in this study.

Procedure

The questionnaires were distributed by mail, and there were two postings; that is, an initial lack of response prompted a second request to complete and return the form. The results outlined below are grouped for ease of interpretation in thematic blocks, but the questions within these blocks were, on the questionnaire itself, interspersed with one another. Results were analysed using chi-square and analysis-of-variance techniques. Unless otherwise noted, 'no responses' have been omitted from the calculations, and, generally, where there were no differences detected among the three groups, only overall results are given.

Results

Background data

Among group G, the average age was 69 years (range = 35 to 89), among group GS it was 61 (22 to 86), and among group GL it was 57 (30 to 82). The groups were very evenly split between men and women; thus, in group G 50.0% were females, in group GS 51.1%, and in group GL 55.5%. Group G was the least well-educated, with 89.2% having high school education or less (10.8% had at least some college education). For the GS group, these percentages were 81.6% and 18.3%. The GL group was the best-educated — 41.6% had at least some third-level education.

Among all groups, most women described themselves as housewives and most men as farmers. However, many in the G and GS groups described themselves simply as 'retired'. Among the GL group, there were slightly more holding higher-status jobs, and the most common of these was teacher. Among group G, 94.9% were born on Cape Breton Island, as were 89.6% of the GS group. Only 14.8% of the GL group were Cape Breton-born, but the remainder were all from mainland Nova Scotia.

Some 80.7% of the group G respondents knew where their forebears originated, as follows: 26.2% from Barra, 11.5% from Uist, 32.8% from other isles, 21.3% from Inverness and 8.2% from other parts of Scotland. Among the GS group, 81.5% knew where their ancestors came from: 29.7% from Barra, 16.8% from Uist, 21.8% from other isles, 21.8% from Inverness and 9.9% from the rest of Scotland. Similarly, 81.5% of group GL knew their origins: 19.1% from other isles (i.e. not Barra or

Uist), 47.6% from Inverness and 33.3% from other areas of Scotland. Somewhat fewer in two of the three groups knew just when their forebears had arrived in Canada (62.8% of group G, 61.5% of group GS, and 85.2% of group GL), but the arrival times were very consistent across groups, more than three-quarters of the ancestors having come between 1810 and 1830.

No question about religion was put to respondents. However, we can assume that all three groups are comprised largely of Roman Catholic persons. There are two reasons for this assumption. First, MacKinnon (1979a, 1985b) has observed, simply, that most eastern Nova Scotia Scots are Catholic. Secondly, there is the fact that most of the respondents' forebears came from Catholic areas of Scotland — Barra and Uist being largely Catholic sections, as are parts of Inverness.

In group G, 30.8% had English as a first language, 53.8% had Gaelic, and 15.4% reported learning Gaelic and English together as children. Among the GS group, the percentages were 77.0% English, 16.3% Gaelic and 6.7% Gaelic/English. In group GL, these figures were 77.7% English, 11.1% Gaelic and 11.2% Gaelic/English. In the G group, 58.3% of the native English speakers had Gaelic as a second language. This percentage was 37.5% for group GS and 23.8% for the GL group. It should be noted here, however, that we cannot assume equal levels of Gaelic-as-a-second-language here since the actual question asked was 'Do you know any other language?' (but see also below). Unsurprisingly, all native Gaelic speakers had English — there are no monolingual Gaelic speakers.

Gaelic competence and use

Respondents were asked to rate their understanding of Gaelic on a 4-point scale (from 1 = 'not at all' to 4 = 'perfectly'). The average ratings here were 3.82 (G), 2.79 (GS) and 2.70 (GL). A one-way analysis of variance revealed an overall F-value of 32.29 (df = 2,156; $p < 0.001$), and subsequent Newman-Keuls tests indicated that the group G rating was significantly different from the other two. Respondents next rated their Gaelic speaking ability on a 5-point scale (from 1 = 'not at all' to 5 = 'fluently'). The averages obtained were 4.72 (G), 3.00 (GS) and 2.90 (GL). Here, analysis revealed an F-value of 47.08 (df = 2,156; $p < 0.001$) and, again, Newman-Keuls tests showed that group G were significantly higher than the other two groups.

Subjects were also asked to rate their Gaelic reading ability, on a

3-point scale (on this and subsequent 3-point scales higher numbers indicate greater ability). Here the averages were 2.16 (G), 1.73 (GS) and 2.05 (GL) — the overall F-value was 4.92 (df = 2,156; $p < 0.001$). Newman-Keuls tests showed that the group G ratings were significantly different from the GS ratings. Respondents were further asked *how* they had learned to read — in particular, whether they learned formally with textbooks and/or lessons, or whether they were self-taught, aided by friends and relatives, etc. A chi-square analysis showed no significant differences among the three groups, but there did exist a marked pattern. Omitting the 'no responses', we observe that, among the G group, half learned formally and half informally; however, formal learning was reported by 66.7% of group GS and by 81.8% of group GL. Finally here, there were no differences detected among the groups with regard to the possession of Gaelic-language reading materials at home (71.5% had such materials).

Respondents were next asked if they could write Gaelic; no significant differences were detected among the groups on a 3-point scale (G mean = 1.64; GS mean = 1.41; GL mean = 1.60). Group G reasserted their superiority, however, in the ability to sing in Gaelic. On a 3-point scale, their average was 2.70 (GS mean = 1.93; GL mean = 1.75). One-way analysis of variance revealed an F-value of 23.79 (df = 2,156; $p < 0.001$), and Newman-Keuls tests confirmed that the group G mean was significantly different from the other two.

The three groups were also differentiated in terms of immediate forebears speaking Gaelic. Among group G, 96.0% reported that their parents and most or all of their grandparents knew Gaelic. This percentage dropped to 77.5% for the GS group, and 60.0% for group GL ($\chi^2 = 13.82$; df = 2; $p < 0.01$).

We note no significant differences among the groups when they were asked if they would speak Gaelic at home, at work, in town or on holiday — 77.5% said that they use or have used Gaelic in all or most of these settings (clearly, taking previous information into account, the opportunities and the levels of Gaelic would differ).

In answer to the question 'Which language sounds better to you?' 82.3% of group G said Gaelic, none said English, and 17.7% indicated no preference. Among the GS group, 52.5% said Gaelic, 31.3% said English and 16.2% had no preference, while among the GL group these percentages were 35.7%, 42.9% and 21.4% respectively ($\chi^2 = 21.54$; df = 4; $p < 0.001$). A similar pattern emerged in response to the question 'Which language do you prefer to use?' Here, 68.9% of group G said

Gaelic, 24.4% said English and 6.7% said 'either'. Percentages for the GS group here were 25.3%, 67.5% and 7.2% respectively; for group GL these figures were 20.0%, 73.3% and 6.7% respectively ($\chi^2 = 26.90$; df = 4; $p < 0.001$).

Respondents were also asked if they had ever felt uneasy or ashamed speaking Gaelic. Those answering 'yes' constituted 8.2% of group G, 29.6% of group GS and 25.0% of group GL ($\chi^2 = 8.07$; df = 2; $p < 0.05$). When asked further how this happened, only a very few (24) answered; across all three groups there was an even split between being uneasy because of ridicule from others, and being uneasy simply because of lack of fluency.

Evaluations of Gaelic

Respondents were asked if local Gaelic was different from that spoken elsewhere; overall, 47.4% said 'yes'. When asked how it differed from other varieties only a few answered, and these mentioned pronunciation differences, and differences deriving from variations in Scottish provenance. However, in response to another question, 46.6% of respondents said that there were words and expressions unique to the local variety. Subjects were also asked where they thought the best Cape Breton Gaelic was spoken. There was a fairly wide range of responses here, but 38.1% overall chose Inverness county.

On a 3-point scale, respondents rated the difficulty of learning Gaelic vis-à-vis English. There were no group differences detected and the overall average rating was 1.54 — i.e. a tendency to see Gaelic as more difficult than English. Similarly, no group differences emerged when respondents evaluated the quality of Nova Scotia Gaelic as opposed to Scottish Gaelic. The overall rating was 1.97 on a 3-point scale — i.e. almost exactly on the mid-point, indicating that the two varieties (or, more accurately, two groups of varieties) were seen to be of equivalent quality.

Current status, transmission and survival of Gaelic

There was agreement across the three groups that the older generation sees Gaelic as more important than does the younger; 82.8% agreed with this. Similarly, the groups agreed that it was useful but not essential for children to learn the language (the average rating on a 3-

point scale was 1.89, where a rating of 2 was the useful-but-not-essential mid-point). Nonetheless, most (91.6%) agreed that Nova Scotia schools should offer courses in Gaelic, and 71.6% said that either the school, or the school and home in combination should lead in the teaching of the language (28.4% here opted for the home alone).

Respondents were asked two questions about changes in the importance of Gaelic in the area. Across all three groups, the most common perception was that a knowledge of the language now was as important as it used to be (average rating of 1.71 on a 3-point scale ranging from 1 = 'more important' to 3 = 'less important'). A similar average rating (1.69) was found when subjects were next asked to compare the importance of Gaelic now with its future importance. Thus, taken together, these two questions revealed a generally static perception of the language over time, although in each case there was a very slight tendency to see Gaelic as increasing in importance, from the past to the present, and from the present to the future.

Subjects were given a list of agencies and were asked to indicate which have helped or could help Gaelic to survive; these agencies were the school, Gaelic or Highland societies, Gaelic festivals, the church, home teaching, the media, the Cape Breton Gaelic College, and community Gaelic classes. Across the groups many opted for some combination of school, home and community classes (38.0%), but the majority (55.5%) simply ticked *all* the possibilities.

Respondents in all three groups agreed (82.2%) that intermarriage between Gaelic speakers and English speakers had affected the status of Gaelic, in so far as Gaelic tended to be subordinate in such situations and was not often passed on to the children. Finally, the subjects were asked to state the reasons they would give to someone for learning Gaelic. Overall, 46.5% gave reasons relating to the preservation of a distinctive heritage, while another (and not unrelated) group of responses (42.8%) centred upon enjoyment, knowledge for its own sake and the beauty of the language. Interestingly, only 8.4% mentioned the use of Gaelic in talking to others.

Questions for the GL group

Asked why they were now studying Gaelic, 52.6% gave reasons relating to heritage, while the others stressed enjoyment and knowledge *per se*. Again, we note that no one mentioned actually speaking the language. However, when questioned about the use they *hoped* to make of Gaelic, 41.7% did mention conversing with other Gaelic speakers — another 41.7% stressed enjoyment, and 16.7% specifically mentioned learning Gaelic so as to be able to read in the language. The average time spent studying Gaelic was 3¼ years, and all respondents said that they planned to continue their studies in the future.

Comments added to the questionnaire

The comments reproduced below represent, in the main, sentiments expressed by several respondents in each of the three groups; some of them are given in the form of direct quotations.

(a) Group G

(1) 'My generation are all anxious for the future of Gaelic. But the younger people are not getting a chance to participate in any Gaelic society — it's always seniors.'
(2) 'I would like to see a revival in the Gaelic language in Nova Scotia but I do not think there is enough interest among the younger people.
(3) 'Just like myself and Jessie, we can both speak Gaelic. Still, we didn't speak it to them. Now two of them are gone out west and they would like it and regret they haven't got it.'
(4) Many respondents noted that Gaelic will die out, while others expressed general hopes for the language in the future.
(5) Many observed (with 1 and 2 above) that young people are uninterested in Gaelic, but some claimed that there *was* some degree of interest among the young.
(6) A common observation was that the language must be taught at school if it is to have any chance of survival.
(7) Several reported punishment for speaking Gaelic, and one was quite explicit: 'When I attended school in 1915–20 you got a strapping with a leather strap if caught speaking Gaelic.'
(8) 'In the interests of religion, music and culture I commend the valiant efforts that are being made to preserve the Gaelic heritage.'

(b) Group GS

(9) 'Sorry to say, but I believe that Gaelic will continue to decrease without the language being spoken in the home. I don't see much future for Gaelic even when a few short courses are taught in

schools — the home use is what counts.'

(10) 'Gaelic will last in Nova Scotia for another 15 years. The older generation who have Gaelic and those who have lost it downgrade it as unimportant, or just to sing a few old songs.'

(11) 'I believe that people are now realising that Gaelic is starting to disappear with the older people, and although they have not been very interested in the past do not want to see it fade out altogether.'

(12) Several respondents noted that there are few young married couples with Gaelic.

(13) Several made the observation noted above — the need to have Gaelic in the schools.

(14) Many observed that Gaelic is dying and is not spoken in the home which provides the only avenue of survival (see (9)). Again, however, there were general hopes expressed for the future (see (4)).

(15) 'It seems your questions are directed wholly at the Gaelic language. The continuance of Scottish culture will not be promoted or should not be promoted on Gaelic language. It is not where it is at with the prevailing interest . . . Language is the living culture of a people. However, for the Scots many other aspects of their culture are near and dear to their hearts. Emphasis on the Gaelic language will I feel bring small returns. Studies in Celtic history I think are very important. Music (pipes, drums, fiddle) — all this is part of the make-up of our culture.'

(16) Several respondents noted that Gaelic needs more exposure on radio and television.

(17) 'In my youth, people speaking Gaelic were considered backward and were discouraged from speaking it' (see (7)).

(c) Group GL

(18) 'I fear it will be lost. As part of our heritage it and other customs should be preserved.'

(19) 'As much as I would like to believe otherwise, I feel that Gaelic as a spoken language doesn't have much of a chance.'

(20) 'I sometimes think the sudden interest in Gaelic is nothing more than a fad or a gimmick to promote tourism.'

(21) 'I have found a reluctance on the part of native speakers to become involved in furthering use of Gaelic. I feel there is potential for survival and growth if what is almost a guilt complex is shed for an attitude of pride, and willingness to impart Gaelic to one and all who show interest.'

(22) Several respondents noted that the language now has only 'cultural value'.

(23) 'I started going to this school in Antigonish nearly three years ago, the first evening I was there I did not have an idea what to expect, so thinking it was just speaking Gaelic and learning it that way. The class was already in progress and almost before I was introduced, I started to tell a story. And when I finished with it, a Sister spoke up and said we are here a year and a half and this is the first story we have heard. And now I am here almost two and a half winters and have not told another story and have not heard another story told, so without speaking the Gaelic we will never learn to converse in it. I could tell a story the first night I was there easier than I can now because conversation or story telling is not the thing at our school. The way I see it anyway. Now about the school expanding or getting a few more to attend. One thing I see about it is that if we get any others to attend it has to come from the people in the class to get their own children or near relatives to attend the class. There are a few here who have children living in town and if they cannot get their children to take up the Gaelic how can anyone else be induced to learn the language, who have only a slight background of it?' (This comment is from a man in his 70s and, since he made it, story-telling *has* been encouraged and he has participated.)

Discussion

In terms of respondents' age, educational level and occupation, results here confirm earlier reports. There is a progression across the three groups such that group G subjects — the most capable in Gaelic — are the oldest, least well-educated and most likely to have (or to have had) jobs in the semi-skilled domain (i.e. that 'ethnic core' described by MacKinnon, 1985a, 1985b). Group GL, the students of the language, are the youngest (however, the average age here is 57), best-educated and most likely to have skilled occupations. Group GS subjects fall between the other two here.

Most of the respondents knew where their forebears originated — and the places cited confirm the Catholic nature of the present sample — but considerably more among the GL group knew just when ancestors had come to Canada. It can be argued here that such detail is more likely to be sought by those learners who are making the most active commitment to the language. In any event, it is clear that the ancestors of present respondents arrived in Nova Scotia in the heyday of Scottish emigration.

The information obtained about linguistic competence also confirms the expected differences among the three groups; group G are the most likely to have Gaelic as their mother tongue or second language. The complete absence of any Gaelic monolinguals, even in group G, in combination with earlier information from MacKinnon (1979a, 1985a), suggests that, indeed, the last few such speakers are now gone.

Understandably, group G respondents are the best at speaking and understanding Gaelic, although their superiority does not extend to reading; here, group G were slightly but not significantly better than the Gaelic learners group (they *were* significantly better than group GS, however) and, not surprisingly, were most likely to have rather informally acquired reading ability. In terms of writing, too, the G group is only equivalent to the other two, and for all groups writing is obviously the weakest aspect. These results support previous information about Gaelic being mainly an oral language in Nova Scotia, and about Gaelic literacy levels being low (Anderson, 1973; Campbell & MacLean, 1974; Kelly, 1980). Members of all groups appear to have made use of whatever Gaelic they possessed across a variety of domains, and groups were logically differentiated in terms of preferred language. It is interesting, however, that one-quarter of the G group said that they prefer to use English (the much higher percentages in groups GS and GL obviously relate to lower levels of Gaelic competence) — this may be taken as a telling indicator, since group G are clearly the most proficient in the language.

The local Gaelic was seen as different from other varieties, but not lower in quality. Respondents are thus apparently content with their own varieties and do not see some Scottish variant as a superior standard. In fact there is the suggestion that a particular region of Cape Breton — Inverness county — provides a standard for Nova Scotia Gaelic. It is likely that the Inverness variety was seen as important here because this largely Catholic area has traditionally been the stronghold of the language, as Campbell observed (1948).

On other important points, respondents in the three groups tended to agree that older people place more importance on Gaelic than do the younger; that it would be a good thing if children were learning the language at school; that intermarriage weakens Gaelic; and that various agencies could assist in the survival of the language. There was also a general feeling that Gaelic was maintaining its importance, perhaps even becoming slightly more important. However, in the face of the evidence, this can perhaps be put down as a hope rather than a statement of fact.

MacKinnon (1985a: 6) has noted that ideals or hopes here 'fail to be matched in the realities of everyday life, and the language and culture continue to weaken'. We also observe that very few people — except some among the GL group — gave ordinary communication as a reason for learning the language. Most responses here centred upon the language as a facet of general Scottish heritage. This may indicate a change in status for Gaelic, from a communicative to a symbolic language (see Edwards, 1985; see also MacKinnon (1982, 1985a) on Gaelic as a 'cultural' rather than a community language).

The responses to questionnaire items were essentially reinforced, and sometimes expanded, in the comments which all subjects were encouraged to add. Thus we observe a feeling that the language decline is going to continue, together with a *hope* that this decline might be arrested, largely through educational intervention. There were also suggestions that preservation of Scottish culture in Nova Scotia should not be linked to attempts to maintain the language. Two other interesting features here are, first, the reported punishment (or at least discouragement) in the past for using Gaelic (this supports earlier information from the Cape Breton context, and is reminiscent of other Celtic situations; see Edwards, 1985) and, second, the view that native speakers themselves are not always the strongest active supporters of language maintenance — again reminiscent of settings elsewhere.

In summary, the results of this study, taken together with previous reports and findings, strongly support the list of points given in the introduction, as follows:

First, Gaelic in Nova Scotia, as a language in decline, is essentially associated with older speakers. While most respondents clearly would like to see the younger generation take more of an interest, and while some suggest that there *is* some such interest, the facts relating to the transmission of the language are clear (see also Dorian (1986: 561) on 'the deliberate non-transmission of the ancestral language to young children . . . a theme repeated with dreary frequency').

Second, Gaelic is a language of rurality. It is described as the language of 'toil, hardship and scarcity' by Dunn (1974); this is remarkably similar to Ó Danachair's (1969) labelling of Irish, in its rural *Gaeltacht* context, as a variety of 'penury, drudgery and backwardness'. It is difficult for a language to shake off these associations when the very rurality which gives rise to them also provides the firmest, and perhaps only, foothold.

Third, it is clear that bilingualism in the Nova Scotia Gaelic context has indeed been a temporary way-station on the road to English monolingualism for the vast majority.

Fourth, it seems that the decline of Gaelic cannot be halted since it is the result of large-scale social dynamics involving out-migration, decreasing geographical isolation and the overwhelming socioeconomic clout of a powerful linguistic neighbour. For example, the fact that educational programmes never provided strong support for Gaelic is partly simply due to the power of English but, more subtly perhaps, also due to the lack of desire — even in days gone by when Gaelic had considerable strength. Again, there is an obvious parallel with Ireland here, where nineteenth-century Irish-speaking parents largely acquiesced in the English education of their children.

Fifth, there has been very little *active* support for Gaelic revival, and what there has been has not emanated primarily from within the dwindling native-speaker group — group G in the present study. Group GS are also not pushing the language, and the GL group are personally committed (to varying extents, of course) but show no signs of larger activity on behalf of Gaelic. Dorian (1986: 560) observed that little language loyalty may be exhibited by native speakers of languages in decline, that there exists a 'lightly regretful pragmatism which gives rise to general protestations about the regrettable loss of the language unaccompanied by efforts to halt that loss'. We have seen, in this connection, MacKinnon's (1985a) observation that general cultural loyalty is greater than specific language loyalty among Cape Breton Gaelic speakers. Dorian also goes on to mention that 'strongly negative' attitudes to declining languages are often found. This is something more active than merely low language loyalty. However, we find no particular evidence of this in the present study. Indeed, in surveying several language situations, Edwards (1985: 51) found that 'reasons behind non-transmission are not related to some personal repudiation of the language but rather to pragmatic assessments of the likely utility of competing varieties'. This presumably relates to that 'regretful pragmatism' noted by Dorian.

Sixth, and relatedly, those learning Gaelic now are obviously very few in number, tend to be middle-aged or older, and can hardly be seen as the vanguard of language revival.

Seventh, there *is* considerable evidence of the continuity of Scottish culture — and Scottish cultural stereotypes — in Nova Scotia, and some respondents specifically acknowledged this. This is clearly not dependent upon knowledge and use of Gaelic. Again, we observe cultural loyalty in the relative absence of language loyalty (see also MacKinnon, 1979a, 1985a).

Eighth, several respondents noted that the media should contain more Gaelic; the current situation of course is of English-medium coverage throughout the province, which has the effect of rendering Gaelic less important still.

Ninth, the situation of the language in Nova Scotia clearly shows language shift as a result of perceived necessity.

Tenth, while respondents did not comment specifically upon language-as-a-symbol, they did indicate in their reasons for learning Gaelic that the language had become a cultural, symbolic entity. MacKinnon (1982, 1985a) clearly suggests this as the most likely continuing role for Gaelic — and current dynamics in Nova Scotia make this quite plausible.

To these ten points we can add two more emerging from the present study: *eleventh*, the oral nature of a language, in conjunction with low levels of literacy, may limit its spread and contribute to its decline; and *twelfth*, an interesting defense for languages in decline is the association claimed between them and spiritual or religious values. Comment (8) in this study (see above) suggests such an association, and other respondents touched upon the theme. We also have the quotation already cited from Campbell & MacLean (1974: 178) in which Gaelic is seen as a guide to righteousness, truth, honour and spirituality. Exactly the same sentiments have been produced for Irish. Thus, in 1916, Fullerton (1916: 6) said that 'the Irish language is the casket which encloses the highest and purest religion'; in 1947, O'Donoghue (1947: 24) observed that 'Irish is the instrument and expression of a purely Catholic culture'.

Finally, can we say anything here about the relationship between language and group identity (Edwards, 1985)? I would suggest that Scottish-Canadians, in Nova Scotia at least, maintain many cultural trappings (MacKinnon (1985a) speaks of a 'lively' Gaelic culture). These trappings reflect the power of symbolic ethnicity which, itself, can be a quite enduring phenomenon. The maintenance of these trappings is clearly *not* generally allied to the maintenance of the Gaelic language. It may be argued that such manifestations are 'superficial' (Kelly, 1980) or that they represent only some ethnic 'residue' — nonetheless, they do exist and continue, they support a sense of Scottishness, and they do not rely upon linguistic continuity. Some of the respondents' comments accented this (see, as an example, comment (15), above), as did the responses to the question about reasons for learning Gaelic — where only a very small number mentioned the *use* of Gaelic, most stressing heritage.

Taken together these points illustrate a continuity of culture without a continuity of original group language in its ordinary, communicative sense. We should perhaps disagree slightly with MacKinnon (1985a) when he describes a 'pitiful' adoption of a Lowland identity. What seems to be happening is a change in life-style, language, etc. brought about by larger social forces, such that any adaptations made are based upon pragmatic considerations. Besides, the cultural adaptations made by Gaelic speakers in Cape Breton are in the direction of an Anglo-Canadian mainstream, not particularly to a Scottish Lowland one. In any event, we should always try to understand change in life-style, to understand those group markers which are more susceptible to alteration (like language) and those which are more enduring (see Edwards (1985) for a general discussion). In this way we may hope to come more realistically to grips with an identity that is dynamic, where elements within the cultural boundaries change with altered environmental conditions (see Barth, 1969), rather than to try and maintain an essentially static perspective which might, in some extreme form, enshrine cultures in amber.

Acknowledgements

I wish to acknowledge the provision of grants from the Multiculturalism Directorate, Department of the Secretary of State, Ottawa and from the St Francis Xavier University Council for Research which supported this research and writing. I also wish to thank the following individuals for their assistance: Moira Calderwood, Suzanne de Larichelière, Nancy Dorian, James Kelly, Margaret MacDonnell, Kenneth MacKinnon, Elizabeth Mertz, John Shaw, Douglas Stallard and Seosamh Watson.

References

ANDERSON, A. B. 1973, The Scottish tradition in Canada: its rise and fall. Paper presented at the Seventh Colloquium on Scottish Studies, University of Guelph, October.

BARNARD, F. (ed.) 1969, *J. G. Herder on Social and Political Culture*. Cambridge: Cambridge University Press.

BARTH, F. (ed.) 1969, *Ethnic Groups and Boundaries*. Boston: Little, Brown.

BUMSTED, J. M. 1981, The beginnings of Highland settlement in Atlantic Canada: Covehead, Scotchfort, Pictou, 1770–1775. Unpublished paper.

— 1982, *The People's Clearance: Highland Emigration to British North America, 1770–1815*. Edinburgh: Edinburgh University Press.

CAMPBELL, D. and MACLEAN, R. *Beyond the Atlantic Roar: A Study of the Nova Scotia Scots*. Toronto: McClelland & Stewart.

CAMPBELL, J. L. 1948, Scottish Gaelic in Canada. *An Gaidheal* 43(6), 69–71.

COWAN, M. 1963, *Humanist without Portfolio: An Anthology of the Writings of Wilhelm von Humboldt*. Detroit: Wayne State University Press.

DORIAN, N. 1982, Language loss and maintenance in language contact situations. In R. LAMBERT and B. FREED (eds) *The Loss of Language Skills* (pp. 45–59). Rowley, Massachusetts: Newbury House.

— 1986, Gathering language data in terminal speech communities. In J. FISHMAN, A. TABOURET-KELLER, M. CLYNE, BH. KRISHNAMURTI and M. ABDULAZIZ (eds) *The Fergusonian Impact. Volume 2: Sociolinguistics and the Sociology of Language* (pp. 555–95). Berlin: Mouton de Gruyter.

DUNN, C. W. 1974, (First edition, 1953) *Highland Settler*. Toronto: University of Toronto Press.

EDWARDS, J. R. 1985, *Language, Society and Identity*. Oxford: Basil Blackwell.

FISHMAN, J. 1972, *Language and Nationalism*. Rowley, Massachusetts: Newbury House.

FOSTER, F. G. 1983, The Gaeldom of Tir-Nua — The Newfound Land: Scots Gaelic in Western Newfoundland. In S. CLARKE and R. KING (eds) *Papers from the Sixth Annual Meeting of the Atlantic Provinces Linguistics Association* (pp. 176–93). St John's: APLA.

FULLERTON, R. 1916, *The Prudence of St. Patrick's Irish Policy*. Dublin: O'Brien & Ards.

GANS, H. 1979, Symbolic ethnicity: the future of ethnic groups and cultures in America. *Ethnic and Racial Studies* 2, 1–20.

GREENE, D. 1981, The Atlantic group: Neo-Celtic and Faroese. In E. HAUGEN, J. MCCLURE and D. THOMSON (eds) *Minority Languages Today* (pp. 1–16). Edinburgh: Edinburgh University Press.

KELLY, J. C. 1980, A sociographic study of Gaelic in Cape Breton, Nova Scotia. Concordia University: Unpublished MA Thesis.

MACDONALD, N. 1982, Preserving language is essential. *The Casket* (Antigonish), 1st December.

MACDONALD, N. 1987, Putting on the kilt: the Scottish stereotype and ethnic community survival in Cape Breton. Paper presented at the Ninth Biennial Conference of the Canadian Ethnic Studies Association, Halifax, October.

MACDONELL, M. 1981, Those who remember. In R. O'DRISCOLL (ed.) *The Celtic Consciousness* (pp. 655–8). Toronto: McClelland & Stewart.

MACEACHEN, A. J. 1977, Let us not give up the Gaelic. *The Casket* (Antigonish), lst December.

MACINNES, D. 1977–8, The role of the Scottish Catholic Society in the determination of the Antigonish Movement. *Scottish Tradition* 7/8, 25–46.

MACKINNON, K. 1979a, Vanishing Scots — Renascent Gaels? Unpublished paper.

— 1979b, Gaelic language and culture in Gaelic-speaking Cape Breton communities. Unpublished paper.

— 1982, Cape Breton Gaeldom in cross-cultural context: the transmission of ethnic language and culture. Paper presented at the Sixth Congress of the International Association of Cross-Cultural Psychology, Aberdeen, July.

— 1985a, Erosion and regeneration in Gaelic speech communities: some transatlantic comparisons. Paper presented at the Conference of the Iona Foundation, St Columba's, Prince Edward Island, July.

— 1985b, Gaelic in Cape Breton: Language maintenance and cultural loyalty in the case of a Canadian 'non-official language'. Paper presented at the Second Biennial Conference of the Canadian Studies in Wales Group, Gregynog Hall, University of Wales, July.

MacLean, L. 1985, Cape Breton Gaelic surprises linguist. *Chronicle-Herald* (Halifax), 25th June.

MacLean, R. A. 1978, The Scots: *Hector's* cargo. In D. Campbell (ed.), *Banked Fires: The Ethnics of Nova Scotia* (pp. 51–72). Port Credit, Ontario: Scribbler's Press.

MacLeod, C. I. N. 1958, The Gaelic tradition in Nova Scotia. *Lochlann* 1, 235–40.

MacPherson, J. A. 1985, The Gaelic diaspora: a Canadian perspective. Paper presented at the Conference of the Iona Foundation, St Columba's, Prince Edward Island, July.

Mertz, E. 1989, Sociolinguistic creativity: Cape Breton Gaelic's linguistic 'tip'. In N. Dorian (ed.) *Investigating Obsolescence: Studies in Language Death*. Cambridge: Cambridge University Press.

Millward, H. A. 1980, Regional patterns of ethnicity in Nova Scotia: A geographical study. Unpublished paper.

Ó Danachair, C. 1969, The Gaeltacht. In B. Ó Cuív (ed.) *A View of the Irish Language* (pp. 112–21). Dublin: Government Stationery Office.

O'Donoghue, D. 1947, Nationality and language. In Columban League (ed.), *Irish Man — Irish Nation* (pp. 20–8). Cork: Mercier.

Prebble, J. 1969, *The Highland Clearances*. Harmondsworth, Middlesex: Penguin.

Shaw, J. 1977, The Gaelic revival in Cape Breton. *West Highland Free Press*, 16th and 23rd September.

Sinclair, D. M. 1950–1, Gaelic in Nova Scotia. *Dalhousie Review* 30, 252–60.

Smith, A. 1971, *Theories of Nationalism*. London: Duckworth.

Stephens, M. 1976, *Linguistic Minorities in Western Europe*. Llandysul: Gomer.

Taylor, W. 1986, Scottish culture focus of new tourism campaign. *Chronicle-Herald* (Halifax), 22nd April.

Wilson, B. 1982, Over the sea from Skye . . . *The Sunday Times*, 6th June.

Withers, C. W. J. 1984, *Gaelic in Scotland 1698–1981: The Geographical History of a Language*. Edinburgh: John Donald.

11 Language Made Visible: Representation in Geolinguistics

J. E. AMBROSE AND C. H. WILLIAMS

This volume has been concerned with interpreting the plight of threatened minority cultures and has investigated the factors which conduce to language decline and language revival. Our representation, critical if sympathetic in its stance, has been primarily through the use of the written text.

In this penultimate chapter we will seek to investigate other forms of representation which are perhaps more a feature of conventional human geographic accounts of languages in contact: the use of maps and diagrams. This transposition of word and image is significant, for maps and diagrams, too, are a form of language. The concerns of the linguistic map-maker can be seen to mirror the more general debate about methods in the social sciences, and particularly those in the developing discipline of geolinguistics, but it will be contended that practitioners of geolinguistics have not, as yet, clearly recognised the complete role and value of illustration, nor have they been able to exploit it to the full. The same can be said of illustrations as of words: used without a full understanding of their meaning, they can confuse rather than clarify the message. The Tower of Babel has its illustrative equivalent!

If it is indeed the case that illustration is such a central support of geolinguistics, it is all the more important that its potential and limitations are understood. Macaulay (1985), in an article entitled 'Linguistic Maps: visual aid or abstract art?', stresses what he perceives to be limitations. He thanks the map-makers for 'the elegant works of art that grace my coffee-table and intrigue my visitors'. At the same time, he produces, from the areas of phonology and dialect-mapping, a series of illustrations which serve to show how most language maps stop short of the levels of analysis and interpretation which should be expected of them if they are to be seen as making an undisputed contribution to the study of linguistics. As data-gathering exercises, the *Atlas of English Sounds* (Kolb, 1979) or the *Linguistic Atlas of Scotland* (Mather & Speitel, 1975; 1977) can hardly fail to impress; but their makers, Macaulay implies, clearly see their brief to be that of the laying out of descriptive information for the use of others, rather than the task of providing interpretation. Cartographers then express disappointment when their maps are ignored or under-used by the wider academic community (Macaulay, 1985: 172).

Most of what follows will relate specifically to maps and their uses, rather than to diagrams more generally. This is because criticisms such as those quoted are directed particularly towards language maps, their makers and perhaps also their users. While such critical comment must be taken seriously, it may stem, in part, from a misapprehension that the process of map making is a descriptive rather than an analytical one — that it fails to reflect, in its procedures, the full range of activity of the social sciences. The range of functions which map making can fulfil is ambitiously large, as Figure 11.1 contends, and covers everything from the initial data collection to its analysis, in space and over time, and the presentation and interpretation of results. It must be admitted that it would take a very unusual map indeed to accomplish all of these at the same time, but we would contend that each stage is perfectly capable of being achieved by cartographic means.

The reality of the cartographic contribution to geolinguistics does not always match these ideals. It is not that language maps are a rarity, nor even that existing maps are unsatisfactory — just that they tend not to fulfil the complete range of the functions on Figure 11.1. Readers opening nearly any recent book on dialectology, for example, will discover, first, a heavy dependence upon map support, but those maps will be almost certain to be examples of either stage 2 or stage 5 on Figure 11.1. Only rarely will they serve a directly analytical purpose. Secondly, the great majority will represent static patterns (such as locations), using punctiform, linear or areal symbols, and will not convey the interactive and dynamic character of language use.

It is not that the art and science of linguistic mapping is not developing; a number of workers have given it a great deal of attention. One of the most tireless is R. Breton. Scarcely a continent seems to have escaped his attention since the mid-1970s, and his forays into the portrayal of language patterns in economically 'less-developed' areas are a particularly valued addition to the literature (Breton, 1989). One of the more significant

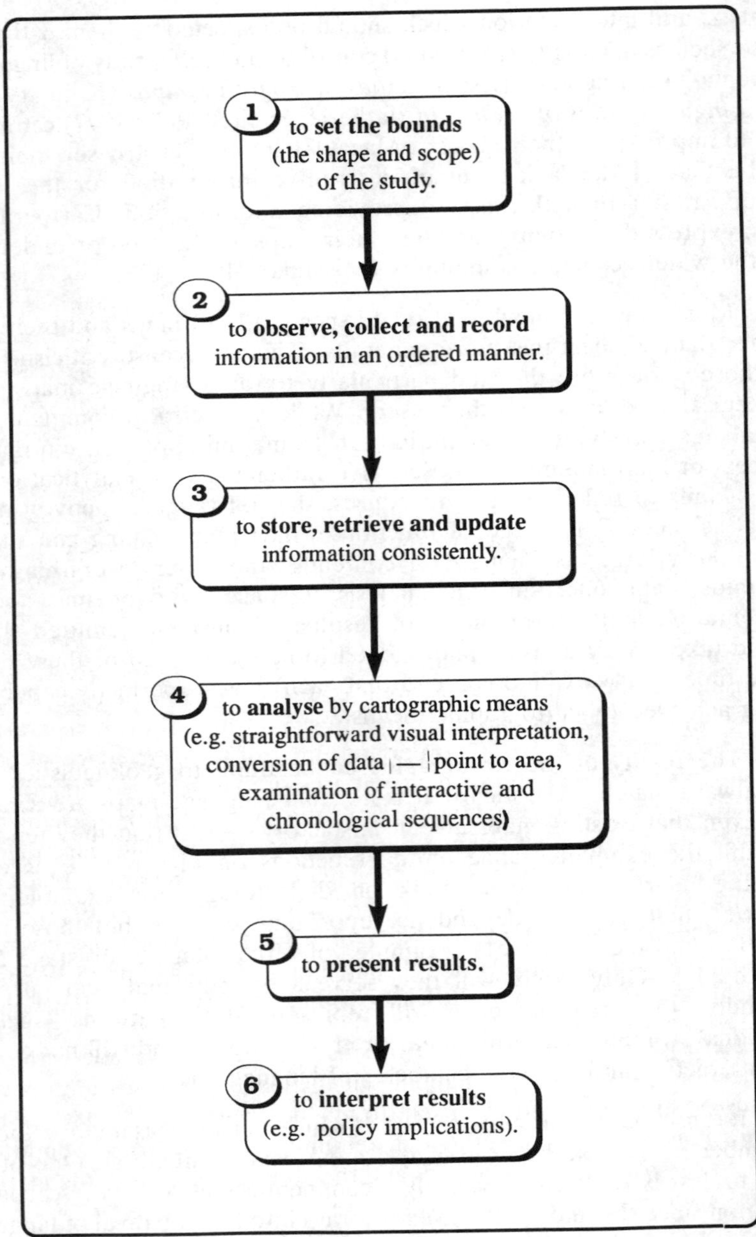

FIGURE 11.1 *The function of maps in geolinguistics*

aspects of his work is his willingness to encompass a range of scales, adjusting his technique to suit world patterns or the large-scale depiction of areas of a few hundred square kilometres. Breton is unusual in having given innovative thought to ways of depicting language dynamics (such as diffusion). It is interesting, though, that when he does so, he almost always replaces maps with diagrams, at a smaller, more general scale and of more abstract form than his static language maps.

It would be misleading, however, to come to the conclusion that maps are more suited to static, descriptive, geolinguistic patterns and diagrams to dynamic and analytical ones. Such is the variety of mapping techniques, in fact, that it is difficult to generalise about them at all. From the vast array of cartographic methods found in a selection of published material, the examples in Figure 11.2 are presented, to reinforce this impression of variety. We have adopted, as a brief means of classification, two conventions common in cartography: a typology of 'point, line and area symbols' and a differentiation between methods which are 'qualitative' or 'quantitative' in approach. Amongst the many other efforts to classify linguistic maps one of the more notable is perhaps that of Chambers & Trudgill (1980), quoted by Macaulay (1985), who distinguish between 'display maps' and 'interpretative maps'. The latter term is a reminder that to draw a language map can involve an element of analysis. Sometimes the results can be surprising, to the map maker as well as to the subsequent user. Personal experience, for example, includes the drawing of maps of two separate sets of information in the Welsh Borderland: first, of the percentage of people able to speak Welsh; then of their patterns of Welsh use in practice. The methodology in that case amounted to little more than the careful visual comparison of the two maps, but it revealed that language-planning approaches based only evidence of percentages of speakers would be a quite inappropriate strategy, at least in that locality (Ambrose, 1979). Crude though the process might have been, it helped lead the way towards a realisation that the existing basis of spatial language planning in Wales was deficient, and to that extent, at least, it fulfilled an analytical function.

Returning to Macaulay's criticisms, it could be asked, with some justification, why language mapping, if it indeed possesses an analytical potential, so often restricts itself to its descriptive role. Two sets of reasons suggest themselves, the first stemming from the broad relationship between geography and linguistics and the second inherent in the mapping process itself.

At a general level, there is the whole question of the compatibility of linguistics and geography, whose relationship rather rarely seems like a true 'meeting of minds'. Perhaps one of the roots of the problem is that those who possess expertise in techniques such as phonetic transcription cannot necessarily be expected to have the same level of experience of the rudiments of map construction, whilst those well-trained in cartography are similarly poorly versed in basic linguistic and phonetic methods. Linguists venture into the world of map making and geographers into the realms of linguistics, but rarely is there genuine co-operation in the setting-up of goals and methods. The problems of the linguists are compounded by the fact that, as Figure 11.2 illustrates, the choice of potential cartographic methods is so wide that few conventions for language mapping have yet been established. Individuals such as Breton, working in a genuine spirit of experiment and against a background of cartographic styles which are often culturally or nationally distinctive, are obliged to employ mapping techniques without recourse to clear standards of comparability. The International Phonetic Alphabet is not yet matched in the field of cartography.

More specifically, it could also be that the process of constructing language maps has included a number of constraints which have devalued their contribution to linguistic study. Not the least of these is that map makers face an ever-present problem of resources, in terms of money and labour. There is no doubt that acquiring language data is time-consuming, and to turn them into maps often requires a much more voluminous sample than has been the norm in linguistics. The increasing of the sample size usually means, in turn, the simplification of the data, to the dismay of linguists. Often, only the most basic and general information (for example, numbers of speakers of a language) reaches the stage of mapping. On most occasions the degree of compromise is far greater than so far implied, and the makers of maps are obliged to rely on ready-gathered statistics, collected for administrative purposes but adapted, as far as possible, to academic ends. As an example of this, cartographic users of the language census data for Scottish Gaelic and Welsh are long used to the restricted range of evidence at their disposal. The census usefully documents several of the quantitative aspects of the ability to speak these languages, but almost wholly neglects the more qualitative assessment of their state of survival (for example, the domain-related frequency of their use). Elsewhere, better progress has been made — not least in Canada, with the use of a sophisticated census linguistic data source. The process of map making, as outlined on Figure 11.1, is an active and potentially influential one. At best, it can be a vital ingredient in the framing of language policy (as, for example, in the case of the drawing-up of Canada's bilingual districts (Cartwright, 1971)).

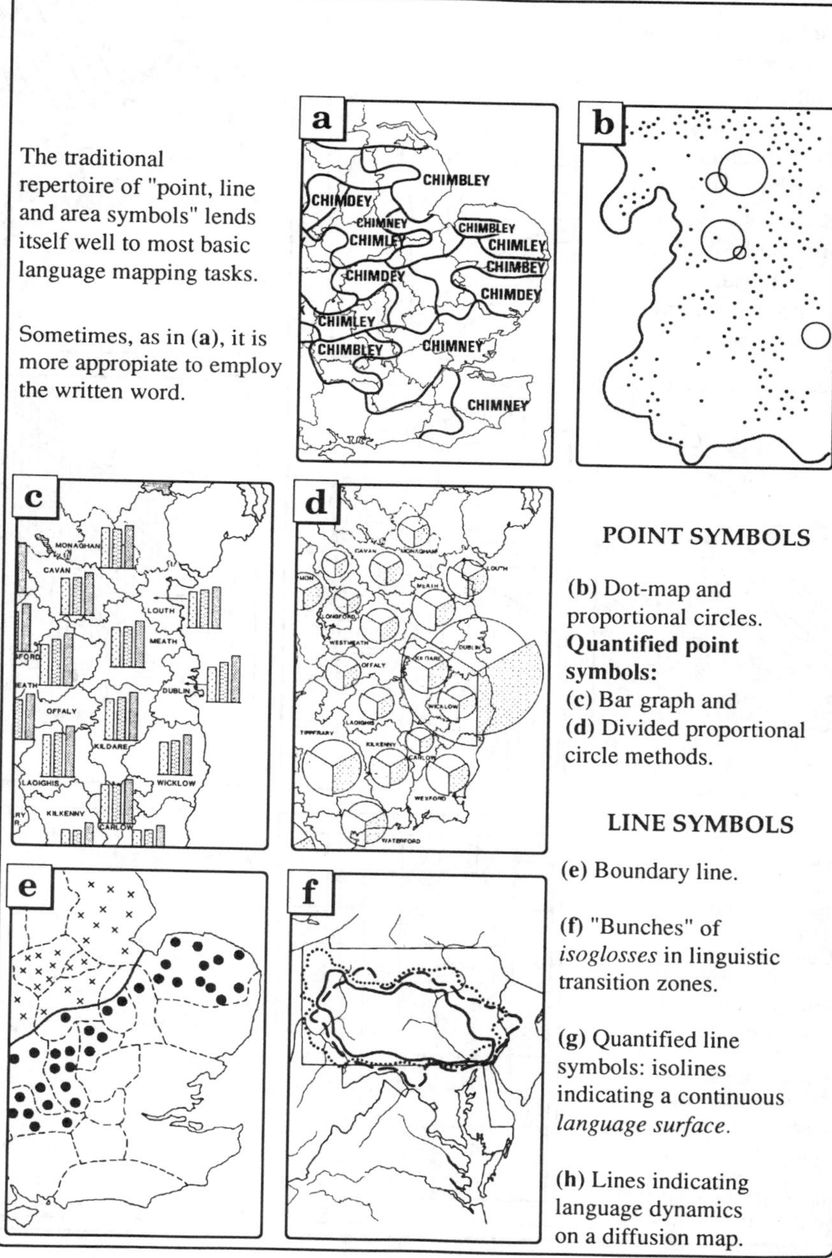

FIGURE 11.2 *A selection of commonly used language mapping techniques*

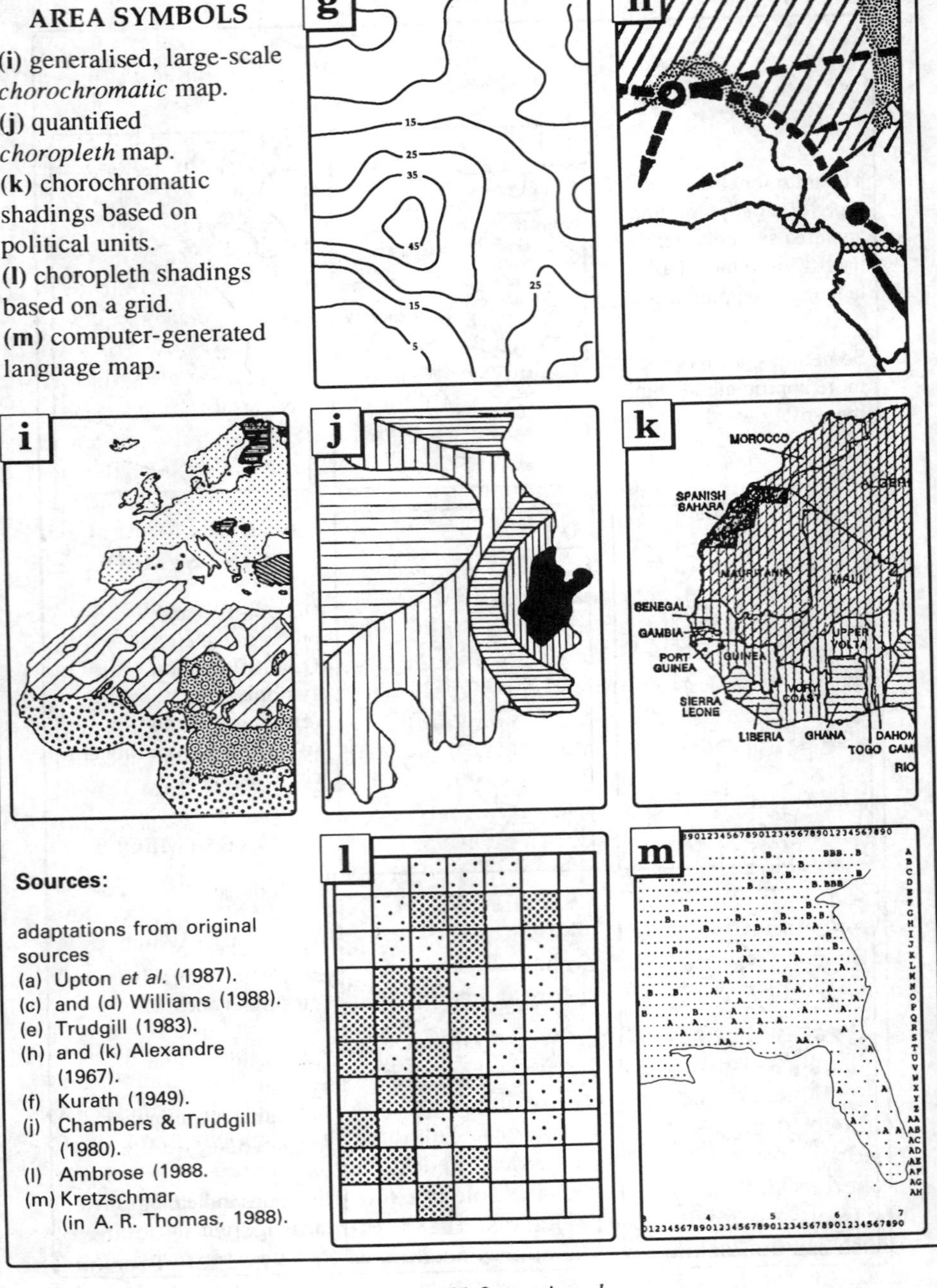

FIGURE 11.2 *continued*

The accumulating evidence is that maps can make useful servants in linguistic study, but that they are not without the potential to disappoint and even to deceive their users, not to mention their makers. Stages 1 and 6, on Figure 1, perhaps best illustrate that observation. Stage 1 (the selection of the precise area to be mapped, together with the units which comprise it) is a task frequently given less consideration than it deserves. Existing administrative areas, such as counties, with their internal divisions into civil parishes or similarly-sized components, are the usual, pragmatic compromise in Wales and Scotland, regardless of the fact that their boundaries may be irregularly-shaped, largely arbitrary and subject to variation over time. Yet, by stage 6, such units may have become transformed, by some miraculous process, into districts for the administration of language policy. The formulation of spatial language policy reveals itself as a highly pragmatic process: 'culture regions', 'zones of linguistic collapse', 'bilingual districts' and a host of other areal designations originate partly in a quasi-random process in which people can become net beneficiaries or losers, depending upon chance factors of location and the meanderings of boundaries.

If boundaries are deceptive, so too are scales. The question of scale, fundamental to most geographical study, furnishes at least part of the explanation for such patchy progress in the drawing of analytical language maps. It is necessary, in most conventional forms of map making, to group together information into areal units — a problem in that linguistic processes operate, for the most part, at the level of the individual speaker. It is a source of ceaseless frustration to map makers that official language data sources provide information in aggregate form (for quite understandable motives of confidentiality, it must be admitted) using units ranging from randomly aggregated grid-squares to postal districts, but quite incompatible with the needs of analytical cartography. This incompatibility of scale is another of the contributory factors which could be seen as casting cartographers in the role of secondary observers of linguistic processes, rather than agents of their understanding.

A case drawn from the Welsh language area can illustrate this scale problem. Welsh is one of Europe's best-documented minority languages. A sequence of census information, since the end of the nineteenth century, forms the basis of numerous national and regional maps of its regional strengths and weaknesses, and is supplemented, in turn, by numerous studies of the language's role in education, cultural and political life (Betts, 1976; Pryce & Williams, 1988). In many respects, details of Welsh are not lacking; yet the emergence of a co-ordinated set of regional and local policies for the Welsh language has been slow. One of the contributory factors, it can be argued, is a gap in the understanding of the local, areal processes operating to affect the language. Some of the missing evidence merely calls for a different scale of map compilation, analysis and presentation.

Figure 11.3 represents one such alternative. It takes a section of countryside in the central Welsh Borderland (see top map) and illustrates Welsh-speaking ability (by households) at two dates, a dozen years apart. The section covers a range of topography and incorporates parts of some four or five civil parishes. The parish scale is not especially important, however: the processes occurring over the period are clearly operating at a much more local level. Language planners would need to be aware of the changing fortunes of the farming industry, of house prices, journeys to work and the availability of schools and social services, if any clear picture of the fortunes of Welsh were to be achieved. No one could pretend that the data are conceptually sophisticated — only that they are mapped at a scale commensurate with the highly complex changes taking place in this area.

The short time period between the two dates in Figure 11.3 reveals the degree of social upheaval — and associated linguistic change — now taking place in this locality, and also provides some more general lessons in methodology. In cases where we have to compromise on detail, one measure in particular can be taken to increase the value of linguistic mapping; that is, to create a 'time series' — a sequence of data sets for the same place. Figure 11.3 clearly demonstrates the need for such a quickly generated sequence: decisive patterns of change can take place within short time periods. If that is a general feature, then elaborate policies directed solely at language can become outdated even before they have time to be implemented. Such policies must be tailored clearly to the needs of the locality, and be part of an overall strategy for local development; and they cannot simply be imposed 'from the top downwards' — by deriving a national–regional language policy and applying it locally — if they are to have any realistic chance of success. An element of successful language planning is the ability to anticipate the changes which are likely to occur in any particular area. In the past, Welsh language census data, mapped at the national scale, have enabled a relatively accurate process of linguistic 'sophology' to be undertaken, in order to predict which areas are next likely to experience severe pressures of anglicisation (Williams, 1980; 1989). The main obstacle to repeating that exercise at the scale of the locality, though it is inherently a rather more complex exercise, is the rarity of sufficiently detailed time

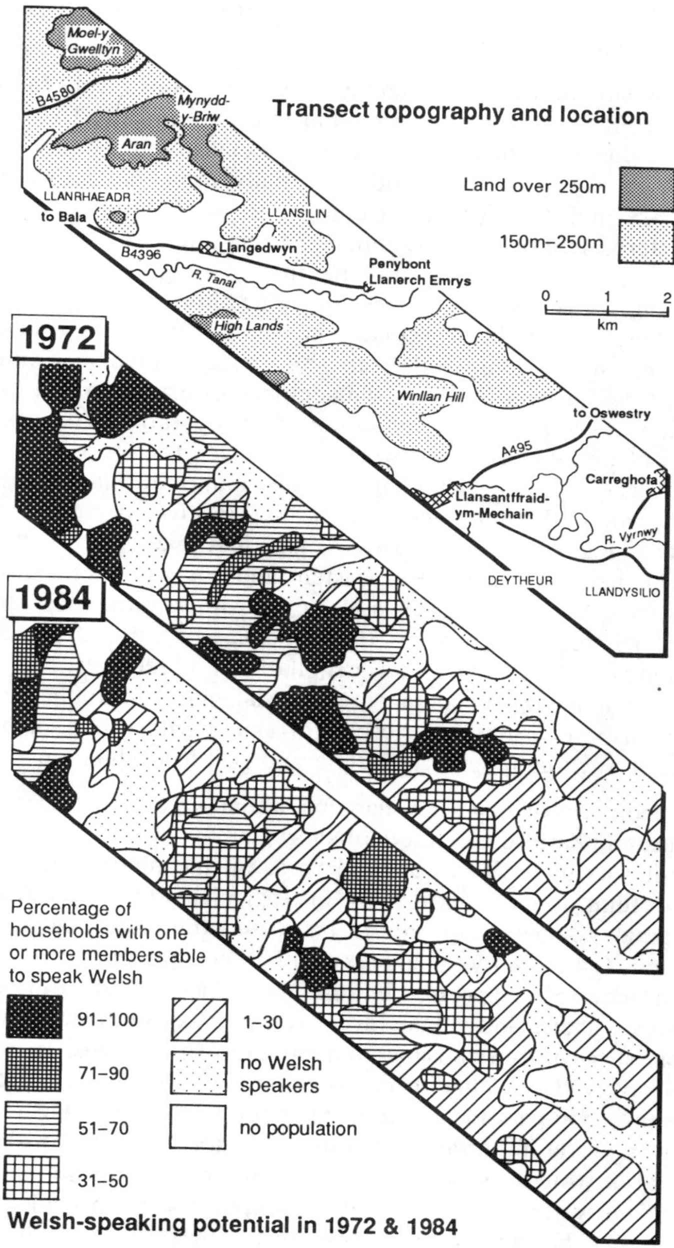

FIGURE 11.3 *Recent changes in the potential for Welsh speaking*

series such as that on Figure 11.3. The question is, could there be any prospect of such developments?

If the situation in such relatively simple cases as bicultural Wales is lamentable, it is even more deplorable that we tend not to possess the linguistic evidence to make accurate judgements about areas of the world where more rapid, complex and potentially more disruptive linguistic changes are underway (as, for example, in such multicultural cities as Manilla, Jerusalem or Kuala Lumpur). Major cities are often the context for competing language groups in their struggle for survival and recognition, for access to services, for education or for the legalisation of their language in the workplace, in commerce and in industry. The ecology of language shift has been ably demonstrated in a number of Western cities such as Toronto, Philadelphia, Amsterdam and Montreal, but we have little by the way of sustained, comparative research into the structure of multilingual cities world-wide. Even the most basic mapped data concerning the total numbers and distribution of language groups is absent, let alone the more geolinguistically sensitive concerns as to when and where language switching or language loss takes place within urban areas. This need for accurate, consistent and finely tuned language maps will become even more pressing as societies witness more inter-urban and international migration, and as the principles of cultural pluralism are increasingly employed to counter assimilationist tendencies. For the truth remains that languages in contact are often languages in conflict, especially when linguistic divisions are closely correlated with other socio-cultural differences, such as religion, life-style and political affiliation.

The picture of linguistic mapping which we have presented is one which has emphasised the frequent shortcomings of the medium, as well as stressing its undoubted potential uses. Of the many functions which maps can fulfil, the analytical ones, in particular, are under-represented. Language mapping still appears to be at an exploratory stage, with few conventions (particularly to aid cross-cultural comparison) yet established. Resource shortages, expressed in time, money and expertise, have meant slow progress, and individual inventiveness has not been matched, in many cases, by official and government mapping agencies. In particular, this has involved a failure to derive systems with a sufficient flexibility of scale to encompass local and more general processes, and insufficient recognition of the importance of constantly monitoring linguistic change. In general, it would not be unfair to say that most language mapping has traded quantity for quality, as well as simplifying much evidence to the point where it becomes difficult to perceive the processes taking place. No wonder that linguists often fail to recognise the potential of drawing language maps. A classic example of this inevitable compromise between ambitious ideals and more mundane results was recently provided in the production of the map of the lesser-used languages of the European Community, which forms our final case study.

In 1987 the European Bureau for Lesser-Used Languages (EBLUL) commissioned a map of such languages in the European Community. Preparation of an EC language map to complement those already produced for political administrative units, population, agriculture and other themes was a daunting and complex task, for whilst information is generally available on the size and distribution of the nine official Community languages, together with other State languages, such as Irish, the equivalent data for lesser-used languages are lacking. Yet at least one in every six citizens of the EC speaks a lesser-used language. It has been estimated that of the Community's 321 million inhabitants, some 50 millions speak a lesser-used language (O'Riagain, 1989).

The first problem, as in Figure 11.1, was one of definition. What are the appropriate geographical units, and what constitutes a lesser-used language? Is Scots in the United Kingdom, or Polish in the Federal Republic of Germany, a legitimate use of the term, in comparison, say, with Breton in France, or Sard in Italy? Is Galician, which linguistics would accept as being Portuguese, to be considered a lesser-used language, merely because it happens to be the version of Portuguese spoken in north-west Spain? Again there is the classic problem, in linguistics, of differentiating between a dialect and a language: for example, should Valencian be considered as an autochthonous language, or as a variant of Catalan? For that matter, can one justify the designation of Catalan, spoken by over eight million people, as a lesser-used language?

The answers to these questions were largely determined by political, rather than purely linguistic, considerations. As the EBLUL is comprised of representative committees from the member states of the EC, it is their definitions of what they consider to be lesser-used languages within their state, which count, not the criteria as defined by professional linguists. Thus, for example, though Letzburgish is the national language of Luxembourg, it is also a lesser-used language there, for it is overshadowed by French, German and English as working languages.

As with all other means of imparting information, linguistic cartography depends upon good quality data. Unfortunately there is great variation in the usefulness of data, whose quality declines progressively, in general terms, from north to south and from west to east across the territory of the Community. Thus whilst both Scotland and Wales have a century-long tradition of asking language questions in their decennial census (Pryce & Williams, 1988), Euskadi, Catalonia and Brittany have only recent and very modest sociolinguistic surveys of language affiliation available, though in the Catalan and Basque cases it is fair to say that the Autonomist governments are doing their best to provide an historical overview of the changes in the fortunes of Catalan and Euskera, and have established a comprehensive census data base on knowledge of speaking, reading and writing these languages. However, for many of the lesser-used language communities, such as Vlak, Macedonian and Turkish in Greece, or the Langues d'Oc in France (Sérant, 1965), much of the current information available in the literature is based on a combination of guess-work, inspired scholarship and partisan estimates. Inevitably, then, we are faced with a choice of either displaying detailed language distributions for north and west Europe, leaving southern and south-eastern Europe relatively sparsely-covered, or of reducing the overall level of representation to the lowest common denominator for the whole of the map.

This is not a new problem in cartography. The relationship between representation and reality is one of the most intractable and complex problems, common to many forms of expression, whether it be in fine art, sculpture, music or image-creation in map form. J. S. Keates (1982) surveys the myriad forms by which cartographic signs and symbols may be used to generalise and simplify a multi-dimensional reality in two-dimensional space. He cites Petchenik's (1975: 86) observation that most people acknowledge that a single 'map' (in the same way as a single picture) 'can "tell" more than hundreds of words, yet our vocabulary is deficient in trying to state what the map "tells"'. We need more sensitive interpretations of the sign language of maps, for despite the enormous developments in psycho-linguistics as it pertains to thought and language, our visual representation of reality is still hindered by our impoverished language of 'explanation'.

Modes of signifying cognitive and non-cognitive (or referential and expressive) items are also subject to the use of general or classificatory concepts, such as colour choice or symbolic representation. To cite an example, conventional cartographic practice in Europe has associated specific countries with particular colour representation. Thus France has commonly been depicted by a blue hue, Britain by red or pink, and Ireland by green. In addition, national atlases have often heightened the propaganda effect by using bold colours for their own country, as well as by centring the map projection there. The most significant examples of suggestive or persuasive maps are perhaps those produced by the National Socialists in their development of *Geopolitik* (Herb, 1989:

289–303), but less extreme practices of manipulative representation still abound in contemporary map production.

The conventional choice of colour representation would suggest green for the Celtic territories, red for Latin/Romance countries and blue for Germanic areas. However, in this case such conventions had to be overturned for technical reasons. Given that on the EBLUL map the lesser-used languages which are derived from the same base language are to be represented in a variant shade of that base language (for example, Catalan from Latin, English from Low German), then the language grouping with the largest number of radiants determined the colour selection. Thus the Latin-based lesser-used languages numbered 18, the Germanic radiants seven and the Celtic only six. Therefore green was used for the Latin group, because it has the widest range of easily-distinguishable printed densities, while blue and red were employed for the Germanic and Celtic groups respectively.

Once such necessary production decisions have been made, we may turn to broader questions and ask what messages are being conveyed by the resultant map. Is it suggesting that within the territories depicted the lesser-used language is dominant, or residual, or potential? Are the boundaries of the language territory to be depicted as current or historical, formal or informal? Do they denote official support and recognition for the language? To what extent do they mask the degree of functional bilingualism, by depicting only the lesser-used language, rather than all the significant languages, in any particular area?

The answer depends to a large extent upon the part of the map under consideration. In northern and western Europe the linguistic territories tend to incorporate both historical core areas and regions within which the lesser-used languages operate as recognised, legitimate mediums of communication. However, in parts of Mediterranean Europe, particularly Greece, the very existence of certain minority groups is a matter of current debate. Thus any attempt to designate the territory of Slav speakers as 'Bulgarian', 'Macedonian' or 'Slav-Macedonian' will be contentious and, in the absence of self-reported census information, largely dependent upon historical and social evidence. Are the Pomacs, for example, to be considered as a separate language group, or are they Bulgarian-speaking Muslims who differ from their fellow Greek Slavs only in religion? Equally contentious is the designation of Arvanite/ Arberesch and Vlak areas, for although their distribution at the time of the War of Independence in 1821 was well-understood, their current distribution pattern is far less certain, and yet they need to be represented as a significant linguistic group by some symbol or means.

Data on such groups have not been collected systematically in the past, partly because of the paucity of the means of gathering state-wide information on social issues, and partly because past political expediency has deemed the recognition of such groups to be a strategically-sensitive matter. The current situation is that as a result of the Greek government's disquiet about the disclosure of such information, based as it is upon non-governmental sources, the publication of the map has been delayed subject to amendment. In the light of such difficulties, will purely technical improvements, such as better data-gathering techniques and computer-aided recording of information, be able to make any positive contribution to the future prospects of geolinguistic representation?

In the general area of geography and cartography there is already, of course, a considerable history of computer use. More specifically, in the field of geolinguistics, it is now over a decade since Orton & Dieth (1962) first suggested that the *Survey of English Dialects* should be coded into machine-readable form, to expedite its progress, and as Figure 11.2(m) reminds us, computer-based linguistic maps are now with us, in their thousands. In some cases, official agencies, Census Canada in particular, have adopted digital storage and processing of linguistic information, making the effective manipulation and scale transformation of mapped data an altogether more realistic prospect.

It would be far from the truth, however, to imply that computer-based geolinguistic mapping represents a universal success. Instead, it can be taken as an example of the broader resource problems which such technology brings to light. The capability of computer mapping of language information presupposes a data-collection process which is consistent, copious and accurate. That may be an unduly large assumption. A recently published volume (Maguire, 1989), assessing the general role of computers in geographical study, considers the chronological sequence of key problems which have faced computer users. Initial problems of obtaining the computer hardware itself were supplanted by those of gaining access to suitable software, such as mapping programs. As these became available, there arose a shortage of suitably trained personnel, and finally, inevitably, there occurred an extreme proliferation of data (Maguire, 1989: 4). It might be argued that the last-mentioned is scarcely a problem; such a proliferation was, in some respects, one of the very objectives of computer use. It only assumes the complexion of a problem if the accuracy and consistency of the information becomes difficult to maintain; and as explained earlier, that has been one of the traditional problems with linguistic data. The remedy, in the longer term, calls for a large work-force, consistently trained in matters of linguistic field observation and recording, together with levels of financial support which are, unfortunately, quite alien to the experience of most non-governmental geolinguists.

To set against that, the revolution in information technology makes possible (as it has in other fields of geography) the creation of continuously augmented and updated linguistic data banks, rather than the spasmodic 'snap-shots' to which language geographers have become accustomed. Such frameworks for data storage and retrieval also provide the possibility of solving another of the problems mentioned earlier, in the context of the Welsh example in Figure 11.3. It was contended there that an understanding of the complex patterns of linguistic change, and perhaps also the formulation of an appropriate local policy response, demanded the acquisition of similarly detailed, current information on a wide array of socio-economic indicators which were affecting the local language position. The possibilities raised by data banks for combining previously unrelated information, while they would demand both caution and sophistication on the part of the user, open exciting prospects of more flexible local policy responses, together with new academic opportunities (for example, detailed studies of domain-related language use).

Computer-aided linguistic mapping (in the broader sense of 'mapping' implied by Figure 11.1) requires, in short, a parallel revolution in attitudes on the part of geolinguists. It has already been pointed out that language mapping is beset by problems of inconsistency in the way that data are stored, processed and presented. In the light of new opportunities to remedy such difficulties, it would be ironic if we, with our common interest in language and communication, allowed technology merely to amplify the level of Babel and further to hinder the passage of what Bottiglioni (1954) referred to as 'the word in the immediacy of its poetic creation'.

References

ALEXANDRE, P. 1967, *Langues et Langage en Afrique Noire*. Paris: Payot.

AMBROSE, J. E. 1979, A geographical study of language borders in Wales and Brittany. Unpublished PhD thesis, University of Glasgow.

AMBROSE, J. E. and WILLIAMS, C. H. 1988, On measuring language border areas. In C. H. WILLIAMS (ed.) *Language in Geographic Context*. Clevedon: Multilingual Matters.

BETTS, C. 1976, *Culture in Crisis: The Future of the Welsh Language*. Wirral: Ffynnon Press.

BOTTIGLIONI, G. 1954, Linguistic geography: achievements, methods and orientations. *Word* 10, 375–87.

BRETON, R. 1989, Indices Numériques et Représentations Graphiques de la Dynamique des Langues. Paper presented at the *Deuxième Colloque International sur la Diffusion des Langues*, CIRB, Québec, 9–12 April, 1989.

CARTWRIGHT, D. 1971, *Bilingual Districts: The Elusive Territorial Component in Canada's Official Languages Act.* Discussion Papers in Linguistics 1. Stoke-on-Trent: Staffordshire Polytechnic, Department of Geography and Recreation Studies.

CHAMBERS, J. K. AND TRUDGILL, P. 1980, *Dialectology*. Cambridge: Cambridge University Press.

HERB, G. H. 1989, Persuasive cartography in Geopolitik and National Socialism. *Political Geography Quarterly* 8(3), 289–303.

KEATES, J. S. 1982, *Understanding Maps*. Harlow: Longman.

KOLB, E. B. *et al.* 1979, *An Atlas of English Sounds*. Bern: Francke.

KRETZSCHMAR, W. A. Jr 1988, Computers and the American linguistic atlas. In A. R. THOMAS (ed.) *Methods in Dialectology*. Clevedon: Multilingual Matters.

KURATH, H. 1949, *A Word Geography of the Eastern United States*. Ann Arbor: University of Michigan Press.

MACAULAY, R. K. S. 1985, Linguistic maps: visual aid or abstract art? In J. M. KIRK *et al.* (eds) *Studies in Linguistic Geography: The Dialects of English in Britain and Ireland*. London: Croom Helm.

MAGUIRE, D. J. 1989, *Computers in Geography*. Harlow: Longman Scientific and Technical.

MATHER, J. Y. and SPEITEL, H. -H. 1975, *Linguistic Atlas of Scotland* volume 1. London: Croom Helm.

— 1977, *Linguistic Atlas of Scotland* volume 2. London: Croom Helm.

Ó'RIAGÁIN, D. 1989, The European Bureau for Lesser-Used Languages: its role in creating a Europe united in diversity. In T. VEITER (ed.) *Fédéralisme, Régionalisme et Droit des Groupes Ethniques en Europe*. Vienna: Braumuller.

ORTON, H. and DIETH, E. 1962, Survey of English dialects. Department of English Language and Medieval English Literature, University of Leeds.

PETCHENIK, B. B. 1975, Cognition in cartography. *Proc. Int. Sym. on Computer-Assisted Cartography and Cartographica* 19 (1977).

PRYCE, W. T. R. and WILLIAMS, C. H. 1988, Sources and methods in the study of language areas: a case study of Wales. In C. H. WILLIAMS (ed.) *Language in Geographic Context* (pp. 171ff). Clevedon: Multilingual Matters.

SÉRANT, P. 1965, *La France des Minorités*. Paris: Laffont.

TRUDGILL, P. 1983, *On Dialect*. Oxford: Basil Blackwell.

UPTON, C., SANDERSON, S. and WIDDOWSON, J. 1987, *Word Maps: A Dialect Atlas of England*. Beckenham: Croom Helm.

WILLIAMS, C. H. 1980, Language contact and language change: a study in historical geolinguistics. *Welsh History Review* 10, 207–38.

— 1988, Language planning and regional development: Lessons from the Irish Gaeltacht. In C. H. WILLIAMS (ed.) *Language in Geographic Context*. Clevedon: Multilingual Matters.

— 1989, The anglicisation of Wales. In N. COUPLAND (ed.) *English in Wales* (pp. 19–47). Clevedon: Multilingual Matters.

12 Conclusion: Sound Language Planning is Holistic in Nature

COLIN H. WILLIAMS

We are conscious that the largely underdeveloped field of geolinguistics and its parent discipline of Geography has much to offer co-workers in the Sociology of Language and Sociolinguistics. Our focus has been upon linguistic minorities in decline, but our approaches and methodologies are capable of wider application to most situations of language contact. Although geographers have long been fascinated by society-environment relations, it is very evident that cognate research in all the other Social Sciences is also now addressing the role of space, context, environment and ecology in influencing human behaviour and intention in all its myriad forms. Conventionally, scholars such as Fishman (1966; 1989) and Romaine (1989) interested in language maintenance, shift and death have offered transitional models which follow a classic pattern identified by early anthropologists and human geographers (e.g. Paul Vidal de la Blache, 1848–1914, or E. G. Bowen, 1900–83). The model has been refined and given its own specialist terminology, but essentially its dynamism and central processes remain unchanged. Romaine (1989) has specified it thus:

> The classic pattern is that a community which was once monolingual becomes transitionally bilingual as a stage on the way to eventual extinction of its original language. Thus language shift involves bilingualism (often with diglossia) as a stage on the way to monolingualism in a new language. [cf. Bowen & Carter, 1975] Although the existence of bilingualism, diglossia and code-switching are both often cited as factors leading to language death, in some cases code-switching and diglossia are positive forces in maintaining

> bilingualism. Swiss German and Faroese may never emerge from diglossia, but are probably in no danger of death. (Romaine, 1989: 39)

Unfortunately the same confidence cannot be expressed in relation to contemporary Gaelic whether in Scotland, Nova Scotia or, dare one say, Ireland. The other major Celtic languages of Breton and Welsh are also not entirely secure. However, to varying degrees, they are subject to popular support and to comprehensive language planning in ever-expanding social and occupational domains. But how strong are languages in decline? How do we measure their degree of popular support? What are the chief influences determining rates of language shift? These questions have animated the contributors to this volume, and John Edwards has come closest to applying with great clarity the universal concepts of language decline (cf. Hindley, 1987).

It is customary to divide the factors influencing languages under threat into internal (social-psychological) and external (socio-economic and political). A modification of this rather simple and in my view untenable division, has been the development of scales of ethnolinguistic vitality, a concept advanced by Giles, Bourhis & Taylor (1977) and refined by Bourhis (1979; 1983) and others (Allardt & Landry 1987). Many of the conventional external factors have been addressed in this volume in an attempt to demonstrate the salience of Mackey's (1988) observations on language territoriality and geolinguistic distinctions. In a parallel discussion Suzanne Romaine (1989) had drawn attention to the significant factors which can be implicated in, but do not necessarily determine the fate of a minority language, among which are:

> the numerical strength of the group in relation to other minorities and majorities, social class, religious and educational background, settlement patterns, ties with the homeland, degree of similarity between the minority and majority language, extent of exogamous marriage, attitudes of majority and minority, government policy toward language and education of minorities, and patterns of language use. (Romaine, 1989: 39–40)

Judged by these measures, many of the language communities addressed in this volume can be described as 'terminal speech communities' and the focus questions of Dorian's (1989: 8–9) recent excellent collection apply very well to their situation. In the four areas identified by Dorian, namely assessing language skills, accounting for the range of language skills, interpreting change within certain speech forms, and predicting the effects of sudden dissolution or resistance, it is the latter phenomenon which relates most closely to our concerns. We have demonstrated that the cessation of home language transmission is a combination of the closer socio-economic integration of the respective communities into the state system and beyond, together with a tacit group-wide change in values and norms which effectively undermines the autonomous rationale for an out-moded and under-subscribed culture. Once this 'trauma' of lack of social confidence and economic purchase becomes internalised by individuals, families, organisations and whole communities, then, as Ambrose & Williams (1981) make clear there ensues a social collapse or 'tip' in the language. However, this structural transition is by no means uniform across space or through time and we need empirical investigation of the several stages of the collapse process. The Welsh pattern is not untypical of many others discussed in this volume. Consider this description:

> Levels of Welsh-speaking ability may stay near a hundred per cent over a long and uninterrupted period. Next, over a period of a few decades in this border region, a rapid change of fortune seems to overtake the language. There is a sudden crisis involving the whole numerical basis of Welsh speaking within some parishes, while others nearby remain apparently unaffected, even though experiencing strongly similar economic, demographic and other circumstances. Such a pattern presents a problem, both for those seeking a coherent language-planning policy for the region, and for the speakers themselves . . . Planning policies, as well as being variable from one part of the region to another, must be adaptable at short notice in order to accommodate the suddenly changing fortunes of the language in any locality. (Ambrose & Williams, 1981: 59–61)

However, before adequate remedial planning is adopted we need a firm and unequivocable discussion about the correct application of language planning alongside other forms of appropriate planning. It is all too evident in the cases discussed herein that too little attention has been paid to the needs of the communities, the language issues have often been separated from other issues and the consequence has been niggardly and piecemeal reform of the socio-economic conditions which sustain the communities. No wonder, then, that resistance and conflict are intimately involved in the struggle for cultural survival, for at root we are describing a power relationship between a dominant culture and a subordinate culture. Far from being neutral in this struggle the state is often deeply implicated in the attempt to eradicate former vestiges of minority cultures for they speak of the mal-integration of the state and its constituent peoples. Moreover, it is economically disfunctional to have an internal labour force, differentiated by language, religion or some other cultural marker which threatens to inhibit the smooth development of the production processes, with all its ramifications for economic autarchy as the counterpart of political sovereignty.

We thus need a sustained investigation of the relationship between the modern state, its constituent minorities and the role of language planning. Clearly a conclusion to a detailed set of cameos like this is not the place to instigate such a debate, but one can point to certain limitations inherent in language planning to counter the more optimistic, and at times, naive view of its potency as a technical fix for most of the ailments of shrinking minority languages. A case has been presented throughout this volume for a more integrated, inter-disciplinary approach to the context which structures the fate of language communities. It is evident that in societies like Canada, Belgium and Spain aspects of bilingual and multicultural planning have been incorporated as central features of public policy decision-making. The success of their application to lesser-used language communities has been determined more by the macro-political context than by the micro-level adaptation of language planning principles and techniques. However, one should not accept the growth of language planning uncritically and assume that it is always a positive element in minority language communities. Language planning is not a neutral activity and too often in past applications it has engendered ambiguous or contradictory attitudes, both within the local state and its constituents. I do not wish to argue that language planning has no role in bolstering the use of lesser-used languages — far from it. If we consider the judicious development of formal bilingual education, the extension of lesser-used languages into new domains, such as public administration, the law and the media, then there is ample room for supporting the coherent adoption of basic language and social planning principles (Williams, 1989). However, it is evident that there are also new and often unanticipated consequences of adopting language planning principles uncritically which may be framed in a series of questions for further investigation.

In Western social science, planning has been formed within a positivist, developmental epistemology. The whole thrust behind planning in all its myriad forms since the 1960s has been to equip it so as to cope with growth and expansion, with congestion and with 'progress'.

In contemporary society so many aspects of planning are now concerned with contraction, with a culture which emphasises the comprehensive rationalisation of scarce resources and with competition.

Does this necessarily make language planning a handmaiden for policies of nation/state congruence? Within governmental circles the needs of a minority language in terms of educational provision, recruitment of bi- or tri-lingual personnel etc. are pitted against the competing needs of hospital provision, or water care or social services. Language is sectionalised rather than being a medium through which these other services are provided to linguistically distinct regions of the state. What consequence will this sectionalisation have for the ultimate realisation of the goals of the minority community? This is an especially crucial question for we have two simultaneous trends at work. The first is the re-definition of the relationship between the individual, the minority language community and the state, whereby the state has recognised an obligation to honour the rights of selected autochthonous minorities after decades, if not centuries, of political agitation. The second is the expanding nature of state involvement in all aspects of social and economic life so that many other group rights and self-defined minorities are making equal demands on the state's legislature and exchequer. In such an environment it is clear that minority language groups can be conceived as special interest groups, one amongst many worthy charitable organisations such as those dealing with homelessness, child abuse, poverty, disablement and religious tolerance. Rather than being seen as prior to these other activities, language representation is deemed to be either co-equal, or secondary in importance. Given that so much of a modern infra-structure is established by government departments and finances it is clearly essential that bilingual services within the lesser-used language community be provided as part of the state's remit. We may legitimately ask if language planning then serves to redefine, relocate and redirect the central thrust of language politics into an accommodative rather than a conflictual mode of operation? For once language needs become established as a state recognised function they become subject to the same rules that govern other state provision. What role does language planning have in distancing individuals, and even whole communities, from the construction of the rules which govern inter-group or local-state relationships?

In consequence of the development of formal language planning agencies we witness the growth of a technical intelligentsia to staff and expand these agencies. Are élitism, a new professional/technocratic intelligentsia, and a burgeoning bureaucracy, the necessary progeny of the recent marriage between language activists and the local/central power brokers? We are used to treating minority languages as vehicles of resistance to an often uncaring or hostile state government, but are not yet fully equipped to deal with the minority language as the language of power, of establishment positions, in short of governance. What consequence will this entail for the internal class relations within the language community itself? Can the language issue be mobilised as the basis for rapid social advancement within the new order, and if so with what consequence for the form and direction of language politics and language planning?

These are vital questions which we are only just beginning to ask in such contexts as Wales, Catalonia and Euskadi, although Québec has experienced three decades of such debates along these lines. They are pertinent questions for many of the language communities described in this volume, because it is precisely at the level of government involvement that the difficulties of 'saving' the socio-cultural environment which sustains the language, need to be addressed. However, as we have also demonstrated, the critical mass needed to animate the many reforms advocated by professional language planners is daily diminishing. We may soon be faced with the ultimate irony of language minorities; a dedicated, well trained and resourceful, if small, professional class, backed to a limited extent by the authority and finances of the local state, ready to resuscitate the dying patient, only to discover that the patient has discharged itself and quit the scene of its demise.

If this tragic farce is not to be repeated in all the cases described in this volume, then two lessons must be learned. A language will survive only so long as its speakers derive warmth, humour, socio-economic gain, status, and psychological satisfaction from its habitual use. If, by contrast, a neighbouring, competitive language performs these functions more effectively then it is rational to switch languages, especially if that second language is also a vehicle of social advancement and equal opportunity within the larger state. The second lesson is that individuals are not wholly autonomous beings. The choice described in the first lesson is structured by the wider context within which individuals and language communities operate. It is therefore of the utmost importance that linguists, language planners and language activists recognise that their combined efforts, though significant in their own right, depend upon the vagaries of macro-economic, political and social forces, over which they have little or no control. However, the efficacy of their reforms and formulations will be enhanced greatly if they take due account of these forces and attempt to harness their impact to the needs of the constituent language group members they seek to serve. This is not a recipe for introversion, nor a prediction of the ultimate collapse of the linguistic minorities discussed above. Rather it is a recognition of the realistic difficulties faced by minority group members who must, at the very least, be offered a future which is commensurate with majority language speakers in most, if not all, domains. If some language groups are unable to offer such a future and disappear as a result, then so be it. I would far rather favour a situation where some aspects of a culture fall into disuse, than preserve an outmoded culture in aspic which would deny children access to the knowledge and opportunities offered by full participation in the modern world. However, the choice need not be framed in such stark, zero-sum terms. Given the combined resources of a critical mass of language supporters and a sympathetic local state, all of the language minorities analysed in this volume have a future. Ultimately it is not technology nor the market-place which determines the shape of that future, but the people themselves. Yet their sovereignty is clearly fashioned both by the nature of the political system they inhabit, and by the degree of majoritarian tolerance exhibited within the state. Language minorities will never be entirely free from the impediment of relative powerlessness — such is their lot in life. But they can be made more free than they are at present, and one of the prerequisites of the call to liberty is a clear specification of the goals of the community, and of the scale of the difficulties which must be faced and overcome if such goals are to be realised as social action. My hope and conviction is that volumes such as this add to our understanding of such difficulties, and thereby frame the choices we make in a more realistic manner.

References

Allardt, R. and Landry, R. 1987, Contact des langues, vitalité ethnolinguistique subjective et comportement ethnolangagier. *Colloque Contacts des Langues: Quels Modèles*? Nice: IDERIC.

Ambrose, J. E. and Williams, C. H. 1981, On the spatial definition of minority: scale as an influence on the geolinguistic analysis of Welsh. In E. Haugen *et al. Minority Languages Today*. Edinburgh: Edinburgh University Press.

Andersen, R. 1988, *The Power and the Word*. London: Paladin.

Bourhis, R. Y. 1979, Language and ethnic interaction: a social psychological approach. In H. Giles and B. Saint-Jacques (eds) *Language and Ethnic Relations*. Oxford: Pergamon Press.

— 1983, Language attitudes and self-reports of French–English language usage in Québec. *Journal of Multilingual and Multicultural Development* 4, 163–79.

Bowen, E. G. and Carter, H. 1975, Some preliminary observations on the distribution of the Welsh language. *The Geographical Journal* 140, 432–40.

Dorian, N. C. (ed.) 1989, *Investigating Obsolescence: Studies in Language Contraction and Death*. Cambridge: Cambridge University Press.

Fishman, J. A. (ed.) 1966, *Language Loyalty in the United States*. The Hague: Mouton.

— 1989, *Language and Ethnicity in Minority Sociolinguistic Perspective*. Clevedon, Avon: Multilingual Matters.

GILES, H., BOURHIS, R. and TAYLOR D. M. 1977, Towards a theory of language in ethnic group relations. In H. GILES (ed.) *Language, Ethnicity and Intergroup Relations*. London: Academic Press.

HINDLEY, R. 1987, Geolinguistics. *Area* 19(4), 378–9.

MACKEY, W. 1988, Geolinguistics: its scope and principles. In C. H. WILLIAMS (ed.) *Language in Geographic Context* (pp. 20–40). Clevedon, Avon: Multilingual Matters.

ROMAINE, S. 1989, *Bilingualism*. Oxford: Blackwell.

WILLIAMS, C. H. 1989, New domains of the Welsh language. Education, planning and the law. In G. REES and G. DAY (eds) *Contemporary Wales* 3, 41–76.

Appendix: International Seminar on Geolinguistics

Speakers, discussants and particants

Ms J. Adams, Geography and Recreation Studies, Staffordshire Polytechnic
Dr J. Ambrose, Geography and Recreation Studies, Staffordshire Polytechnic
Professor H. Carter, Geography, University College of Wales, Aberystwyth
Professor D. Cartwright, Geography, University of Western Ontario
Professor J. Edwards, Psychology, St Francis Xavier University
Mr M. Grover, Multilingual Matters Ltd, Clevedon
Dr R. Hindley, School of European Studies, Bradford University
Dr H. L. Humphreys, French, St David's University College, Lampeter
Mr C. James, Planning, Gwynedd County Council
Professor G. Kay, Geography and Recreation Studies, Staffordshire Polytechnic
Cathlin Macaulay, Glasgow
Dr K. MacKinnon, Sociology, Hatfield Polytechnic
Dr J. MacLaughlin, Geography, University College, Cork
Ms D. Morris, Sociology, UCNW, Bangor
Mr D. Pratts, Geography and Recreation Studies, Staffordshire Polytechnic
Dr W. T. R. Pryce, The Open University in Wales, Cardiff
Mr D. H. Rogers, Geography, UCW, Aberystwyth
Cllr. R. Swann, Geography and Recreation Studies, Staffordshire Polytechnic
Mr K. Thompson, Director, Staffordshire Polytechnic
Mr R. Tolley, Geography and Recreation Studies, Staffordshire Polytechnic
Professor J. de Vries, Sociology, Carleton University
Dr P. White, Geography, University of Sheffield
Professor C. H. Williams, Geography and Recreation Studies, Staffordshire Polytechnic
Dr S. W. Williams, Geography and Recreation Studies, Staffordshire Polytechnic
Dr C. W. J. Withers, Geography, College of St Paul and St Mary

Index

Note: Page references in italics indicate tables, figures and maps.